SIXTH EDITION
Mastering Written English
The COMP-LAB Exercises

Mary Epes
Michael G. Southwell
York College/CUNY

Prentice
Hall

Upper Saddle River, NJ 07458

Library of Congress Cataloging-in-Publication Data

Epes, Mary.
 Mastering written English : the comp-lab exercises / Mary Epes, Michael G.
 Southwell.– 6th ed.
   p. cm.
 Includes index.
 ISBN 0-13-030415-8 (alk. paper)
 1. English language–Self-instruction. 2. English language–Textbooks for foreign
 speakers. 3. English language–Grammar–Problems, exercises, etc. 4. English
 language–Written English–Problems, exercises, etc. I. Southwell, Michael G. II. Title.

PE1112.3 .E64 2001
808'.042–dc21
                                                        00-047832

Editor-in-Chief: *Leah Jewell*
Acquisitions Editor: *Craig Campanella*
Editorial Assistant: *Joan Polk*
AVP and Director of Production and Manufacturing: *Barbara Kittle*
Managing Editor: *Mary Rottino*
Project Manager: *Lisa M. Guidone*
Prepress and Manufacturing Manager: *Nick Sklitsis*
Prepress and Manufacturing Buyer: *Benjamin D. Smith*
Cover Designer: *Jayne Conte*
Proofreader: *Rainbow Graphics*
Director of Marketing: *Beth Gillett Mejia*
Marketing Manager: *Rachel Falk*

This book was supplied as camera ready copy by the authors.
The text was printed by Courier Kendallville.
The cover was printed by Phoenix Color Corp.

 © 2001, 1997 by Prentice-Hall, Inc.
A Division of Pearson Education
Upper Saddle River, New Jersey 07458

Printed in the United States of America

10 9 8 7 6 5 4 3 2 1

ISBN 0-13-030415-8

Prentice-Hall International (UK) Limited, *London*
Prentice-Hall of Australia Pty. Limited, *Sydney*
Prentice-Hall Canada, Inc., *Toronto*
Prentice-Hall Hispanoamerica, S. A., *Mexico*
Prentice-Hall of India Private Limited, *New Delhi*
Prentice-Hall of Japan, Inc., *Tokyo*
Pearson Education Asia Pte. Ltd., *Singapore*
Editoria Prentice-Hall do Brasil, Ltda., *Rio de Janiero*

Table of Contents

How To Use This Book
To the Teacher v
To the Student xii

Section 1:   **Practicing the Writing Process** 1
      Phase One: Plan and Draft
      Phase Two: Revise
      Phase Three: Edit and Proofread

Section 2:   **Practicing the Editing Process** 29
   Module 1:   **Mastering Writing Conventions** 31
      Marking Paragraphs
      Using Capital Letters
      Using Punctuation
      Using Abbreviations
      Using Numbers
      Solving One-word/Two word Problems
      Using Spelling Rules
      Avoiding Wrong Words
      Using Sound-alike Words

   Module 2:   **Understanding Simple Sentences** 65
      Finding Verbs
      Finding Subjects
      Verb Phrases
      Verbs in Contractions
      Words Easily Confused with Verbs

   Module 3:   **Understanding More Complicated Sentences I** 87
      Joining Words and Compound Sentences
      Expansion Words and Complex Sentences

   Module 4:   **Understanding More Complicated Sentences II** 109
      Noun-expansion Words and Complex Sentences
      Punctuating Sentences with Noun-expansion Words
      That and Complex Sentences

   Module 5:   **Using Nouns and Pronouns** 127
      Recognizing Nouns
      Determiners and Noun Endings
      Writing Plural Nouns
      Noncount Nouns
      Singular and Plural Pronouns
      Other Pronoun Forms
      Avoiding Sexist Language

   Module 6:   **Making Present-tense Verbs Agree** 159
      Present-tense Verbs
      Making Verbs Agree
      Making Verbs Agree in More Complicated Sentences
      The Irregular Verb *BE*: Present Tense

Module 7:   *Mastering Past-tense Verbs* 183
Irregular Past-tense Verbs
Regular Past-tense Verbs
The Irregular Verb *BE*: Past Tense
Using Appropriate Tenses

Module 8:   *Recognizing and Fixing Run-ons* 207
Recognizing Run-ons
Understanding Transition Words
Fixing Run-ons I
Fixing Run-ons II
Fixing Run-ons III

Module 9:   *Recognizing and Fixing Fragments* 229
Recognizing Fragments
Fixing Fragments
Fixing Fragments Caused by Noun-expansion Words

Module 10:   *Mastering Verb Phrases I* 247
Verb Phrases with Modal Helping Verbs
Verb Phrases with *DO*
Verb Phrases with *HAVE*

Module 11:   *Mastering Verb Phrases II* 275
Verb Phrases with *BE*
Verb Phrases with *BE* in Active Sentences
Verb Phrases with *BE* in Passive Sentences

Module 12:   *Mastering Expansion* 297
Using Possessive Forms
   Possessive Noun Forms
   Possessive Pronoun Forms
   Avoiding Other Problems with Apostrophes
Using Adjectives and Adverbs
   Expansion with Adjectives and Adverbs
   Placement of Adverbs in Sentences
   Using Adjectives and Adverbs in Comparisons
Using Other Expansion
   Placement of Noun and Verb Expansion
   Noun Expansion with *ING* Words
   Noun Expansion with Past Participles
   Dangling Expansion
Using Parallel Parts

Answers 333

Index 410

How To Use This Book
To the Teacher

In this 6th edition of *Mastering Written English*, we have for the first time included a discussion of the entire writing process. We did this in response to suggestions from some long-time users as well as reviewers. So Section 1 of this book is focused on drafting and revising papers; Section 2 is focused, like previous editions, on editing those papers.

Placed at the beginning of the text, this new section gives students a clear and immediate sense of the difference between drafting and revising (the first two phases of the writing process) and editing for correctness (the third phase). Subsequently, paper assignments in each module reinforce what students have begun to learn in the new Section 1 about the writing process, as well as what they are learning and have learned about editing

Like the rest of the book, Section 1 has a self-instructional format; it has been designed so that portions of it may be assigned for students to work on by themselves. However, students' work on each step of the writing process should be reviewed in the classroom, in small group sessions, in the writing laboratory, or in one-on-one conferences where students can get feedback on their own efforts and learn from what others have done. And of course, you should not overlook your obligation to monitor students' progress on their papers through the rest of the semester. Even though they should be able to work by themselves on learning to edit their papers effectively, they will continue to rely on you for help with the planning, drafting, and revising steps in the writing process.

The New Climate for Grammar Instruction

The edition of *Mastering Written English* immediately preceding this one appeared at a time of renascent interest in, and recognition of the importance of, grammar instruction in the teaching of writing. Since then the imposition of statewide writing standards and standardized tests has further heightened teachers' interest in **a new and more effective approach to grammar instruction**, one that can measurably reduce error and even improve overall writing quality. This more effective approach has been variously dubbed a "pedagogical grammar," a "writer's grammar," or a "usage grammar." This "new" grammar can be described as follows:

- Eliminating vague, imprecise, and unreliable rules, the new grammar **accurately** identifies what good writers **do** when they write.
- It reduces the myriad categories of formal grammar to a minimum, and includes only those necessary for students to understand and to correct their most serious and frequent errors.
- It's presented in clear, everyday language which students who are unacquainted with or confused by traditional grammatical terminology may readily grasp and apply.
- Its rules are **operational**, making clear how the written language **works**, so that students can use it not only in editing their writing for correctness, but also in improving it stylistically.
- Its mastery is facilitated first through practice that uses a range of approaches, like sentence-combining, focused proofreading, and varieties of sentence- and paragraph-transformations, and then through students' editing their own writing for the rules they have just practiced.

The New Grammar and *Mastering Written English*

From its first edition, *Mastering Written English* has used most of the features of the new grammar:

- Our rules are **operational** ones, with minimal grammatical terminology, and limited to what students need to know to understand and avoid their characteristic mistakes.
- The distinction between the **visual** and the **linguistic** features of written English is integral to the organization and pedagogy of our work. In this edition, Module 1 deals with the purely visual features of the written code, and the other nine with its grammatical component.
- The features we stress the most are essentially 16 of the 20 errors in written English which the oft-cited Connors-Lunsford study (*College Composition and Communication*, 1988) identified as **actually occurring** most frequently in college writing. We also give close attention to those errors which Maxine Hairston's ground-breaking study (*College English*, 1981) found most highly stigmatized.
- We provide **extensive practice** in increasingly complex contexts, using the full range of sentence and paragraph transformations.

Beyond the New Grammar

Mastering Written English offers important advantages over other textbooks using the new grammar:

- *Mastering Written English* is **self-instructional**. Except for the writing assignments in each module (discussed below), every single exercise, no matter how complex, has an unambiguous answer at the back of the book. Students may correct their own work, exercise by exercise, and then periodically apply what they have learned in the process to their own writing, using the rules and analytic tools they have mastered step by step. **No other text provides such sophisticated exercises with unambiguously right and wrong answers.**

- This self-teaching method enables students to move ahead at their own pace, spending as much or as little time necessary to master a particular rule. Moreover, in the process of correcting their own work, students learn four important lessons: ① to notice fine details of the written code, ② to read and follow instructions carefully, developing perceptual skills lacking in most students in basic and developmental writing, ③ to learn from their own mistakes, and ④ to identify their own specific weaknesses in the production of standard written English. At the same time teachers' work-load is greatly reduced in that they have only to spot-check students' work on the modules for accuracy. While keeping abreast of students' progress in mastering the rules of written English and applying them to their own writing, teachers are freed up to teach aspects of writing which can only be communicated by a teacher, and through interaction with other writers and readers.

- Advocates of the new grammar have not yet come to focus on the critical importance of a thoroughly **systematic and incremental approach** in teaching grammatical structures to inexperienced writers. The order in which our chosen features are presented has been dictated by linguistic theory and experience. Just as each module builds logically and incrementally on what has gone before, so too each exercise is carefully ordered and crafted so as to call only on knowledge already mastered. Sensitive to the mindlessness of mere repetition, we have tried, even within exercises, to design each item so as to present a slight advance, a discernibly new challenge beyond the item that came before. Further, in this systematic approach, teachers at all times are aware of what students have learned and what they have yet to learn, and may mark errors accordingly. This helps students to recognize their responsibility for avoiding errors that they have learned to identify and correct.

- Advocates of the new grammar continue to rely almost completely on a purely cognitive or conceptual approach. But studies have shown that inattention to visual details in writing in combination with oral language habits (rather than ignorance of a rule) is the root of most errors in writing. We have tackled this problem through consciousness-raising exercises, making students aware of the **kinds** of errors they are apt to overlook, especially in certain semantic and phonetic contexts. These **perceptual** exercises begin in the introductory section *To the Student*, and continue throughout, as for example in Module 5 in regard to dropped plural *S* endings, and in Module 7 in regard to omitted *ED* inflections. As mentioned above, the self-teaching approach, enabling students to correct their own work, supports the development of this important writing and proofreading skill.

Innovations in This 6ᵗʰ Edition

1. **The target population has been broadened:**

   In general, by including somewhat more advanced work, by de-emphasizing some of the more elementary material, by increasing the emphasis on sentence construction (the most persistent problem in the writing of so-called regular college composition students), and by providing more opportunities for students to apply what they learn in their own writing, this edition is now suitable for courses ranging from basic writing to those college composition courses which include less practiced writers. And because of the book's self-instructional format, it can accommodate this range when it occurs within one class: it can be used by some students in the class, and not by others; some students can be assigned one set of modules, others a different set.

2. **An entire new section trains students in the writing process:**

   We have added an entire new section on the writing process. Placed at the very beginning of the book, this section trains students in all the steps of the writing process, and helps them to experience the important differences between revising their ideas for greater effectiveness and editing their writing for correctness. Thus it prepares them for writing the papers they will be assigned as they move through the book (see item #3 below).

3. **The transfer of editing skills to students' own writing has been facilitated:**

   In this edition, students begin each module by choosing one of two topics and developing it into a paper of four or more paragraphs, practicing the planning, drafting, and revising steps in the writing process as they learned them in Section 1. The topics themselves and the special instructions that accompany them insure that students will use the targeted feature of the module repeatedly in their own freely composed writing. They will then edit their draft paper for this feature in systematic stages as they work through the module. At the end of the module, after they have finished editing for this module's feature, they will edit their draft for features covered in prior modules, and then will prepare a final copy to hand in.

   Because of the inclusion of the new Section 1 on the writing process, the instructions for these writing assignments have been made less detailed and less explicit than they were in the 5ᵗʰ edition, giving students more responsibility for the development and organization of their papers. These writing assignments therefore give students a chance not only to practice using the module feature in their own writing, but also to improve their composing skills and (beginning with Module 2) to practice the kinds of expository and argumentative writing required by many introductory college courses.

4. **The sentence analysis modules have been reordered:**

The simplified but powerful approach to sentence-analysis which was used in the previous edition and proven there to be effective, continues. But now students work on correcting sentence problems (fragments and run-ons) after their work on nouns and verbs. This change is likely to improve learning in both areas.

The new method of sentence analysis, central as it is to our new approach, calls for further explanation. It is based on the same linguistic premise as the successful sentence-combining pedagogy, namely, that all written sentences are composed of "kernel" (or "simple") sentences connected by three kinds of "connecting" words (what we call joining, expansion, and noun-expansion words). Once students have learned to identify each verb (with a circle), its subject (with a box), and every connecting word (with a +), and once they have mastered the principle that between a capital letter and a period the number of simple sentences must always be one more than the number of connecting words, they hold the key to the structure of every conceivable sentence. The utter simplicity of the concept, along with its mode of dramatically clear marking, makes it instantly transferable to student writing. And they can apply it directly to their own writing, without their having to rewrite, diagram, or add any obtrusive clutter. Even before students do specific work on run-ons and fragments, they begin to recognize and correct these problems. For a fuller understanding of this syntax for writers, we invite you to take the short course offered in the *Instructor's Manual* that accompanies this book.

5. **Students are provided with information that will help them to perform successfully on various statewide tests of grammar and writing:**

This edition now includes almost all of the topics covered in these tests. In Module 5 on nouns and pronouns, new topics include pronoun case, reflexive pronouns, advanced pronoun reference, and avoiding sexist language. In Module 12, new and more difficult aspects of expansion are presented. At this point in the term students, having mastered the overall framework of the sentence, can readily understand the function of any piece of expansion within that framework. These new aspects include problems with adjectives and adverbs, misplaced and dangling expansion, with special emphasis on present and past participial expansion, and using parallel parts.

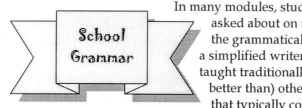 In many modules, students are alerted to the terms that they might be asked about on these system-wide or state-wide tests. By relating the grammatical **concepts** of *Mastering Written English* (taught using a simplified writer's grammar) to the technical **terms** of grammar taught traditionally, we prepare them to perform as well as (if not better than) other students on the identification and correction tasks that typically constitute such tests. We call these terms "school grammar," and highlight them as we did in this paragraph.

6. **The new design is more user-friendly:**

An attractive new interior design highlights rules more incisively and uses a more conversational tone so that students absorb the material more readily and are less intimidated by what might be considered its technical nature.

Heightening Student Motivation and Monitoring Their Progress

1. The goal of each exercise is highlighted so that students are motivated to do it purposefully.

2. Scoring grids are provided for each module and paper assignment. They keep students aware of the level of their control of the targeted feature in their own writing, their performance on the related exercises, and the probable connection between such control and such performance. They make it easy for teachers to check students' satisfactory completion of modules and to score their writing assignments. Teachers may choose to grade the final writing assignment for overall quality as well as correctness, or to grade for correctness only, or use some other measure.

3. Rules Summary pages for students' reference at the beginning of each module facilitate review and application of rules to their own writing.

What You Need to Know about Using This Book

Before students begin work on the content of this course, make sure they have read the section To the Student that follows, and have done the exercises it contains. We urge you to read this introductory material yourself, as it gives information about how to use this book that is as important to you as it is to your students. Additionally, it will show you what you should require of your students if they are to be successful in using the self-instructional approach.

In particular, To the Student contains six exercises focusing on the specific skills your students need to get the most out of the exercises in the book and then to apply this learning to their own writing. Five of these exercises they can check themselves, but the sixth, a deceptively simple copying exercise, requires someone else to check it. Students have therefore been instructed to hand it in to you. If you do check and return it, you, like teachers who have used this exercise in previous editions of *Mastering Written English,* are likely to get important information about how each student tends to work on writing tasks. You may also be surprised at how hard many students find so seemingly easy an exercise. We urge you not to miss the chance to gain information quickly about the writing skills and work habits of your students.

Once you understand how your students will be — or should be — using this self-instructional book, you will need to make decisions in the following areas:

*   **What parts of the book will you assign, and in what order?** We urge you to consider assigning the entire book in order to less practiced writers, since later modules are built on what has been taught in earlier ones. But teachers of more advanced students could easily assign only parts of the book, and assign them in a different order.

    On page 30, the back of the cover page for Section 2, you will find a chart which students can use for keeping track of when their assignments are due. You might want to ask students to fill this in during the first week of class.

*   **What will you expect students to hand in to you?** Your answer here could range from "nothing" to "everything." "Nothing" is what most students using other textbooks are used to, but it provides you with no information whatsoever about how much students are actually doing and learning. If students hand in "everything," there is no reason for you to do anything more than ① check that they have

completed everything, and ② spot check their answers to see whether they are checking their own work carefully. If you use the book in association with a Writing Lab, these duties can usually be assigned to lab personnel. **At a minimum**, you should expect students to hand in the paper they have worked on in each module. You can read this quickly to see whether students ① continue to use and become more competent in their use of the steps in the writing process, ② now control the feature they have been working on, and ③ continue to control the features they have previously worked on.

In planning your supervision of the self-instructional component of the semester's work, you will find it helpful to examine the scoring sheets at the beginning of each module and decide how or if you want to use their various check-off boxes in evaluating students' efforts and success in doing the exercises and writing the module Paper. At this point you may want to consider to what extent you wish to incorporate the Paper assignments (students will have a chance to write ten fully developed Papers and several shorter ones during the term) into your classroom instruction and activities.

* **How will you supplement the book's instruction in the writing process?** As we have stressed above, this will normally be your most important class activity, and (much more so than their work on correctness) something that students need your help with.

For additional practical help in using this book more effectively, and especially in managing the self-teaching method, the *Instructor's Manual* will be helpful. Teachers have told us that it is a source of many useful approaches, fun lessons, and time-saving procedures. If you have not received your copy, write to:

Faculty Services
Prentice Hall
One Lake Street
Upper Saddle River, NJ 07458

Write to Us

The authors will be grateful for your comments and suggestions. Write to either of us at:

Department of English
York College/CUNY
Jamaica, NY 11451

Or send e-mail to MEpes@aol.com or Southwell@york.cuny.edu.

Or visit our web site at http://www.prenhall.com/epes.

Acknowledgments

The authors would like to acknowledge the valuable contributions made by their long-time co-author **Carolyn Kirkpatrick** to the first four editions of *Mastering Written English*.

We acknowledge also the help of reviewers who either commented on the 5th edition with a view to improving this 6th edition, or made comments about this manuscript: **Shirley Hart Berry** of Cape Fear Community College, **Carlotta W. Hill** of Oklahoma City Community College, **Jill A. Lahnstein** of Cape Fear Community College, **Jeffrey Maxson** of Rowan University, **Sara McLaughlin** of Texas Tech

University, **Bonnie Ronson** of Hillsborough Community College, and **Maria Alene Van Valkenburg** of Ivy Tech State College.

As in the past, we give special thanks to **Stan Frick** of Midlands Technical College for his thoughtful suggestions, ever since the very first edition. His suggestions have had a profound effect on this edition in particular.

Finally, we would like to thank our new editor **Craig Campanella** for his expertise in coordinating this complicated project, and in offering suggestions which have helped us to make this edition more attractive and useful. We also want to thank his assistant **Joan Polk** for taking care of many important details.

Thanks also to Lillian.

Mary Epes
Michael Southwell

How To Use This Book
To the Student

Mastering Written English is a **self-teaching** book, designed so that you can learn from it by yourself, at your own speed.

Although you may need a teacher's help in focusing, organizing, and revising your ideas on paper, you can learn how to edit for correctness on your own. By doing the exercises in Section 2 of this book, and checking your work against the Answers, you can teach yourself a lot about how to write more correctly, more clearly, and more effectively.

This self-teaching approach places the responsibility for learning this aspect of writing on you. If you accept this responsibility, and work carefully and thoughtfully, you'll soon find yourself beginning to master your own written English.

The Parts of This Book

Table of Contents

How To Use This Book
  To the Teacher v
  To the Student xii

Section 1:	*Practicing the Writing Process* 1
	Phase One: Plan and Draft
	Phase Two: Revise
	Phase Three: Edit and Proofread

Section 2:	*Practicing the Editing Process* 29
Module 1:	*Mastering Writing Conventions* 31
	Marking Paragraphs
	Using Capital Letters
	Using Punctuation
	Using Abbreviations
	Using Numbers
	Solving One-word/Two word Problems
	Using Spelling Rules
	Avoiding Wrong Words
	Using Sound-alike Words

Module 2:	*Understanding Simple Sentences* 65
	Finding Verbs
	Finding Subjects
	Verb Phrases
	Verbs in Contractions
	Words Easily Confused with Verbs

Module 3:	*Understanding More Complicated Sentences I* 87
	Joining Words and Compound Sentences
	Expansion Words and Complex Sentences

Module 4:	*Understanding More Complicated Sentences II* 109
	Noun-expansion Words and Complex Sentences
	Punctuating Sentences with Noun-expansion Words
	That and Complex Sentences

Module 5:	*Using Nouns and Pronouns* 127
	Recognizing Nouns
	Determiners and Noun Endings
	Writing Plural Nouns
	Noncount Nouns
	Singular and Plural Pronouns
	Other Pronoun Forms
	Avoiding Sexist Language

Module 6:	*Making Present-tense Verbs Agree* 159
	Present-tense Verbs
	Making Verbs Agree
	Making Verbs Agree in More Complicated Sentences
	The Irregular Verb *BE*: Present Tense

If you look at the Contents on page iii above, you'll see that the book is divided into two main sections. The second section is divided into chapters or modules, each on a different writing problem.

What is Section 1 about?

_____

What page does Section 2 begin on? _____

How many modules are there in Section 2? _____

Answers

Exercise 0.1

1. A girl with three younger **brothers** often has a difficult childhood.
2. In the early evening, the fireworks factory was rocked by a **powerful** explosion.
3. When his mother walked in with a tiny bundle in her arms, Gerald rushed up to get a good look at his new baby **sister**.
4. The **best** way to prepare this sauce is to beat it vigorously for three minutes.
5. Victor, an experienced **electrician** from Czechoslovakia, wants to join the local electricians' **union**.

Exercise 0.2 The three mistakes that you cannot hear, but must actually see, are the word *sail*, the incorrect capital letter *P* in *Property*, and the missing capital letter *W* in *whatever*.

Buying property is **is even** riskier than buying used **cars**. For example, a store **by** the library in **in** my neighborhood is going to **be** put up for **sale** soon. The owner, Hank Dawson, **may** try to get **$90,000** for **it**, but the value of the **property** is actually much less than that. A building inspector **was** in the basement recently and saw termites. He checked the beams and found **they** were completely rotten and ready to collapse. Buyers, beware! **Whatever** claims Dawson makes about that building, you can bet **your** bottom dollar they're **not** true.

Exercise 0.3

From the 1920s through the 1950s, cigarette smoking was considered **a** harmless and even glamorous habit. Stars of **the** silver screen, wearing tuxedos and evening gowns, lighted **each** other's cigarettes in night club scenes. Film detectives chain-smoked as **they** solved their cases. The children in many pictures sneaked **their** first puffs behind the garage. **But** modern audiences watching old movies on TV find these scenes disturbing.

Exercise 0.4

From the 1920s through the 1950s, cigarette smoking was **considered** a harmless and even glamorous habit. Stars of the silver screen, **wearing** tuxedos and evening gowns, lighted each other's **cigarettes** in night club scenes. Film detectives chain-smoked as they **solved** their cases. The children in many pictures **sneaked** their first puffs behind the garage. But modern audiences **watching** old movies on TV find these scenes disturbing.

Exercise 0.5

From the 1920s through the 1950s, cigarette smoking was considered a harmless and even glamorous habit. Stars of the **silver** screen, wearing tuxedos and evening gowns, lighted each other's cigarettes in night club scenes. **Film** detectives chain-smoked as they solved their cases. The **children** in many pictures sneaked their **first** puffs behind the garage. But **modern** audiences watching old movies on TV find these scenes **disturbing**.

The Answers to all the exercises are at the end of the book. Find these Answers now.

What page do the Answers begin on? _____

Letting you check your own answers provides important practice in helping you to be sure that you are **seeing** what you have actually written.

If you copy from the Answers, you are cheating yourself out of this chance to improve your writing by learning from your mistakes.

How to Use This Book

1 Mastering Writing Conventions

NAME _____

As you complete each exercise, record your number of mistakes below.

1.1 ____	1.8 ____	1.15 ____	1.22 ____	1.29 ____
1.2 ____	1.9 ____	1.16 ____	1.23 ____	1.30 ____
1.3 ____	1.10 ____	1.17 ____	1.24 ____	1.31 ____
1.4 ____	1.11 ____	1.18 ____	1.25 ____	1.32 ____
1.5 ____	1.12 ____	1.19 ____	1.26 ____	1.33 ____
1.6 ____	1.13 ____	1.20 ____	1.27 ____	1.34 ____
1.7 ____	1.14 ____	1.21 ____	1.28 ____	1.35 ____

EXERCISES	INSTRUCTIONS	CHECKING OF EXERCISES	
❏ Complete	❏ Followed carefully	❏ Careful	❏ Green pen not used
❏ Incomplete	❏ Not careful enough	❏ Not careful enough	❏ Mistakes not corrected

PAPER B	EDITING PAPER B FOR THIS MODULE'S WORK
❏ Doesn't follow the instructions; write a NEW Paper B.	❏ Careful ❏ Not careful enough
❏ Skips some instructions; COMPLETE everything.	OVERALL EVALUATION OF PAPER B
❏ Too short; add MORE	❏ Excellent ❏ Good ❏ Acceptable ❏ Not acceptable

COMMENTS

At the beginning of each module is a cover page on which you can keep a record of the number of mistakes you make on each exercise.

Keeping this record accurately will help you to see which rules you have trouble understanding or which are hardest for you to apply consistently. This record may also help your teacher or tutor to see where your problems are.

Turn to the cover page for Module 1. How many exercises are in Module 1? _____

Rules Summary for Module 1	
1A	Mark the beginning each paragraph clearly by indenting or by skipping a line.
1B	Use capital letters only for the following: 1 the first letter of a sentence; 2 the word *I*; 3 the first letter of a specific name (and its title); and 4 the first letter of a word made from a name.
1C 1 2 3 4	Use correct and clear punctuation. Use a <u>period</u> after a <u>statement</u>, and a <u>question mark</u> after a <u>question</u>. <u>Don't</u> put space <u>before</u> punctuation. <u>Do</u> put space <u>after</u> punctuation. Use an <u>apostrophe</u> to show where letters have been omitted in contractions. Use quotation marks whenever you use someone else's exact words.
1D	Avoid most abbreviations.
1E	Spell out the numbers *one* through *ten*. Use numerals for numbers above *ten*.
1F	Don't write what should be one word as two words, or what should be two words as one word.
1G 1 2 3 4	Use spelling rules to spell many words correctly. When to put *I* before *E* When to change *Y* to *I* When to double the final consonant before adding an ending How to spell words ending in *ING*
1H 1 2 3 4 5	Don't confuse words that sound alike but have different meanings. *THEN/THAN* *TO/TOO/TWO* *ITS/IT'S* *YOUR/YOU'RE* *THEIR/THEY'RE/THERE*

On the back of each cover page is a Rules Summary, containing an outline of what you'll be learning in the module. Each rule is lettered. Some rules may have numbered subparts.

You will use this summary to check how accurately you have applied the rules of the module in your own writing, and to correct your mistakes.

What is the last lettered rule in Module 1?
_____

How many numbered subparts does it have?
_____

Each module follows the same general method of instruction. Find each of these parts in Module 1 now:

- a **paper assignment** near the beginning. This is always shaded.

    What page is the assignment for Paper B on? _____

- a **rule** or general concept that you need to understand. This is always in a box. Then some **examples**, with explanations of how they illustrate the rule.

- one or more **short exercises**, to check that you understand the rule. You will check your answers to these exercises by yourself, so that you can find out whether you really do understand the rule.

    What is the first of these short exercises in Module 1? Write its number here: _____

- several **longer exercises**, where you can practice applying the rule. Again, you will check your answers yourself, so that you can find out whether you really know how to use the rule.

    What is the first of these longer exercises? Write its number here: _____

- one or more **shaded Editing Practice exercises** where you check the paper that you wrote at the beginning of the module, to see whether you can use the rule you've been learning to fix any mistakes you may have made.

    What page is Editing Practice B.1 on? _____

Notice that each page in the book is perforated, so you can tear it out easily. You will find it easiest to check your work if you tear out the exercises, so you can compare what you wrote to the Answers.

Your instructor may ask you to hand in the entire module after you've finished it. Or he or she may want you to hand in only the final paper.

School Grammar

Mastering Written English will teach you a simplified grammar, one which is aimed at helping you to improve your own writing. Nevertheless, you can use it to help prepare yourself for the identification and correction tasks on system-wide and state-wide standardized tests of grammar and writing. We call the traditional terms "school grammar," and highlight them with this symbol.

Even though we won't be asking you to identify dangling modifiers or coordinating conjunctions, then, if you pay attention to these sections of this book, you should be able to connect the **concepts** you are learning here to the traditional **terms**, and so you should be able to do well on those tests.

What You Need Before You Begin

Here is what you need to have before you begin:

1. Two different colored pens (use a blue or black one to work with, and a green one to check your answers with);
2. Plenty of 8½ by 11 inch loose leaf paper to write your papers and longer exercises on;
3. A three-ring loose leaf notebook (to keep your papers and completed exercises in); and
4. A good dictionary.

Get these materials now, and have them ready before you go on.

The Skills You Need to Use This Book Successfully

To learn from the self-instructional method used in this book, and in fact to do **any writing** assignment successfully, these are the skills you will need to acquire if you don't already have them:

1. To read and follow directions exactly
2. To proofread closely
3. To check your answers carefully
4. To copy passages accurately
5. To use your dictionary effectively

In doing the following exercises, you will practice skills 1-4. This practice will steer you toward success in using the self-instructional approach for the rest of this semester.

First, let's find out how good your skills already are in the first three essential areas.

Proofreading seems as if it should be easy. When you're reading someone else's writing, errors jump right out at you. Unfortunately, that doesn't happen when the writing is your own. Since you already **know** what you mean by what you've written, your eye just glides right past omitted or incorrect letters, words, and punctuation marks.

One of the most effective ways to proofread is to **read out loud**. Train your eye and ear to work together. Listen to the sound of your voice as you look closely at the words. Have any words been left out? Have any parts of words been left out? Do the words on the page mean what you intended?

Exercise 0.1	Checking proofreading skills in sentences

① Read each sentence out loud. ② Underline any words that are incorrect. ③ Write the entire correct word in the space above the line. Follow this model:

God
The motto of the Treasury Department is "In <u>Gold</u> We Trust."

1. A girl with three younger bothers often has a difficult childhood.

2. In the early evening, the fireworks factory was rocked by a powderful explosion.

3. When his mother walked in with a tiny bundle in her arms, Gerald rushed up to get a good look at his new baby sitter.

4. The beat way to prepare this sauce is to beat it vigorously for three minutes.

5. Victor, an experienced electricity from Czechoslovakia, wants to join the local electricians' onion.

Before checking your work, re-read the instructions, and answer these questions:

- Did you read each sentence out loud? _____
- How many corrections did you make? _____ (You should have made six.)

Now tear this page out along the perforations. Then find the Answers in the back of the book and line up this exercise with the appropriate answer. Compare what you wrote to what is printed in the Answers. Be sure to check **every detail**, including spelling and word endings. Fix any mistakes you made like this:

- Don't just mark a mistake wrong or add a letter. Use your green pen to **write in the entire correct answer** above the mistake. Cross out in green any answer that is incorrect.

- After you've checked your work, stop to think about **why** you made a particular mistake. Were you in a rush to finish? Or did you misunderstand a rule, or forget it? Checking your work thoughtfully will let you know whether you need to slow down or perhaps to study the rules more closely (with special attention to the examples) before you go on.

You probably did pretty well in finding the mistakes in Exercise 0.1, because mistakes are easy to see in isolated sentences. However, the next exercise may be more difficult. The kinds of mistakes in it confuse readers much more than the obvious ones you just saw. But these are just the kinds of mistakes that writers have the hardest time seeing when they proofread their own work.

| Exercise 0.2 | Checking proofreading skills in a paragraph |

The following paragraph contains no errors. Read it carefully before you go on.

> Buying property is even riskier than buying used cars. For example, a store by the library in my neighborhood is going to be put up for sale soon. The owner, Hank Dawson, may try to get $90,000 for it, but the value of the property is actually much less than that. A building inspector was in the basement recently and saw termites. He checked the beams and found they were completely rotten and ready to collapse. Buyers, beware! Whatever claims Dawson makes about that building, you can bet your bottom dollar they're not true.

Here is the same paragraph, but full of mistakes, as a careless student might have copied it. **Without looking back at the original paragraph,** proofread this version carefully. Mark mistakes like this: ① Cross out any word that has been repeated. ② If a word has been omitted, insert a ∧, and write the missing word in the space above the line. ③ Underline each incorrect word, and correct it in the space above the line. The first three mistakes have been corrected for you.

> *even* *cars*
> Buying property is ~~is~~ ∧ riskier than buying used <u>car</u>. For example, a store be the library in in my neighborhood is going to by put up for sail soon. The owner, Hank Dawson, my try to get $60,000 for, but the value of the Property is actually much less than that. A building inspector saw in the basement recently and saw termites. He checked the beams and found the were completely rotten and ready to collapse. Buyers, beware! whatever claims Dawson makes about that building, you can bet you bottom dollar they're true.

Before checking your work, answer these questions:

1. How many corrections did you make in Exercise 0.2? _____
2. The paragraph in Exercise 0.2 contained 10 mistakes, not counting the three that were corrected for you. If you didn't find all 10, proofread the paragraph again, reading it **out loud**, word by word. **Listen** for mistakes as you read it. Now how many did you find? _____
3. If you still didn't find all 10, proofread the paragraph once again, this time comparing it to the original. **Look** for mistakes as you compare it. (There are three mistakes that you must actually **see**.) Now how many did you find? _____

Now turn to the Answers to check your work. Be sure that you:

- corrected everything that was wrong;
- corrected it in the right way; and
- didn't change anything that was already right.

If you over-corrected, use your green pen to **cross out** the change that you should not have made.

Remember that learning from your mistakes is a very important part (maybe even the most important part) of this self-teaching method. If you don't use a different-colored pen when you correct your work, it will be hard for you to locate your mistakes. It will also be hard for you to review.

Exercise 0.3	Checking proofreading skills in another paragraph

The following paragraph contains no errors. Read it carefully before you go on.

> From the 1920s through the 1950s, cigarette smoking was considered a harmless and even glamorous habit. Stars of the silver screen, wearing tuxedos and evening gowns, lighted each other's cigarettes in night club scenes. Film detectives chain-smoked as they solved their cases. The children in many pictures sneaked their first puffs behind the garage. But modern audiences watching old movies on TV find these scenes disturbing.

Here is the same paragraph, but full of mistakes, as a careless student might have copied it. **Without looking back at the original paragraph**, proofread this version carefully. Mark mistakes like this: ① If a word has been omitted, insert a ∧, and write the missing word in the space above the line. ② Underline each incorrect word, and correct it in the space above the line.

> From the 1920s through the 1950s, cigarette smoking was considered harmless and even glamorous habit. Stars of silver screen, wearing tuxedos and evening gowns, lighted other's cigarettes in night club scenes. Film detectives chain-smoked as solved their cases. The children in many pictures sneaked first puffs behind the garage. Modern audiences watching old movies on TV find these scenes disturbing.

Before checking your work, answer these questions:

1. How many corrections did you make in Exercise 0.3? _____
2. The paragraph in Exercise 0.3 contained six mistakes. If you didn't find all six, proofread the paragraph again, reading it **out loud**, word by word. **Listen** for mistakes as you read it. Now how many did you find? _____
3. If you still didn't find all six, proofread the paragraph once again, this time comparing it to the original. **Look** for mistakes as you compare it. Now how many did you find? _____
4. What one kind of error is repeated over and over by the writer of the paragraph in Exercise 0.3?

_____

Now turn to the Answers to check your work.

Exercise 0.4	Checking proofreading skills in another paragraph

Here is the same paragraph, as it might have been copied by another careless student. **Without looking back at the original paragraph**, proofread this second version carefully. Mark mistakes like this: ① If a word has been omitted, insert a ∧, and write the missing word in the space above the line. ② Underline each incorrect word, and correct it in the space above the line.

From the 1920s through the 1950s, cigarette smoking was consider a harmless and

even glamorous habit. Stars of the silver screen, wear tuxedos and evening gowns,

lighted each other's cigarette in night club scenes. Film detectives chain-smoked as they

solve their cases. The children in many pictures sneak their first puffs behind the garage.

But modern audiences watch old movies on TV find these scenes disturbing.

Before checking your work, answer these questions:

1. How many corrections did you make in Exercise 0.4? _____
2. The paragraph in Exercise 0.4 contained six mistakes. If you didn't find all six, proofread the paragraph again, reading it **out loud**, word by word. **Listen** for mistakes as you read it. Now how many did you find? _____
3. If you still didn't find all six, proofread the paragraph once again, this time comparing it to the original. **Look** for mistakes as you compare it. Now how many did you find? _____
4. What one kind of error is repeated over and over by the writer of the paragraph in Exercise 0.4?

_____

Now turn to the Answers to check your work.

Exercise 0.5	Checking proofreading skills in another paragraph

Here is the same paragraph, as it might have been copied by yet another careless student. **Without looking back at the original paragraph**, proofread this third version carefully. Mark mistakes like this: ① If a word has been omitted, insert a ∧, and write the missing word in the space above the line. ② Underline each incorrect word, and correct it in the space above the line.

From the 1920s through the 1950s, cigarette smoking was considered a harmless and

even glamorous habit. Stars of the sliver screen, wearing tuxedos and evening gowns,

lighted each other's cigarettes in night club scenes. Flim detectives chain-smoked as they

solved their cases. The childern in many pictures sneaked their frist puffs behind the

garage. But modren audiences watching old movies on TV find these scenes distrubing.

Before checking your work, answer these questions:

1. How many corrections did you make in Exercise 0.5? _____
2. The paragraph in Exercise 0.5 contained six mistakes. If you didn't find all six, proofread the paragraph again, reading it **out loud**, word by word. **Listen** for mistakes as you read it. Now how many did you find? _____
3. If you still didn't find all six, proofread the paragraph once again, this time comparing it to the original. **Look** for mistakes as you compare it. Now how many did you find? _____
4. What one kind of error is repeated over and over by the writer of the paragraph in Exercise 0.5? (Yes, it's a spelling mistake, but **what kind** of spelling mistake?)

Now turn to the Answers to check your work.

Check off here which exercise you found most difficult:

❑   0.3   (missing words)
❑   0.4   (missing endings)
❑   0.5   (reversed letters)

Your answer to this question suggests the kinds of mistakes you tend to miss in your own writing. Proofread for these kinds of mistakes with special care.

Now let's practice the 4th skill in the list on page xv above. In many exercises, you must pay close attention to details as you make small but important changes while copying sentences and paragraphs. This kind of practice helps you to be more accurate in all of your own writing.

Copying, like proofreading, seems as though it should be easy. But as with proofreading, you need to pay very careful attention to details in order to copy successfully. Let's check how well you can copy a paragraph.

Exercise 0.6	**Copying a paragraph**

Mark a piece of paper Exercise 0.6, and copy the following paragraph exactly onto it. Don't worry about making your lines the same as these, but otherwise don't change anything.

> We often remember, or think we remember, being told not to use the word "I" in our writing. I think this advice is foolish. Sure, I can avoid the word "I," by avoiding writing about my concerns. But why would I ever want to do this? I can't write successfully about something that is of no concern to me; no one can. If I write about something that matters to me, I know I'll have plenty to say, while the ideas will come very hard if I don't care about the subject. And if I care about what I write, I don't make a lot of foolish mistakes that reveal my lack of attention and make me look silly. Further, when what I write means something to me, it can mean something to others as well; they care (or don't care) along with me. So why avoid the word "I"? The advantages of using it are too many.

Hand in your completed **Exercise 0.6** so your teacher can check it for you.

The 5th skill in the list is **using your dictionary effectively.** In many exercises throughout this book, you will need to use a dictionary, so make sure you have a good one. Any paperback dictionary with the word *College* in its title should be fine.

You will need your dictionary to check your spelling, to make sure that the forms of various words are correct, and to make sure that you are using the correct word, the word that means exactly what you are trying to say. Your teacher may give you some additional practice in putting your dictionary to good use in editing your writing.

The rest of this book will help you review the most important rules of written English. But rules are useless unless you can apply them in your own writing. The self-teaching method of these exercises helps bridge this gap between **learning** the rules and **applying** them. So do the skills that you have worked on here.

Good luck with your work in *Mastering Written English!* We hope that you, like the many other students who have used these exercises, will find this self-teaching method both helpful and interesting.

Section 1

Practicing the Writing Process

The Steps in the Writing Process

Phase 1: Plan and draft your paper

1. Plan your paper.
   - Choose your topic.
   - Narrow your topic to a main point, and state it in a complete sentence.
   - Free write or make a list to get ideas about your topic.
   - Plan your paragraphs by selecting and arranging supporting ideas.
2. Write a draft of your paper.

Phase 2: Revise your draft

1. Check your ideas.
   - Delete ideas which repeat others or don't support your main point.
   - If necessary, add more supporting ideas to show that your main point is true.
   - Add examples, details, and facts to make each supporting idea more convincing.
2. Check the order of your ideas.
   - Rearrange ideas to put them in the most effective logical order.
   - Use words that show the logical relationships among your ideas.
3. Check your paragraphs.
   - Make sure that each supporting idea has its own paragraph.
4. Make a clean copy of your revised draft, and then revise it again until you are completely satisfied with it.

Phase 3: Edit and proofread

1. Edit to fix mistakes in writing conventions, sentence structure, and grammar.
2. Make your final copy.
3. Proofread your final copy.

Practicing the
Writing Process

NAME _____

After you have completed this section of *Mastering Written English*, write here whatever you think might be helpful for ycur teacher to know about what you did while practicing the writing process, such as what you found most helpful, what you had most difficulty with, which tasks you think you completed most successfully, least successfully, etc.

PAPER A
❏ Doesn't follow the instructions; write a NEW Paper A.
❏ Skips some instructions; COMPLETE everything.
❏ Too short; add MORE

OVERALL EVALUATION OF PAPER A
❏ Excellent ❏ Good ❏ Acceptable ❏ Not acceptable

COMMENTS

In this book we focus on the kind of writing that's required in college and on the job. Here are the main characteristics of this kind of writing:

1. It's usually written in response to a specific assignment.
2. It's written for someone other than the writer to read.
3. It's intended to convey ideas or information.
4. It focuses on one main point (or central idea).
5. It's organized in a logical way.
6. It's developed well enough to be convincing.
7. It uses standard written English.

We call this kind of writing either **expository** (which explains or describes how or why something is true by giving information—examples, details, and facts) or **argumentative** (which gives reasons supported by examples, details, and facts why something should be done or why something has happened).

Writing like this is not easy; it's the product of a process with a surprising number of steps. However, almost all students who practice these steps can improve their writing significantly.

The Structure of Expository and Argumentative Writing

As you probably know already, expository or argumentative writing, even though it focuses on one main point, normally has three distinct parts: an **introduction**, a **body**, and a **conclusion**. Whether it consists of one paragraph or many, writing like this always has these three parts.

So in a one-paragraph paper, the introductory sentence will probably express the main point of that paragraph, the body sentences will all tell how or why that one idea is or should be true, and the final sentence will comment on it or re-emphasize it. You may have noticed little one-paragraph essays as advertisements, as thumb-nail movie reviews, and as blurbs on book jackets. For examples in this book, see Exercises 1.16 and 4.13.

Letters are a special kind of shorter and simpler writing. They usually are intended to give information rather than argue something, and they usually are much more informal than the kind of college writing that you will hand in. Still, even a quick note to a friend containing directions for going somewhere will tend to have the same general structure: some kind of introduction telling what you'll be writing about, then the information itself, and then some kind of conclusion.

Most college-level writing, of course, has more than one paragraph. A writer usually devotes a brief introductory paragraph to stating a main point, several longer paragraphs to developing each idea or argument that supports that main point, and a short concluding paragraph reflecting on or summarizing the main point. But the structure remains the same as in a shorter paper or a letter:

Introduction	the main point (a sentence or brief paragraph)
Body	supporting ideas (each in a separate longer paragraph)
Conclusion	comment/summary (a sentence or brief paragraph)

The Steps in the Writing Process: An Overview

Phase 1: Plan and draft your paper

1. Plan your paper.
    - Choose your topic.
    - Narrow your topic to a main point, and state it in a complete sentence.
    - Free write or make a list to get ideas about your topic.
    - Plan your paragraphs by selecting and arranging supporting ideas.
2. Write a draft of your paper.

Phase 2: Revise your draft

1. Check your ideas.
    - Delete ideas which repeat others or don't support your main point.
    - If necessary, add more supporting ideas to show that your main point is true.
    - Add examples, details, and facts to make each supporting idea more convincing.
2. Check the order of your ideas.
    - Rearrange ideas to put them in the most effective logical order.
    - Use words that show the logical relationships among your ideas.
3. Check your paragraphs.
    - Make sure that each supporting idea has its own paragraph.
4. Make a clean copy of your revised draft, and then revise it again until you are completely satisfied with it.

Phase 3: Edit and proofread

1. Edit to fix mistakes in writing conventions, sentence structure, and grammar.
2. Make your final copy.
3. Proofread your final copy.

Don't be discouraged by the number of steps in this process. After you have practiced these steps several times as you write papers for this course, you will find yourself going on automatically to the next step without looking at the list. This happens because this three-phase approach is the **natural** way to do a good job on this kind of writing.

This process will become natural more quickly if you keep the following points in mind:

1. There are **three distinctly different phases** in this process, and writers who do these steps in order — first Phase 1, then Phase 2, and finally Phase 3 — save time and effort. In particular, it's important to notice that fixing mistakes is one of the very last parts of the writing process. Paying attention to them any sooner interferes with the more important phases of the total process.

2. Within the first two phases, **the order of the smaller steps sometimes changes** because different assignments may require different approaches.

3. At different times in this process, you are writing for **different readers**. You write your first draft for just one reader — you yourself. Its purpose is to help you yourself to see what you're thinking and

want to express. Then you need to revise your wording so that others can understand it in the same way that you do, and use that wording in your final copy, which others will read.

4.   You will often want to go back and **repeat certain steps** until you get that aspect of your paper right.

Practicing the Writing Process

Now we'll help you to practice the writing process as described above by doing an assignment with the help of a role model (we'll call her Silvia Sawyer), a student enrolled in Composition 101. Before **you** do any of the steps in the writing process, you will first have a chance to see what **she** does as she writes her paper.

Before you begin any writing assignment, make sure you have read and understood the instructions, and carefully reviewed the topics offered. Some topics may be suitable for expository writing, others for argumentative papers, and some for either, depending on what your main point turns out to be.

Below are the instructions for Silvia's and your writing assignment, Paper A. These instructions are similar to those you will see in the various papers you will write in each of the 12 modules in this book.

You will be writing Paper A throughout the rest of this section. Once you have completed it, you should understand better how to organize and develop all the other papers from Paper B in Module 1 to Paper M in Module 12.

Paper A	*Practicing the Writing Process*
Assignment	Write a well-organized, well-developed paper on one of the following topics:
	The supreme spectator sport A law that should be changed A difficult choice An extraordinary marriage An experiment that failed A dangerous idea
Get Ready	On a piece of scratch paper, free write on your chosen topic, first to narrow it to one specific example if necessary, and then to get ideas to use in developing your paper. Don't stop until you have plenty of ideas. Draw a line across the page when you have finished free writing.
	Read over your free writing, and decide on your main point. Write it in one complete sentence below the line.
	Plan your paragraphs by selecting enough supporting ideas from your free writing to make your main point interesting, clear, and convincing to a reader. Write your supporting ideas in a numbered list below your main point.
Draft	On another piece of scratch paper, write an introduction to your draft telling what your main point is.
	Then write at least one paragraph for each of your supporting ideas. Be sure to include enough examples, details, and facts to make your reader understand and believe each idea.

	Write your conclusion.
Revise	Revise your draft in any way you can to make your paper better. Make sure that you have written at least four paragraphs, including your introduction and conclusion.
Edit	After you have finished revising your ideas, check your draft carefully, and fix any mistakes with your green pen.
Make Final Copy	Mark another piece of paper Paper A, and write the final copy of your paper on it, or print out a clean copy on your word processor.
Proofread	Read your final copy **out loud.** Correct any mistakes neatly by hand. If you used a word processor, enter your corrections, and print out a corrected final copy.

Now let's get ready to use the instructions above to write Paper A.

Phase 1: Plan and Draft your Paper

Some students, when they get a paper assignment, take out a piece of paper and simply start writing right away. These students don't usually write very good papers, because writing a paper is too hard for most people to be able to do it well in just one try. But it's not hard to write a good paper if you **plan** your paper before you try to write even one word. Phase 1 of the writing process teaches you how to plan your paper **before** you write your first draft.

1.1	*Plan your paper.* ● **Choose your topic.**

Sometimes you are given just one topic to write on, as in an essay exam and in some of the writing assignments in this book. For this assignment, however, you will have a choice. Here again are the possible topics:

The supreme spectator sport
A law that should be changed
A difficult choice
An extraordinary marriage
An experiment that failed
A dangerous idea

If you already know something about one of these topics, or have recently read something about it, that information gives you a distinct advantage. You will find out below that Silvia chooses her topic and her main point partially because she has just finished reading something about it. It is therefore sometimes helpful before you choose a topic, or at least before you begin writing about one, to get as much information about it as you can, from the Library, from the Internet, or from some other source. The more you know about a topic the easier it will be for you to develop it, and the more interesting and convincing your paper will be.

Silvia chooses her topic: Silvia Sawyer, the student in whose steps you will follow, decides which topic she wants to write on, and puts a check mark ✓ next to her choice:

✓ An extraordinary marriage

You may want to look up some information about whichever topics interest you before you choose one.

 You choose your topic: Think about the remaining five topics, and choose one that interests you and that you know something about. When you are ready, write your topic here:

1.₁	*Plan your paper.* ● **Narrow your topic to a main point,** **and state it in a complete sentence.**

There is one basic principle you need to keep in mind as you're thinking about what you'll write: **A topic isn't a main point.** A **topic** is typically a large general idea about which you will need to say something; it's often expressed in just a few words.

You will usually find it much easier to discover a good main point by first narrowing your general topic either to a **specific example** of this general idea or to some **limited aspect** of it. Sometimes you may get an assignment where it isn't necessary to narrow your topic in this way. But most college topics will require this step.

After you have narrowed your topic, you can determine your **main point**. However, in writing your main point based on a specific example or limited aspect of the topic, there are three essential qualities or criteria for a good main point that you should always keep in mind:

- After it's narrowed down, a good main point must still be about an idea that can be discussed for four or five paragraphs; in other words, it must still be general enough so that it can be developed adequately.

- A good main point is still about the given general topic, even though it discusses only one aspect or example of that topic; in other words, it must not get off the topic.

- A good main point is normally expressed in a complete sentence.

Here are some examples illustrating these important criteria of a good main point.

Topic	dangerous people
Specific example	people who oppose gun control
Main point #1	People who oppose gun control put my life in danger.
Main point #2	People who oppose gun control have good arguments on their side.

Main point #1 is a good one. While narrowing the topic to a specific group of dangerous people (those who oppose gun control), it's still about the original given topic, "dangerous people," and it's still broad enough to discuss for several paragraphs. Main point #2 is not a good one. Although it is a sufficiently general idea for a paper, it gets off the given topic, "dangerous people."

Here is another example:

Topic	gun control
Limited aspect	people who oppose gun control
Main point #1	People who oppose gun control put my life in danger.
Main point #2	People who oppose gun control make me mad.

Main point #1 is a good one. It limits the topic to one aspect of gun control, but it's still general enough to be developed adequately, and it doesn't get off the track of the given topic, "gun control." Main point #2 isn't a good one. It seems to be about the given topic, but it doesn't express an idea that the writer is likely to be able to develop for four or five paragraphs.

To sum up: in both of these cases the topic is a large general idea, expressed in a few words; the specific example or limited aspect is a smaller but still general idea, and still expressed in just a few words; and the main point is a complete sentence telling what specifically you want to show or prove is true about the topic. Your main point will be your topic sentence, the most important sentence in your paper, and the basis for everything you are going to write about your topic. So it's important for you to understand the difference between a good main point and one that's not good because it's too broad or too limited or unclear or off the topic.

Often it's easy to narrow a topic so that you can write a main point. But at other times you may need to do some additional reading or writing about your topic before you can pin down what you want to write about it. Frequently the best way to get ideas about your topic is to **free write** about it. If you don't know what free writing is or haven't used it before now, you'll learn about it beginning on page 12 below.

Let's see how Silvia narrows her topic, and writes it as a main point.

 Silvia narrows her topic by choosing a specific example: Silvia has plenty of ideas already about interesting marriages, so she doesn't need to do reading or free writing in order to narrow her topic. She simply thinks of some specific marriages that she has found interesting and writes them down:

My parents' marriage
President Roosevelt's and his cousin Eleanor's marriage
Joanne Woodward's and Paul Newman's marriage

Silvia's first choice to write about is her parents' marriage, but then she realizes that it isn't really extraordinary. She admires Joanne Woodward and Paul Newman as a husband and wife team of actors, but she decides she doesn't know enough about their private lives. Finally she chooses Franklin Roosevelt's and his cousin Eleanor's marriage because she recently read an article about this famous couple in *The New Yorker* magazine, and she remembers many things about their marriage that made it both interesting and extraordinary. She puts a check mark ✓ next to her choice:

✓ President Roosevelt's and his cousin Eleanor's marriage

To avoid becoming confused later on, Silvia has to remember that, even though she has narrowed her topic, it's still about an **extraordinary marriage**. She is not free to write everything she knows about the Roosevelts, but only about what made their marriage extraordinary. In the same way, if she had chosen "A dangerous idea" for her topic and had narrowed it to her cousin George's idea about private schools, her paper would be about this one dangerous idea, and not about her cousin George in general or about private schools in general.

 Silvia writes down her main point: Since her topic was "an extraordinary marriage," Silvia can easily see that the purpose of her paper is to convince her readers that the Roosevelts' marriage was indeed extraordinary. So she simply writes down that idea in a complete sentence. This statement of her main point will eventually be the topic sentence of her paper, letting her readers know at the very beginning of her paper what her purpose is.

Franklin and Eleanor Roosevelt had an extraordinary marriage.

 You narrow your chosen topic: First write your chosen topic for Paper A below. Then write three possible specific examples or limited aspects of it.

your chosen topic: _____

a specific example or limited aspect: _____

another specific example or limited aspect: _____

another specific example or limited aspect: _____

Read over the examples or aspects you wrote above. Think about which one of them you know most about, which one will be easiest for you to develop into an interesting and convincing paper. Then put a check mark ✓ next to your choice.

Now you are ready to turn your narrowed topic into a main point. To do this successfully, remember the qualities of a good main point, and how it will control everything you write from this point on. Although you have already narrowed your topic, your main point must still be on track for your chosen topic, it must still be general enough to write at least four paragraphs about, and it must be a complete sentence.

 You write down your main point: Look back at the specific example or limited aspect of your topic that you chose. Using that idea, write your main point on the line below, in a complete sentence. Like Silvia, you will later use this sentence as a topic sentence for your paper.

_____

_____

Now we're ready for the next step in planning a paper.

1.1	***Plan your paper.*** ● **Free write or make a list to get ideas about your topic.**

In doing some assignments, you may want to do research or free write **first** as a way of discovering just what main point you want to make.

But if (as in this assignment) you can find your main point without any additional reading or writing, then it's better to write it down immediately, as you just did, and then free write to get ideas about this more narrowly focused idea rather than about your broader topic.

Free writing means writing down as fast as you can any information that you have on a topic and any ideas that pop into your head about it as you write. It means writing **without stopping** for as long as necessary to get going on your topic. When you free write, in order to write quickly and not forget your ideas, you should pay no attention to correctness or style—to matters of vocabulary, spelling, or grammar—as long as you can understand what you have written. Remember, you are the only reader this free writing will have. The major goal of the writing process at this point is to line up enough ideas and supporting facts and examples to be able to plan a draft of your paper, and to do this quickly, without worrying about exactly how you are going to write those ideas down later.

Making a list is just another form of free writing, but instead of writing your ideas about your topic in sentence form, you simply make a list of them as they come to mind. Both methods are useful for quickly getting ideas about your topic from your head to the page. Both can help you to get in touch with your ideas, to identify your main point if you don't already know what it is, and to get down on paper some of the examples, details, and facts which can help support it.

 ***S**ilvia free writes to get ideas:* What writers need for an effective paper is lots of examples, details, and facts. So Silvia jots down anything at all that seems to be related to her main point in any order that she thinks of it. She doesn't worry about writing complete sentences or spelling words correctly. This is what she writes in six or seven minutes:

Franklin→handsome, sociable. Eleanor→shy, physically unattractive. An odd couple. For a long time nothing unusual about their marriage–six kids. They begin to drift apart. Then E finds out about F's affair. She sticks with him anyway. But now she feels free to get a life of her own. children mostly grown so she begin to travel alot–gets interested in social issues, makes lots of new friends. F gets polio–paralyzed. E helps him in his political career by travelling. She gets to know a lot of smart people. They help F with his campaings for Gov of NY, and then Pres. Wins support for his programs for restoreing propsperity. Then during WWII, F has no time for his programs for ordinary Americans, but E won't let him forget them–he learns to listen to her. From her friends and her travels E gets to know a lot about social and economic conditions around the country especially during the Depression. Her advice influences him, he listens to her. He passes her ideas along to congressmen, new domestic bills get passed even during the war. They stick together, he pays attention to her ideas because they think alike.

***Y**ou free write to get ideas:* Using a piece of scratch paper, free write about your main point as quickly as you can, for at least six or seven minutes. Or, if you prefer, make a list of ideas. Even if some of the ideas don't seem to support your main point, don't pause or stop writing. Later these ideas may remind you of something else that you can use. Just get as much down on paper as you can in a short time.

After doing free writing, you and Silvia should have lots of ideas to use in supporting your main point and developing your paper. Now you need to select which of those ideas will be best to use in your paper, and how to arrange them.

1.1	*Plan your paper.* • **Plan your paragraphs by selecting and arranging supporting ideas.**

***S**ilvia plans her paragraphs:* Silvia reads over her free writing to find some useful ideas, examples, and details. She underlines four items that she thinks will help her show that her main point is true:

An odd couple
During World War II F learns to listen to her
Free to get a life of her own
During the Depression E's advice influences him

She thinks about how each one can support her point, and then rejects the third one because it doesn't seem to be connected to her main point.

Next, Silvia thinks about what order these three ideas should be in. Since she is telling a kind of story, she decides to put them in chronological order—the order in which the events happened. Since they aren't in the right order now, she numbers them in the margin of her free writing to show the correct order.

1 An odd couple
3 During World War II F learns to listen to her
2 During the Depression E's advice influences him.

Because Silvia is using chronological order, she knows her readers will expect some kind of signals (like *first, second,* etc., or *last year, now,* etc.) that will help them follow what she's telling them. So she notes the time clues she can use later—the Depression, World War II.

Silvia now has finished her planning, and has a rough outline of her paper. To make sure that she understands it clearly, she draws a line across the page below her free writing, and copies over her plan. First she writes her topic as a title (capitalizing the important words). Then she writes her main point in a complete sentence. Finally she lists her three supporting ideas:

An Extraordinary Marriage

Franklin and Eleanor Roosevelt had an extraordinary marriage.

1   *They were an odd couple.*
2   *During the Depression E's advice influenced F*
3   *During WW II he learns to listen to her.*

Silvia is now ready to write the first draft of her paper. Because she has planned her paper carefully, it will be fairly easy. She will begin with an introduction telling her main point. She will develop each of her three supporting ideas into one of the three paragraphs she plans for the body of her paper. She knows she will need to explain and support them with examples, details, and facts, and she will need to show clearly how they're connected to her main point. Finally, she will add on some kind of concluding thought.

 You plan your paragraphs: Read over your free writing or list to find those ideas that can do one thing: show that your main point is true. Underline the more promising ones. If you don't have enough ideas to get started, do some more free writing, focusing on **why** and **how** your main point is true. When you have enough ideas, number them in the margin in the order in which you will write about them. Then copy your main point (in one complete sentence) and three or more supporting ideas on the lines below.

Main point: _____

_____

1 _____

2 _____

3 _____

4 _____

Now that you have finished your planning, you, like Silvia, are ready to write your draft. Like her, you will start with an introduction telling your main point. You will develop each of your supporting ideas into paragraphs, explaining them with examples, details, and facts, and showing clearly how they support your main point. And finally, you will add a conclusion. If you have planned your paper carefully, writing this draft will be easy.

1.2	**Write your draft.**

A draft, or first draft, is what most students call the first version of their paper. Here are some hints about how to write a good one:

- **Do not stop to fix mistakes**. Remember that fixing mistakes is the last phase of the writing process. Paying attention to them any sooner interferes with the more important phases of the total process.

After all, this first draft is for just one reader—you yourself. Its purpose is to find some kind of language for your ideas that makes sense to you, and to develop and organize them so you yourself can better see what you're thinking and want to express. Later you will revise and correct this draft with your readers in mind so that they too can see what you mean and be convinced by what you have written.

- If you are writing by hand, **add new sentences or new phrases in the margins** and use arrows to show where they fit. If you are using a word processor, of course, insert additions where they belong.

- **Stop whenever you think you have enough** supporting ideas and details to convince your reader that your main point is true.

- **Don't worry if your ideas become jumbled**. You will have a chance to re-organize them in Phase 2.

You write your first draft: This time don't wait for Silvia. Working from your plan, write your first draft on a piece of scratch paper. Use your main point as a topic sentence in an introduction. Then just keep writing until you have written down all the ideas on your list, plus any more that you think of as you write. Remember to start a new paragraph whenever you start writing about a new item on your list or any other new supporting idea that you decide to discuss. Of course, you will need to add details and examples to make each of your ideas convincing. Add a conclusion.

Silvia writes her first draft: Using her plan, Silvia writes an introduction. In each of the three paragraphs for her supporting ideas, she adds further details that help to show that the Roosevelts' marriage was extraordinary. Then she writes a conclusion. Here is her first draft:

An Extraordinary Marriage

Franklin and Eleanor Roosevelt had an extraordinary marriage.

Early photographs of the couple show a handsome, charming young Franklin and a serious, shy, and not very attractive Eleanor. People wonder how they could have fallen in love with each other in the first place. In their early years together, Eleanor loved being a wife and mother, and bore and raised six children while Franklin pursued his career in the Navy and in politics. In the meantime, the strength he had admired in Eleanor now seemed like stubbornness, and she began to find his sociability simply boring. Then she discovered her husband's affair with her own social secretary. He begged her not to divorce him, she agreed, but only because she believed so strongly in his gift for politics and in his future as a great President.

According to this agreement, Eleanor was now free to have a life of her own. She made many friends, gave speeches, and wrote articles. When Franklin became paralysed by polio from the waist down, his wife went where his lifeless legs could not take him, she

15

shared what she had learned from her journeys, and in this way gave him a better understanding of the enormous problems of the Depression.

In the years after Pearl Harbor, when the President was frantically busy with the world war now raging on two fronts, the First Lady travelled hundreds of thousands of miles to gather facts about conditions in rural and urban America.

Both Franklin and Eleanor, as husband and wife, were able to rise above each other's flaws and even to go on loving each other for their best qualities. The result was an extraordinary marriage.

Phase 2: Revise your Draft

We can learn a lot about revising by noticing the problems in somebody else's writing and seeing how they can be fixed. So let's try reading and criticizing Silvia's first draft before we begin to work on yours.

Don't forget that at this stage of the writing process it's a waste of time to try to correct mistakes in grammar or spelling, since these words and sentences may not even appear in the final draft. Worse, editing for mistakes is a serious distraction from the important and quite different job we're about to do, **fixing ideas**. So if we happen to notice any mistakes, we should just ignore them. What we are examining now are Silvia's ideas only, and asking how these ideas can be made clearer and more interesting and convincing to a reader.

Before we begin, let's look again at the first two steps in the revision process. Here they are, each followed by questions we need to answer about Silvia's draft before it can be effectively revised.

2.1	*Check your ideas.* ● **Delete ideas which repeat others or don't support your main point.** ● **If necessary, add more supporting ideas to show that your main point is true.** ● **Add examples, details, and facts to make each supporting idea more convincing.**

* Is each idea distinctly different from all others, or are some ideas simply repeated in the same or different words? Does every idea help to show that your main point is true, or are there any ideas which may be related to the topic but not to the main point?

* Are there too few supporting ideas to convince a reader that the main point is true?

* Are there too few examples, details, and facts to help a reader understand and believe each of the supporting ideas?

2.2	***Check the order of your ideas.*** ● **Rearrange ideas to put them in the most effective logical order.** ● **Use words that show the logical relationships among your ideas.**

- Are any ideas or details in the wrong place? Are they arranged in chronological order, or order of ascending or descending importance? Or in some other recognizable and logical order?

- Are transition words needed to help you follow the writer's logic? Where?

Now apply these rules and questions by evaluating Silvia's draft.

 You criticize Silvia's first draft: Go back to Silvia's first draft on page 15, and put a line in the left margin next to any place where you find the kinds of problems described in the two rules above. Make notes in the right margin about what's wrong and how to fix it.

 Silvia criticizes her own first draft: She puts a line next to passages that she needs to fix and makes notes in the margin on what she needs to add, delete, explain, or change.

Franklin and Eleanor Roosevelt had an extrordinary marriage.	*My main point may come as a surprise to some people – this idea needs some explanation. Expand this paragraph.*
Early photographs of the couple show a handsome, charming young Franklin and a serious, shy, and not very attractive Eleanor. People wonder how they could have fallen in love with each other in the first place. In their early years	*So why <u>did</u> they get married? Needs more details to make readers believe they were really in love.*
together, Eleanor loved being a wife and mother, and bore and raised six children while Franklin pursued his career in the Navy and in politics. In the meantime,	*These facts make their marriage sound pretty ordinary – contradicts my main point. Cut? No, this <u>is</u> part of this marriage. Rewrite.*
the strength he had admired in Eleanor now seemed like stubbornness, and she began to find his sociability simply	*This sentence hints at why they were attracted to each other in the first place – idea belongs more toward the beginning?*

boring. Then she discovered her husband's affair with her own social secretary. He begged her not to divorce him, she agreed, but only because she believed so strongly in his gift for politics and in his future as a great President.

OK, but why didn't he want a divorce? Explain.

According to this agreement, Eleanor was now free to have a life of her own. She made many friends, gave speeches, and wrote articles. When Franklin became paralysed by polio from the waist down, his wife went where his lifeless legs could not take him, she shared what she had learned from her journies, and in this way gave him a better understanding of the enormous problems of the Depression.

Not clear how these facts relate to the main idea — their extraordinary marriage. But it does relate to it. Got to show the connection.

In the years after Pearl Harbor, when the President was frantically busy with a world war now raging on two fronts, the First Lady traveled hundreds of thousands of miles to gather facts about conditions in rural and urban America.

This part doesn't give enough background for the reader to understand the importance of this to the American public.

But did he pay attention to her? Needs to be connected to main idea. Also paragraph too skimpy — add more information about these important years.

Both Franklin and Eleanor, as husband and wife, were able to rise above each other's flaws and even to go on loving each other for their best qualities. The result was an extraordinary marriage.

More than extraordinary — it also helped the country. Add to this — more details.

Do you agree with Silvia's notes on her draft? Do you have different comments? Write them here.

_____

_____

_____

_____

_____

_____

Y_ou criticize your own draft:_ Look back at the first two steps in the revision process, and the questions that relate to each, on page 16 above. You may find it useful to tear that page out along the perforations and keep it in front of you as you continue.

Next do as Silvia did: Put a line next to each problem with ideas that you see in your draft, and then write what's wrong and how to fix it in the margin.

2.3	*Check your paragraphs.* ● **Make sure that each supporting idea has its own paragraph.**

• Do any paragraphs have two or more supporting ideas in them? Should any paragraphs be combined with others? Should some long paragraphs become two or more paragraphs?

S_ilvia checks her paragraphs:_ Now that she has pretty well figured out what changes and additions are needed, Silvia reconsiders the structure of her paper by making a more detailed plan or outline for the paragraphs in her final draft. Each numbered idea below represents a separate paragraph. Each one has its own specific purpose, but at the same time supports the overall main point of her paper. This new plan shows that some of the material that was originally in her third paragraph is now in her fourth. She also lists the intentions she has worked out for each paragraph, as well as the conclusion.

Main point	*The Roosevelt marriage is extraordinary.*	*I'll add more to turn this into a short introductory paragraph with more background information.*
Idea 1	*They are an odd couple—extraordinarily different from each other.*	*Once I explain more about the reasons why they were first attracted to each other, this idea will make a well developed and pretty convincing second paragraph.*
Idea 2	*A crisis changes Eleanor's own life, but also gets her ready for a different role–a whole new and wonderful relationship with Franklin.*	*If I want to make this into a convincing third paragraph, I need to explain what Eleanor's new personal and public life had to do with her husband's political career.*

Idea 3	*Especially after Franklin's paralysis, there's plenty to show that they had a whole new kind of life together.*	*By combining two shorter paragraphs and adding more facts, I can build this up into a strong fourth paragraph.*
Conclusion	*They were able to rise above each other's flaws and go on loving each other.*	*With a bit more added on, this idea will make a good, short concluding paragraph.*

You check your own paragraphs: Just as Silvia did, reconsider the structure of your paper by revising the plan you wrote for your first draft. See if you can write a sentence that sums up the central idea of each paragraph you have written (or are now planning to write) in support of your overall main point. You may not want to use this sentence in the paragraph itself, but writing it down will help you focus on the idea you're trying to get across in that paragraph. It will also help you to see how or if the paragraph supports your main point. And it will help you to see what more you need to say to make it clear to your reader **how** the paragraph supports your main point.

Write your revised plan on another piece of scratch paper. Make sure that you have written down the point of each of your supporting paragraphs in a clear, complete sentence.

Once you have completed your first review of your ideas and paragraphs, and made a new plan for your paper, you are ready to go ahead and write your revision.

Silvia writes her final revision: Using her marginal notes and other markings made on her first draft, along with her revised plan, Silvia rewrites her paper, adding, deleting, changing, rearranging, and sorting her material into somewhat different paragraphs. To carry out all her ideas for revision, she has to rewrite her paper several times. Below is her final revision.

An Extraordinary Marriage

Because of all the new information about the Roosevelts that has been published during the past ten years, the American public has begun to realize that the marriage of President Franklin Delano Roosevelt to his cousin Eleanor was extraordinary, particularly as a marriage that began early in the 20th century.

When people look at the early photographs of the couple, they marvel that these two got married in the first place. They wonder how the handsome, charming young Franklin and the serious, shy, and not very attractive Eleanor could have fallen in love with each other. Their attraction to each other, however, is not as strange as it seems. In that period of his life, the future President felt a need for the sincerity and moral strength he found in Eleanor. As for her, with very little love and not much fun when growing up, she was flattered by his boundless charm and delighted by his socialability. These and other strongly contrasting qualities always made them a kind of odd but striking couple.

It appears, however, that the first sixteen years of this couple's marriage was no different from most marriages of that period. In their early years together, Eleanor loved being a wife and mother, and bore and raised six children while Franklin pursued his career in the Navy and in politics. Then Eleanor discovered her husband's affair with her own social secretary. He begged her not to to divorce him, because at that time a divorce would have ended his political career, she agreed, but only because she believed so strongly in his gift for politics and in his future as great President. From this time on, she felt free to spend her time and her enormous energies in pursuing a new career as an agitator for social change and human rights. The shy and insecure Eleanor was transform into a different kind of partner, capable of helping her husband in new and important ways.

When Franklin became paralysed by polio from the waist down, the Roosevelt marriage progressed into its final and most remarkable phase, which lasted the rest of their lives together. During his campaigns for high office and his four terms as President, his wife became his eyes and ears all over the country. She went where his lifeless legs could not take him, she shared what she learned from her journies, and in this way gave him a better understanding of complicated national issues. Without her, he might not have been able to solve the enormous problems of the Depression. In the years after Pearl harbor, when the President was frantically busy with the world war now raging on two fronts, the First Lady travelled hundreds of thousands of miles to gather facts about social and economic conditions in rural and urban America. Whenever she returned to the White House, she succeeded in getting her husband to pay attention again to domestic affairs and to continue the reforms he had begun before the war.

Both Franklin and Eleanor, as husband and wife, had the power to rise above each other's flaws, to recognize the other's remarkable gifts, and even to go on loving each other for their best qualities. The result was an extraordinary marriage, of benefit not only to themselves but to many Americans for years to come.

Y*ou comment on Silvia's final revision:* If you notice that Silvia's draft still has mistakes in written English, continue to ignore them. But you will certainly notice that the **content** has changed a lot. Compare this version of Silvia's paper to her first draft. If you think some or all of Silvia's changes are improvements, explain in the right margin next to the change how it improves the paper. If you notice improvements in Silvia's choice of words, comment on that too. If you see new ways of improving the paper, other changes that Silvia should have made, write these comments and suggestions also in the margins. Finally, go over the three steps in the revising process once more to see if Silvia missed something she should have fixed.

Before you begin to revise your draft, think about each of the following four points.

1. ***Stick to the point:*** Study your first draft, the notes you made on it, and your new plan, with the leading idea of each of your main paragraphs spelled out in clearly written sentences. As Silvia did, use this plan to revise your draft as a paper with as many paragraphs as you need to adequately **develop each of your supporting ideas**, and to help you **stick to the point** of each paragraph and to the point of the paper as a whole.

2. ***Use plenty of details:*** Remember, as you work on the paragraphs in the body of your paper, that each supporting idea can be effective only when readers see **lots of examples, details, and facts** that make it clear and convincing.

   Consider the difference between Silvia's first draft and her final revision, and you will realize that the main problem she had to solve in her revision was the lack of enough details (explanations, facts, and examples) to convince her reader that her claims about the Roosevelts' marriage were true.

3. ***Show connections:*** Make sure that you have clearly explained the **connection** between your supporting ideas and your main point. Showing the relationships between and among your ideas is important if your readers are going to be able to follow your meaning. Connecting words like *because* and *although* and transitional words like *therefore* and *however* are very helpful in making these relationships clear to your reader.

   You'll remember that the next most serious problem in Silvia's first draft was her repeated failure to show the connection between some important aspects of her topic and her main idea. Notice how her use of *because* in several sentences in her revision connects these facts with explanations that make these facts more believable. Notice also how Silvia's use of the transition word *however* at the beginning of the third paragraph of her revision solves a problem she discovered in her first draft (see page 18 above). That word alone tells the readers of her revision that Eleanor's contentment as a wife and mother is not presented as evidence of an extraordinary marriage but simply to show that this marriage had its conventional features too.

   Even though Silvia's suggesting that the marriage was conventional would seem to contradict her main point that it was extraordinary, it is a fact that an honest reporter should not ignore. Also it's a smart idea to include such material because it **anticipates objections** that a knowledgeable reader might have to her main point. When you use this strategy (reporting facts that seem to contradict your main point), just make sure your reader understands that such statements are "concessions to the opposition," and not details intended to support your main point. Using words like *although* and *however* will make this clear.

Later on in this book you will learn a lot about how to use connecting and transition words to bring out the precise relationships between and among your sentences and paragraphs and main point. Since you are sure to need some of these words in revising Paper A, **look now at page 224** for a list of these words, and choose those you need to show how your ideas are connected and related one to the other.

4. ***Ignore mistakes:*** Remind yourself once more **not to stop to think about correctness** (grammar, spelling, etc.), but to focus entirely on writing and rewriting your ideas in clear sentences and well-developed paragraphs.

 You write your first revision: Keeping in mind the four points above, revise your first draft. Don't worry about your draft becoming messy; changes show that you are working on improving your paper.

2.4	Make a clean copy of your revised draft, and then revise it again until you are completely satisfied with it.

• Is your draft so messy that you can hardly read it?

• Once you have copied it over so that you can read it clearly, are you satisfied with it?

 You criticize your second draft, and then revise it further as necessary: When you have finished your second draft, read it over slowly and carefully, checking to make sure that you have applied all parts of the three steps in the revision process to your paper, and answered the questions related to them (see page 16 above).

As part of polishing your revision, try to improve your choice of words (use your dictionary and thesaurus) and the readability of your sentences (ask a friend to mark any confusing sentences, and then try to rewrite them more clearly). In these ways, continue to revise your paper until you feel sure that your reader will be convinced by what you've written, and not confused by it in any way.

Revise your paper still further if you find other ways to improve it, and copy it over again if it becomes too messy to read easily.

Phase 3: Edit and Proofread

Now that you know for sure which words and sentences will actually appear in your paper, it's time to consider matters of **correctness in written English**. Let's see how this phase is distinctly different from the phases you have just completed.

• In **Phase 1**, you were writing mostly for **yourself**, trying to pin down the ideas you needed to develop your topic, and writing them down so you could read them over and think more about them.

- In Phase 2, you focused on how you could develop your main point with enough supporting ideas to make it persuasive, and then how to develop your supporting ideas with enough specific examples and details to make them clear and convincing to **others**.

- Now in Phase 3, you will be trying to present your ideas in a form that will **not distract your readers** from their meaning.

In this final phase, you need to make sure of the following:

- that every stroke of your pen or tap on the keyboard has translated the sounds of spoken English into that visual code known as writing conventions — **correct spelling, punctuation, capitalization,** etc.

- that your **sentences** are complete, clear, and correctly punctuated, and

- that you have used the **grammatical forms** that all readers expect to see in this kind of writing.

3.1	**Edit to fix mistakes in writing conventions, sentence structure, and grammar.**

Editing is very different from **revising**. When you revise your writing, you are rewriting to make the **content** of your writing stronger and better, to make the **ideas** clearer and better organized, and to improve **the way they are expressed** by choosing more accurate, colorful, and interesting language. When you edit your writing, you are looking for mistakes, those things about writing that are either **right** or **wrong** according to the rules of written English.

Although you need a teacher to help you master the process of drafting and revising, editing is a skill you can and actually must **teach yourself**. You do this by learning rules, and then practicing applying them on your own. Only **you** can memorize them initially, and only **you** can practice using them until they become mostly automatic when you write. No one can do this job for you. As you have learned the basics of other skills, like basketball or playing computer games perhaps, you can learn to write correct English on your own. Once you have taught yourself the basic rules or procedures, and how to apply them, it's all a matter of practice, practice, and self-correction so that you can find out what you're still doing wrong and be on the alert to avoid it. It's a skill you can master this semester by carefully doing the modules in this self-instructional book.

Let's practice editing skills by looking for mistakes in writing conventions, syntax, and grammar in Silvia's paper. Here is a list of her 11 mistakes:

- In **writing conventions**:
  one mistake in using capital letters (you will learn about these in Module 1)
  six mistakes in spelling

- In **sentence structure**:
  two mistakes, both run-ons (see Module 8)

- In **grammar**:
  one mistake in subject-verb agreement (see Modules 6 and 7)
  one mistake in verb forms (see Module 11)

You *edit Silvia's final revision:* Look for these mistakes in Silvia's paper now, and as you find each one, put a check in the left margin. Then correct it with your blue or black pen by underlining what's wrong and writing in your correction above the line. (If you notice any obviously accidental mistakes like omitted or repeated words that Silvia failed to catch in proofreading, ignore these for now.)

If you were not able to find many of the eleven mistakes listed above, then there's a lot you need to learn from this book. However, if you do all the exercises in this book carefully, by the end of the semester you should be able to find such mistakes easily, even in your own writing.

After you have found all the mistakes you can in Silvia's paper and tried to fix them, turn to the Answers for **Section 1** on page 334 to see how many corrections you got right, and how many you missed. (It will be easer to do that if you tear out the pages with Silvia's paper neatly along the perforations so that you can easily line it up with the Answers.)

How many of Silvia's mistakes did you find and fix correctly? _____
How many did you find but not fix correctly? _____
How many changes did you make that were unnecessary or perhaps wrong? _____
How many mistakes were you unable to find? _____

Now with your **green** pen, fix the mistakes in Silvia's paper that you missed or fixed wrongly.

 You *edit your own final revision:* Look for mistakes in these areas:
- spelling and other writing conventions (capitals, commas, periods, apostrophes)
- sentence structure (run-ons and fragments)
- subject-verb agreement and other verb mistakes

Correct any mistakes you found in your final revision with your green pen. When you are finished, fill in the number of mistakes you found and corrected: _____

3.2	**Make your final copy.**

 You *recopy your corrected draft*: Incorporate all your changes and corrections as you write your final copy, or print out a final corrected copy on your word processor.

3.3	**Proofread your final copy.**

Proofreading and **editing** are both ways of finding and correcting mistakes, but the mistakes that you look for in each of these two processes are different. The mistakes that you looked for when you were **editing** were mistakes that break the **rules** all writers must follow when they write for readers, not for themselves. In your own writing, if you made these kinds of mistakes, it was either because you don't know what the rules are, or because writing is complicated, and you became confused about the rules.

Or you may have made them because you sometimes write the way you speak, forgetting that what's OK in speech is not always correct in writing.

In contrast, the mistakes you look for when you **proofread** are **accidental** mistakes, like omitted words, or important endings on words, ones you may never leave off when you speak. They are mistakes that you immediately know how to fix once you notice them on the page. The problem is **seeing** these mistakes, especially in reading your own final copy. You know exactly what you mean to say; your mind supplies what's missing, and it's hard for you to see that it's not actually there on the page, or that somehow you have miscopied it. (You have already worked on mistakes like these in *To the Student* on pages xvi-xx above.)

It's always easier to see someone else's mistakes rather than your own, so let's practice proofreading on Silvia's paper.

 Y*ou proofread Silvia's final copy:* In Silvia's paper, look for those same slips of the pen that you worked on in *To the Student:* omitted and repeated words, reversed letters in simple words, and other accidental mistakes that Silvia made in her final copy, and then failed to notice when she proofread it. There are two such mistakes in Silvia's final revision. Find and correct them now in the same way as you corrected her other mistakes.

When you have finished proofreading Silvia's paper, check your answers in the back of the book, and, if you missed any, correct them with your green pen.

The following two-part process is the best way to see your own accidental mistakes, the kind you make when you are focused on your meaning rather than the written words on the page, or when you are writing quickly as when you are simply copying what you have already written:

1. Read your paper **out loud** one time to make sure you haven't left out words or endings or even entire sentences. Remember that reading out loud lets you **hear** as well as **see** your accidental mistakes, like:

    *   reversed letters
    *   omitted punctuation like apostrophes
    *   missing words
    *   repeated words

2. Read it out loud again, but this time begin with the last sentence and not only look at and pronounce but also **touch** each word with your finger. Continue to read your paper backwards in this way, sentence by sentence, using all your senses—sight, hearing, touch—as you check for mistakes made in copying, ones that may not have been in your other drafts.

 Y*ou proofread your own final copy:* If you make your proofreading corrections neatly and legibly, you don't need to recopy your paper. However, if you're using a word processor, enter your corrections, and print out a final clean copy.

Your teacher will tell you whether he or she wants you to hand in this entire section of *Mastering Written English* or just the final copy of the paper you have now completed. For now, tear out all the pages of this section carefully along the perforations and keep them in your three-ring loose leaf notebook, along with the drafts of your paper and your final copy.

Looking Ahead

Throughout this course, you will continue to practice these steps in the writing process at the beginning and end of each module. All the other modules focus on the third phase of the writing process — fixing your mistakes — because this is the phase you can learn by yourself from a self-instructional book like this one. In class, your teacher will help you with the other two phases. But it's up to you to learn how to edit by first mastering the rules of written English and then applying them to your writing. You will be able to do this if you follow all the instructions carefully and complete each module on time. Keep in mind that interesting, well-organized content and correctness are **both** essential to pass this course and to succeed in most of your other college courses.

Section 2

Practicing the Editing Process

Practicing the Editing Process

Use this chart to keep track of when each module is due.

Module	Title	Date due
1	Mastering Writing Conventions Paper B	
2	Understanding Simple Sentences Paper C	
3	Understanding More Complicated Sentences I	
4	Understanding More Complicated Sentences II Paper D	
5	Using Nouns and Pronouns Paper E	
6	Making Present-tense Verbs Agree Paper F	
7	Mastering Past-tense Verbs Paper G	
8	Recognizing and Fixing Run-ons Paper H	
9	Recognizing and Fixing Fragments Paper J	
10	Mastering Verb Phrases I Paper K	
11	Mastering Verb Phrases II Paper L	
12	Mastering Expansion Paper M	

1 Mastering Writing Conventions

NAME _____

As you complete each exercise, record your number of mistakes below.

1.1 _____	1.8 _____	1.15 _____	1.22 _____	1.29 _____
1.2 _____	1.9 _____	1.16 _____	1.23 _____	1.30 _____
1.3 _____	1.10 _____	1.17 _____	1.24 _____	1.31 _____
1.4 _____	1.11 _____	1.18 _____	1.25 _____	1.32 _____
1.5 _____	1.12 _____	1.19 _____	1.26 _____	1.33 _____
1.6 _____	1.13 _____	1.20 _____	1.27 _____	1.34 _____
1.7 _____	1.14 _____	1.21 _____	1.28 _____	1.35 _____

EXERCISES
❑ Complete
❑ Incomplete

INSTRUCTIONS
❑ Followed carefully
❑ Not careful enough

CHECKING OF EXERCISES
❑ Careful ❑ Green pen not used
❑ Not careful enough ❑ Mistakes not corrected

PAPER B
❑ Doesn't follow the instructions; write a NEW Paper B.
❑ Skips some instructions; COMPLETE everything.
❑ Too short; add MORE.

EDITING PAPER B FOR THIS MODULE'S WORK
❑ Careful ❑ Not careful enough
OVERALL EVALUATION OF PAPER B
❑ Excellent ❑ Good ❑ Acceptable ❑ Not acceptable

COMMENTS

Rules Summary for Module 1

1A	Mark the beginning of each paragraph clearly by **indenting** or by skipping a line.
1B	Use **capital letters** only for the following: 1 the first letter of a sentence; 2 the word *I;* 3 the first letter of a specific name (and its title); and 4 the first letter of a word made from a name.
1C 1 2 3 4	Use correct and clear punctuation. Use a **period** after a **statement**, and a **question mark** after a **question**. **Don't** put space **before** punctuation. **Do** put space **after** punctuation. Use an **apostrophe** to show where letters have been omitted in contractions. Use **quotation marks** whenever you use someone else's exact words.
1D	Avoid most **abbreviations**.
1E	Spell out the **numbers** *one* through *ten.* Use numerals for numbers above *ten.*
1F	Don't write what should be **one word** as two words, or what should be **two words** as one word.
1G 1 2 3 4	Use **spelling rules** to spell many words correctly. When to put *I* before *E* When to change *Y* to *I* When to double the final consonant before adding an ending How to spell words ending in *ING*
1H 1 2 3 4 5	Don't confuse words that **sound** alike but have different meanings. *THEN/THAN* *TO/TOO/TWO* *ITS/IT'S* *YOUR/YOU'RE* *THEIR/THEY'RE/THERE*

Writing conventions are rules which writers have invented over the centuries to communicate the meaning of spoken language through visual symbols. They include the alphabet, the letters of the alphabet chosen to represent specific words, the use of capital letters to add to the meaning of a word, punctuation marks to suggest the inflections of a speaker's voice or to add additional meanings, and the use of space on the page to project further meanings.

If any of these conventions are not followed in a piece of writing, it becomes hard to read. For example, here is an old inscription on a 17th century tombstone

HERELYETHTHEBODYOFWILLMVOGWELLTHEELDERBURYEDNOV3ANODONI1683

Because it lacks such a basic writing convention as leaving space between words, besides using all capital letters, archaic spelling, and the abbreviation *anodoni* (for the Latin *anno Domini* or "in the year of the Lord"; the modern abbreviation is *AD*), this inscription is almost unreadable. Try to write it here using modern writing conventions.

_____

_____

Check the Answers on page 336 to see how much of it you got right. Correct your answer with your green pen.

Obviously, your readers rely on these conventions to help them understand what you write. This module will teach you what you need to know about writing conventions so that you can meet your readers' expectations. Writers who don't meet readers' expectations run the risk of having their ideas misunderstood or ignored.

School Grammar Questions about writing conventions are very common on system-wide or state-wide tests of school grammar. On these tests, writing conventions are often referred to as *mechanics*, which is just a traditional term for the writing conventions you will be learning about in this module, like capitalization, punctuation, abbreviations, and spelling. If you do the work in Module 1 carefully, you shouldn't have any problems answering questions about *mechanics* on these tests.

Using Module 1 to Edit Your Own Writing

Use Paper B to discover how much you already know about writing conventions. Later in this module, you'll be editing this paper by applying the rules of this module to what you have written.

Because Paper B assigns you to write a letter rather than a typical college-level paper, the steps that you follow in the process of writing it are somewhat different from, and in some ways simpler than, those that you followed in Section 1. Still, you will be using the same three general phases of the writing process: ① planning your letter, ② organizing your information logically and developing it sufficiently, and ③ editing it to fix any mistakes.

You may write this paper by hand. Better yet, use a word processor.

Drafting Paper B	**Using writing conventions**

Assignment

Imagine that on your birthday a rich aunt has taken you to a large shopping mall in a nearby town. Together you have visited a variety of stores, including ones that sell clothing, sports goods, and electronics, where your aunt has paid for anything you wanted, up to a total of $1,000. Your purchases include various items in various quantities. You have just returned from this shopping spree. Write a letter to a friend, describing the shopping trip and giving your friend exact information about your purchases so that he or she can make similar ones.

Get Ready

On a piece of scratch paper, make a list, including your aunt's name, the name and complete address of the shopping mall you visited, the names of at least six stores where you shopped, the items that you chose, how many of each you purchased, and the price of each.

Because you will be writing a letter, you don't need to worry about the parts that are typical of a formal paper: an introduction containing a main point, separate paragraphs for separate ideas, and a conclusion.

Draft

On another piece of scratch paper, write today's date, and then the salutation of your draft letter: *Dear [whoever].*

Then write several paragraphs describing the shopping spree, including all the information you listed above. Be sure to use complete sentences. Include several sentences about those purchases that you know will be especially interesting to your friend. Also quote at least one comment your aunt made about your day together, **using her exact words**.

Write the ending to your letter.

Revise

Check to make sure that you have included all the information required in your letter. Rearrange your facts and details, if necessary, in logical order and in appropriate paragraphs, and rewrite any sentences that are not completely clear.

Keep your draft of Paper B to use later.

Marking Paragraphs

  Mark the beginning of each paragraph clearly by <u>indenting</u> or by skipping a line.

When you start a new paragraph, you show that you want to focus attention on something new, usually on some new aspect of your main point. Every time you start a new idea, you should begin a new paragraph.

1. If you are writing by hand, indent each paragraph about half an inch, or about the width of your thumb.
2. If you are writing with a word processor, indent five spaces.
3. If you are writing single-spaced text, you may leave a blank line between paragraphs without indenting (as we do in this book).

Exercise 1.1	Showing where new paragraphs begin

Read this passage carefully to make sure that you understand it. Mark a piece of your three-hole, loose leaf paper Exercise 1.1, and rewrite this passage onto it as **two paragraphs**, indenting each paragraph distinctly. Start the second paragraph where a new idea begins.

Anglo-Saxon, an old Germanic language, ranks first among many languages that contributed to our modern English vocabulary. This language, spoken by early inhabitants of England, gave us words like <u>cow</u>, <u>pig</u>, <u>plow</u>, <u>walk</u>—common words associated with outdoor life and the activities of farmers and workers. The second most important source of modern English words is Norman French. This language, brought to England by a conquering army, gave us words like <u>beef</u>, <u>pork</u>, <u>study</u>, <u>dance</u>—more refined words associated with life indoors and the pastimes of a ruling class.

Remember to use your green pen to check each exercise as soon as you finish it. Write in any necessary corrections, and then write your number of mistakes on the cover page.

Using Capital Letters

1B	Use <u>capital letters</u> only for the following: 1 the first letter of a sentence; 2 the word *I*; 3 the first letter of a specific name (and its title); and 4 the first letter of a word made from a name.

<u>Did</u> I get the right answer?
> *Did* is capitalized because *D* is the first letter of a sentence.
> *I* is a capital letter because *I* is always capitalized.

The retired <u>general</u> teaches at a local <u>college</u>.
> *General* and *college* aren't capitalized because they aren't parts of specific names.

Does <u>General Gibson</u> teach at <u>Pomona College</u>?
> *General* is capitalized because it's a title used with a specific name.
> *Gibson*, *Pomona*, and *College* are capitalized because they're specific names.

My brother is studying <u>sociology</u> and <u>English</u> at a <u>Nigerian</u> <u>university</u>.

Sociology isn't capitalized because it isn't part of a specific course name.

English and *Nigerian* are capitalized because they're made from the names *England* and *Nigeria*.

University isn't capitalized because it isn't part of the name of a specific university.

Exercise 1.2   Inserting missing capital letters

Underline each word that should begin with a capital letter, and write the entire correct word in the space above the line.

1. when roberto goes to college, he will study psychology and spanish.

2. has your mother made an appointment with the doctor?

3. today i went to see dr. alston.

4. my youngest uncle is an engineer for the sperry corporation.

5. the house where aunt sally was born is on narcissus street.

Exercise 1.3   Correcting misused capital letters

Underline each word that should not begin with a capital letter, and write the entire correct word in the space above the line.

1. St. Mary's is the only Church in the Neighborhood that has a Raffle every Friday night.

2. Our math Professor owns stock in the Railroad which the Metropolitan Transit Authority took over.

3. The local High School improved its Curriculum by offering new courses in Geography and requiring

    four years of Spanish or another Foreign Language.

The following exercise is your first chance to look for mistakes in Paper B and to correct any mistakes you find.

Editing Practice B.1   Checking paragraphs and capital letters in your own writing

1. Get your draft of Paper B.
2. Review Rule 1A, and then check to make sure that you clearly indented each of your paragraphs. Fix any mistakes with your green pen.
3. How many mistakes did you make in using Rule 1A? _____
4. Review Rule 1B, and then check the first letter of each word to make sure it is correct (either a capital letter or a lower-case letter). Fix any mistakes with your green pen.
5. How many mistakes did you make in using Rule 1B? _____
6. How many mistakes did you fix altogether? _____ Your ability to find and fix mistakes in your own writing shows how much you've learned so far.

Keep your draft of Paper B to use again later.

Using Punctuation

1C	Use correct and clear punctuation.

College costs are rising , This means that many students can't attend full-time .

It isn't clear whether the punctuation mark in the middle is a comma or a period. And it isn't clear whether the letter *T* in *This* is capitalized. So it isn't clear whether this is two correct sentences or a run-on (which would be an error).

1C1	Use a <u>period</u> after a <u>statement</u>, and a <u>question mark</u> after a <u>question</u>.

Is the game over **?**
A question mark is used because this sentence asks a question.

I asked whether the game was over **.**
A period is used because this sentence makes a statement. It tells what I asked.

Don't forget the period or question mark at the end of the last sentence in a paragraph.

Exercise 1.4	**Using correct capital letters and punctuation**

① Underline each word that should begin with a capital letter, and rewrite it correctly in the space above the line. ② Write in the correct punctuation mark clearly at the end of each sentence.

1. is it time to go

2. did he ask if it was time to go

3. he asked if it was time to go

4. they couldn't decide whether to write the letter

5. did loretta write the letter

1C2	<u>Don't</u> put space <u>before</u> punctuation. <u>Do</u> put space <u>after</u> punctuation.

When you're writing by hand, be especially careful to leave a noticeable space (the width of at least one letter) after punctuation.

When you're writing with a word processor, put two spaces at the ends of sentences and after colons. Put one space after other punctuation marks.

When I looked at her, □ she turned away from me. □□ Then she started to run.
The □ marks where there are spaces.

Parentheses ( ) and quotation marks " " are exceptions to the rule about spacing. Never put a space after the first or before the second parenthesis or quotation mark.

My brother □ (the one with the beard) □ asked, □ "Where are you going?"
The □ marks where there are spaces.

1C3	Use an <u>apostrophe</u> to show where letters have been omitted in contractions.

it is	it □ s	it's
are not	aren □ t	aren't
do not	don □ t	don't

Apostrophes show where the letters i and o have been omitted.

| will not | w □ n □ t | won't |

The contraction won't is irregular.

Contracted forms are more informal than uncontracted forms, but they're usually acceptable in college and business writing.

Exercise 1.5	Using contractions correctly

Write these two-word forms as contractions.

1. it is   _____

2. does not   _____

3. is not   _____

4. I am   _____

5. do not   _____

6. will not   _____

Exercise 1.6	Using contractions correctly in a paragraph

Rewrite each underlined pair of words as a contraction in the space above the line.

<u>It is</u> amazing how much <u>we are</u> able to learn about the so-called good old days from old

mail order catalogues. <u>Here is</u> a sampling of their ads between 1912 and 1932:

Model H Motor Car, $348: "<u>We will</u> refund every penny if it <u>will not</u> go 15 miles an hour."

Baby Grand Piano, $118: "<u>She is</u> a beauty. Delivery? <u>It is</u> free!"

Two-piece Bathing Suits, $1.63: "<u>They are</u> the latest—backless and skirtless." And a model says, "<u>Where is</u> your courage? <u>I am</u> wearing one. <u>It is</u> the cat's pajamas."

Bargains? <u>You are</u> wrong. A person <u>who is</u> making ten dollars an hour today <u>would not</u> have made five dollars a day when these ads were printed.

Exercise 1.7	**Fixing incorrect contractions**

This paragraph contains contractions that are incorrect because they are missing apostrophes. Underline each incorrect contraction, and correct it in the space above the line.

If youre on a diet, its likely that youre counting calories. However, nutritionists are now saying that calories arent necessarily bad for a person whos trying to lose weight. Theyve discovered that carbohydrates like potatoes, bread, and cereals have lots of calories, but theyre full of nutrition, so they dont add pounds quickly. On the other hand, fats like butter arent nutritious at all, so its easy to gain weight by eating them. Even worse, most people dont realize how much fat theyre getting in cheese, meat, and ready-made foods. So if youre dieting, youd do well to remember this: Fats what makes you fat.

1C4	**Use <u>quotation marks</u> whenever you use someone else's exact words.**

My grandmother used to say, "Don't wear white before Easter."
  The words inside the quotation marks are the **exact words** that my grandmother used.

"White will be the most the popular color in next winter's wardrobe," a fashion columnist wrote recently.
  The words inside the quotation marks are taken from a Philadelphia newspaper.

Most quotations are introduced by or followed by a comma.

In American usage, the closing quotation marks come **after** the period or comma that ends the quotation.

> My grandmother used to say, "Don't wear white before Easter."
> "White will be the most popular color in next winter's wardrobe," a fashion columnist wrote recently.
>> A comma separates these quotations from the rest of the sentence. The closing quotation marks are written after the period or comma at the end of the quotation.

Exercise 1.8	Fixing quotations

Place quotation marks and commas where they belong.

1. Jeremiah overcame procrastination by repeating to himself Anything worth doing is worth doing badly.

2. Any man's death diminishes me wrote the poet John Donne.

3. The new student muttered I must be in the wrong class as she picked up her books and bolted out the door.

If a complete sentence is quoted, the quotation must begin with a capital letter.

> It was Leo Durocher who said, **"N**ice guys finish last."
>> *Nice* is capitalized because it is the first word of a quoted sentence.

Exercise 1.9	Fixing quotations

Underline each word that should begin with a capital letter, and write the entire correct word in the space above the line.

1. The old saying tells us, "when in Rome, do as the Romans do."

2. According to Murphy's law, "if anything can go wrong, it will."

3. The proverb says, "practice makes perfect," but athletes advise us, "only perfect practice makes perfect."

Editing Practice B.2	*Checking punctuation in your own writing*

1. Get your draft of Paper B again.
2. Review Rules 1C-1C2, and then check the end of each sentence to make sure that you used a clear period or question mark. Pay particular attention to the last sentence in each paragraph. If you used a word processor, check to make sure you followed Rule 1C2 and the exception for parentheses and quotation marks on page 38. Fix any mistakes with your green pen.
3. In all the other parts of your letter, where you did not write sentences (for example, at the end of the date), check to make sure that you have **not** used a period. Fix any mistakes with your green pen.
4. How many mistakes did you make in using Rules 1C-1C2? _____
5. Review Rule 1C3, and then check each contraction to make sure that the apostrophe shows where letters have been omitted. Fix any mistakes with your green pen.
6. How many mistakes did you make in using Rule 1C3? _____
7. Review Rule 1C4, and then check the quotation in your letter (the exact words of your aunt's comment) to make sure you used quotation marks, commas, and capital letters correctly. Fix any mistakes with your green pen.
8. How many mistakes did you make in using Rule 1C4? _____

9. How many mistakes did you fix altogether? _____ Your ability to find and fix mistakes in your own writing shows how much you've learned so far.

Keep your draft of Paper B to use again later.

Using Abbreviations

1D	Avoid most <u>abbreviations</u>.

Most abbreviations make your writing harder to read.

✗   ✗   ✗   ✗

While visiting <u>N.Y.C.</u> last <u>Oct.</u>, we saw <u>&</u> photographed many famous <u>bldgs</u>.
> Avoid abbreviations like these. Never use the ampersand sign & instead of the word *and* in college and business writing.

While visiting <u>New York City</u> last <u>October</u>, we saw <u>and</u> photographed many famous <u>buildings</u>.
> Spelled out words are easier to read.

Some abbreviations are appropriate in college and business writing:

*   The abbreviations *AM* and *PM* (or *am* and *pm*) are normally used with numerals to write the time of day.

*   Titles like *Mr., Mrs., Ms., Sgt., Prof.,* and *Dr.* are normally abbreviated to write specific names.

*   The abbreviation *etc.* is usually acceptable.

*   Abbreviations like *St., Ave.,* and *Blvd.,* and the two-letter postal abbreviations of state names, are normally used with numerals to write specific addresses.

Use a period after most abbreviations. But if an abbreviation is the last word in a sentence, don't use two periods.

A few very common abbreviations, usually written with capital letters, like *USA* (for *United States of America*), *TV* (for *television*), *AM* and *PM* (or *am* and *pm*, for times of the day), *NYC* and *LA* (for the cities), and postal state abbreviations (like *NY* for *New York* and *CA* for *California*), are written without periods.

<u>Dr.</u> Mulero has mail delivered to his new address: 725 Tulip <u>St.</u>, Floral City, <u>FL</u> 33417.
> *Dr.* is abbreviated because it's a title used with a specific name.
> *St.* and *FL* are acceptable abbreviations because they're parts of a specific address.
> The postal abbreviation *FL* is written without a period.

Many children in the <u>USA</u> watch too much <u>TV</u>.
> The abbreviations *USA* and *TV* are written without periods.

Many <u>doctors</u> have offices in expensive locations like Boston's Beacon Hill, New York's
Park <u>Avenue</u>, <u>etc.</u>
> The word *doctors* isn't abbreviated because it isn't a title used with a name.
> The word *Avenue* isn't abbreviated because it isn't part of a specific address.
> When the abbreviation *etc.* comes at the end of a sentence, only one period follows it.

Exercise 1.10	Fixing incorrect abbreviations

Rewrite each sentence, changing abbreviations to their written-out forms. But don't change the
acceptable abbreviations.

1. In Dec. the student govt. will present an Xmas show to raise funds for the trip to S. America.

2. Between Battery Pk. & Greenwich Village, most of the sts. in N.Y.C. have names instead of numbers.

3. Dr. Farley's new address is 15722 Princess St., River Falls, MN 55203.

Using Numbers

1E	Spell out the <u>numbers</u> *one* through *ten*. Use numerals for numbers above *ten*.

There were <u>26</u> actors on stage and <u>six</u> people in the audience when the show began.
> The number *26* is written with numerals because it's more than *ten*.
> The number *six* is spelled out because it's less than *ten*.

For most college and business writing, there are a few exceptions to this rule:

*   It's usually acceptable to spell out numbers that can be written as one word, especially round
    numbers like *thirty, a hundred,* or *a thousand*. But it's never wrong to use numerals for round numbers
    like these: *30, 100,* or *1000.*

*   Always spell out numbers at the beginning of a sentence.

- Numbers in addresses and dates are never spelled out.

- Times on the hour and even-dollar prices may be spelled out, but times and prices are normally written with numerals.

- Numerals are normally used when counting with numbers like *4th, 11th, 22nd,* and *33rd.*

- Numbers in lists and in scientific and technical writing are usually not spelled out.

<u>Nineteen</u> people gathered in front of <u>6</u> Main Street at <u>3:00</u> on July <u>4</u>, 1997.
  Nineteen is spelled out because it's at the beginning of a sentence.
  The time *3:00* could also be spelled out as *three o'clock* because it's a time on the hour.
  But *6* is not spelled out because it's in an address, and *4* is not spelled out because it's in a date.

I paid <u>$6</u> for that book and <u>$1.95</u> for this magazine.
  The price *$6* could also be spelled out as *six dollars* because it's an even-dollar price.

Exercise 1.11	Fixing mistakes in abbreviations and numbers

Underline each error in abbreviations and numbers, and write the correct word or number in the space above the line.

1. I read only 3 chapters of the book Mrs. Duff lent me, & then I lost it.

2. The prof. in my govt. class assigned one hundred and thirty-three pp. of homework for Tues.

3. When I was 6 yrs. old, we moved to a quiet st. in Phila.

4. 90 people began to picket in front of 10 Downing St., London, on March 9, 1997.

5. She told me to take 1 teaspoonful of cough medicine every four hrs. for the next 48 hours.

Solving One-word/Two-word Problems

1F	Don't write what should be <u>one word</u> as two words, or what should be <u>two words</u> as one word.

Some words are always written in either a two-word form or a one-word form.

Here are some common phrases that should always be written as two words:

a lot in fact	all right no one	even though

Here are some common words that should always be written as one word:

furthermore however	myself nevertheless	whereas throughout

Other words are sometimes written as one word and sometimes written as two words, depending on what they mean.

Bill wrote to his mother <u>every day</u>.
> In this sentence, *every* and *day* are two words. They mean "on every single day."

Ginny wore her <u>everyday</u> clothes.
> In this sentence, *everyday* is one word. It means "ordinary" or "commonplace."

If you're not sure whether a word should be written as one word or as two, use your dictionary to look up the one-word form. If the one-word form doesn't have the meaning you want, then you should write the two-word form.

Exercise 1.12   Using one-word and two-word forms correctly

① Look up the given one-word form in your dictionary, and write in its definition. ② Then fill in the appropriate one-word and two-word forms.

1. everyday / every day

    Everyday means _____

    a. _____ most people do their jobs and care for their families.

    b. These _____ activities require commitment, even dedication.

2. nobody / no body

    Nobody means _____

    a. The court declared Judge Crater dead even though _____ was ever found.

    b. Jane had nothing and _____ to call her own.

3. sometimes / some times

    Sometimes means _____

    a. For criticizing your parents, _____ are better than others.

    b. You are _____ exasperating.

Exercise 1.13   Fixing one-word/two-word mistakes

Underline each word that should be two words, or two words that should be one word, and write the entire correct word or words in the space above the line. For help, use your dictionary.

Health care costs so much nowadays that people worry alot about taking care of them selves. Infact, everyday expenses are so heavy now that almost no body (my self included) has any money put a side for health emergencies. How ever, I had a high fever to day and decided that maybe I should see my doctor, who gave me an anti biotic. She said I maybe allright by to morrow. I certainly hope so, for I donot want to miss an other day at work.

Editing Practice B.3   *Checking other conventions in your own writing*

1. Get your draft of Paper B again.
2. Review Rule 1D, and then check each abbreviation to make sure it is correct. Fix any mistakes with your green pen.
3. How many mistakes did you make in using Rule 1D? _____
4. Review Rule 1E, and then check each number (either a numeral or spelled out) to make sure that it is correct. Fix any mistakes with your green pen.
5. How many mistakes did you make in using Rule 1E? _____
6. Review Rule 1F, and then check each one-word/two-word form to make sure that it is correct. Pay particular attention to the 11 problem forms listed on pages 43-44 above: *a lot, all right, even though, in fact, no one, furthermore, however, myself, nevertheless, throughout,* and *whereas.* Fix any mistakes with your green pen.
7. How many mistakes did you make in using Rule 1F? _____
8. How many mistakes did you fix altogether? _____ Your ability to find and fix mistakes in your own writing shows how much you've learned so far.

Keep your draft of Paper B to use again later.

Exercise 1.14   Reviewing writing conventions in a paragraph

Read this passage carefully to make sure that you understand it. ① Mark a piece of paper Exercise 1.14, and rewrite this passage onto it as **one paragraph**, correcting errors in writing conventions. The spelling, grammar, and sentence structure are correct, so **make no other changes**. Hint: The phrase *wonders of the world* should not be capitalized. ② In your rewritten paragraph, underline every change.

In our History class last week, I gave a report on the Golden Gate bridge in California. I'd heard alot about this bridge, but I wasnt really sure of all my facts. when I said the Bridge was one of the 7 wonders of the world, our Professor asked me what the other wonders were.

Infact, i didn't know, but I guessed the Rocky Mts. No one else in the class even tried to guess. Our teacher laughed & said he'd give us a hint. every single one of the seven wonders, he said, was built by man, and each was built at least 2,100 yrs. ago. After a while, some one guessed 1 right answer, those huge stone pyramids in egypt. But no body could name even one of the other six wonders. Can you.

This passage contained 19 errors. How many did you find? _____ If you didn't find all 19, try again before you check your work.

Using Spelling Rules

1G	**Use <u>spelling rules</u> to spell many words correctly.**

Spelling is an important writing convention. Usually there is just one correct way to spell a word, and your readers expect you to use that correct spelling.

You can always use your dictionary to check the spelling of a word you're not sure about, but looking every word up in the dictionary takes time. Here, we'll help you to learn four spelling rules that will help you spell hundreds of common words without having to look them up.

1G1	***IE* and *EI*** **Use *I* before *E*, but** **use *EI* after *C*, and** **use *EI* to sound like *A*.**

We <u>believe</u> the package contains books.
> Use *IE* to spell *believe*. This word follows the basic rule.

We <u>received</u> it today.
> Use *EI* after *C* to spell *received*.

Its <u>weight</u> surprised us.
> Use *EI* to spell *weight* because it sounds like *A*.

This rhyme will help you remember the rule. Memorize it, if you don't know it already:

> I before E,
> Except after C,
> Or when sounded like A (as in *neighbor* and *weigh*).

Exercise 1.15	**Spelling words correctly with *IE* and *EI***

① Write in *IE* or *EI* to spell each word correctly. ② Write in *1*, *2*, or *3* to tell which line of the rhyme explains the word's spelling:

    1 - I before E,
    2 - Except after C,
    3 - Or when sounded like A (as in *neighbor* and *weigh*).

Follow this model:

    a tribal leader: ch <u>*i e*</u>f   line <u>*1*</u>

1. a piece of open land: f __ __ ld   line _____

2. the top of a room: c __ __ ling   line _____

3. the number after seven: __ __ ght   line _____

4. the paper that proves you paid for something: rec __ __ pt   line _____

5. a close companion: fr __ __ nd   line _____

6. to look at something, usually from far off: v __ __ w   line _____

7. they carry blood: v __ __ ns   line _____

Here are four common exceptions to this spelling rule:

either	neither	weird	height

Exercise 1.16   Correcting mistakes with *IE* and *EI*

This paragraph contains many words spelled with *IE* and *EI*. Some of them are correct and some are misspelled. Underline each misspelled word and correct it in the space above the line. For help, use your dictionary.

Do you beleive in magic? When people play the lottery or enter a sweepstakes, they always beleive in their hearts that they're going to win. It's hard to conceive that the odds against winning a sweepstakes are millions to one. Did you ever have a freind who won a big state lottery? Probably not. But most of us have friends and neighbors who consistently play their lucky number and lose. These people might not spend a dime without a receipt, and they would be outraged if a theif took thier hard-earned dollars. However, again and again they decieve themselves and squander money that never can be retreived, all on a brief fantasy of magical gains. (Do you believe that **you** have a lucky number?)

This paragraph contained seven errors. How many did you find? _____ If you didn't find all seven, try again before you check your work.

1G2	**Changing *Y* to *I*** Change *Y* to *I* before adding *ES* or *ED* if a word ends with a consonant + *Y*; but never change *Y* to *I* if the word ends with a vowel + *Y*.

Remember that the letters *A, E, I, O,* and *U* are always **vowels**. *Y* is sometimes a vowel. All the other letters are **consonants**.

Write the five letters that are always vowels here: ____ ____ ____ ____ ____ Write the letter that is sometimes a vowel here: _____

PENNY	Those <u>pennies</u> won't buy much these days.
TRY	Nobody ever <u>tried</u> to do that before.

The words *penny* and *try* end in a *consonant* + *Y*. So change *Y* to *I* before adding an ending beginning with *E*.

PRAY	The farmers <u>prayed</u> for rain.
TOY	The factory makes wooden <u>toys</u>.

The words *pray* and *toy* end in a *vowel* + *Y*. So **do not** change *Y* to *I* before adding an ending.

Exercise 1.17   Changing *Y* to *I*

Add first an *S* or *ES* ending, and then an *ED* ending, to each word.

1. play   _____   _____

2. marry   _____   _____

3. enjoy   _____   _____

4. reply   _____   _____

5. terrify   _____   _____

6. x-ray   _____   _____

1G3	**Doubling final consonants**
	If a word ends with a <u>single vowel + a consonant</u>,
	   and the ending begins with a vowel, double the final consonant.
	But if a word ends with a <u>double vowel + a consonant</u>,
	   or its last syllable <u>isn't accented</u>, do not double the final consonant.

S<u>AD</u>	s<u>a</u>dder, s<u>a</u>dden
FORG<u>ET</u>	forg<u>e</u>tting
PATR<u>OL</u>	patr<u>o</u>lled, patr<u>o</u>lling

Each word ends with a single vowel + a consonant, so double the consonant before adding an ending beginning with a vowel.

FEAR   feared, fearing
PEEL   peeled, peeling
      Each word ends with a double vowel + a consonant, so do not double the consonant.

DIFFER   different, differed
GATHER   gathered, gathering
      Each word has more than one syllable and the last syllable of each word is not accented, so do not double the final consonant.

Exercise 1.18	Doubling the final consonant

Write each word with the given ending.

1. grin + ING   _____

2. rain + ED   _____

3. star + ING   _____

4. matter + ED   _____

5. repel + ENT   _____

6. repeal + ING   _____

7. shop + ED   _____

8. swim + ER   _____

9. prefer + ED   _____

10. cover + ED   _____

1G4	***ING* endings** **If a word ends with a <u>consonant</u> + *E*, drop the *E* before adding *ING*. Never drop *Y* before adding *ING*.**

HOPE   Emma was <u>hoping</u> for a letter.
WRITE   She was <u>writing</u> a note to her sister.
      Each word ends with a consonant + *E*, so the *E* is dropped before adding *ING*.

Don't confuse this with what you learned in Rule 1G3 above: Double the final consonant before adding *ING* if a word ends with a **single vowel + a consonant**.

HOP   A robin was <u>hopping</u> about under my window.
SIT   A wren was <u>sitting</u> on a nearby tree.
Each word ends with a single vowel + a consonant, so double the final consonant before adding *ING*.

Exercise 1.19	Spelling changes with *ING* endings

Fill in the *ING* form of the given word.

1. ROBE   The choir members were _____ in the church vestry.

    ROB   That gang has been _____ shops in this neighborhood.

2. PLAN   _____ next year's schedule is the chairman's responsibility.

    PLANE   The carpenter is _____ the boards.

3. STARE   For Americans, _____ at strangers seems very impolite.

    STAR   Many actors with _____ roles on TV never work in movies.

Do not become confused about words ending with *Y*. Remember the rules you have learned:

Rule 1G2 says: **Do** change *Y* to *I* when adding *ES* or *ED*.
Rule 1G4 says: **Do not** change *Y* to *I* when adding *ING*.

WORRY   Linda <u>worries</u> about every deadline.
              Linda is <u>worrying</u> about the deadline next week.
In *worries*, *Y* is changed to *I* because the ending is *ES*.
In *worrying*, *Y* is not changed to *I* because the ending is *ING*.

Exercise 1.20	Changing *Y* to *I*

Add an *ES* ending, an *ED* ending, and an *ING* ending to each word. Follow this model:

HURRY	*hurries*	*hurried*	*hurrying*
	+ ES	+ ED	+ ING

1. CARRY   _____   _____   _____

2. WORRY   _____   _____   _____

3. TRY   _____   _____   _____

4. REPLY   _____   _____   _____

5.   STUDY   _____   _____   _____

DIE and LIE have irregular ING forms.

DIE   The <u>dying</u> embers glowed.
LIE   <u>Lying</u> under oath is a serious crime.
             Dying is the irregular *ING* form of *DIE*.
             Lying is the irregular *ING* form of *LIE*.

STUDY and *WRITE* have *ING* forms that cause more trouble than any others.

STUDY   <u>Studying</u> is necessary to pass that course.
WRITE   <u>Writing</u> papers is easier on a computer.
             Y is not dropped from *studying* because *Y* is never dropped before *ING*.
             E is dropped from *writing* before *ING*. The *T* is never doubled.

Exercise 1.21	Adding endings in a paragraph

Read this paragraph carefully to make sure that you understand it. ① Mark a piece of paper Exercise 1.21, and rewrite this paragraph onto it, adding the given ending to each word. ② In your rewritten paragraph, underline every change.

READ + ING, 'RITE + ING, and 'rithmetic have been called the three R's of education, the basics that every child should have STUDY + ED and MASTER + ED by the end of elementary school. Now some educators are SAY + ING that the new basics will be READ + ING, WRITE + ING, and COMPUTE + ING. But the computer should not be IDENTIFY + ED only with STUDY + ING arithmetic and numbers. For example, word PROCESS + ING is much more than just TYPE + ING. Young children have TRY + ED USE + ING a word processor before they have even STUDY + ED the alphabet, and their teachers are SAY + ING that WRITE + ING on the computer has HELP + ED them to read sooner and with more UNDERSTAND + ING. A special computer language called *LOGO* APPLY + ES REASON + ING skills by HAVE + ING children draw pictures on the screen. Some people are WORRY + ED that children will become too dependent on machines, but the ones who are WORRY + ING the most are usually not the ones who have TRY + ED to teach in this new way.

Exercise 1.22	Correcting misspelled words

This paragraph contains commonly misspelled words, but no other errors. Underline each misspelled word, and use your dictionary to correct it in the space above the line.

The automobil has changed the landscape and the way we live dramaticly in less than a hundred years. Citys once were built on rivers, with stores clustered on Main Street. Now suburban shoping malls and parking lots sprawl for miles along the highways, and it's not unusal for families to own two or even three cars. Scientists who are studing the enviroment

know that car exaust fumes are a major cause of smog and acid rain. They even beleive that

our reliance on the internal combusiton engine may be contributting to global warming. Yet

many Americans still take thier right to drive for granted, and the avrage person thinks

commuting to work by car is far better than ridding on the mass transit system.

This paragraph contained 14 errors. How many did you find? _____ If you didn't find all 14, try again
before you check your work.

Editing Practice B.4   Checking spelling in your own writing

1. Get your draft of Paper B again.
2. Review Rules 1G–1G4, and then check the spelling of each word, paying particular attention to these four problems: *IE* and *EI*, changing *Y* to *I*, doubling final consonants, and adding *ING* endings. Fix any mistakes with your green pen.
3. How many mistakes did you make in each kind of spelling mistake?

KIND OF MISTAKE	# OF MISTAKES
IE and *EI*	_____
changing *Y* to *I*	_____
doubling final consonants	_____
ING endings	_____
other mistakes	_____

4. How many mistakes did you fix altogether? _____ Your ability to find and fix mistakes in your own writing shows how much you've learned so far..

Keep your draft of Paper B to use again later.

Exercise 1.23   Correcting various errors in writing conventions

① On scratch paper, rewrite this passage **as three paragraphs**, correcting errors in writing conventions and spelling. Underline every change. ② This passage contained 37 errors. How many did you find? _____ If you didn't find all 37, try again before you go on. ③ Mark another piece of paper Exercise 1.23, copy your three paragraphs onto it, and underline every change.

The first & most basic writting convention is the direction of words on the pg. If you dont read any thing but English or some other european language, it probably hasn't occured to you that words maybe arranged in more than 1 way. But at the dawn of History, writing from rt. to left apparently seemed natural for many people. Infact hebrew still runs from right to left, & Japanese runs from top to bottom. The second basic writting convention, standard spelling, followed the invention of the Printing Press in the 15th cent. Handwritten books were scarce and didnt circulate very far. when local writers spelled words the way they pronounced them, thier local readers had no promblem. But printed books traveled to distant neighborhoods, so a standard spelling was gradually developed.

By 1775, when Doctor Samuel johnson published the first dictionary in english, there was usually just one accepted way to spell a word, even though readers were pronounceing it in 2 or 3 different ways. The third basic writing convention, the use of Punctuation marks, wasnt followed consistantly until about two hundred and fifty yrs. ago. For centuries dots were used in random ways, and commas werent used atall. Writters gradually started to use dots as periods or full stops, showing readers where to pause. However, only in modern times were Commas introduced, to indicate the difference between breif pauses and longer ones.

Editing Practice B.5   *Checking writing conventions in your own writing*

1. Get your draft of Paper B again.
2. Check again to make sure that you have already fixed each mistake in writing conventions. If you find any more mistakes, fix them with your green pen.
3. How many more mistakes did you fix? _____ Your ability to find and fix mistakes in your own writing shows how much you've learned so far.

Keep your draft of Paper B to use again later.

Avoiding Wrong Words

When you make a **spelling mistake**, you've written a word that doesn't exist. You've used the wrong letters, or you've written the right letters but in the wrong order. If you try to look up your spelling in the dictionary, you won't find it. When you type it on your word processor, your spelling checker marks it.

However, if you type this sentence on your word processor, "If your comming, call me," only *comming* will be flagged as a mistake, even though *your* in this sentence is also a mistake. *Your* is a correctly spelled word but it has a meaning that's different from what the writer intended. This kind of mistake—using a word that **sounds** just like another word but means something different (in this case, *your* for *you're*)—is probably the most frequently repeated mistake in written English. We call these frequently confused words **wrong words**.

Wrong words are serious mistakes; they can badly confuse a reader about what you mean. In this section, you'll learn how to avoid using wrong words.

Exercise 1.24   Distinguishing between wrong words and spelling mistakes

Wrong words and spelling mistakes are underlined in these sentences. Above each incorrect word, write *WW* for a wrong word or *SP* for a spelling mistake. For help, use your dictionary. Follow this model:

                WW   SP
I gave the book two my frend.

1. Thier class was to large for the room.

2. This television progam has been condemned for it's sex and violence.

53

3. <u>Whose</u> the owner of that <u>vechile</u>?

4. <u>Their</u> is no possible chance of <u>wacthing</u> the fireworks tonight.

5. Marisol likes mathematics more <u>then</u> <u>writting</u>.

In other books, what we call "wrong words" are sometimes called "words frequently confused." In school grammar, they are often called *homonyms*, from the Greek words

School Grammar

for "same name." They are also and more accurately called *homophones*, from the Greek words for "same sound." A homonym or homophone is usually thought of as a word that sounds exactly like some other word with a different meaning (like *its* and *it's*). In this book, though, we use "wrong words" to refer to any words that look or sound enough alike to be confused in writing. One of the most common tasks on system-wide or state-wide standardized tests of school grammar is to distinguish one homonym or homophone from another.

Using More of Module 1 to Edit Your Own Writing

Now let's revise Paper B to discover how much you know already about avoiding wrong words.

Revising Paper B	*Avoiding wrong words*
Assignment	Get your draft of Paper B again.
	Revise Paper B by adding at least one more paragraph telling how you feel about the purchases your aunt's generosity helped you to make, and what you plan to do with them.
Get Ready	On a piece of scratch paper, free write on this topic to get ideas to use in revising your Paper B.
Special Instructions	Use each one of the following 12 words at least once in your revised paper:

      ❏ *their*   ❏ *its*   ❏ *your*   ❏ *to*   ❏ *there*   ❏ *than*
      ❏ *then*   ❏ *they're*   ❏ *too*   ❏ *it's*   ❏ *two*   ❏ *you're*

      First read over your draft of Paper B carefully, to see how many of these 12 words you've already used. Whenever you find one, underline it, and check that word off in the list. Then, as you add at least one more paragraph to Paper B, use the rest of the words, underlining them, and checking them off in the list also.

Keep your draft of Paper B to use again later.

Using Sound-alike Words

1H	**Don't confuse words that <u>sound</u> alike but have different meanings.**

1H1	*THEN* Use *then* to mean *at that time* or *next*, often as the first word in a sentence. *THAN* Use *than* to compare two ideas or things.

She shook the present. <u>Then</u> she opened it.
> This sentence means that she opened the present right after she shook it.

Than is always used with another word showing comparison, like *more, better, rather,* and *sooner.*

Beverly has more money <u>than</u> I do.
> This sentence compares the amount of money that she has to the amount that I have.

Exercise 1.25	**Checking your understanding of *then* and *than***

Fill in *then* or *than.*

1. Sharon liked studying current events better _____ history.

2. _____ she signed up for an archeology course.

3. Her class took a field trip to the Indian pueblos at Santa Clara and Taos in New Mexico;

    _____ , they visited Mesa Verde National Monument.

4. Now Sharon is thinking of majoring in Native American history rather _____ continuing her studies in journalism.

1H2	*TO* Use *to* to mean something like *in the direction of.* And use *to* with a verb form, in an <u>infinitive</u>. *TOO* Use *too* to mean *also,* usually after a comma. And use *too* to mean *excessively* or *more than enough.* *TWO* Use *two* for the number after *one.*

Sheila went <u>to</u> the bank.
> This sentence means that Sheila went toward the bank.

Sheila went <u>to borrow</u> some money.
> This sentence means that Sheila went for the purpose of borrowing some money. *To borrow* is an infinitive.

My brother wanted some cake, <u>too</u>.
> This sentence can mean that my brother wanted cake, and someone else also wanted it. Or it can mean that he wanted cake and he also wanted something else to eat or drink.

It's <u>too</u> windy today for a boat ride.
> This sentence means that it's more windy today than it ought to be for a boat ride.
> Notice that *too* has **more than** one *O* and means **more than** enough.

We ordered <u>two</u> books.
> *Two* tells how many books.

Exercise 1.26	**Checking your understanding of *to*, *too*, and *two***

Fill in *to, too,* or *two.*

1. The celebrated orator Edward Everett spoke _____ the crowd at Gettysburg.

2. He spoke for _____ hours.

3. Abraham Lincoln spoke, _____ .

4. A photographer stood up _____ take Lincoln's picture.

5. By the time he had focused his camera, he was already _____ late.

6. After less than _____ minutes, Lincoln sat down.

7. It was _____ late _____ capture a great moment of history, the Gettysburg Address.

Two groups of words that cause many wrong word problems because they sound alike are **possessive pronouns** and **contractions**. Possessive pronouns mean *belonging to,* and **never** have apostrophes; you'll learn more about them in Module 12. Rule 1C3 above told you that contractions **always** have apostrophes, showing where letters have been omitted.

1H3	*ITS* Use *its* as a possessive pronoun, to mean *belonging to it.* *IT'S* Use *it's* as a contraction of *it is* (or *it has* in verb phrases).

Natalie bought a new rake, and then broke <u>its</u> handle.
> *Its* is a possessive pronoun. The handle belongs to the rake.

<u>It's</u> a shame he couldn't come.
> *It's* is a contraction of *it is.* The apostrophe shows where the letter *I* has been omitted.

<u>It's</u> been a long time since I was here last.
> *It's* is a contraction of *it has.* The apostrophe shows where the letters *H* and *A* have been omitted.

| Exercise 1.27 | Checking your understanding of *its* and *it's* |

Fill in *its* or *it's*.

1. _____ important to check the air pressure in your car's tires every week.

2. And _____ a good idea to have your car serviced every 5,000 miles.

3. You should change _____ oil and oil filter.

4. Every 10,000 miles, your car should have _____ tires rotated.

5. Your car will last longer if _____ not neglected.

1H4

YOUR
Use *your* as a possessive pronoun, to mean *belonging to you*.
YOU'RE
Use *you're* as a contraction of *you are*.

It's <u>your</u> turn now.
  Your is a possessive pronoun. The turn belongs to you.

<u>You're</u> always in my way.
  You're is a contraction of *you are*. The apostrophe shows where the letter *A* has been omitted.

| Exercise 1.28 | Checking your understanding of *your* and *you're* |

Fill in *your* or *you're*.

1. Even if you don't believe in astrology, _____ unusual if you don't know

   what sign of the Zodiac you were born under.

2. Astrologers say that _____ sign in the stars influences

   _____ character and attitudes.

3. For example, if _____ a Leo, _____

   temperament is domineering, like a lion's.

4. And if _____ a Gemini (born under the sign of the twins),

   _____ friends will notice that you have contradictory traits.

5. To tell the truth, doesn't _____ sign of the Zodiac fit you?

1H5	*THEIR* Use *their* as a possessive pronoun, to mean *belonging to them.* *THEY'RE* Use *they're* as a contraction of *they are.* *THERE* Use *there* to mean *at that place.* And use *there* to begin a sentence, with verbs like *is* or *was.*

They waxed <u>their</u> car.
> *Their* is a possessive pronoun. The car belongs to them.

<u>They're</u> my neighbors.
> *They're* is a contraction of *they are.* The apostrophe shows where the letter *A* has been omitted.

Carolyn left her laptop over <u>there</u>.
> *There* tells where she left her laptop computer.

<u>There</u> are three major world powers.
> *There* doesn't mean a particular place; it simply begins the sentence. It is followed by the verb *are*.

They're means *they are.* So **never** write *they're are*, which would have to mean *they are are.*

    ✗
<u>They're are</u> three major world powers.
> Even though *they're* may sound like *there*, it means something completely different, so it's incorrect here.

<u>There are</u> three major world powers.
> This sentence is correct.

Exercise 1.29	**Checking your understanding of *their*, *they're*, and *there***

Fill in *their, they're,* or *there.*

1. Throughout the United States _____ are many young people who dream of a future in professional sports.

2. _____ interested in athletics, not _____ studies.

3. _____ minds are on news stories about huge salaries made by professional athletes.

4. So every day _____ out practicing instead of studying in the library.

5. But _____ are few stories about college players who don't make the pros, or

   about high-paid athletes who lose all _____ money to bad investments.

6. Students should be aware that _____ are few things more important than

   _____ college degrees.

Exercise 1.30	Reviewing words that sound alike

1. Fill in *then* or *than*.

   When you spend more _____ you earn,

   _____ it's time to take out a loan; I'd rather owe money

   _____ do without.

2. Fill in *to, too,* or *two*.

   Ramon goes _____ the school gym _____ swim because the health

   club is _____ expensive. _____ of his friends go there, _____ .

3. Fill in *its* or *it's*.

   _____ strange but true that an insect will often eat

   _____ mate, or even _____ offspring.

4. Fill in *your* or *you're*.

   When _____ anxious, _____

   blood pressure sometimes rises.

5. Fill in *their, they're,* or *there*.

   _____ are millions of men who support equal rights for

   women, and if the Equal Rights Amendment comes up for a vote again,

   _____ going to be _____ at the polls

   to cast _____ votes for it.

Here is a summary of what you've learned about these possessive pronouns and contractions that sound alike:

POSSESSIVE PRONOUNS	CONTRACTIONS	TELLS WHERE, OR STARTS A SENTENCE
its, your, their	*it's, you're, they're*	*there*
The doll lost *its* head. (The head belonged to the doll.)	*It's* lost. (*It is* lost.)	
Your house is nice. (The house belongs to you.)	*You're* nice. (*You are* nice.)	
Their house is old. (The house belongs to them.)	*They're* old. (*They are* old.)	The house is *there* on the corner. (The house is at that place.) *There* is a house for sale.

Exercise 1.31	Reviewing possessive pronouns and contractions

This paragraph contains errors in *its* and *it's*, *your* and *you're*, and *their*, *they're*, and *there*. Underline each error, and correct it in the space above the line.

      If your not in the habit of writing down you're ideas and then proofreading what is

written there on the page, its hard for you to see that, although some contractions and

possessive pronouns sound exactly alike, there very different. People who don't write much

may not use apostrophes at all, because they don't realize their importance. Their simply

not aware that every contraction must have its apostrophe to be correct. On the other hand,

they're are writers who treat apostrophes like confetti. They scatter them around in they're

writing like decorations. But there guilty of confusing there readers even more than the

writers who leave apostrophes out entirely. If your ambitious to become a clear and correct

writer, it's important for you to learn the following apostrophe rule and it's application:

"Their is a group of words called possessive pronouns, which mean *belonging to*. These

words are never written with apostrophes. When you use an apostrophe with a pronoun, its

always a contraction. Contractions can also be written as two words."

This paragraph contained 13 errors. How many did you find? _____ If you didn't find all 13, try again before you check your work.

Exercise 1.32   **Reviewing words that sound alike**

Rewrite each sentence, using the appropriate words and underlining them.

1. your / you're   Where's <u>the</u> textbook <u>that belongs to you</u>? <u>You are</u> sure to need it today.

_____

_____

2. its / it's   This show has lost <u>the</u> popularity <u>belonging to it</u>, and so <u>it is</u> time to take it off the air.

_____

_____

3. to / too / two   Diane struggled <u>in the direction of</u> the bus stop. She was carrying <u>fewer than three</u> big boxes, and had a full shopping bag, <u>also</u>. This luggage was almost <u>excessively</u> heavy for her to handle.

_____

_____

4. their / there / they're   The passengers are picking up <u>the</u> luggage <u>belonging to them</u> in the airport. Two friends are meeting them <u>at that place</u> to drive them home. <u>They are</u> all eager to get going.

_____

_____

Exercise 1.33   **Reviewing words that sound alike**

This paragraph contains many wrong words. Underline each error, and correct it in the space above the line.

Its an interesting fact that many people are much better at speaking then at writing.

Their are some people who can start a riot just by shouting to an angry crowd. But two few

of these born orators are able to write a two-line letter to the newspaper which it's editor

wouldn't find to awkward and ungrammatical to publish. Then there are those who would

rather spend $200 on telephone calls then $2 on stamps. When they pick up a telephone, there chattering away in an instant. And yet when they pick up a pencil, it's likely that

they'll chew it for 20 minutes before their able to write a single word. You may be an

excellent speaker, but unless your able to write your ideas correctly and clearly, your going

to have problems.

This paragraph contained 11 errors. How many did you find? _____ If you didn't find all 11, try again before you check your work.

B esides the 12 especially confusing words we have been working on, there are many other words that sound exactly alike but that have different meanings.

x

Smoking isn't <u>aloud</u> in most classrooms.
> *Aloud* is a mistake for *allowed*. These two words sound alike, but they have very different meanings.

Exercise 1.34   Checking your understanding of other sound-alike words

① Use your dictionary to write in the meanings. ② Then fill in the appropriate words.

1. passed / past   *Passed* is the past-tense form of the verb _____

                     Past means _____

                     Just _____ Rosie's bar, we _____ a big accident.

2. know / no   *Know* means _____

                     No means _____

                     We _____ that you have _____ time to see us.

3. here / hear   *Here* means _____

                     Hear means _____

   _____ comes Joseph to _____ the latest gossip.

4. whose / who's   *Whose* is a possessive form meaning "belonging to _____ "

                     Who's is a contraction for _____

   _____ the student _____ papers are on the table?

5. find / fine   *Find* means _____

                     Fine means _____

                     Harold felt _____ after he was able to _____ the money.

Editing Practice B.6   *Checking your own writing for wrong words*

1. Get your draft of Paper B again.
2. Review Rule 1H, and then check each occurrence of the 12 especially difficult sound-alike words to make sure it is correct. Fix any mistakes with your green pen.
3. Check your letter for other incorrect sound-alike words. Fix any mistakes with your green pen.
4. How many mistakes did you fix altogether? _____ Your ability to find and fix mistakes in your own writing shows how much you've learned so far.

Keep your draft of Paper B to use again later.

Exercise 1.35   **Reviewing everything you've learned so far**

This paragraph contains errors in spelling, wrong words, and other writing conventions. Underline each error, and correct it in the space above the line. For help, use the Rules Summary and your dictionary.

      You hear alot about "the wonders of the world," but only a few people know that this phrase originally refered to seven wonders in the ancient world. Hardly anybody nowadays can name these monuments of early civilization. Their is a good reason for this. Just one of these wonders is still standing, the huge stone pyramids in Egypt. A few people also no about the second wonder, the magnificent terraced gardens which a king of babylon built to please his wife. The thrid wonder, a seated statue of Zeus in a temple at Olympia in greece, was made of ivory & gold, with precious jewels in it's eyes. (If this huge statue could have stood up, it would have hit it's head on the cieling.) Some fragments of the forth wonder, a Temple dedicated to the goddess Diana, were found in turkey about a hundred yrs. ago. Earthquakes destroyed all 3 of the other wonders: a beautiful tomb built for King Mausolus in Turkey, an enormous lighthouse near the coast of Egypt (huge fragments of which were draged from the sea only a few years ago), and a giant statue of Apollo at Rhodes in Greece. The colossal statue at Rhodes must have been more spectacular then the Statue of Liberty. According to an old legend, it stood in the middle of a harbor with its legs spread a part, while ships past between them.

This paragraph contained 20 errors. How many did you find? _____ If you didn't find all 20, try again before you check your work.

Editing Practice B.7 — Checking wrong words in your own writing

1. Get your draft of Paper B again.
2. Check again to make sure that you have already fixed each wrong word. If you find any more mistakes, fix them with your green pen.
3. How many more mistakes did you fix? _____ Your ability to find and fix mistakes in your own writing shows how much you've learned so far.

Writing Your Final Copy of Paper B

Use your final copy of Paper B to demonstrate what you've learned in Module 1 about using writing conventions and avoiding wrong words.

Paper B	Using writing conventions and avoiding wrong words
Make Final Copy	Mark another piece of paper Paper B, and write the final copy of your paper on it, or print out a clean copy on your word processor. Be sure to include all your corrections.
Proofread	Read your final copy **out loud.** Correct any mistakes neatly by hand. If you used a word processor, enter your corrections, and print out a corrected final copy.

Hand in your final copy of Paper B, and the rest of your exercises.

2 Understanding Simple Sentences

NAME _____

After you finish checking each exercise, fill in your number of mistakes.

2.1 _____	2.7 _____	2.12 _____	2.17 _____	2.22 _____
2.2 _____	2.8 _____	2.13 _____	2.18 _____	2.23 _____
2.3 _____	2.9 _____	2.14 _____	2.19 _____	2.24 _____
2.4 _____	2.10 _____	2.15 _____	2.20 _____	2.25 _____
2.5 _____	2.11 _____	2.16 _____	2.21 _____	2.26 _____
2.6 _____				

EXERCISES	INSTRUCTIONS	CHECKING	
❑ Complete	❑ Followed carefully	❑ Careful	❑ Green pen not used
❑ Incomplete	❑ Not careful enough	❑ Not careful enough	❑ Mistakes not corrected

PAPER C
❑ Doesn't follow the instructions; write a NEW Paper C.
❑ Skips some instructions; COMPLETE everything.
❑ Too short; add MORE.

EDITING PAPER C FOR THIS MODULE'S WORK
❑ Careful   ❑ Not careful enough
EDITING PAPER C FOR PREVIOUS WORK
❑ Careful   ❑ Not careful enough
OVERALL EVALUATION OF PAPER C
❑ Excellent   ❑ Good   ❑ Acceptable   ❑ Not acceptable

COMMENTS

Rules Summary for Module 2

2A	Every sentence must have at least one **verb**, and every verb must have a **subject**.
1	Almost all sentences also have **expansion** telling more about the verb or the subject or other words in the sentence.
2B	To find the **verb** in a sentence, find the word that **changes to show different tenses**.
1	A sentence can have **more than one verb**.
2	Use a **comma** to separate three or more words in a series.
2C	To find the **subject** of a verb, find the word that **answers the question *WHO?* or *WHAT?* about the verb**.
1	A verb can have **more than one subject**.
2D	Verbs may be **verb phrases** as well as one-word verbs.
2E	**Contractions** always contain verbs.
2F	Don't confuse verbs with other words that may seem to be verbs.
1	*To* + the base form of a verb is an **infinitive**. An infinitive never changes to show different tenses, so it's not a verb.
2	An *ING* **word** by itself is not a verb.
3	Words that are not verbs sometimes look exactly like words that are verbs.

A simple sentence looks like this:

Subject verb expansion.

W ritten English generally consists of a series of complete sentences, each beginning with a capital letter and ending with a period. In speech, it's not always necessary to use complete sentences, but in writing, complete sentences are almost always needed for a reader to understand what's written on the page. In this module and the next, we'll work on understanding what the parts of a sentence are.

2A	**Every sentence must have at least one <u>verb</u>, and every verb must have a <u>subject</u>.**

In writing, every sentence, even a very short one, must have a verb, and that verb must have a subject.

Armies battled.
Countries collapsed.
Empires arose.

Even these very short sentences are correct because each has a verb (the word that is circled) and each verb has a subject (the word that is boxed).

2A1	**Almost all sentences also have <u>expansion</u> telling more about the verb or the subject or other words in the sentence.**

Expansion can be one word or many words telling more about the verb or the subject or the other words in a sentence. Adding expansion to a sentence gives the reader more information.

Large armies frequently battled over territory.
Countries with fewer resources often collapsed.
Then great empires arose for a while.

These sentences have the same verbs, and those verbs have the same subjects as in the two-word sentences above, but in these longer sentences expansion has added more information.

In school grammar, a sentence (that is, a group of words containing a verb which has a subject) is often called a **clause**. A simple sentence is often called an **independent clause** because it can exist by itself, independently of any other words.

> *School Grammar*

The various pieces of expansion are often called **modifiers**. Modifiers include **adjectives** (like *large* telling more about the subject *armies*) and **adverbs** (like *frequently* telling more about the verb *battled*). Modifiers (or expansion) also include groups of words called *phrases* (like *over territory* telling more about the verb *battled*, and *with fewer resources* telling more about the subject *countries*).

Sometimes on a test you may need to know these terms, but there is no need for you to learn them to be able to write well. In this book, the one word **expansion** covers all these different kinds of modifiers.

Exercise 2.1	**Recognizing verbs, subjects, and expansion**

These three sentences have even more expansion than the sentences above, but they still have the same verbs and subjects. Circle each verb, and box its subject.

1. In the course of history, great armies, led by ambitious generals, sometimes battled for supremacy over weaker countries.

2. These weaker countries, poorly armed and with meager resources, often collapsed before the superior forces of their attackers.

3. Then vast empires, like the Greek, the Roman, and more recently the British, arose as rulers of the earth for centuries.

Remember to use your green pen to check each exercise as soon as you finish it. Write in any necessary corrections, and then write your number of mistakes on the cover page of this module.

Using Module 2 to Edit Your Own Writing

Use Paper C to discover how much you know already about the structure of simple sentences. Later in this module, you'll be checking this paper by applying the rules of this module to what you have written.

You may write this paper by hand. Better yet, use a word processor.

Drafting Paper C	*Using simple sentences*

Assignment   Choose one of these assignments:

- ❑ Describe the kind of clothes that you or someone you know well usually wears during the school year. Explain why you or your close acquaintance wears these clothes, and what these clothes may tell others about you or your acquaintance.

- ❑ Describe an experience that taught you something important.

Get Ready   On a piece of scratch paper, free write on your chosen topic, first to narrow it to one specific example if necessary, and then to get ideas to use in developing your paper. Don't stop until you have plenty of ideas. Draw a line across the page when you have finished free writing.

Read over your free writing, and decide on your main point. Write it in one complete sentence below the line.

Plan your paragraphs by selecting enough supporting ideas from your free writing to make your main point interesting, clear, and convincing to a reader. Write your supporting ideas in a numbered list below your main point.

Draft   On another piece of scratch paper, write an introduction to your draft telling what your main point is.

Then write at least one paragraph for each of your supporting ideas. Be sure to include enough examples, details, and facts to make your reader understand and believe each idea.

Write your conclusion.

Special Instructions Make sure that you have written a clear capital letter at the beginning of each sentence and a clear period or question mark at the end of each sentence. How many sentences did you write? _____ If you didn't write at least 19 sentences, think of more supporting details to add to your paragraphs, and insert additional sentences.

Revise Revise your draft, using the four steps in revision listed on the inside front cover to make your paper better. Make sure that you have written at least four paragraphs, including an introduction and a conclusion.

Keep your draft of Paper C to use later.

Finding Verbs

2B	To find the <u>verb</u> in a sentence, find the word that <u>changes to show different tenses</u>.

There are many tenses. Three of the most common are **present**, **past**, and **future**. The future tense is always a verb phrase, a verb that is more than one word.

> Every night my mother (calls) me on the telephone.
> Last night my mother (called) me on the telephone.
> Tomorrow night my mother (will call) me on the telephone.
>> The verb *call* changes to show three different tenses: present, past, and future. The present-tense verb *calls* and the past-tense verb *called* are one-word verbs. The future-tense verb *will call* is a two-word verb phrase.

Time words are often used to emphasize or reinforce the tense of a verb.

> <u>Every night</u> my mother (calls) me on the telephone.
> <u>Last night</u> my mother (called) me on the telephone.
> <u>Tomorrow night</u> my mother (will call) me on the telephone.
>> Time-words like *every night*, *last night*, and *tomorrow night* help to show the tense of the verb, present, past, or future.

Exercise 2.2	**Finding verbs by changing present tense to past**

① Rewrite each sentence in the past tense, using a one-word verb with a *D* or *ED* ending. ② Circle each verb in both sentences.

1. Every morning the warden talks to the prison inmates.

    Yesterday morning _____

2.   Usually he announces the day's activities.

   Yesterday _____

3.   Often he reminds them about their behavior.

   Recently _____

T he most common kind of verb phrase is a **future-tense verb**, which always uses the helping verb *will* in a verb phrase.

   He will go home soon.
       The future-tense verb *will go* is a verb phrase.

Exercise 2.3	**Finding verbs by changing present tense to future**

① Rewrite each sentence in the future tense, using a two-word verb phrase with *will*. ② Circle each verb in both sentences.

1.   This music soothes my frazzled nerves.

   _____

2.   The instruments convey a peaceful feeling.

   _____

3.   The song tells of quiet relaxation.

   _____

Exercise 2.4	**Finding verbs by changing past tense to present**

① Rewrite each sentence in the present tense, using a one-word verb with no ending. ② Circle each verb in both sentences.

1.   At dawn the birds chirped loudly.

   _____

2.   They disturbed my sleep.

   _____

3.   Then I rolled over anyway for another short snooze.

   _____

Y̶ou've probably heard that verbs are words that show action. It's true that some verbs do show action, but many verbs do not. Trying to find a verb by looking for a word that shows action is unreliable; it won't work very often.

> Hilary (runs) ten miles a day. Her running (is) an inspiration to us.
> Hilary (ran) ten miles a day. Her running (was) an inspiration to us.
> > The verbs *runs* and *ran* show action. The verbs *is* and *was* do not show action, but they are verbs, because they change to show different tenses. *Running* also shows action, but it is not a verb.

So to be sure of finding the verb, don't look for a word that shows action, but for a word that **changes to show different tenses.**

Exercise 2.5	**Finding verbs that don't show action**

① Rewrite each sentence in the past tense, using *were* for the past tense of *are*. ② Circle each verb in every sentence.

1. These horses are sprinters. They gallop at top speed.

    _____

2. They streak across the finish line. Their owners are jubilant.

    _____

3. Sometimes their trainers seem anxious. These mounts are worth millions.

    _____

Exercise 2.6	**Finding verbs by changing present tense to past**

This paragraph contains present-tense verbs. Read it carefully to make sure that you understand it. ① Circle each verb. ② Mark a piece of paper Exercise 2.6, and rewrite this paragraph onto it, using the past tense. Your paragraph will begin *Last year Jane and Walter were...* ③ In your rewritten paragraph, circle each verb.

> This year Jane and Walter are intern doctors at Central Hospital. Medical facts fill their brains, but they have little medical experience, and they are sometimes on duty for 36 hours without a break. Just as they tumble into their beds, their beepers sound, so with bleary eyes, Jane and Walter stagger back to the intensive care unit. Their patients pray hard that they commit no mistakes. But the hospital's staff checks everything that Jane and Walter do. The resident doctor reviews their prescriptions carefully, and the nurse watches closely as their fingers fumble with the intravenous tubes.

2B1	**A sentence can have <u>more than one verb</u>.**

| Exercise 2.7 | Finding more than one verb |

Circle each verb.

John Kennedy became President in 1961 and died from an assassin's bullet in 1963. He

started the Peace Corps, and thousands joined. The Peace Corps volunteers traveled to

many countries, improved medical conditions, taught better farming practices, and served

as ambassadors for the USA. People around the world were grateful for the help of the

Peace Corps and mourned Kennedy's death.

| **2B2** | **Use a <u>comma</u> to separate three or more words in a series.** |

The audience clapped, stamped, and cheered.
Commas separate the series of verbs *clapped, stamped,* and *cheered.*

Occasionally the comma before the *and* in a series is omitted, but it is usually clearer not to omit that comma.

✗ The actors waved, bowed and threw kisses.
The actors waved, bowed, and threw kisses.
The second sentence is clearer.

| Exercise 2.8 | Using commas in a series |

① Circle each verb. ② Insert commas where necessary.

Some gifted people encountered incredible obstacles lost hope and ended their careers.

Vincent Van Gogh, the Dutch artist, painted hundreds of masterpieces sold only one cut off

his ear and finally shot himself. Others, though, pursued their goals succeeded and gained

greater fame. Ludwig van Beethoven, the German composer, lost his hearing kept working

and then wrote some of his greatest musical masterpieces. Sarah Bernhardt, the great

actress, went lame in 1905 lost a leg to gangrene in 1914 but then became famous all over the

world before her death in 1923.

| *Editing Practice C.1* | *Finding verbs in your own writing* |

1. Get your draft of Paper C.
2. Review Rules 2A-2B1.
3. Circle each verb.

Keep your draft of Paper C to use again later.

Finding Subjects

| **2C** | To find the <u>subject</u> of a verb, find the word that <u>answers</u> the question *WHO*? or *WHAT*? about the verb. |

Children play games.
> *Play* is the verb. Ask *WHO or WHAT play games?* *Children* is the subject because it answers the question *WHO or WHAT play games?*

Even though the subject usually comes before the verb in a sentence, **always look for the verb first,** because you can't find the subject reliably until after you've found the verb.

| **Exercise 2.9** | **Finding verbs and subjects** |

Circle each verb, and box its subject.

1. Marvin needs a new battery for his car.

2. He parks his car alongside the store.

3. He is inside for only a minute.

4. That eager policeman gives him a parking ticket.

5. Marvin's new battery is very expensive.

You learned in Rule 2A1 that almost all sentences also have **expansion,** words telling more about the verb or the subject or other words in the sentence. Usually the other words in a sentence besides the verb and its subject are expansion. Be careful not to confuse a verb or subject with expansion.

The black kettle on the stove whistled loudly.
> *Whistled* is the verb, because it can change to show different tenses. It might seem that *stove* is the subject, because it's right next to *whistled*. But *kettle* is the subject, because it tells *WHAT* whistled. *On the stove* is expansion telling *WHERE the kettle is*.

| Exercise 2.10 | Finding verbs and subjects in expanded sentences |

Circle each verb, and box its subject. Be careful not to circle or box any expansion.

1. Time passes.

    Time passes slowly for little children.

    Time passes quickly for old folks.

2. Bridges sway.

    Well-built suspension bridges always sway a little in high winds.

    Poorly built bridges sometimes sway dangerously in hurricanes.

3. People complained.

    Those grouchy people in the next apartment always complained about our parties.

    The frightened people in my building never complained to the police about the drug pushers.

| Exercise 2.11 | Finding verbs and subjects in expanded sentences |

Circle each verb, and box its subject. Be careful not to circle or box any expansion.

1. The leader of the hike arrived without a map.

2. The river between the hikers and the mountains blocked their path.

3. However, the trail along the north side of the river led them to a shallow place.

4. The hikers, with their shoes in their hands, crossed over dry and safe.

5. The hike from the campground to the mountains was a success.

| Exercise 2.12 | Finding verbs and subjects in expanded sentences |

Circle each verb, and box its subject. Be careful not to circle or box any expansion.

1. Sometimes styles of architecture from the distant past become popular again in later centuries.

2. During the 18th and 19th centuries, imitations of ancient Greek and Roman architecture appeared

    everywhere in European and American homes.

3. Wealthy settlers in the South often built homes in the Greek style with triangular roofs and three-story

    classical columns.

4. Some residents of New England preferred Italian villas with Renaissance features, or Gothic Revival houses.

5. Frequently architects will use a wide variety of features from different periods, like pointed Gothic windows, Greek columns, and French mansard roofs, all in the same building.

6. Even for a student of architecture, identification of the main style in a house sometimes is quite difficult.

Sometimes the subject follows the verb, especially when a sentence begins with *here* or *there*. Be especially careful about the subject in this case.

> There (is) ice in the freezer.
>> *WHO or WHAT is in the freezer?* The answer is *ice*, not *There*. So the subject is *ice*, even though *ice* comes **after** the verb *is*.

> Here (comes) Tim.
>> *WHO or WHAT comes?* The answer is *Tim*, not *Here*. So the subject is *Tim*.

Exercise 2.13	Finding the subject when it follows the verb

Circle each verb, and box its subject. Be careful not to circle or box any expansion.

1. Here are some quarters for the toll.

2. There goes their car through the tollgate ahead of us.

3. Here is a twenty-dollar bill for gas.

2C1	A verb can have <u>more than one subject</u>.

> Men , women , and children (ran) toward the stage.
>> *Men, women,* and *children* all tell who ran toward the stage. Commas separate this series of subjects.

Exercise 2.14	Finding more than one subject

Circle each verb, and box each subject. Be careful not to circle or box any expansion.

My aunt and uncle gave us a sofa for our new house. The dog and the cat ripped the fabric on one side with their sharp claws. My mother and sister made a slipcover and hid the damage with it.

Exercise 2.15	Finding verbs and subjects

Circle each verb, and box each subject. Be careful not to circle or box any expansion.

Between 1970 and 1995, angry environmentalists and concerned legislators together campaigned vigorously against waste and pollution. Today many earth-watchers still complain and worry about the condition of the air and the water. On Earth Day, gloomy prophets loudly foretell the End. Influential newspapers and telecasts around the nation echo their pessimistic statements. Yet humans today breathe healthier air and drink purer water than their grandparents or great-grandparents. Unbiased scientists report a one-third reduction in smog since 1972. By comparison with the 1960s, our rivers, lakes, and oceans are now twice as safe. However, environmentalists and other concerned citizens have good reasons for their fears. The next Congress probably will repeal many federal environmental regulations, will cut funding for environmental protection, and thus will reverse the current trend toward a cleaner planet.

Editing Practice C.2	*Finding subjects in your own writing*

1. Get your draft of Paper C again.
2. Review Rule 2C.
3. Box each subject.
4. If you find any places where commas are omitted, insert them with your green pen.

Keep your draft of Paper C to use again later.

Verb Phrases

You already know that a verb can be **one word** (like *went*) or a **verb phrase**, more than one word (like *will go* or *will be going*).

COOK   He cooks breakfast for us.
           He cooked breakfast for us.
     These sentences have one-word verbs.

COOK   He will cook breakfast for us.
           He is cooking breakfast for us.
           He has cooked breakfast for us.
           He might be cooking breakfast for us.
     These sentences have verb phrases.

76

When you look a word up in the dictionary, you look up the **base form** of the word. This is the form of that word without any ending. In this book, we'll show you the base form of a word by writing it in **capital letters**, like COOK in the examples on page 76.

2D	**Verbs may be <u>verb phrases</u> as well as one-word verbs.**

Every verb phrase has two parts: at least one **helping verb**, and a **main verb**. The **first word** in a verb phrase is a helping verb, which shows the tense of a verb phrase. The **last word** in a verb phrase is a main verb, which tells the general meaning of the verb phrase.

WORK   Paula had worked until midnight last night.
        She has worked all day today.

        Paula certainly did work hard last year.
        She always does work hard.

        Paula was working all day yesterday.
        She is working right now.

Had and *has*, *did* and *does*, *was* and *is* are helping verbs. Like one-word verbs, these helping verbs change to show different tenses. These verb phrases are about working.

So to find verb phrases, look for the helping verb, the word that can change to show different tenses.

Here is a list of all helping verbs. Notice that all these helping verbs except *must* and *ought to* can change to show different tenses (or meanings).

Base form	Present tense	Past tense
BE	am is are	was was were
HAVE	has have	had had
DO	does do	did did
	will can shall may must ought to	would could should might

Exercise 2.16	Recognizing one-word verbs and verb phrases

Circle each verb (either a one-word verb or a verb phrase), and box its subject. Be sure to circle all the words in verb phrases, and be careful not to circle any interrupting words.

1. The customers are impatient.

    They are becoming more impatient by the minute.

2. That man has some defective clothing for the Returns clerk.

    He has been in line for an hour already.

3. The woman with the baby is furious.

    Her baby is crying loudly.

4. Over in the stockroom, the Returns clerk does nothing about the angry customers.

    But he does look forward to closing time.

Exercise 2.17	Finding verbs by changing past tense to present

This paragraph contains past-tense verbs. Read it carefully to make sure that you understand it. ① Circle each verb (either a one-word verb or a verb phrase), and box its subject. ② Mark a piece of paper Exercise 2.17, and rewrite this paragraph onto it, using one-word verbs and verb phrases in the present tense. Your paragraph will begin *These days, Americans are changing…* ③ Mark your rewritten paragraph in the same way.

Even ten years ago, Americans were reconsidering their use of alcoholic beverages. People of all ages, anxious about their health, were drinking less. In restaurants, they were ordering white wine or nonalcoholic beer. Equally important, attitudes were changing. Intoxicated people no longer seemed so funny. Comedians cracked fewer jokes about the antics of drunks. In more and more states the police were arresting drunk drivers, and the authorities were giving them stiff fines. Some judges were sending them to prison. Abuse of alcohol was recognized as a threat to health, to life, and to society.

Some verb phrases have more than one helping verb. The helping verbs together determine the tense or precise meaning of the verb phrase.

WORK   Paula has been working here for a year.
        She had been working in the city previously.
        She may have worked there several years.
        She might have been working here sooner except for her injury.
        These verb phrases are about working, but the helping verbs determine the tense or precise meaning.

Exercise 2.18	Finding verb phrases with several helping verbs

Circle each verb phrase, and box its subject.

1. My lawyer will call soon.

    She will be calling about the lawsuit.

2. She will prepare the legal forms today.

    She might have prepared them already this morning.

3. Our case will be heard within two months.

    However, it should have been heard before that bad publicity.

Exercise 2.19	Finding verb phrases in a paragraph

Circle each verb phrase, and box its subject.

The mailman will be here in half an hour. However, he should have been here already

by now. The extra mail for Christmas does slow him down. Also, the snowy weather has

made travel difficult. Still, he has been late with his deliveries every day this week. Maybe

he should start earlier in the mornings. In addition, he could spend less time in the Donut

Shop. He might lose a little weight that way.

Verbs in Contractions

2E	Contractions always contain verbs.

They're in the hall.   They are in the hall.
They aren't ready yet.   They are not ready yet.
The contractions *they're* and *aren't* contain the verb *are*.

The verb in a contraction may be a one-word verb or the helping verb in a verb phrase.

BE   She's here.
COME   She's coming.
In the first sentence, the one-word verb *is* is contracted with the subject. In the second sentence, the verb phrase *is coming* is contracted.

Exercise 2.20	**Finding verbs in contractions**

Circle each verb, and box its subject.

1. Khalil's a clown in the Europa Circus.

2. He wasn't at work today and isn't at home now

3. We're not sure of his whereabouts.

4. Maybe it's just another one of his jokes.

One or more words can go in between the helping verb and the main verb in a verb phrase, even when the helping verb is contracted. When you are marking verb phrases, be careful not to circle these interrupting words.

> WORK   Paula has not worked here for a month.
> Paula hasn't worked here for a month.
> *Not* interrupts the verb phrase *has worked*, even when it is contracted with *has*.

Exercise 2.21	**Finding verb phrases in contractions**

Circle each verb (either a one-word verb or a verb phrase), and box its subject. Be careful not to circle any words that interrupt a verb phrase.

Your brother's been in a car accident. He's not badly hurt, fortunately.

He's being taken to Central Hospital. They'll take good care of him there.

They've got the best Emergency Room around. The police are still investigating

the accident. They're arresting the other driver. She's been charged with drunk

driving. She's on probation from a previous accident. She'd better get a good

lawyer. She'll need one. Right now we're going to the hospital. We'll pick you

up in 15 minutes.

Words Easily Confused with Verbs

2F	**Don't confuse verbs with other words that may seem to be verbs.**

2F1	*To* + the base form of a verb is an <u>infinitive</u>. An infinitive never changes to show different tenses, so it's not a verb.

LIKE   My daughter likes to play soccer.
         She liked to play soccer.
         LIKE changes to show different tenses, so it's a verb. *Play* is part of the infinitive *to play*, which doesn't change, so it isn't a verb.

REQUIRE To become a surgeon requires 16 years of training.
         To become a surgeon answers the question *WHAT requires 16 years of training?* so this infinitive is actually the subject of the verb *requires*.

Exercise 2.22	Distinguishing between verbs and infinitives

① Circle each verb (either a one-word verb or a verb phrase), box its subject, and underline infinitives.
② Rewrite the sentence in the present tense. ③ Mark your rewritten sentence in the same way.

1.   Elaine was hoping to become a successful actress.

_____

2.   To achieve fame had become her one goal in life.

_____

3.   To improve her chances for success, she planned to move from Kansas to Los Angeles.

_____

2F2	An *ING* word by itself is not a verb.

You already know that an *ING* word can be the main verb in a verb phrase with the helping verb *BE*.

DIVE   Jenny is diving into the pool.
         Is diving is a verb phrase. The main verb is *diving*.

But when an *ING* word is used by itself, not as a main verb in a verb phrase, it's not a verb.

PRACTICE Jenny practices diving.
          Jenny practiced diving.
          PRACTICE changes to show different tenses, so it's a verb. *Diving* doesn't change, so it isn't a verb.

ING words often name actions, so they are actually **nouns** rather than verbs. They can therefore be subjects.

TAKE   Diving takes a lot of practice.
         Diving names an action, so it is a noun. And *diving* answers the question *WHAT takes practice?* so it is the subject of the verb *takes*.

ING words can also be used as **expansion**, telling more about other words.

SAVE   <u>Diving</u> quickly, |Jenny| (saved) the <u>drowning</u> boy.
  Diving and *drowning* don't change to show different tenses, so they aren't verbs. *Diving* is expansion telling more about *Jenny*, and *drowning* is expansion telling more about the *boy*.

Exercise 2.23	Distinguishing between verbs and *ING* words

① Circle each verb, box its subject, and underline *ING* words. ② Rewrite the sentence in the present tense. ③ Mark your rewritten sentence in the same way.

1. Elaine liked living in Los Angeles.

   _____

2. However, she hated competing with hundreds of others for one job.

   _____

3. After trying out for dozens of roles without success, she was getting depressed.

   _____

4. Moving back to Kansas started seeming like a good idea.

   _____

2F3	**Words that are not verbs sometimes look exactly like words that are verbs.**

DRINK |They| always (drink) lemonade.
BE |Lemonade| (is) a very refreshing <u>drink</u>.
  In the first sentence, the verb is *drink*. In the second sentence, the verb is *is*, not *drink*.

School grammar gives various complicated names to *ING* words, depending on how they are used. If an *ING* word is used as a noun (for example, as a subject), it's called a **gerund.** If it's used to expand a noun, then it's called a **participial adjective**. If it's used as the main verb in a verb phrase with the helping verb *BE*, it's called a **present participle**. Phrases that begin with *ING* words are called **participial phrases**. However, you don't need to know any of these terms to use an *ING* word correctly. As long as you understand that an *ING* word **by itself** is not a verb, and that it can be the main verb in a verb phrase, then you are not likely to make a mistake using it. However, you will learn more about using *ING* words in Modules 11-12.

School Grammar

| Exercise 2.24 | Distinguishing between verbs and other words |

① Circle each verb, and box its subject. ② Write in *A* or *B* to tell which sentence contains the given verb.

1. A. Long disputes are very frustrating.

   B. My friend Mi-long disputes our plans for February.

   Disputes is the verb in sentence _____.

2. A. We visit Canada to go skiing every year in February.

   B. Our last visit was a catastrophe for Mi-long.

   Visit is the verb in sentence _____.

3. A. She lost her wallet somewhere on the slopes.

   B. The lost wallet contained over $400 in cash.

   Lost is the verb in sentence _____.

| Exercise 2.25 | Finding verbs and subjects in a paragraph |

Circle each verb, and box its subject. Be careful not to circle or box any words that are not verbs or subjects.

Near the Italian town of Modena, a blood-red car rockets around a twisting track and quickly soars to 120 miles an hour. The driver pumps the brakes and careens into a hairpin turn. Skidding briefly, he turns the steering wheel sharply to regain his hold on the road. He roars around the track a few more times and screeches to a stop. The driver steps out grinning. This Ferrari passes.

Enzo Ferrari began producing his racing cars in 1929. His trademark was a prancing black horse, the insignia of the flying ace, Francesco Baracca. Ferrari cars started to win racing championships during the next decade. In 1945 Ferrari designed his first 12-cylinder model for everyday use. He developed a system of checks and controls to produce perfect parts and hired daring engineers to create shovel-nosed hoods and swooping fenders. The result was a powerful and almost indestructible machine. It was also stunningly beautiful.

In every country around the globe, car buffs and drag racers rushed to buy it even at extravagant prices.

The next Ferrari to come out of Modena is likely to cost more than $300,000, and to have a speed of over 200 miles an hour. The Ferrari factory will produce no more than a few thousand of these cars. Consequently, they're sure to vanish from the dealerships within days of their arrival. Then they'll spend their lives cruising over roads at 55 miles an hour — about one-fourth of their capacity. Still, the proud owners of these aristocrats of the road will continue to smile, and to smile again, at the turning heads and staring eyes of envious drivers everywhere.

In this book, we call every group of words that starts with a capital letter and ends with a period a **word-group**. However, not all word-groups are sentences. Remember what Rule 2A says: Every sentence must have at least one verb, and every verb must have a subject. So this is the first (although not the only) requirement for a word-group to be a sentence: to have at least one verb that has a subject. By applying Rule 2A, you take the first step toward recognizing word-groups that are **not** sentences. This is important, because in writing all word-groups should normally be sentences.

> This word-group is a complete sentence.
> But not this one.
>> These are both word-groups because each starts with a capital letter and each ends with a period. The first word-group meets the first requirement for a sentence; it has one verb that has a subject. The second word-group is not a sentence because it has no verb.

> This word-group starts with a capital letter.
> And ends with a period.
>> Again, these are both word-groups, and the first word-group meets the first requirement for a sentence. The second word-group is not a sentence because, although it has a verb, that verb has no subject.

Exercise 2.26   Checking word-groups for verbs and subjects

Circle each verb, and box its subject. Put brackets [ ] around any word-groups that are not sentences.

Moving day is often a nightmare. Especially for people with large families and lots of belongings. To keep things under control, the parents have to make long check-off lists and remember a hundred details. Like not to pack every cup and spoon. After all, everybody needs to eat breakfast, even on moving day. Still nothing seems to go right. The movers arriving at dawn, immediately snatching every chair in sight, and leaving the children and old folks with nothing to sit on. The weather, of course, is always terrible. Essential tools disappear. Boxes break. The dog barking in wild excitement. The children weeping for the

loss of old friends. Anxious to get going, the moving van driver revs up the motor. And

takes off without warning, leaving two closets still full of odds and ends. Finally, at the end

of the exhausting day, the movers arrange the heavy furniture in the living room. And only

then remember to roll out the rug.

How many word-groups have no verbs? _____
How many verbs have no subjects? _____
How many word-groups did you bracket? _____

Editing Practice C.3	*Checking verbs and subjects again in your own writing*

1. Get your draft of Paper C again.
2. Review Rules 2D-2F3.
3. Check your paper again, to make sure that you have circled every verb (either a one-word verb or a verb phrase). Fix any mistakes with your green pen.
4. Check your paper one more time, to make sure that you have boxed every subject, and that each word you boxed really is the subject of a verb. Fix any mistakes with your green pen.
5. How many mistakes did you fix? _____ Your ability to find and fix mistakes in your own writing shows how much you've learned so far.
6. Now check your paper to find any word-group that doesn't have at least one verb, or has a verb without a subject. Since word groups like these are not sentences, put brackets [ ] around them. How many word-groups did you bracket? _____

Writing Your Final Copy of Paper C

Use your final copy of Paper C to demonstrate what you've learned in Module 2 about the structure of simple sentences, and to show how well you're continuing to apply what you've learned previously.

Paper C	*Using simple sentences*
Edit for Previous Modules	Use your dictionary and the Rules Summary for Module 1 to: • Check your use of writing conventions. Fix any mistakes with your green pen.
Make Final Copy	Mark another piece of paper Paper C, and write the final copy of your paper on it, or print out a clean copy on your word processor. Be sure to include all your corrections. Mark your final copy as you did your draft.
Proofread	Read your final copy **out loud.** Correct any mistakes neatly by hand. If you used a word processor, enter your corrections, print out a corrected final copy, and mark it again.

Hand in your final copy of Paper C, and the rest of your exercises.

3 Understanding More Complicated Sentences I

NAME _____

After you finish checking each exercise, fill in your number of mistakes.

3.1 _____	3.5 _____	3.9 _____	3.12 _____	3.15 _____
3.2 _____	3.6 _____	3.10 _____	3.13 _____	3.16 _____
3.3 _____	3.7 _____	3.11 _____	3.14 _____	3.17 _____
3.4 _____	3.8 _____			

EXERCISES	INSTRUCTIONS	CHECKING	
❏ Complete	❏ Followed carefully	❏ Careful	❏ Green pen not used
❏ Incomplete	❏ Not careful enough	❏ Not careful enough	❏ Mistakes not corrected

COMMENTS

Rules Summary for Module 3

3A	The **joining words** *and*, *but*, *or,* and *so* can make **compound** sentences by connecting two or more related simple sentences.
1	In a compound sentence, always use a **comma** in front of the connecting word.

Sentences connected with joining words look like this:

+

Subject verb **,** connecting word subject verb.

3B	**Expansion words** like *when*, *because*, and *if* can make **complex** sentences by connecting two or more related simple sentences. Expansion words change one sentence into **expansion** of the other.
1	The expansion in a complex sentence can be at either the **end** or the **beginning** of the sentence.
2	When the expansion in a complex sentence is at the beginning of the sentence, use a **comma** to separate it from the rest of the sentence.
3C	The number of simple sentences contained in a compound or complex sentence always should be one more than the number of connecting words.

Sentences connected with expansion words look like this:

+

Subject verb **,** connecting word subject verb.

+

Connecting word subject verb **,** subject verb.

In Module 2, you worked on understanding the structure of simple sentences. But many (or most) sentences are more complicated; they often consist of two or more related simple sentences connected together into one longer sentence. To understand these more complicated sentences, you must learn to recognize **connecting words**, which are used to **connect simple sentences together**. In this module and in Module 4, you'll learn about the following:

- two kinds of more complicated sentences:
  - compound sentences
  - complex sentences
- four kinds of connecting words:
  - the joining words *and, but, or,* and *so*
  - expansion words like *when, because,* and *if*
  - noun-expansion words like *who, which,* and *that*
  - *that* (when it answers the question *WHAT?*)

Using Modules 3 and 4 to Edit Your Own Writing

Use Paper D to discover how much you know already about the structure of more complicated sentences. Later in this module and in Module 4, you'll be checking this paper by applying the rules of this module to what you have written.

You may write this paper by hand. Better yet, use a word processor.

Drafting Paper D	*Using more complicated sentences*
Assignment	Choose one of these assignments:
	❑ Describe a serious mistake that you (or your friend, or a member of your family) once made that had serious consequences for you (or your friend or your family). Be sure to include a description of the mistake, its causes, and its consequences.
	❑ Describe an accident in which several people were involved, something that happened to you, or somebody that you know well, or something that was in the news. Be sure to include a description of what happened and how it affected the lives of the people involved.
Get Ready	On a piece of scratch paper, free write on your chosen topic, first to narrow it to one specific example, and then to get ideas to use in developing your paper. Don't stop until you have plenty of ideas. Draw a line across the page when you are finished free writing.
	Read over your free writing, and decide on your main point. Write it in one complete sentence below the line.
	Plan your paragraphs by selecting enough supporting ideas from your free writing to make your main point interesting, clear, and convincing to a reader. Write your supporting ideas in a numbered list below your main point.
Draft	On another piece of scratch paper, write an introduction to your draft telling what your main point is.

Then write at least one paragraph for each of your supporting ideas. Be sure to include enough examples, details, and facts to make your reader understand and believe each idea.

Write your conclusion.

Special Instructions   This is a topic about the relationship between an incident and its consequences, so make sure that you have made that connection clear. Words like *and, but, or, so, when, before, after, although, because, since, if, unless, so that, whether, who, which,* and *that* are useful to show such relationships and connections. Make sure that you have used at least 15 of these kinds of words in your paper. Write additional sentences if necessary.

Revise   Revise your draft, using the four steps in revision listed on the inside front cover to make your paper better. Make sure that you have written at least four paragraphs, including your introduction and conclusion.

Keep your draft of Paper D to use later.

Joining Words and Compound Sentences

You already know that we often use the word *and* to join subjects, verbs, and other words within simple sentences:

Hector and Achilles were warriors in Homer's epic poem the *Iliad*.
And joins the subjects *Hector* and *Achilles*.

Hector fought and died in the Trojan war.
And joins the verbs *fought* and *died*.

The words *but* and *or* also can join verbs and other words within sentences:

Hector fought bravely but was killed in the end.
But joins the verbs *fought* and *was killed*.

Warriors may die or may survive to fight again.
Or joins the verbs *may die* and *may survive*.

Besides joining subjects, verbs, and other words within sentences, words like *and, but,* and *or* can also be used to join together two or more related simple **sentences**. When they are used like this, to join not words but simple sentences, they are called **connecting words**.

3A	**The <u>joining words</u> *and*, *but*, *or*, and *so* can make <u>compound sentences</u> by connecting two or more related simple sentences.**

When the joining words *and, but, or,* and *so* connect two or more related simple sentences together, they create what we call a **compound sentence**.

To understand the difference between a **compound sentence** and a **simple sentence**, consider these examples:

The [Greeks] **and** [Trojans] (fought) a long war.
> This is a **simple** sentence because it has no connecting words. The joining word *and* in this sentence is **not** a connecting word because it joins two **subjects**, not **sentences**.

The [Trojans] (fought) hard **but** (lost) the war.
> This is also a **simple** sentence because it has no connecting words. The joining word *but* in this sentence is **not** a connecting word because it joins two **verbs**, not **sentences**.

The [Trojans] (fought) hard, **but** the [Greeks] (won)
> This is a **compound** sentence because it has two simple sentences connected together by the joining word **but**. In this sentence the joining word **but** is a **connecting word** because it connects two simple sentences.

When we analyze a compound sentence in order to understand it, we mark the connecting word with a +.

[Hector] (fought) fiercely. [Achilles] (was) even more ferocious.
> These two simple sentences are related, so they can be connected.

+

[Hector] (fought) fiercely, but [Achilles] (was) even more ferocious.
> The connecting word *but* makes the two simple sentences into a compound sentence.

Let's review the process of analyzing compound sentences like these. Follow the three steps below to mark this sentence:

The Trojans fought bravely, but the Greeks won the Trojan War.

1. Circle each verb.

    - *Fought* and *won* can both change tense, so they are verbs. You should have circled them.

2. Box its subject.

    - *Trojans* tells WHO fought, so it is the subject of the verb *fought*. You should have boxed it.
    - *Greeks* tells WHO won, so it is the subject of the verb *won*. You should have boxed it.

3. Put a + over each connecting word.

    - *But* is the word that connects the two sentences. You should have put a + over it.

Marking the sentence like this makes it easy to see that this compound sentence consists of two simple sentences and one connecting word:

+

The [Trojans]① (fought) bravely, but the [Greeks]② (won) the Trojan War.

Use this three-step method in doing the following exercises.

91

Exercise 3.1   Understanding compound sentences

① Circle each verb (either a one-word verb or a verb phrase). ② Box its subject. ③ Put a + over each connecting word.

1. Friday was payday, so we went out last night.

2. I went to the movies, and my brother went to a concert.

3. The movie was terrible, but the concert was outstanding.

4. I'll go to a concert next week, or I'll stay home.

Remember to use your green pen to check each exercise as soon as you finish it. Write in any necessary corrections, and then write your number of mistakes on the cover page.

Be careful not to confuse compound sentences with simple sentences that have two subjects or two verbs.

> Hector and Achilles fought at Troy.
> Hector fought and died for Troy.
> These warriors fought for Troy and Greece.
>> These aren't compound sentences but rather simple sentences with two subjects or two verbs or two other words joined by *and*. The joining word *and* isn't a **connecting** word in these sentences.

Exercise 3.2   Distinguishing between simple and compound sentences

One sentence is simple and the other is compound. ① Circle each verb (either a one-word verb or a verb phrase). ② Box its subject. ③ In the compound sentence, put a + over the connecting word. Be careful **not** to mark any joining word that doesn't connect **sentences**. ④ Write in *A* or *B* to tell which sentence is compound.

1. A. Mahinder was born in India but now lives in Los Angeles.

    B. His family emigrated in 1990, but he didn't come here until last year.

    Sentence _____ is a compound sentence.

2. A. He had been attending college in New Delhi, and he was living with his uncle.

    B. He was studying electronics and wanted to work with computers.

    Sentence _____ is a compound sentence.

3. A. Mahinder had excellent grades but wasn't very good at writing.

    B. He applied for a job at Air India, but they wouldn't hire him.

    Sentence _____ is a compound sentence.

4. A.   Then he moved to Los Angeles and joined his family's business.

   B.   Now he manages a printing shop, so he never has to write anything.

   Sentence _____ is a compound sentence.

Exercise 3.3	**Distinguishing between simple and compound sentences**

① Circle each verb. ② Box its subject. ③ In compound sentences, put a + over the connecting word. Be careful not to mark any joining word that doesn't connect sentences.

Frequently Henry has bored his friends by telling and retelling the story of his first driving lesson. As a once-told tale, it's actually rather amusing. Henry arrived for his lesson and found his instructor dozing at the wheel. Sleepily he moved over, and Henry took his place in the driver's seat. His instructor then smiled encouragingly and pointed to the ignition key and the accelerator. Henry hesitantly turned the key and stepped on the gas. The motor started to run, and he looked at his instructor with amazement. Next, the instructor taught him how to shift gears. Henry shifted into "Drive" and held on tight to the wheel. The car jerked, and then it slowly edged forward. Henry looked anxiously ahead. A truck and a car with a "Wide Load" sign were creeping toward him at 20 miles an hour. Quickly he slammed on the brakes, and his instructor almost went through the windshield. Telling Henry to stop, the instructor began to open the car door. Henry tried to obey, but he stepped on the accelerator instead of the brake. Henry had a new instructor for his next lesson.

3A1	**In a compound sentence, always use a <u>comma</u> in front of the connecting word.**

+

Many [immigrants] (expect) to find good jobs in the USA **,** but often [they] (have) no training for the best jobs.

   A comma is used in front of the connecting word *but* in this compound sentence.

Never use a comma **after** the connecting words *and, but,* and *or.* Always use a comma **in front of** these connecting words.

✗

They take low-paying jobs but **,** then they are very unhappy.
The comma is used incorrectly in this compound sentence.

+

They take low-paying jobs **,** but then they are very unhappy.
The comma is used correctly in this compound sentence.

Exercise 3.4	**Writing compound sentences**

① Circle each verb, and box its subject. ② Connect the two simple sentences into one compound sentence, using the given joining word with a comma in front of it. ③ Mark your rewritten sentence in the same way.

1.   Ching-si wants to be a stock broker.
    but   She doesn't speak English very well yet.

_____

_____

2.   She knows a lot about economics.
    so   She's optimistic about her future.

_____

_____

3.   She has a great personality.
    but   Many people can't understand her speech.

_____

_____

4.   Her parents want her to go to college to learn English better.
    or   Maybe she can study at a language school.

_____

_____

The joining word *and* joins two ideas that are **similar**. The joining word *but* joins two ideas that are **contrasted**. The joining word *or* joins two ideas that are **alternatives**, a choice between two possibilities. The joining word *so* joins two ideas to show that the second idea is **a result** of the first idea.

Exercise 3.5	Using the appropriate connecting word

① Circle each verb, and box its subject. ② Connect the two simple sentences into one compound sentence, using the most appropriate joining word from the list at the right. Check off each word as you use it, and use each word only once. Make sure that your compound sentence makes sense. ③ Mark your rewritten sentence in the same way.

❑ and
❑ but
❑ or
❑ so

1. In the prosperous 1960s, gasoline was plentiful and cheap.
    The big, gas-guzzling American cars were popular.

    _____

    _____

2. By the 1970s, gas prices had soared.
    American cars still had very low gas mileage.

    _____

    _____

3. In the 1980s, Detroit needed to start making more economical cars.
    Imported cars would put them out of business.

    _____

    _____

4. In recent years, American cars have offered good values.
    They have regained their earlier popularity.

    _____

    _____

Editing Practice D.1	Finding compound sentences in your own writing

1. Get your draft of Paper D.
2. Circle each verb (either a one-word verb or a verb phrase), and box its subject.
3. Review Rule 3A.
4. Look for four compound sentences in which you used one of the joining words *and, but, or,* and *so* as connecting words. Put a + over each connecting word in these sentences. Be careful not to mark any joining word that doesn't connect sentences.
5. If you didn't find four compound sentences, create more by connecting two related simple sentences, changing them if necessary so that they sound natural. Or insert new compound sentences into Paper D. Mark these sentences also.
6. Check each compound sentence to make sure that you have punctuated it correctly. Fix any mistakes with your green pen.

7. Review the meanings of the joining words on page 94 above. Then check each compound sentence to make sure that you have used the most appropriate connecting word. Fix any mistakes with your green pen.

8. Your ability to use these sentences shows how much you've learned so far.

Keep your draft of Paper D to use again later.

Expansion Words and Complex Sentences

3B	<u>Expansion words</u> like *when*, *because*, and *if* can make <u>complex</u> sentences by connecting two or more related simple sentences. Expansion words change one sentence into <u>expansion</u> of the other.

Expansion words like *when*, *because*, and *if,* like joining words, can connect two or more related simple sentences together into what we call a **complex sentence**.

Accidents happen. Roads are slippery.
These two simple sentences are related, so they can be connected.

+

Accidents happen when roads are slippery.
The connecting word *when* makes the two simple sentences into a complex sentence.

Complex sentences are different from compound sentences: When expansion words make a complex sentence, they turn one sentence into **expansion**, a group of words which expands the meaning of the other sentence by explaining the relationship between them. This kind of expansion answers questions like *WHEN? WHERE? HOW? WHY?* or *UNDER WHAT CONDITION?* about the other sentence. The expansion and the other sentence work together to create the meaning of the complex sentence.

+

Accidents happen when roads are slippery.
The expansion word *when* turns the sentence *roads are slippery* into expansion that tells **when** accidents happen.

Putting parentheses around the expansion may help make the structure of this kind of sentence clearer.

+

Accidents happen (when roads are slippery).
The parentheses may make it easier to recognize the expansion.

Let's review the process of analyzing complex sentences like these. Follow the two steps below to mark this sentence:

Drivers will have accidents if they are not alert.

1. Circle each verb, and box its subject (we don't need to separate these two steps).

- *Will have* and *are* can both change tense, so they are verbs. You should have circled them.
- *Drivers* tells WHO will have accidents, so *drivers* is the subject of *will have*. You should have boxed it.
- *They* tells WHO are not alert, so *they* is the subject of *are*. You should have boxed it.

2. Put a + over each connecting word.

- The expansion word *if* connects the two sentences. You should have put a + over it.

Marking the sentence like this makes it easy to see that this complex sentence contains two simple sentences and one connecting word:

Drivers <u>will have</u> accidents if they <u>are</u> not alert.

The connecting word turns one of the simple sentences into expansion; putting parentheses around it may help make the structure of this kind of sentence clearer.

Drivers <u>will have</u> accidents (if they <u>are</u> not alert).

Use this two-step method in doing the following exercises.

Exercise 3.6   **Understanding complex sentences**

① Circle each verb, and box its subject. ② Put a + over each connecting word. You may find it helpful to put parentheses around expansion.

1. I asked my brother if he would go with me to the drugstore.

2. He wanted to know when I was going to leave.

3. I left without him because he was watching soap operas on TV.

Remember, the expansion word turns one sentence into **expansion** of the other sentence. Expansion answers questions like *WHEN? WHERE? HOW? WHY?* or *UNDER WHAT CONDITION?* about the other sentence. The expansion and the other sentence work together to create the meaning of the complex sentence.

Accidents <u>happen</u> (when roads <u>are</u> slippery).
The expansion *when roads are slippery* tells **when** accidents happen.

Exercise 3.7   **Understanding the meaning of complex sentences**

① Circle each verb, and box its subject. Put a + over each connecting word. You may find it helpful to put parentheses around expansion. ② Write in what the expansion tells about the other sentence.

1. Jacques will gain weight if he doesn't exercise.

   If he doesn't exercise tells under what _____ Jacques will gain weight.

2. When he moved to Seattle, therefore, he bought a bicycle.

    When he moved to Seattle tells _____ he bought the bicycle.

3. He's getting fat anyway because it rains too much to ride the bike very often.

    Because it rains too much to ride the bike very often tells _____ he's getting fat.

4. Now he always drives when he needs to go someplace.

    When he needs to go someplace tells _____ he drives.

5. Jacques wants to move soon because he worries about getting too fat.

    Because he worries about getting too fat tells _____ he wants to move.

So far you have worked with just three common expansion words: *when, because,* and *if.* Here is a list of almost all of the most common expansion words:

telling WHY or UNDER WHAT CONDITION		
although as because even though	for if since so that	though unless whereas whether
telling WHEN		
after as as soon as	before once until	when whenever while
telling WHERE		
where	wherever	

Exercise 3.8   Using appropriate expansion words

① Circle each verb, and box its subject. ② Connect the two simple sentences into one complex sentence, using the most appropriate expansion word from the list at the right. Make sure that your complex sentence makes sense. Check off each word as you use it, and use each word only once. ③ Mark your rewritten sentence in the same way. You may find it helpful to put parentheses around expansion.

❑ after
❑ before
❑ so that
❑ unless
❑ while

1. I wanted to visit the Grand Canyon. I saw that show about it on TV.

2. I bought some books about geology. I could learn more about it.

    _____

3. I got more and more excited about going. I was reading the books.

    _____

4. However, I need to save some more money. I'll be able to go.

    _____

5. I should have enough by next month. My bills this month are too high.

    _____

You learned in Module 2 that **joining words** like *and, but,* and *or* are not always used as connecting words. In the same way, **expansion words** like *when, because,* and *if* are not always used as connecting words.

> We canceled our meeting because of the weather.
> *Because of the weather* is expansion telling WHY, but *because* doesn't connect two simple sentences.

> After lunch, we'll reschedule the meeting.
> *After lunch* is expansion telling WHEN, but *after* doesn't connect two simple sentences.

Be sure not to mark an expansion word with a + unless it connects two sentences.

Exercise 3.9 — Understanding simple and complex sentences

One sentence is simple and the other is complex. ① Circle each verb. ② Box its subject. ③ In the complex sentence, put a + over the connecting word. You may find it helpful to put parentheses around expansion. Be careful not to mark any expansion word that doesn't connect sentences. ④ Write in *A* or *B* to tell which sentence is complex.

1. A. Mustafa is going to buy a telephone answering machine after lunch.

    B. He decided this after he missed a call about a new job.

    Sentence _____ is a complex sentence.

2. A. He has been trying to get another job since last Christmas.

    B. He has been unhappy since he began working nights and weekends.

    Sentence _____ is a complex sentence.

3.   A.   Often he doesn't get home until his children leave for school.

     B.   Then he just goes to sleep until dinnertime.

          Sentence _____ is a complex sentence.

3B1	**The expansion in a complex sentence can be at either the <u>end</u> or the <u>beginning</u> of the sentence.**

+

The ceremony will begin (when the bride arrives).
The expansion *when the bride arrives* is at the end of the sentence.

+

(When the bride arrives), the ceremony will begin.
The expansion is at the beginning of the sentence, so the connecting word *when* is the first word in the sentence.

Even if the connecting word is at the beginning of the sentence, it still connects the two sentences, and is still marked with a + .

Exercise 3.10	Understanding complex sentences

① Circle each verb, and box its subject. ② Put a + over each connecting word. You may find it helpful to put parentheses around expansion.

If Sangeeta can save enough money, she will soon be able to buy a car. She needs it

badly because now she has to work evenings and weekends. Since her job is in an isolated

neighborhood, she is nervous about taking public transportation to work at night. Although

her friend, Mustafa, has been traveling with her, he will probably quit his job soon. If he

can get a good job, he wants to work in the daytime. However, Sangeeta prefers working

nights, because she makes more money that way.

3B2	**When the expansion in a complex sentence is at the beginning of the sentence, use a <u>comma</u> to separate it from the rest of the sentence.**

+

(If the bride doesn't arrive soon) , the ceremony will be canceled.
The expansion *if the bride doesn't arrive soon* is at the beginning of the sentence, so a comma is used to separate it from the rest of the sentence.

100

Exercise 3.11   Moving expansion to the beginning of the sentence

① Circle each verb, box its subject, and put a + over each connecting word. You may find it helpful to put parentheses around expansion. ② Rewrite the sentence, moving the expansion to the beginning of the sentence, and using a comma to separate it from the rest of the sentence. ③ Mark your rewritten sentence in the same way.

1. Sangeeta may have to quit her job if she can't buy a car.

   _____

2. She will have to travel alone on the bus as soon as Mustafa quits.

   _____

3. The trip makes her very nervous because few people are on the bus late at night.

   _____

Exercise 3.12   Writing sentences with expansion words

① Circle each verb, and box its subject. ② Connect the two simple sentences into one complex sentence, using the given expansion word. ③ Mark your rewritten sentence in the same way.

1.   The newspapers are criticizing the merchants.
   because   They oppose the boycott.

   _____

   _____

2. if   The boycott continues.
            Some merchants will lay off workers or even go out of business.

   _____

   _____

3. after   A teenager was falsely accused of shoplifting.
            The local block association asked the residents to shop elsewhere.

   _____

   _____

Exercise 3.13   Choosing the appropriate connecting word

① Circle each verb, and box its subject. ② Connect the two simple sentences into one complex sentence, using the most appropriate expansion word from the list at the right. Check off each word as you use it, and use each word only once. Make sure that your complex sentence makes sense and is punctuated correctly. ③ Mark your rewritten sentence in the same way. You may find it helpful to put parentheses around expansion.

- ❏ although
- ❏ because
- ❏ once
- ❏ so that
- ❏ until

1. Maria Callas stood out among opera singers.
   She was slender and attractive.

   _____

   _____

2. Her performances had great passion.
   Audiences around the world adored her.

   _____

   _____

3. She lived only for her art.
   She met the billionaire shipowner Aristotle Onassis.

   _____

   _____

4. Her public remained faithful for a while.
   Her vocal powers were declining.

   _____

   _____

5. Callas fell apart completely.
   Onassis ditched her for Jackie Kennedy.

   _____

   _____

Rules 3A and 3B tell you that joining words and expansion words can connect two **or more** simple sentences. Even when a sentence contains more than two simple sentences, mark it in the same way.

Exercise 3.14   Understanding sentences in a paragraph

Circle each verb, and box its subject. Put a + over each connecting word. You may find it helpful to put parentheses around expansion.

People and information continue to hurtle through space at higher and higher speeds. When John Adams traveled from Boston to Williamsburg in the 1770s, he was on the road for more than a week. Today the trip takes 90 minutes by plane. After Andrew Jackson was elected President in 1828, a month went by before some voters heard the news. Today most people know the new President's name before the polls close. However, one notable exception to this law of progress is the daily mail. The pony express delivered mail in the 19th century faster than some modern mail trucks. Back in the 1940s, the postman came to my great-grandmother's house twice a day unless there was a big snowstorm. When she mailed a letter in the late afternoon, it usually arrived the next morning at a friend's house 50 miles away. If her friend wrote back that morning, Great-Grandma sometimes got her reply the same day. This service used to cost just six cents. Today I pay over $11 for Express Mail, and it sometimes can take several days to arrive anyway. In fact, although it runs up my phone bill, I often fax a letter or send e-mail because the mails are so undependable. Today's postal service seems to be an example of progress in reverse.

Editing Practice D.2	**Finding complex sentences in your own writing**

1. Get your draft of Paper D again.
2. Review Rule 3B.
3. Look for four complex sentences in which you used one (or more) of the 23 expansion words listed on page 98 above as connecting words. Put a + over each expansion word in these sentences. Be careful not to mark any word that doesn't connect sentences.
4. If you didn't find four complex sentences, create more by connecting related simple sentences from Paper D, changing them if necessary so that they sound natural. Or insert new complex sentences into Paper D. Mark these sentences also.
5. Check each complex sentence to make sure that you have punctuated it correctly. Fix any mistakes with your green pen.
6. Review the meanings of the expansion words on page 98 above. Then check each complex sentence to make sure that you have used the most appropriate connecting word. Fix any mistakes with your green pen.
7. Your ability to use these sentences shows how much you've learned so far.

Keep your draft of Paper D to use again later.

In school grammar, connecting words like *and, but, or,* and *so* are called **coordinating conjunctions**, and connecting words like *because, when,* and *if* are called **subordinating conjunctions**. And when an expansion word turns simple sentences into expansion, school grammar calls that piece of expansion an **adverbial clause** or a **dependent clause** or a **subordinate clause**. Except perhaps for the purpose of naming these sentence structures on standardized tests, there is no need for you to learn these terms. If you can show on Paper H that you can use connecting words correctly, that's all that matters.

When one sentence contains two or more connected simple sentences, here's a rule that will help you make sure that your sentences are correct.

3C	**The number of simple sentences contained in a compound or complex sentence always should be one more than the number of connecting words.**

According to this rule, **one** connecting word can connect **two** simple sentences:

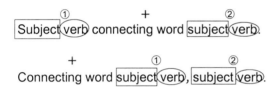

Two connecting words can connect **three** simple sentences:

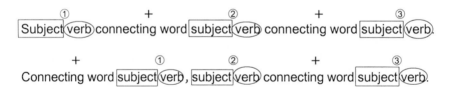

Exercise 3.15   Understanding sentences with several connecting words

① Circle each verb, and box its subject. Put a + over each connecting word. Be careful not to mark any word that doesn't connect simple sentences. You may find it helpful to put parentheses around expansion. ② Fill in the number of simple sentences and connecting words. These sentences are all correct, so make sure that the number of simple sentences you have marked is one more than the number of connecting words you have marked.

1. Saving money is hard when inflation is high, because everything costs a lot.

   This entire sentence contains _____ simple sentences and _____ connecting words.

2. Interest rates on savings are also high when inflation is high, so that savings can grow quickly if you can manage to save.

   This entire sentence contains _____ simple sentences and _____ connecting words.

3. Because economics seems hard and boring, many people don't understand the importance of saving, so that their financial situation gets worse rather than better.

   This entire sentence contains _____ simple sentences and _____ connecting words.

4. If you can save money, you will be protecting yourself against rising prices, and you will have a more comfortable life in the future.

   This entire sentence contains _____ simple sentences and _____ connecting words.

Exercise 3.16	Finding word-groups that are not correct sentences

① Circle each verb, box its subject, and put a + over each connecting word. You may find it helpful to put parentheses around expansion. ② Examine carefully the structure of each word-group. In some, the number of simple sentences is one more than the number of connecting words, so these word-groups are correct sentences. In some others, the number of simple sentences is **not** one more than the number of connecting words, so these word-groups are **not** correct sentences. In still others, there is no verb, or there is a verb with no subject, so these word groups are **not** correct sentences. ③ Answer the questions after each word-group.

1. Because they enjoyed so much wealth and power, the English royal families often behaved outrageously, their subjects from time to time simply had to kill or to exile them.

   How many simple sentences does this word-group contain? _____
   How many connecting words does it have? _____
   This word group ❏ is ❏ is not a correct sentence.

2. After Henry VIII divorced his first wife and beheaded the second, burying the third, and beheading the fourth.

   How many simple sentences does this word-group contain? _____
   How many connecting words does it have? _____
   This word group ❏ is ❏ is not a correct sentence.

3. The Stuart kings, the descendants of Mary Queen of Scots, one of them by the name of Charles I getting his head chopped off, and another by the name of James II fleeing to Ireland and eventually to France.

   How many simple sentences does this word-group contain? _____
   How many connecting words does it have? _____
   This word group ❏ is ❏ is not a correct sentence.

4. Queen Victoria seemed to be a model of propriety, but her son Albert, later to be Edward VII, was notorious for his exploits with women.

   How many simple sentences does this word-group contain? _____
   How many connecting words does it have? _____
   This word group ❏ is ❏ is not a correct sentence.

5. Perhaps the most celebrated episode relating to the English monarchy in the 20ᵗʰ century when Edward VIII renounced his throne to marry an American divorcee.

    How many simple sentences does this word-group contain? _____
    How many connecting words does it have? _____
    This word group ❑ is ❑ is not a correct sentence.

6. When in 1992 two of her sons' marriages broke up and her main home was almost destroyed by fire, Queen Elizabeth II pronounced that year an *annus horribilis*.

    How many simple sentences does this word-group contain? _____
    How many connecting words does it have? _____
    This word group ❑ is ❑ is not a correct sentence.

Exercise 3.17	Finding word-groups that are not correct sentences

① Circle each verb, box its subject, and put a + over each connecting word. You may find it helpful to put parentheses around expansion. ② Remember: word-groups with no verb, or with a verb with no subject, or where the number of simple sentences is **not** one more than the number of connecting words, are not correct sentences. Put brackets [ ] around any word-group that is not a correct sentence.

Robert E. Lee, as Commander-in-Chief of the Confederate Army of Northern Virginia, made only one serious mistake in his otherwise brilliant military career. However, that mistake was a disastrous one. A failure of judgment resulting in the deaths of thousands.

For the first two years of the American Civil War, Lee had taken enormous risks against overwhelming odds, but consistently his tactics had triumphed over the caution of the Union generals. Hence, with high hopes in the summer of 1863, he led his devoted troops into Pennsylvania to crush the blundering Army of the Potomac. Clashing at Gettysburg, rebels and Yankees fought fiercely for two long days, thousands were killed and many more were wounded on both sides. Although, when night fell on the second day, neither side could claim victory. Nevertheless, at that point the federal troops had one distinct advantage, they had fled to high ground, where they ranged their batteries along the ridge overlooking Lee's encampment.

On the third day, after the Confederate commander had devised one plan after another to surprise and outwit the federals, only to find his plans foiled by their unanticipated counterattacks along a five-mile battle front. In the late afternoon, a desperate Lee ordered his officers to lead their surviving troops in parade formation across a mile-wide open field in direct line with Union cannon and rifles at the ready. According to Lee's plan, in a flanking movement, his troops would converge on a clump of trees on the far side of the field. Then storm up an embankment and slaughter and rout the enemy in hand to hand combat. Since they had total confidence in the wisdom of their commander, his soldiers marched forward obediently, with drums beating and battle flags flying. Until enemy fire cut them down like blades of grass and turned the field into a bloody carpet of the dead and dying. Afterwards this incredibly daring but foredoomed assault was known as Pickett's Charge. Because the main division participating in the attack happened to be under the command of General Pickett. Later still, when the war was over, historians pronounced this ghastly blunder the turning point of the Civil War.

How many word-groups have no verbs? _____
How many verbs have no subjects? _____
How many word-groups have too many connecting words? _____
How many word-groups have too few connecting words? _____
How many word-groups did you bracket? _____

Editing Practice D.3   **Finding word-groups that are not correct sentences**

1. Get your draft of Paper D again.
2. Look carefully at each word-group that has no connecting words. If any word group doesn't have at least one verb, or has a verb without a subject, it is not a sentence. Put brackets [ ] around it
3. Review Rule 3C.
4. Look carefully at each word-group that has connecting words like *when, because,* and *if.* If any word-group doesn't have one simple sentence more than the number of connecting words, it is not a correct sentence. Put brackets [ ] around it.
5. How many word-groups did you bracket altogether? _____

Keep your draft of Paper D to use again in Module 4. Now hand in your exercises, and go on to Module 4.

NAME _____

After you finish checking each exercise, fill in your number of mistakes.

4.1 _____	4.4 _____	4.7 _____	4.10 _____	4.13 _____
4.2 _____	4.5 _____	4.8 _____	4.11 _____	
4.3 _____	4.6 _____	4.9 _____	4.12 _____	

EXERCISES	INSTRUCTIONS	CHECKING	
❏ Complete	❏ Followed carefully	❏ Careful	❏ Green pen not used
❏ Incomplete	❏ Not careful enough	❏ Not careful enough	❏ Mistakes not corrected

PAPER D	
❏ Doesn't follow the instructions; write a NEW Paper D.	EDITING PAPER D FOR THIS MODULE'S WORK
❏ Skips some instructions; COMPLETE everything.	❏ Careful ❏ Not careful enough
❏ Too short; add MORE.	EDITING PAPER D FOR PREVIOUS WORK
	❏ Careful ❏ Not careful enough
	OVERALL EVALUATION OF PAPER D
	❏ Excellent ❏ Good ❏ Acceptable ❏ Not acceptable

COMMENTS

Rules Summary for Module 4

4A	The **noun-expansion words** *who*, *which*, and *that* make **complex** sentences by connecting two or more related simple sentences. They change one sentence into **expansion of a noun** in the other.

Sentences connected with noun-expansion words look like this:

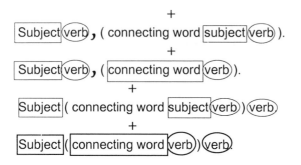

4B	*That* can connect two simple sentences when the second sentence answers the question *WHAT?* after verbs like *SAY, THINK,* and *HOPE.*

Sentences connected with *that* look like this:

Subject verb connecting word subject verb.

In Module 3 we worked on understandingmpound sentences, which are created by using joining words to connect two or more simple sentences, and complex sentences, which are created by using expansion words to connect two or more simple sentences. Now we'll work on another kind of complex sentences, those created by using noun-expansion words.

Noun-expansion Words and Complex Sentences

As you probably already know, nouns are **words that name things**. Those things may be real things (**objects** like *book* or **persons** like *Sheila*) or abstract things (**ideas** like *love* or **actions** like *dancing*). These nouns can appear almost anywhere in a sentence, as the subject of the verb, after the verb, or in expansion.

The new player on the team scored the winning point in the game.
> This sentence contains four nouns. ① The noun *player* is the subject. ② The noun *team* is part of the expansion *on the team*, telling more about *player*. ③ The noun *point* comes after the verb, and tells what was scored. ④ The noun *game* is part of the expansion *in the game*, telling more about *point*.

4A	The <u>noun-expansion words</u> *who, which,* and *that* make <u>complex</u> sentences by connecting two or more related simple sentences. They change one sentence into expansion of a noun in the other.

The **noun-expansion words** *who, which,* and *that,* like the expansion words *when, because,* and *if,* can connect two or more related simple sentences together into a complex sentence, again by turning one sentence into expansion. This kind of expansion answers questions like *WHICH?* or *WHAT KIND?* about **nouns**.

The new player scored a point. Fans will talk about it for a week.
> These two simple sentences are related (*it* in the second sentence refers to *point* in the first sentence), so they can be connected.

The new player scored a point which fans will talk about for a week.
> The noun-expansion word *which* connects the two simple sentences, and turns the sentence *fans will talk about it for a week* into expansion telling more about the *point*.

Let's review the process of analyzing complex sentences like these. Follow the two steps below to mark this sentence:

We cheered the only point which the new player scored.

1. Circle each verb, and box its subject. (We don't need to separate these two steps.)

- *Cheered* and *scored* can both change tense, so they are verbs. You should have circled them.
- *We* tells WHO cheered, so *we* is the subject of *cheered*. You should have boxed it.
- *Player* tells WHO scored, so *player* is the subject of *scored*. You should have boxed it.

111

2. Put a + over each connecting word.

- The noun-expansion word *which* connects the two sentences. You should have put a + over it.

Marking the sentence like this makes it easy to see that this complex sentence contains two simple sentences and one connecting word:

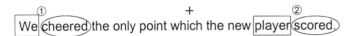

The connecting word turns one of the simple sentences into expansion; putting parentheses around it may help make the structure of this kind of sentence clearer.

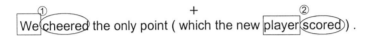

Use this two-step method in doing the following exercises.

Exercise 4.1	Understanding sentences with noun-expansion words

① In the two simple sentences, circle each verb (either a one-word verb or a verb phrase), and box its subject. ② In the complex sentence, circle each verb, box its subject, and put a + over each connecting word. You may find it helpful to put parentheses around expansion.

1. Last week, Raj bought a new television set. He is watching it now.

   Last week, Raj bought a new television set which he is watching now.

2. Raj avoids certain programs. His wife dislikes them.

   Raj avoids certain programs that his wife dislikes.

3. Still, he always watches *Baywatch*. He enjoys it very much.

   Still, he always watches *Baywatch,* which he enjoys very much.

It's a little harder to use noun-expansion words than the other kind. You may have noticed in the previous exercise these two differences:

1. The noun-expansion word isn't just inserted; it actually replaces one of the words already in the original sentence.

   The new player scored a point. Fans will talk about it for a week.
      These two simple sentences are related (*it* in the second sentence refers to *point* in the first sentence), so they can be connected.

   x

   The new player scored a point which fans will talk about it for a week.
      This sentence is incorrect, because *which* hasn't replaced *it*.

2. Because the noun-expansion word refers to a noun, it must be put right next to that noun.

X

The new |player| (scored) a point |fans| (will talk) about <u>which</u> for a week.
     This sentence is incorrect, because the noun-expansion word *which* isn't right next to the noun *point*.

So, to use noun-expansion words correctly, you need to do two things: ① Replace one of the words already in the sentence, and ② Put the connecting word right next to the noun it refers to.

The new |player| (scored) a point. |Fans| (will talk) about it for a week.

+

The new |player| (scored) a point which |fans| (will talk) about for a week.
     This sentence is correct. The noun-expansion word *which* replaces *it*, and is right next to *point*.

Exercise 4.2   Writing sentences with noun-expansion words

① Circle each verb (either a one-word verb or a verb phrase), and box its subject. ② Connect the two simple sentences into one complex sentence, using the given noun-expansion word. ③ Mark your rewritten sentence in the same way. You may find it helpful to put parentheses around expansion.

1.   Retirees want long-term health care.
  that   Many of them can't afford it.

_____

_____

2.   Therefore, they pay close attention to legislation.
  which Their elected representatives are considering it.

_____

_____

3.   They write their Senators frequent letters.
  which The Senators read them carefully.

_____

_____

4.   The Senators will vote for programs.
  that   Their constituents want them.

_____

_____

5.   In turn, the retirees will cast their own votes.
  which The Senators want them just as much.

_____

_____

One thing that's especially hard about this kind of expansion is that **the expansion word can be the subject** of the verb in the expansion. So one word is functioning in two ways in these sentences.

The |fans| (cheered) the player. |She| (scored) the point.

|

+

The |fans| (cheered) the player |who| (scored) the point.

> The noun-expansion word *who* replaces *she*, and is right next to *player*. *Who* is both the connecting word and the subject of the second verb.

|Mary| (scored) the point. |It| (won) the game.

|

+

|Mary| (scored) the point |which| (won) the game.

> The noun-expansion word *which* replaces *it*, and is right next to *point*. *Which* is both the connecting word and the subject of the second verb.

Let's review the process of analyzing complex sentences like these. Follow the three steps below to mark this sentence:

> The coach congratulated the player who won the game for us.

1. Circle each verb. (Because these sentences are complicated, we'll separate marking the verb and the subject.)

    - *Congratulated* and *won* can both change tense, so they are verbs. You should have circled them.

2. Box its subject.

    - *Coach* tells WHO congratulated, so *coach* is the subject of *congratulated*. You should have boxed it.
    - Because *who* refers to *player* (the word that tells WHO won the game), *who* is the subject of *won*. You should have boxed it.

3. Put a + over each connecting word.

    - *Who* is both the subject of *won* and the word that connects the two sentences. You should have put a + over it.

Marking the sentence like this makes it easy to see that this complex sentence contains two simple sentences and one connecting word:

> ①   + ②
> The |coach| (congratulated) the player |who| (won) the game for us.

The connecting word turns one of the simple sentences into expansion; putting parentheses around it may help make the structure of this kind of sentence clearer.

> ①   + ②
> The |coach| (congratulated) the player (|who| (won) the game for us) .

114

Use this three-step method in doing the following exercises.

Exercise 4.3   Understanding sentences with noun-expansion words

① In the two simple sentences, circle each verb, and box its subject. ② In the complex sentence, circle each verb, box its subject (remember that the noun-expansion words *who*, *which*, and *that* can be subjects), and put a + over each connecting word. You may find it helpful to put parentheses around expansion.

1. I met a woman. She knew you in high school.

   I met a woman who knew you in high school.

2. She still remembers the basketball team. It won the state championship.

   She still remembers the basketball team that won the state championship.

3. You were dating Shawn. He was the center on that team.

   You were dating Shawn, who was the center on that team.

4. She is now married to Shawn. He is a high school teacher.

   She is now married to Shawn, who is a high school teacher.

5. They live in an apartment. It is right around the corner.

   They live in an apartment which is right around the corner.

We use the expansion word *who* to refer to **people**, and the expansion word *which* or *that* to refer to **things**.

He is a doctor who is famous world-wide.
Who is used to refer to *doctor*, who is a person.

The doctor performed an operation which lasted for six hours.
Which is used to refer to *operation*, which is a thing.

Exercise 4.4   Choosing *who* or *which*

① Fill in *who* or *which* to connect the two simple sentences. ② Circle each verb, box its subject, and put a + over the connecting word. You may find it helpful to put parentheses around expansion.

1. This car is the one _____ cost $13,000 three years ago.

2. My uncle is the salesman _____ sold it to me.

3. Now I need to replace the tires _____ came with the car.

4. My uncle introduced me to his brother-in-law, _____ sells tires cheap.

Exercise 4.5	Creating more complicated sentences

① Circle each verb, and box its subject. ② Connect the two simple sentences into one complex sentence, using one of the noun-expansion words *who* or *which*. ③ Mark your rewritten sentence in the same way. You may find it helpful to put parentheses around expansion.

1. I have a sister. She is now afraid of dogs.

    _____

2. Years ago, we had a pet cocker spaniel. It used to sleep on my sister's bed.

    _____

3. One night she had a nightmare. It awoke her from a deep sleep.

    _____

4. Her sudden movement startled the sleeping dog. It instinctively bit her arm.

    _____

5. Now she won't even visit our parents. They still have dogs.

    _____

In sentences with noun-expansion words, when the expansion tells more about the **subject** of the sentence, it comes **in the middle of the sentence**. This happens because the connecting word must be put next to the word it refers to. The resulting complex sentence may seem confusing.

The [player] (scored) the winning point. [She] (joined) the team yesterday.

The [player] [who] (joined) the team yesterday (scored) the winning point.
> The noun-expansion word *who* replaces *she*, and is right next to *player*, so the expansion *who joined the team yesterday* comes in the middle of the sentence. *Who* is both the connecting word and the subject of the verb *joined*.

Putting parentheses around expansion may help make the structure of this kind of sentence clearer.

The [player] ([who] (joined) the team yesterday) (scored) the winning point.
> The parentheses may make it easier to recognize the expansion.

This kind of complex sentence is the hardest to understand. But if you mark the parts of sentences carefully, then even complicated sentences like this one will not confuse you.

Let's review the process of analyzing complex sentences like these. Follow the four steps below to mark this sentence:

The player who made three fouls was ejected from the basketball game.

1. Circle each verb. (Because these sentences are complicated, we'll separate marking the verb and the subject.)

    *   *Made* and *was ejected* can both change tense, so they are verbs. You should have circled them.

2. Box its subject.

    *   *Player* tells WHO was ejected, so *player* is the subject of the verb *was ejected*. You should have boxed it.
    *   Because *who* refers to *player* (the word that tells WHO made three fouls), *who* is the subject of *made*. You should have boxed it.

3. Put a + over each connecting word.

    *   The noun-expansion word *who* connects the two sentences. You should have put a + over it.

4. Put parentheses around the expansion to make the structure of the sentence clearer.

    *   *Who made three fouls* is the expansion. You should have put parentheses around it.

Marking the sentence like this makes it easy to see that this complex sentence contains two simple sentences and one connecting word, with the expansion in the middle:

The player (who made three fouls) was ejected from the basketball game.

Use this four-step method in doing the following exercises.

Exercise 4.6	Understanding more complicated sentences

① In the two simple sentences, circle each verb, and box its subject. ② In the complex sentence, circle each verb, box its subject (remember that the expansion words *who*, *which*, and *that* can be subjects), put a + over each connecting word, and put parentheses around expansion.

1. Concerts are very popular. They feature Irish music.

    Concerts which feature Irish music are very popular.

2. Aly Bain is a well-known Irish fiddler. He plays with The Boys of the Lough.

    Aly Bain, who plays with The Boys of the Lough, is a well-known Irish fiddler.

3. Phil Cunningham often plays with Aly. He writes songs and plays the accordian.

    Phil Cunningham, who writes songs and plays the accordian, often plays with Aly.

4. A concert is at Music Hall tomorrow. It features them.

    A concert which features them is at Music Hall tomorrow.

Remember: noun expansion must directly follow the noun it tells more about. If you put it in the wrong place, your sentence may not make sense. Drawing an arrow between related words will help you avoid this kind of mistake.

The [man] (was driving) a truck. [He] (saw) the accident.
> The arrow shows how these two simple sentences are related. *He* in the second sentence refers to *man* in the first sentence, so the two sentences can be connected by the noun expansion word *who*.

The [man] (was driving) a truck [who] (saw) the accident.
> This sentence is incorrect, because the noun-expansion word *who* isn't right next to the noun *man*. *Who saw the accident* is expansion telling more about the *man*, not the *truck*. This sentence doesn't make sense.

The [man] [who] (saw) the accident (was driving) a truck.
> Now that the expansion directly follows *man*, this sentence makes sense.

The [man] ([who] (saw) the accident) (was driving) a truck.
> The parentheses make the structure of this sentence clearer.

Exercise 4.7	**Connecting sentences with *who* or *which***

① Circle each verb, and box its subject. ② Draw an arrow between the two related words. ③ Connect the two simple sentences into one complex sentence, using *who* or *which*. Make sure your complex sentence makes sense. ④ Mark your rewritten sentence in the same way, and put parentheses around expansion.

1. The airport is very modern. It recently opened in Denver.

   _____

2. Passengers praise the baggage-handling system. They use the terminal.

   _____

3. This system is now working well. It moves bags on conveyer belts.

   _____

4. Last year, though, Dan Stoddard lost all his bags. He used the airport on its first day.

   _____

   _____

5. The bags have never been found. He lost them that day.

   _____

Punctuating Sentences with Noun-expansion Words

Punctuating sentences with this kind of expansion can be difficult. Sometimes the expansion contains **information which is needed** to answer the question *WHICH?* about the noun. In this case, **commas should not be used** around the expansion. At other times, the expansion contains **extra information which is not needed** to answer the question *WHICH?* about the noun. In this case, **commas should be used** around the expansion. You may have heard terms like **restrictive** and **non-restrictive** used about this kind of expansion.

+
My brother (who lives in Michigan) has a beard.
> I have two brothers, one of whom lives in Michigan, so the expansion *who lives in Michigan* **is** needed to tell *which brother*, and **commas should not be used**.

+
My brother, (who lives in Michigan), has a beard.
> I have one brother, who by the way lives in Michigan, so the expansion *who lives in Michigan* is **not** needed to tell *which brother*, and **commas should be used**.

Exercise 4.8 — Using commas with noun expansion

① Check off whether the expansion is or is not needed, and whether commas should or should not be used. ② Draw an arrow between the two related words. ③ Connect the two simple sentences into one complex sentence, using *who* or *which*, and using commas if needed. Make sure your complex sentence makes sense. ④ Mark your rewritten sentence in the same way, and put parentheses around expansion.

1. The surgeon saved a young girl's life. He had developed the new procedure.

   The expansion ❑ is ❑ is not needed to tell *which*, so commas ❑ should ❑ should not be used.

2. This young girl had a rare heart malformation. She came from Ecuador.

   The expansion ❑ is ❑ is not needed to tell *which*, so commas ❑ should ❑ should not be used.

3. Her heart was ready to fail. It was too weak to pump effectively.

   The expansion ❑ is ❑ is not needed to tell *which*, so commas ❑ should ❑ should not be used.

4. The operation cost $30,000. It saved her life.

   The expansion ❑ is ❑ is not needed to tell *which*, so commas ❑ should ❑ should not be used.

5. The local newspaper raised all the needed money. It told the girl's story on page 1.

    The expansion ❑ is ❑ is not needed to tell *which,* so commas ❑ should ❑ should not be used.

Exercise 4.9	Connecting more sentences with *who* or *which*

Read these simple sentences carefully to make sure that you understand them. ① Circle each verb, and box its subject. ② Draw arrows between the related words. ③ Connect each set of three simple sentences into one complex sentence, using *who* or *which,* and using commas if needed. Make sure to **change the second and third sentences into expansion of the first**, so that your complex sentence makes sense. ④ Mark your rewritten sentence in the same way, and put parentheses around expansion.

1. Antonio Vivaldi wrote music.
    He lived in 17th century Italy.
    The music still moves audiences.

2. He worked for years at an orphanage.
    The orphanage housed girls.
    The girls sang and played instruments.

3. The girls must have been excellent musicians to play his music.
    They performed in Vivaldi's orchestra.
    His music still demands great skill.

4. Vivaldi's *Gloria* was performed last night by some local girls.
    It contains some of his most beautiful music.
    They didn't do such a good job with it.

Editing Practice D.4	**Checking noun expansion in your own writing**

1. Get your draft of Paper D again.
2. Review Rule 4A.
3. Look for four complex sentences in which you used one (or more) of the noun-expansion words *who*, *which*, and *that* as a connecting word. Put a + over each noun-expansion word in these sentences. Be careful not to mark any word that doesn't connect sentences.
4. If you didn't find four complex sentences with these words, create more by connecting related simple sentences from Paper D, changing them if necessary so that they sound natural. Or insert new complex sentences into Paper D. Mark these sentences also.
5. Check each complex sentence to make sure that you have punctuated it correctly. Fix any mistakes with your green pen.
6. Your ability to use these sentences shows how much you've learned so far.

Keep your draft of Paper D to use again later.

That and Complex Sentences

You already know that the noun-expansion word *that* is used like *which*, to connect simple sentences by changing one sentence into expansion of a noun in the other. It answers the question *WHICH?* in sentences like this, because it's telling more about another noun.

+

I put some money in a bank that later failed.

> *That later failed* is expansion that answers the question *WHICH bank?*

That can also be used to connect sentences in a different way.

4B	***That* can connect two simple sentences when the second sentence answers the question *WHAT?* after verbs like *SAY, THINK,* and *HOPE*.**

You may have heard the term **noun clause** used about this kind of construction.

Mr. Hicks tells me something. Intelligence is unimportant.

> The second sentence answers the question *Mr. Hicks tells me WHAT?*

+

Mr. Hicks tells me that intelligence is unimportant.

> So the connecting word *that* can be used to connect the sentences. *That intelligence is unimportant* answers the question *WHAT does Mr. Hicks tell me?*

+

I think that Mr. Hicks is wrong.

> *That Mr. Hicks is wrong* is a noun clause answering the question *WHAT do I think?*

There are dozens of other verbs that use noun clauses with *that* like this: *STATE, BELIEVE, ASK, ANNOUNCE, INSIST, WRITE, READ, FEAR, SHOUT, DREAM,* and *HEAR,* to mention just a few. You can recognize these verbs easily, because the answer to the question *WHAT?* always comes after them.

In school grammar the noun-expansion words *who, which,* and *that* are called **relative pronouns,** and the pieces of expansion they create are called **adjective clauses** because, like adjectives, these clauses answer the question *WHICH?* about nouns. However, the connecting word *that* as used in Rule 4B above is a **conjunction,** and it does **not** turn a simple sentence into expansion (as the expansion word *that* does). The simple sentences that follow the conjunction *that* in the examples above are called **noun clauses** because they act like nouns by answering the question *WHAT?* after verbs like *SAY, THINK,* and *HOPE.* On standardized tests, just remember that **adjective clauses** are expansion created by *who, which,* and *that* to tell more about nouns, and that **noun clauses** answer the question *WHAT?* after verbs like *SAY, THINK,* and *HOPE.*

So that you won't confuse these two kinds of clauses, we will use the term **noun clause** for the simple sentence that answers the question *WHAT?* after verbs like *SAY, THINK,* and *HOPE.*

Exercise 4.10   Understanding sentences with *that*

That is used to connect these sentences in two different ways. ① Circle each verb, box its subject, and put a + over each connecting word. You may find it useful to put parentheses around expansion. ② If *that* creates expansion telling more about a noun, write in *WHICH.* If it creates a noun clause, write in *WHAT.*

1. Some people believe that environment and heredity influence behavior equally.

    The noun clause beginning with *that* answers the question _____ *do some people believe?*

    However, according to recent research, the genes that we inherit are the strongest factor in shaping our

    character and personality.

    The expansion beginning with *that* answers the question _____ *genes?*

2. Psychiatrists have found that the behavior of identical twins often turns out the same despite great

    differences in their life experiences.

    The noun clause beginning with *that* answers the question _____ *have psychiatrists found?*

    The studies that psychiatrists have published recently on this subject are therefore very discouraging to

    parents.

    The expansion beginning with *that* answers the question _____ *studies?*

3. Studies that gather data on identical twins show that home environment and education make little

    difference in human development.

The expansion beginning with *that* answers the question _____ studies?

The noun clause beginning with *that* answers the question _____ do the studies show?

In speech and even in writing, the connecting word *that* is sometimes not expressed, but it is always understood.

$+$

The |weatherman| believes *that* a |hurricane| is coming.

> *That* can be omitted in a sentence like this, where it connects the two simple sentences. The noun clause answers the question *WHAT does the weatherman believe?*

That can also be omitted in noun expansion, so long as it's not the subject of the verb.

$+$

The |help| *that* |he| promised has arrived.

> *That* can be omitted in a sentence like this, where it connects the two simple sentences. *That he promised* is expansion telling more about the *help*.

$+$

The |money| that was stolen has been returned.

> *That* can't be omitted in a sentence like this. *That was stolen* is expansion telling more about the *money*.
> *That* can't be omitted because it's the subject of the verb *was stolen*.

Exercise 4.11   Understanding sentences where *that* is understood

① Circle each verb, and box its subject. ② Insert the connecting word *that* with a ∧, and put a + over it. You may find it helpful to put parentheses around expansion.

1. My boss says I have to work overtime.

2. But the extra money I earn from overtime just isn't worth it.

3. I know I need to spend more time with my family.

4. Last night I decided to tell my husband I'm looking for a different job.

5. He was happy about the decision I had made.

Editing Practice D.5   Checking *that* in your own writing

1. Get your draft of Paper D again.
2. Review Rule 4B.
3. Look for three complex sentences in which you used the connecting word *that* (or in which *that* is understood) to answer the question *WHAT?* Put a + over each connecting word in these sentences. Be careful not to mark any word that doesn't connect sentences.
4. If you didn't find three complex sentences with *that*, create more by rewriting sentences from Paper D, changing them if necessary so that they sound natural. Or insert new complex sentences with *that* into Paper D. Mark these sentences also.
5. Your ability to use these sentences shows how much you've learned so far.

Keep your draft of Paper D to use again later.

Exercise 4.12   Connecting simple sentences in various ways

Read these simple sentences carefully to make sure that you understand them. ① On scratch paper, connect each set of sentences into one complex sentence, using the given connecting words and any necessary punctuation. Make sure that your complex sentences make sense. ② Mark another piece of paper Exercise 4.12, and copy your complex sentences onto it in paragraph form. ③ Mark your rewritten paragraph as you have learned to.

1.   Michaelangelo was a 16th century sculptor.
     who   He also painted.

2.   His huge paintings on the Sistine Chapel ceiling are in all art history books.
     but   His marble statues are even more famous.

3. because   Marble was plentiful in the hills not far from Florence.
              He always used this beautiful stone.

4. while   He was planning his statues.
              He seemed to hear voices.
     which   They came from within the blocks of marble.

5.   One day he was painting a prince's portrait.
     which   He wanted to finish it before sunset.
     when   His helpers carried in a large chunk of marble.

6. after   They left.
              Michaelangelo continued to paint.
     but   He sensed the presence of an invisible person in the room.

7. when   He turned and saw the marble.
              He understood.

8. as   He touched the rough surface.
              Michaelangelo felt a figure.
     which   It moved in the marble.

9.   It was Moses the prophet.
     who   He was waiting for Michaelangelo to set him free.

10.   The prince would have to wait.
     who   He had ordered the painting.
     because At this moment a more important person was giving Michaelangelo orders.

Exercise 4.13   Finding word-groups that are not correct sentences

① Circle each verb, box its subject, and put a + over each connecting word. You may find it helpful to put parentheses around expansion. ② Remember: word-groups with no verb, or with a verb with no subject, or where the number of simple sentences is **not** one more than the number of connecting words, are not correct sentences. Put brackets [ ] around any word-group that is not a correct sentence.

Cockroaches are perhaps the most durable form of life on earth. They do well in cathedrals, in grass huts, and in swanky duplex apartments. Or any other place in the world which is habitable by humans. Roaches will eat almost anything. Including leather, glue, paper, and even the starch in bookbinding. So that office storerooms and public libraries are among their preferred residences. They're able to live 50 days without food and 14 days without water. In fact, after years of eating huge doses of supermarket roach-poisons, some populations of roaches become immune to them. And pass this immunity on to their descendants. Who then go on to die of advanced old age. Exterminators praise the effectiveness of some powerful anti-roach chemicals, like hydroprene, which renders juvenile roaches sterile. And amidinolhydrazone which roaches are not likely to recognize as poison because it acts so slowly. Nevertheless, according to cynical apartment dwellers, if nuclear war comes, all life on earth will probably become extinct—with one exception, cockroaches will survive and will thrive on nuclear waste and radioactive dust.

How many word-groups have no verbs? _____
How many verbs have no subjects? _____
How many word-groups have too many connecting words? _____
How many word-groups have too few connecting words? _____
How many word-groups did you bracket? _____

Editing Practice D.6   *Finding word-groups that are not correct sentences*

1. Get your draft of Paper D again.
2. Look carefully at each word-group that has connecting words like *who, which,* and *that*. If the number of simple sentences in this word-group is not one more than the number of connecting words, then it is not a correct sentence. Put brackets [ ] around it.
3. How many word-groups did you bracket? _____
4. What is the total number of word-groups that you put brackets around in Paper D? _____

Writing Your Final Copy of Paper D

Use your final copy of Paper D to demonstrate what you've learned in Modules 3-4 about the structure of compound and complex sentences, and to show how well you're continuing to apply what you've learned previously.

Paper D	*Using compound and complex sentences*
Edit for Previous Modules	Use your dictionary and the Rules Summary for Module 1 to: • Check your use of writing conventions. Fix any mistakes with your green pen.
Make Final Copy	Mark another piece of paper Paper D, and write the final copy of your paper on it, or print out a clean copy on your word processor. Be sure to include all your corrections. Mark your final copy as you did your draft.
Proofread	Read your final copy **out loud.** Correct any mistakes neatly by hand. If you used a word processor, enter your corrections, print out a corrected final copy, and mark it again.

Hand in your final copy of Paper D, and the rest of your exercises.

5 Using Nouns and Pronouns

NAME _____

After you finish checking each exercise, fill in your number of mistakes.

5.1 _____	5.8 _____	5.14 _____	5.20 _____	5.26 _____
5.2 _____	5.9 _____	5.15 _____	5.21 _____	5.27 _____
5.3 _____	5.10 _____	5.16 _____	5.22 _____	5.28 _____
5.4 _____	5.11 _____	5.17 _____	5.23 _____	5.29 _____
5.5 _____	5.12 _____	5.18 _____	5.24 _____	5.30 _____
5.6 _____	5.13 _____	5.19 _____	5.25 _____	5.31 _____
5.7 _____				

EXERCISES	INSTRUCTIONS	CHECKING	
❑ Complete	❑ Followed carefully	❑ Careful	❑ Green pen not used
❑ Incomplete	❑ Not careful enough	❑ Not careful enough	❑ Mistakes not corrected

PAPER E
❑ Doesn't follow the instructions; write a NEW Paper E.
❑ Skips some instructions; COMPLETE everything.
❑ Too short; add MORE.

EDITING PAPER E FOR THIS MODULE'S WORK
❑ Careful   ❑ Not careful enough
EDITING PAPER E FOR PREVIOUS WORK
❑ Careful   ❑ Not careful enough
OVERALL EVALUATION OF PAPER E
❑ Excellent   ❑ Good   ❑ Acceptable   ❑ Not acceptable

COMMENTS

Rules Summary for Module 5

5A	Use an appropriate **determiner** and add an *S (or ES)* ending to make most nouns **plural**.
1	Make necessary **spelling** changes when making a noun plural.
2	To make an **irregular** noun plural, change the whole word.
5B	Do not try to make **noncount** nouns plural.
5C	Use a **singular pronoun** to refer to a singular noun, and a **plural pronoun** to refer to a plural noun.
5D	Use a pronoun form that's correct for how it's used in a sentence.
5E	Use a **reflexive** pronoun with *–self* or *–selves* to refer back to the subject or an earlier word.
5F	Use a pronoun form in the same **person** as the word it refers to.
5G	Avoid sexist language in using feminine and masculine pronouns.

In the previous two modules, you learned about verbs and subjects, and about how they work together to form sentences. In the next three modules, you'll learn about the forms of individual words within sentences. We'll start with **nouns** and **pronouns**.

Recognizing Nouns

Nouns are words that **name things**. They can name real things, **things** that can be touched (**objects** like *book* or *car*, or **people** like *Emanuel* or *cousin*). Nouns can also name things that can't be touched (**abstract ideas** like *freedom* or *happiness*, and **actions** like *running*).

But it's not always possible to tell, just from this definition, whether a word all by itself is a noun. For example, think about these five words; are they nouns?

skate   laugh   rose   swimming   bank

These words may or may not be nouns. What's important is how each word is used in a sentence. When you know that, you'll know whether each word is a noun.

Exercise 5.1   Telling the difference between nouns and other kinds of words

① Circle each verb (either a one-word verb or a verb phrase), and box its subject. ② Write in *A* or *B* to tell in which sentence the word is a noun.

1. A. The Brinkers skate to work.
    B. Hans lost a skate.
        Skate is a noun in sentence _____.

2. A. They always laugh at him.
    B. But he'll have the last laugh.
        Laugh is a noun in sentence _____.

3. A. She knelt and picked a rose.
    B. She rose from her knees and gave it to me.
        Rose is a noun in sentence _____.

4. A. Mark is swimming in the championship meet.
    B. Swimming in this championship will make him famous.
        Swimming is a noun in sentence _____.

5. A. He was sleeping on the bank of the river.
    B. I usually bank at Acme Savings & Loan.
    C. A bank shot is the hardest one in billiards.
        Bank is a noun in sentence _____.

Remember to use your green pen to check each exercise as soon as you finish it. Write in any necessary corrections, and then write your number of mistakes on the cover page of this module.

Using Module 5 to Edit Your Own Writing

Use Paper E to discover how much you know already about using nouns and pronouns. Later in this module, you'll be checking this paper by applying the rules of this module to what you have written.

You may write this paper by hand. Better yet, use a word processor.

Drafting Paper E	*Using nouns and pronouns*
Assignment	Choose one of these assignments:
	❑ Think of a family or another group of at least four members, all of whom you know well. Describe the behavior of one member of this group: how his or her behavior has affected the other members, both individually and as a group. As an example of this person's behavior (good or bad), describe in detail one particular incident when at least four members of the group were present and involved.
	❑ Think of situations where men and women sometimes or typically work together: business, education, politics, the church, health care, child raising, etc. Choose one and describe the roles men and women tend to assume. Consider why you think they assume these roles, and what your own views of these roles are
Get Ready	On a piece of scratch paper, free write on your chosen topic, first to narrow it to one specific example if necessary, and then to get ideas to use in developing your paper. Don't stop until you have plenty of ideas. Draw a line across the page when you have finished free writing.
	Read over your free writing, and decide on your main point. Write it in one complete sentence below the line.
	Plan your paragraphs by selecting enough supporting ideas from your free writing to make your main point interesting, clear, and convincing to a reader. Write your supporting ideas in a numbered list below your main point.
Draft	On another piece of scratch paper, write an introduction to your draft telling what your main point is.
	Then write at least one paragraph for each of your supporting ideas. Be sure to include enough examples, details, and facts to make your reader understand and believe each idea.
	Write your conclusion.
Special Instructions	Underline each noun. How many nouns did you use altogether? _____
Revise	Revise your draft, using the four steps in revision listed on the inside front cover to make your paper better. Make sure that you have written at least four paragraphs, including an introduction and a conclusion.

Keep your draft of Paper E to use later.

Determiners and Noun Endings

Nouns often name things that can be counted. We call nouns that name one thing **singular**, and we call nouns that name more than one thing **plural**.

There are two ways to tell whether nouns are singular or plural:

1. Almost every noun has a **determiner**, a word that tells **how many** and shows whether a noun is singular or plural.

2. Almost every noun either has **an ending** (which makes it plural), or has **no ending** (which makes it singular).

The determiner and the ending work together to make a noun singular or plural:

> one book_
>> *One* is a determiner showing that the noun is singular. *Book* has no ending, which also makes it singular.

> two books
>> *Two* is a determiner showing that the noun is plural. *Books* has an ending, which also makes it plural.

Exercise 5.2   Recognizing nouns as singular or plural

① Underline each determiner. ② Write *S* over each singular noun and *P* over each plural noun.
③ Underline the ending on each plural noun. Follow this model:

P	*S*
two books	one book

1. one fork   many forks

2. seven speeches   a speech

3. a task   some tasks

4. three apples   an apple

There are several kinds of determiners. The first kind of determiner tells **how many exactly**. This kind of determiner includes all numbers, *a* or *an* (which mean *one*), and words like *both* (which means *two*).

Some determiners telling how many exactly	
Singular	**Plural**
one a an	two three seven 46 1,550

Exercise 5.3   Recognizing nouns with determiners telling how many exactly

① Underline each determiner. ② Write S over every singular noun and P over every plural noun.
③ Underline the ending on each plural noun.

1.   A tree may have 17,000 leaves.

2.   Sixty-three persons crowded into one room.

3.   Both ideas were discussed for seven hours.

A second kind of determiner tells **how many in general**, but not how many exactly. A few of these determiners are unusual. *Every* seems as though it should be plural, but it is actually singular, because it means something like *each one individually*. A negative determiner like *not any* may seem as though it is neither singular nor plural, but it is actually plural, because it means something like *none of them*. *No* can be used with either singular or plural nouns. Finally, plural nouns may be used with no determiner; this means something like *all of them in general*.

Some determiners telling how many in general	
Singular	**Plural**
each	some all several many most
every no	not any no
	[no determiner]

Exercise 5.4   Recognizing nouns with determiners telling how many in general

① Underline each determiner. ② Write S over every singular noun and P over every plural noun.
③ Underline the ending on each plural noun.

1.   Each suitcase was searched by several guards.

2.   Some neighbors donated many cakes.

3.   Every delivery was delayed for days.

4.   Some neighborhoods allow no businesses.

5.   Most cars now have airbags.

A third kind of determiner tells **which** as well as how many. There are only three determiners like this. These determiners are different from those you've worked with so far, because each singular determiner has just one specific plural form: *These* is the plural form of the singular determiner *this*, and *those* is the plural form of the singular determiner *that*. You can't use these determiners interchangeably. Notice also that *the* has the same form in the singular and plural.

Determiners telling <u>which</u>	
Singular	**Plural**
this that the	these those the

Exercise 5.5 **Recognizing nouns with determiners telling <u>which</u>**

① Underline each determiner. ② Write *S* over every singular noun and *P* over every plural noun. ③ Underline the ending on each plural noun.

1. These tools are needed for that job.

2. This boy liked those games.

3. The worker paid the fees.

4. I bought this book and these magazines.

5. She owns that car and those bicycles.

6. I have the pen and the pencils right here.

You learned in Modules 2-4 about **expansion**, words or groups of words telling more about other words. Many nouns have expansion, usually between the determiner and the noun.

> <u>A fireman</u> rescued <u>three children</u> from <u>that rooftop</u>.
> This sentence contains three nouns, each of which has an appropriate determiner telling how many.

> A <u>courageous</u> fireman rescued three <u>frightened</u> children from that <u>blazing</u> rooftop.
> *Courageous, frightened,* and *blazing* are expansion telling more about the three nouns.

In some languages, expansion may be singular or plural, just like nouns. But in English, expansion **never** has a plural form.

> *x*
> I interviewed <u>three others candidates</u> for the job.
> *Others* is incorrect, because expansion never has a plural form.

> I interviewed <u>three other candidates</u> for the job.
> This sentence is correct.

Exercise 5.6	Recognizing determiners with expanded nouns

① Underline each determiner. ② Write *S* over every singular noun and *P* over every plural noun.
③ Underline the ending on each plural noun.

1. I ate a broiled pork chop and three ripe peaches yesterday.

2. I gave her twelve yellow mums and one beautiful red rose.

3. Some talented housewives made this prizewinning quilt.

Writing Plural Nouns

You learned on page 131 above about the two ways to tell whether a noun is singular or plural:

1. Almost every noun has a **determiner**, a word that tells **how many** and shows whether a noun is singular or plural.

2. Almost every noun either has **an ending** (which makes it plural), or has **no ending** (which makes it singular).

To write a correct singular or plural noun, you will need to keep these same two things in mind: the determiner, and the ending on the noun.

5A	Use an appropriate <u>determiner</u> and add an <u>*S* (or *ES*) ending</u> to make most nouns <u>plural</u>.

If you want to write a plural noun, you will need an appropriate determiner, and you will usually need to add an ending. Most plural nouns have an *S* ending. This *S* ending makes a SSS or ZZZ sound on the plural noun. Remember that expansion never has a plural form.

CAT   one gray cat   <u>two</u> gray cat<u>s</u>
          The plural noun *cats* has an appropriate determiner and an *S* ending, which makes a SSS sound.

DOG   a brown dog   <u>some</u> brown dog<u>s</u>
          The plural noun *dogs* has an appropriate determiner and an *S* ending, which makes a ZZZ sound.

Some plural nouns are more complicated.

*   Nouns that **end with a SSS or CH or SH sound** are pronounced with an extra syllable when they are plural. These nouns need an *ES* ending to make the extra syllable.

    MESS   a big mess   <u>three</u> big mess<u>es</u>
    BRANCH   one broken branch   <u>several</u> broken branch<u>es</u>
    WISH   a secret wish   __ secret wish<u>es</u>
              Each of these plural nouns has an appropriate determiner and an *ES* ending, which makes an extra syllable.
              Remember that you may use no determiner with a plural noun to mean something like *all of them in general*.

134

- Nouns that end with a SSS sound may **end in E already**. These nouns are still pronounced with an extra syllable when they are plural, but they need the regular *S* ending (not an *ES* ending) to make the extra syllable.

> FACE   one dirty face   a few dirty face<u>s</u>
> This plural noun has an appropriate determiner and an S ending, which makes an extra syllable.

- The plural forms of nouns that **end in SK or SP or ST** are hard to pronounce. But they do not add an extra syllable. So use the regular *S* ending (never an *ES* ending) to make them plural.

> MASK   a Halloween mask   several Halloween mask<u>s</u>
> GHOST   one scary ghost   many scary ghost<u>s</u>
> WASP   one vicious wasp   a hundred vicious wasp<u>s</u>
> Each of these plural nouns has an appropriate determiner and an S ending, without an extra syllable.

- The plural forms of nouns that **end in O** are irregular. Some have an *S* ending and some have an *ES* ending, but the *ES* ending never adds an extra syllable. Using an apostrophe + *S* is **never** correct to form a plural of a noun ending in *O*.

> ✗
>
> POTATO a baked potato   several baked potato<u>'s</u>
>   a baked potato   several baked potato<u>es</u>
> DISCO   one crowded disco   many crowded disco<u>s</u>
> Each of these plural nouns has an appropriate determiner and an S or ES ending, without an extra syllable.

Exercise 5.7	Writing plural nouns

Say the plural form of the given noun out loud, and then fill it in.

1. TRUCK   those speeding _____

2. VAN   some delivery _____

3. KISS   a few passionate _____

4. DISH   these dirty _____

5. RACE   three exciting _____

6. GASP   many loud _____

7. RISK   those bad _____

8. NEST   the bird _____

9. TOMATO   six ripe _____

10. RADIO   their loud _____

Now let's practice writing plural nouns in sentences. To do this correctly, you'll have to be able to do these two things:

1.   Choose an appropriate determiner.
2.   Add the correct ending to the noun.

Follow the nine steps below to rewrite this sentence:

> That small girl won a big prize.

---

1.   Underline each noun.

   • *Girl* and *prize* both name things, so they are nouns. You should have underlined them.

2.   *That* is the determiner for *girl*. Write its plural form. Don't forget the capital letter.

   • *Those* is the plural form of *that*. You should have written *Those* (with a capital letter).

3.   Write *small* without changing it.

4.   Say the plural form of *girl* out loud, and then write it with the appropriate ending.

   • The plural form of *girl* needs the regular *S* ending. You should have written *girls*.

5.   Write *won* without changing it.

6.   *A* is the determiner for *prize*. Write its plural form.

   • Almost any of the plural determiners would be appropriate: *two, three, some, many,* etc. You could even use no determiner, to mean something like *all of them in general*. Make sure that you wrote a correct plural determiner by checking the charts beginning on page 131 above.

7.   Write *big* without changing it.

8.   Say the plural form of *prize* out loud, and then write it with the appropriate ending.

   • The plural form of *prize* has an extra syllable but already ends in *E*, so it needs the regular *S* ending. You should have written *prizes*.

9.   Don't forget the period.

   • You should have written *Those small girls won some big prizes*. But *many big prizes* or *two big prizes* or even just *big prizes* would also be correct.

Use this step-by-step method in doing the following exercises.

Exercise 5.8 Writing plural nouns in sentences

① Underline each noun. ② Rewrite the sentence, making each noun plural. ③ In your rewritten sentence, underline each change.

1. That battered old chair sold for a dollar.

   _____

2. Each young participant received this framed certificate.

   _____

3. This powerful computer beat a leading chess champion in one game.

   _____

4. A spiteful reviewer forced this fine show to close.

   _____

5. That new-born panda died in an American zoo.

   _____

6. One local TV station televised the X-rated film.

   _____

7. A silver spoon disappeared along with that uninvited guest.

   _____

8. A true artist must have designed this beautiful garden.

   _____

9. That teenager spent one hour at a disco yesterday.

   _____

Sometimes plural nouns need spelling changes. You learned some of these spelling rules in Module 1. Go back and review Module 1 now if you need to.

5A1	Make necessary <u>spelling</u> changes when making a noun plural.

Rule 1G2 says:
Change *Y* to *I* before adding *ES* if a word ends in a consonant + *Y*.

  COPY a clear copy   <u>ten</u> clear cop<u>ies</u>
       Copies is spelled with an *I*, not a Y.

To make the plural form of most nouns ending in *IFE* or *F*, change the *F* to *V* and add an *S* or *ES* ending.

WIFE   one overworked wife   two overworked wi<u>ves</u>
THIEF   a common thief   many common thie<u>ves</u>
                Wives and *thieves* are spelled with a *V*, not an *F*.

There are a few nouns ending in *F* where the *F* doesn't change to *V* in the plural. The most common ones are *beliefs*, *chiefs*, and *handkerchiefs*. When in doubt, look up the word in your dictionary. If no special plural form is listed, just make the noun plural in the usual way, by adding an *S* ending without changing *F* to *V*.

Exercise 5.9	**Writing plural nouns with spelling changes**

Fill in the plural form of the given noun. For help, use your dictionary.

1.   BABY   some crying _____

2.   KNIFE   six sharp _____

3.   BELIEF   most religious _____

4.   MEMORY   those fond _____

5.   WIFE   both my cousins' _____

Another thing that makes writing correct plural nouns difficult is that some nouns are **irregular**. This means that you can't predict the plural form just by looking at the singular form.

5A2	**To make an <u>irregular</u> noun plural, change the whole word.**

If you don't already know the plural form of an irregular noun, you'll have to look it up in your dictionary. But never add the regular *S* or *ES* plural ending to an irregular noun.

                                            ✗
MOUSE   one blind mouse   three blind mice<u>s</u>
                                       three blind mice
        Mice is the plural form of the irregular noun *MOUSE*. This form has an appropriate determiner but no ending.

Most of the mistakes students make with irregular nouns are caused by just three words. If you check these words carefully when you proofread your writing, you should be able to avoid many mistakes.

MAN   one man   some men
WOMAN   a woman   many women
CHILD   this child   these children

Fill in the singular and plural forms of these three irregular nouns, to make sure that you know them:

CHILD   a crying _____   two crying _____

WOMAN   that young _____   those young _____

MAN   one married _____   two married _____

Exercise 5.10   Writing plural irregular nouns

Fill in the plural form of the given irregular noun. For help, use your dictionary.

1. FOOT   four big _____

2. MAN   several athletic _____

3. CHILD   three happy _____

4. TOOTH   two loose _____

5. WOMAN   both elderly _____

6. MEDIUM   all the news _____

Exercise 5.11   Writing plural nouns in sentences

① Underline each noun. ② Rewrite the sentence, making each noun plural. ③ In your rewritten sentence, underline each change.

1. The young woman wrote a mystery story.

   _____

2. That stylish man liked this plaid wool scarf.

   _____

3. A clever girl fixed this broken shelf.

   _____

4. This naughty child broke that expensive dish.

   _____

5. The new secretary made an extra copy for the boss upstairs.

   _____

Nouns after *of* and *of the,* especially after *one of the,* are often plural. *Of* and *of the* often mean that you are talking about part of a group.

     BICYCLE   one of the bicycles
                     several of the bicycles
          One of the and *several of the* mean that there is a group of bicycles, so *bicycles* is plural.

But you need to think carefully about the meaning of what you're writing. Sometimes *of the* refers to a part of one thing. In this case, the noun will not be plural.

>   BICYCLE   the seat of the bicycle
>   *The seat of the* refers to a part of one bicycle, not a group of bicycles, so *bicycle* is singular.

Exercise 5.12   Using nouns after *of* and *of the*

Fill in the appropriate form of the given noun.

1. DISH   Leora broke one of her mother's favorite _____ .

                      The handle of the _____ broke off.

2. TEST   Another of those awful _____ was given yesterday.

                      Part of that _____ gave me a lot of trouble.

3. QUESTION   One of the _____ was especially tricky.

                      The first word of the _____ puzzled me.

4. KNIFE   Every one of those _____ needs sharpening.

                      The blade of the _____ rusted in the rain.

5. RADIO   We won one of those portable _____ as a prize.

                      Almost immediately, the tuning knob of the _____ broke.

As you already know, many mistakes in writing remain uncorrected, not because writers don't know how to fix a mistake when they see it, but because they simply don't see it. A missing *S* ending is one of these hard-to-see mistakes. In paragraphs it's much harder to see these small mistakes than in separate sentences. So try to do these paragraph exercises with special care; they can help you to train your eye to see those small but important *S* endings. These paragraph exercises give you valuable practice as preparation for proofreading your own writing.

Exercise 5.13   Fixing noun plural errors in a paragraph

① Underline each noun. ② Correct each error in noun forms (including determiners and expansion) in the space above the line.

All Austrian are fascinated by elaborates timepieces. In Vienna, many street have two

or three shops that sell fancy watch of all shapes and sizes, plus clocks made of gold, silver,

porcelain, and many other precious material. In the Clock Museum are two astronomical

clock, each as big as a room, and several timepiece so tiny that you can't read the number on

their faces without a magnifying glass. The most famous Viennese timepiece is the Anker

Clock. Three floor above the street, twelve life-sized statue of Austrian nationals heroes

march across its enormous face. When these clock strikes the hour, melody by many

Viennese musical geniuses salute these historical figure.

This paragraph contained 14 errors. How many did you find? ____ If you didn't find all 14, try again
before you check your work.

Exercise 5.14   **Fixing noun plural errors in another paragraph**

① Underline each noun. ② Correct each error in noun forms in the space above the line.

Both parent of the newborn quadruplets were returning home from the hospital. For

the first 24 hour, two of their four tiny baby had struggled for their lifes. Although still in

incubators, now they all seemed to be doing well. So at this moment the parents were

worrying more about the many huge bill that were piling up. The mother was asking herself

why she had taken those fertility pill. And where, they both wondered, would they get the

cash for all the thing on their shopping list — diapers, blanket, shirt, pins, bottle, and

countless other basic item? Approaching the front door, the couple saw that all the light

were shining in the three rooms of their small house. At first, they were afraid that burglars

had been there, but as they looked around inside, their eye widened with surprise. In the

living room were all their neighbor. On the floor were four box, each filled with baby

clothes, toy, and medical supply. Among other thing were four pairs of bootys, matching

sweaters and caps in four differents color, and even four little hairbrush. When they picked

up a big brown envelope, their neighbor all shouted, "Open it!" More than 50 check fell out

on the table. For a couple of months, anyway, their worrys about money were over.

This paragraph contained 24 errors. How many did you find? ____ If you didn't find all 24, try again
before you check your work.

Editing Practice E.1   ***Fixing noun mistakes***

1. Get your draft of Paper E.
2. Check to make sure that you have underlined every noun, and that you haven't underlined any word
    that is not a noun. If you find any more nouns, mark them with your green pen.
3. Review Rules 5A–5A2.

4.   Check to make sure that each determiner and each noun is correct, either singular or plural. Fix any mistakes with your green pen.

5.   How many mistakes did you fix? _____ Your ability to find and fix mistakes in your own writing shows how much you've learned so far.

Keep your draft of Paper E to use again later.

Noncount Nouns

You've been working with nouns naming real things, things that can be touched, objects like *table,* or people like *sister.* We call these **count nouns.** Because these things can be counted, the nouns have both singular and plural forms.

> TABLE   <u>This table </u>is an antique.
> <u>These tables </u>are antiques.
> Tables are pieces of furniture which can be counted, so *TABLE* has both a singular and a plural form.

But some nouns name things that can't be touched, abstract ideas like *information* or *happiness,* actions like *running,* or collections of things like *furniture* or *traffic.* We call these **noncount nouns.** Because these things can't be counted, the nouns don't have plural forms.

> *x*
> FURNITURE Some furnitures are ugly.
> Some furniture is ugly.
> Furniture is a collection of items. We may be able to count **pieces of furniture** (like *tables*), but we can't count furniture in general. So *FURNITURE* doesn't have a plural form.

5B	**Do not try to make <u>noncount</u> nouns plural.**

Noncount nouns, like count nouns, usually have determiners. Some determiners, like *some* or *no,* can be used with either plural or noncount nouns. You can also use no determiner with either plural or noncount nouns. But use *much* instead of *many* for noncount nouns, and use *little* instead of *few* for noncount nouns.

Some determiners for count and noncount nouns		
For count nouns		**For noncount nouns**
one	many some [no determiner]	much some [no determiner]
	few no	little no

Exercise 5.15	Understanding count and noncount nouns

Fill in *many* plus the plural form for count nouns, or *much* plus the base form for noncount nouns. Follow this model:

	BOOK	*many books*
	KNOWLEDGE	*much knowledge*

1. IDEA _____

   INFORMATION _____

2. EQUIPMENT _____

   TYPEWRITER _____

3. SLICE _____

   BREAD _____

4. ACCIDENT _____

   LUCK _____

Fill in *few* plus the plural form for count nouns, or *little* plus the base form for noncount nouns. Follow this model:

	BOOK	*few books*
	KNOWLEDGE	*little knowledge*

5. LEISURE _____

   HOBBY _____

6. CRY _____

   CRYING _____

7. TRAFFIC _____

   CAR _____

8. ASSIGNMENT _____

   HOMEWORK _____

Some words may be either count nouns or noncount nouns, depending on their meaning in a particular sentence. Usually, nouns that refer to general or abstract ideas are noncount nouns, while nouns that refer to specific ideas or events or objects are count nouns.

EXPERIENCE   Janet has <u>much experience</u> with bookkeeping.
Janet had <u>many interesting experiences</u> on her trip across the country.
Experience in the first sentence is a general idea, so it can't be counted. *Experiences* in the second sentence are specific events, so they can be counted.

Exercise 5.16   Choosing between count and noncount nouns

Fill in the appropriate form of the given noun.

1. INTEREST   Sophia has no _____ in spelunking.

    Sophia has so many _____ that she hardly has time to sleep.

2. TIME   Most of the _____ it's better to keep your temper.

    How many _____ must I tell you not to do that?

3. EXPERIENCE   _____ may be the best teacher.

    We usually can learn the most from our bad _____ .

4. WRITING   Many of his _____ have been translated into Polish.

    He likes _____ at night.

5. LIGHT   All of the _____ had gone out.

    But the room was filled with the _____ of the moon.

Like count nouns, noncount nouns are often used after *of* or *of the*. But unlike count nouns, noncount nouns don't have plural forms.

COCKTAIL   They drank <u>a lot of cocktails</u>.
COCKTAIL is a count noun; it has a plural form.

MILK   They drank <u>a lot of milk</u>.
MILK is a noncount noun; it doesn't have a plural form.

Exercise 5.17   Choosing between count and noncount nouns with *of* and *of the*

Fill in the appropriate form of the given noun.

1. APARTMENT   Neither of the _____ was big enough for a family of four.

2. STEEL   A lot of the _____ for the new building had rusted.

3. WOMAN   Each of the _____ thought that her child was the most intelligent one in the class.

4. INFORMATION   How much of the _____ was useful for your paper?

5. COMEDY   .   That is one of the best _____ the drama club has ever staged.

6. MILK   Two quarts of whole _____ daily is no longer recommended, even for adolescent boys.

7. HOMEWORK   Our teacher gave at least two assignments of _____ every week.

8. LUCK   Happy coincidences are examples of good _____ .

9. HOUSE   The roofs of the _____ were blown off in the storm.

10. CELERY   We bought a big bunch of _____ .

Exercise 5.18   Fixing noun plural errors in a paragraph

① Underline each noun. ② Correct each error in noun forms in the space above the line.

Joe and Gloria often switched work-role before they had their first two childrens.

About three time a month, Gloria used to bring home several of her friend from work, and

Joe would prepare fancy meal for them. He specialized in dish they could get their teeths

into. One night he served thick French onion soup to his two guest. As he mixed their

drink, he gave them some advices about cooking: "When I sliced these onion, I used the

sharpest of all my knife. Always cut the cheese into small pieces. Three dash of salts should

be enough for a quart of soup. Keep many different spice on your shelfs." The women said

that his soup was one of the best feast they had ever eaten. Gloria gave her husband two big

kiss as a reward, and after dinner she helped him clean up the mess. The other two woman

went home and told their mens to make onion soup for them. The next night angry

stomping, several loud crash, and excited cry were heard in the kitchens of these lady. Later

they told Gloria that onion soup had turned their happy marriages into complete wreck.

This paragraph contained 24 errors. How many did you find? _____ If you didn't find all 24, try again before you check your work.

Editing Practice E.2   *Fixing more noun mistakes*

1. Get your draft of Paper E again.
2. Check again to make sure that each noun is underlined. If you find any more nouns, mark them with your green pen.
3. Review Rule 5B.
4. Check again to make sure that each determiner and each noun is correct, either singular or plural, or noncount. Fix any mistakes with your green pen.
5. How many more mistakes did you fix? _____ Your ability to find and fix mistakes in your own writing shows how much you've learned so far.

Keep your draft of Paper E to use again later.

Singular and Plural Pronouns

Pronouns are words that are used to refer to nouns. Like nouns, pronouns have singular and plural forms.

5C	Use a <u>singular pronoun</u> to refer to a singular noun, and a <u>plural pronoun</u> to refer to a plural noun.

The <u>woman</u> sold <u>her</u> car, and then <u>she</u> bought a truck.
    The singular pronouns *her* and *she* refer to the singular noun *woman*.

The <u>women</u> sold <u>their</u> cars, and then <u>they</u> bought trucks.
    The plural pronouns *their* and *they* refer to the plural noun *women*.

The <u>factory</u> replaced <u>their</u> equipment.
    The plural pronoun *their* refers to singular *factory*, so it is incorrect.

The <u>factory</u> replaced <u>its</u> equipment.
    The singular pronoun *its* refers to singular *factory*, so it is correct.

Exercise 5.19   **Writing plural nouns and pronouns**

① Underline each noun. ② Rewrite the sentence, making each noun plural (unless it is a noncount noun), and making whatever other changes are necessary. ③ In your rewritten sentence, underline each change. Follow this model:

This man lost his wallet.

Those men lost their wallets.

---

1. This woman sold her guitar.

    _____

2. That farmer needed advice about his problem.

    _____

3. The lawyer won her case.

    _____

4. That boy asked for hockey equipment for his birthday.

    _____

5. The constant gossiping of this neighbor annoyed that child.

    _____

6. A student tried to steal the final exam from that sealed box.

    _____

Remember that you can use plural nouns with no determiner, when you mean something like *all of them in general.* But every singular noun must always have a determiner.

Exercise 5.20	Writing singular nouns and pronouns

① Underline each noun. ② Rewrite the sentence, making each noun singular (unless it is a noncount noun), and making whatever other changes are necessary. ③ In your rewritten sentence, underline each change.

1. Those children caught butterflies with their nets.

    _____

2. These women earned their master's degrees.

    _____

3. Because their wives had gone camping, those men ate out a lot.

    _____

4. These cars stalled in traffic, and their drivers couldn't start them.

    _____

5. Those choirs needed some new music for their radio programs.

    _____

6. The new tenants built some furniture for their apartments.

    _____

| **Exercise 5.21** | **Fixing errors in pronoun reference** |

All the pronouns refer to the underlined words. ① Underline each pronoun. ② Correct each error in pronoun reference in the space above the line.

1. For his first twelve years, a little <u>boy</u> is learning how to understand what is said to him, to do

    what they can see others doing, and to make sense out of their world. If love surrounds

    them, they are likely to be loving in return. If he never sees anything but violence, he may

    grow up to think and act violently.

2. These days a young <u>woman</u> has many opportunities open to her. They can get married and

    become a housewife, or seek a career. Or she can do both. However, they must realize the

    difficulties of being a good mother to her children and getting ahead on their job at the same

    time.

3. Responsible <u>teachers</u> make an effort to interest, as well as to instruct, her students. She may

    take the children on trips, or she may plan class projects. For example, they can help their

    students to hold a science fair or to raise a family of gerbils. She obviously must keep order

    in class, but the classroom should also be a place where their students have fun. If they can

    succeed in this, both she and her students will look forward to school every day.

| **Exercise 5.22** | **Writing plural nouns and pronouns in a paragraph** |

Read this paragraph carefully to make sure that you understand it. ① Underline each noun. ② Mark a piece of paper Exercise 5.22, and rewrite this paragraph onto it, making each noun **plural** (unless it is a noncount noun), and making whatever other changes are necessary. ③ In your rewritten paragraph, underline every change.

       A rich local citizen recently bought a beautiful old house. He fixed it up as a

museum and opened it to the public. A teacher took her fourth grade class to visit this

mansion. She asked the guide to give her some information about the family who once lived there. The guide told her and her class all about the man and the woman who had

built this house long ago.

| Exercise 5.23 | Writing singular nouns and pronouns in a paragraph |

This paragraph continues the paragraph in Exercise 5.22. Read it carefully to make sure that you understand it. ① Underline each noun. ② Mark a piece of paper Exercise 5.23, and rewrite this paragraph onto it, making each noun **singular** (unless it is a noncount noun), and making whatever other changes are necessary. ③ In your rewritten paragraph, underline every change.

Several children wanted to know more about the ornate furniture. It included tiny

carved desks, some huge beds, cradles made of jet black wood, and several grandfather

clocks which still kept perfect time. Two boys thought they heard ghostly whispering in

the locked closets. Later on, in their English classes, those students made up spooky

stories about the ghosts who still sat at those fancy desks, and rocked those black

cradles, and slept in those big beds.

| *Editing Practice E.3* | *Fixing more noun and pronoun mistakes* |

1. Get your draft of Paper E again.
2. Underline each pronoun.
3. Review Rule 5C.
4. Check to make sure that each pronoun is correct, either singular or plural. Fix any mistakes with your green pen.
5. How many mistakes did you fix? _____ Your ability to find and fix mistakes in your own writing shows how much you've learned so far.

Keep your draft of Paper E to use again later.

Other Pronoun Forms

Unlike nouns, pronouns have not only singular and plural forms, but other forms also. The form of many pronouns depends on how they are used in a sentence.

I stepped on the cat. It bit me.
> *I* and *me* both refer to the same person. This first person pronoun has different forms, depending on whether it is used as the subject of the verb or after the verb.

She called him. He called her right back.
> *She* and *her* both refer to the same person, and *him* and *he* both refer to the same person. These third person pronouns have different forms, depending on whether they are used as subjects or after the verb.

5D	Use a pronoun form that's correct for how it's used in a sentence.

Choose *I, she, he, we,* and *they* when these pronouns are used as the **subjects** of verbs. Choose *me, her, him, us,* and *them* when these pronouns come **after the verb** or **after a preposition.** Remember that prepositions are words like *in, on, before, after, between* ,etc. — words showing location or relationship.

> (He)(sat) between them and her.
>> *He* is correct because it is the subject of the verb *SIT*. *Them* and *her* are correct because they come after the preposition *between.*

Sometimes in everyday speech, or even on television, we hear pronoun forms that don't follow these rules. These incorrect pronouns are most common when the words are used in pairs (that is, coupled with a noun or another pronoun). But these pronoun forms should not be used in writing.

>   ✗   ✗
> Her and me thought the show was great.
>   ✗
> I'll call either he or Nina.
>   ✗
> It was a secret between we and them.
>> All these sentences contain pronoun forms that are incorrect in writing.

To decide which pronoun form is correct, you should test each of the two pronouns by separating them. You would not say, *Her thought the show was great* or *Me thought the show was great,* so a sentence like *Her and me thought the show was great,* even if you might hear it in speech, is incorrect in writing.

> She thought the show was great.
> I thought the show was great.
> She and I thought the show was great.

> I'll call him.
> I'll call Nina.
> I'll call either him or Nina.

> It was a secret between us.
> It was a secret between them.
> It was a secret between us and them.
>> The underlined pronouns are correct.

Exercise 5.24   Fixing pronoun forms

Mentally separate the paired noun and pronoun forms, to decide which ones are correct and which ones are incorrect. Underline each error in pronoun forms and correct it in the space above the line.

1. The invitations were addressed to Elizabeth and I.

2. Julia Roberts starred in *Erin Brockovich,* in which Albert Finney and her won a case against polluters.

3. My mother and me talk on the telephone at least once a week.

4. A large fence ran along the property line between we and the Mercados.

5. Leave the package with the receptionist or I.

6. Just between you and I, Harriet and him get on my nerves.

7. She and I consider him and his wife to be our best friends.

Another group of pronouns with special forms is **reflexive pronouns**. These pronoun forms all end in *–self* or *–selves*. We call them reflexive because they are used to refer (or reflect) back to the subject or an earlier word in the sentence.

5E	Use a <u>reflexive</u> pronoun with *–self* or *–selves* to refer back to the subject or an earlier word.

Joe asked <u>himself</u>, "Is this job really worth my time?"
>   The reflexive pronoun *himself* refers back to *Joe.*

The couple decided to remodel the kitchen by <u>themselves</u>.
>   The reflexive pronoun *themselves* refers back to *the couple.*

Because reflexive pronouns always must refer back to an earlier word, any reflexive pronoun that doesn't have a word to refer back to is incorrect. In this case, you should use the correct regular pronoun form, not a reflexive pronoun.

Joe and <u>myself</u> calculated the expense of remodeling.
Joe and I calculated the expense of remodeling.
>   Because the reflexive pronoun *myself* has no word to refer back to, it is incorrect. *I* is correct as the subject.

Reflexive pronouns can also be used to supply emphasis:

I <u>myself</u> am not sure what to believe.
>   The reflexive pronoun *myself* refers back to and emphasizes the subject *I.*

Reflexive pronouns are always one word.

She was talking to <u>her self</u>.
She was talking to <u>herself</u>.
>   The one-word reflexive pronoun *herself* is correct.

In speech we sometimes hear the forms *hisself* and *theirself* (or *theirselfs* or *theirselves*). These forms are incorrect in writing.

They did it <u>theirselfs</u>.
They did it <u>themselves</u>.
> The reflexive pronoun *theirselfs* is incorrect, but *themselves* is correct.

Exercise 5.25	**Fixing reflexive pronouns**

Underline each error in pronoun forms, and correct it in the space above the line.

1.   The young defendant decided to fire his lawyer and represent hisself at the hearing.

2.   The members of the criminal justice system are their selves responsible for this entire fiasco.

3.   What their worst enemies wouldn't do, these young criminals did to themselfs.

4.   The judge reviewed the facts with the lawyer and myself.

5.   After the trial, we asked ourselfs, "Was justice served?"

6.   The boys' parents and myself were determined to appeal the verdict.

Pronouns also change forms according to whom they are referring: the writer (or speaker) herself or himself (we call this **first person**), the person the writer is writing to (we call this **second person**), or the person about whom the writer is writing (we call this **third person**).

	first person	second person	third person
singular	I / me	you	he / him she / her it / it [any noun]
plural	we / us	you	they / them [any noun]

5F	**Use a pronoun form in the same <u>person</u> as the word it refers to.**

<u>Students</u> may not enter unless <u>you</u> have a pass.
> This sentence is incorrect because the second person pronoun *you* cannot refer back to third person *students*.

Students may not enter unless they have a pass.
    This sentence is correct because the third person pronoun *they* refers back to third person *students*.

Exercise 5.26	Fixing errors in pronoun reference

All the pronouns refer to the underlined words. Underline each pronoun, and correct each error in the space above the line

1. People don't function well under pressure, because then you don't feel like doing anything at all.

2. The counselor taught the students to have confidence in yourself.

3. When we grow up, you often see your parents differently.

Avoiding Sexist Language

5G	Avoid sexist language in using feminine and masculine pronouns.

She and *her* are feminine pronouns because they refer to females. *He* and *him* are masculine pronouns because they refer to males. Pronouns like *it* and *they* do not have specific gender associations.

Sexist language is language that seems to say that one gender is more important than the other, or that only males — or only females — perform certain roles. Such language should be avoided.

A teacher should use words that her students understand.
    The singular pronoun *her* may be in the correct form, but it is sexist, since it ignores the fact that many teachers are male.

A student, nevertheless, must broaden his vocabulary.
    The singular pronoun *his* may be in the correct form, but it is sexist, since it ignores the fact that many students are female.

Exercise 5.27	Recognizing sexist pronouns

These sentences contain sexist pronouns. Draw an arrow from each pronoun to the word to which it refers, and put a question mark **?** over each sexist pronoun.

1. A good cook always keeps her knives handy.

2. A writer often chooses themes from his own life.

3. When a professor does research for an outside agency, he should inform the University about his activities.

Sometimes people try to avoid sexist singular pronouns by using both feminine and masculine pronouns. But this usually creates awkward sentences which are clumsy and can create confusion.

> A parent should not punish <u>his or her</u> child harshly if <u>he or she</u> wants the child to trust <u>him or her</u>.
>> These pronouns are in the correct form, and they are not sexist, but the sentence is extremely awkward.

It is usually best to use plural pronouns rather than singular sexist pronouns.

> Parents should not punish <u>their</u> children harshly if <u>they</u> want the children to trust <u>them</u>.
>> These pronouns are in the correct form, and avoid sexism by using plural forms that include both males and females.

Exercise 5.28   Avoiding sexist pronouns

Rewrite each sentence, avoiding awkwardness by using plural nouns and pronouns.

1. <u>A young person</u> ought to choose <u>his or her</u> first employment carefully, because <u>he or she</u> will most likely continue in the same general line of work in which <u>he or she</u> started.

    Young people _____

    _____

2. In heavy traffic, a <u>bicycle rider</u> should not go through red lights. <u>He or she</u> may cause accidents by surprising drivers or pedestrians who don't expect to see <u>him or her</u> in the intersection. Such a reckless cyclist may endanger <u>himself or herself</u>, as well as others.

    In heavy traffic, bicycle riders _____

    _____

    _____

Exercise 5.29   Fixing errors in pronoun forms and pronoun reference

This paragraph contains errors in pronoun forms and pronoun reference. Underline each error, and correct it in the space above the line.

Taxpayers who receive orders to report to the Internal Revenue Service with his tax

records may feel that the government is out to get him. I received such a summons last

summer. I called a friend who is an accountant, and they told me not to worry. Then I

called another friend, but they just congratulated themselves that the problem wasn't theirs.

So I went through my files and put it in order. At the big gray IRS building the following

Tuesday, you waited for half an hour until a clerk called your name. Then the clerk told me to follow them. My auditor was a severe woman who greeted me with a frown.

Somehow, when a woman is in a position of authority, they can seem even more

intimidating than a man would be. I sat down, reached for my papers, and dropped it all

over the floor. When I recovered, the auditor started checking my return. Two hours later,

she said, "Your tax return is fine." By then her and I felt like old friends. Mrs. Harris had

learned things about I and my life that nobody else knew. She said that I had done a fine job

on my tax return, better than most taxpayers do preparing it by them self. I realized with

relief that if I ever had to deal with officials at the IRS again, I wouldn't be afraid of her.

This paragraph contained 16 errors. How many did you find? _____ If you didn't find all 16, try again
before you check your work.

Exercise 5.30	Fixing errors in noun and pronoun forms and reference

This paragraph is about a typical black serviceman. Underline each error in nouns and pronouns, and
correct it in the space above the line.

According to a *New York Times* report, the typical black serviceman is upbeat about

their career in the Army. He finds that the pay is better and that he enjoys more job

satisfaction than they would as civilian employees. Although there is still some

discrimination, the chances are good that they can eventually win promotion. However, on

the downside, they will sometimes have trouble getting a white subordinate to obey him.

Also, he may have to prove hisself not only equal to all his white counterpart, but superior to

them. Overall, however, a black servicemen generally feels they would have succeeded no

better, and in some instances not as well, in civilian life.

This paragraph contained 10 errors. How many did you find? _____ If you didn't find all 10, try again
before you check your work.

Exercise 5.31   Fixing errors in noun and pronoun forms and reference

This paragraph is about women in the armed forces. Underline each error in nouns and pronouns, and correct it in the space above the line.

Female officers, also interviewed by *New York Times* reporters, were somewhat negative about life in the armed forces. They said their biggest problems centered on getting her male superiors or subordinates to accept them as soldiers or sailors or a Marine with the same rights and duties as their male counterparts. Most of these woman complained that getting the men under her to follow her orders was often difficult. Black service women asserted that they were often treated unfairly, not because they were black, but because they were woman. Some of the women interviewed protested vehemently against the laws which still exclude her from certain combat operations, and consequently from some senior command positions and higher pay.

This paragraph contained seven errors. How many did you find? _____ If you didn't find all seven, try again before you check your work.

Editing Practice E.4   *Fixing mistakes in pronoun forms and reference*

1. Get your draft of Paper E again.
2. Make sure that you have underlined every pronoun.
3. Review Rules 5D, 5E, 5F, and 5G.
4. Check to make sure that each pronoun is correct in the following ways:
   - Is it in the correct form for how it is used in the sentence?
   - If it's a reflexive pronoun, is its form correct? Does it refer back to an earlier word in the sentence?
   - Is it in the same person (first, second, or third) as the word it refers to?
   - Is it sexist in its use of feminine and masculine pronouns?
5. Fix any mistakes with your green pen. How many mistakes did you fix? _____ Your ability to find and fix mistakes in your own writing shows how much you've learned so far.

Writing Your Final Copy of Paper E

Use your final copy of Paper E to demonstrate what you've learned in Module 5 about nouns and pronouns, and to show how well you're continuing to apply what you've learned previously.

Paper E	*Using nouns and pronouns*
Edit for Previous Modules	After you have finished revising your ideas, use your dictionary and the Rules Summaries for previous modules to:

- Check your use of writing conventions. Fix any mistakes with your green pen.

- Circle each verb (either a one-word verb or a verb phrase), box its subject, and put a + over each connecting word.

- Check the structure of each word-group. If any word-group doesn't have at least one verb, or has a verb without a subject, it is not a sentence. Put brackets [ ] around it. How many word-groups like this did you bracket? _____

- Check the structure of each word-group again. If any word-group doesn't have one simple sentence more than the number of connecting words, it is not a correct sentence. Put brackets [ ] around it. How many word-groups like this did you bracket? _____

Make Final Copy   Mark another piece of paper Paper E, and write the final copy of your paper on it, or print out a clean copy on your word processor. Be sure to include all your corrections. Mark your final copy as you did your draft.

Proofread   Read your final copy **out loud.** Correct any mistakes neatly by hand. If you used a word processor, enter your corrections, print out a corrected final copy, and mark it again..

Hand in your final copy of Paper E, and the rest of your exercises.

6 Making Present-tense Verbs Agree

NAME _____

After you finish checking each exercise, fill in your number of mistakes.

6.1 _____   6.6 _____   6.11 _____   6.16 _____   6.21 _____

6.2 _____   6.7 _____   6.12 _____   6.17 _____   6.22 _____

6.3 _____   6.8 _____   6.13 _____   6.18 _____   6.23 _____

6.4 _____   6.9 _____   6.14 _____   6.19 _____   6.24 _____

6.5 _____   6.10 _____   6.15 _____   6.20 _____   6.25 _____

EXERCISES	INSTRUCTIONS	CHECKING	
❏ Complete	❏ Followed carefully	❏ Careful	❏ Green pen not used
❏ Incomplete	❏ Not careful enough	❏ Not careful enough	❏ Mistakes not corrected

PAPER F
❏ Doesn't follow the instructions; write a NEW Paper F.
❏ Skips some instructions; COMPLETE everything.
❏ Too short; add MORE.

EDITING PAPER F FOR THIS MODULE'S WORK
❏ Careful   ❏ Not careful enough
EDITING PAPER F FOR PREVIOUS WORK
❏ Careful   ❏ Not careful enough
OVERALL EVALUATION OF PAPER F
❏ Excellent   ❏ Good   ❏ Acceptable   ❏ Not acceptable

COMMENTS

Rules Summary for Module 6

6A	Make present-tense verbs **agree** with their subjects.
1	Add **no ending** to make a present-tense verb agree with **a plural subject (or *I* or *you*).**
2	Add **an S ending** to make a present-tense verb agree with **a singular subject (but not *I* or *you*).**
6B	Use *am* to make *BE* agree with *I* in the present tense.
	Use *is* to make *BE* agree with **a singular subject (but not *I* or *you*)** in the present tense.
	Use *are* to make *BE* agree with **a plural subject or *you*** in the present tense.

In the next two modules, as well as in Modules 10-11, you will learn more about the various forms that verbs have in written English. Some of these forms may be different from the ones that seem natural to you in talking, or different from the ones you hear when others talk. But using these standard forms consistently makes written communication less confusing and less distracting. All readers and writers, not just your teachers, expect to see these forms in writing.

Present-tense Verbs

A one-word present-tense verb tells **what usually happens or is generally true.**

GO   Tyrone goes to bed early on weekdays.
        The present-tense verb *goes* tells what Tyrone usually does.

NEED   Tyrone needs plenty of sleep.
        The present-tense verb *needs* tells what is generally true about Tyrone.

Students often think that a present-tense verb tells about the present. But we usually use a **verb phrase** to tell what is happening right now.

SLEEP   Tyrone is sleeping late today.
        The present-tense verb phrase *is sleeping* tells what Tyrone is doing right now.

In this module, we will focus mostly on **one-word verbs.**

Present-tense verbs are difficult to use correctly because their forms change, depending on whether their subjects are singular or plural. This change is called **verb agreement.**

TRAVEL The Petersons travel every summer.
        Ms. Peterson travels every summer.
        The present tense of *TRAVEL* has two different forms. *Travel* (with no ending) agrees with its plural subject *Petersons*, and *travels* (with an *S* ending) agrees with its singular subject *Ms. Peterson*.

Exercise 6.1	Understanding verb agreement

The paragraph in the **left** column has **plural** subjects, so the verbs have one form, with **no endings.** The paragraph in the **right** column has **singular** subjects, so the verbs have another form, with *S* endings.
① Circle each verb, and box its subject. ② In the paragraph on the right, put a diamond ◇ around the *S* ending on each verb. The first sentence in each paragraph has been marked for you.

Every day some very fast planes leave Heathrow Airport in London. They arrive in New York only three hours later. The seats cost a lot. But some business people need to meet deadlines. So they take these planes to save time. They complete their business in New York quickly. Often they return home the same day.

Every day a very fast plane leaves Heathrow Airport in London. It arrives in New York only three hours later. A seat costs a lot. But Colin Walker needs to meet deadlines. So he takes this plane to save time. He completes his business in New York quickly. Often he returns home the same day.

Remember to use your **green pen** to check each exercise as soon as you finish it. Write in any necessary corrections, and then write your number of mistakes on the cover page.

Using Module 6 to Edit Your Own Writing

Use Paper F to discover how much you know already about making present-tense verbs agree with their subjects. Later in this module, you'll be checking this paper by applying the rules of this module to what you have written.

You may write this paper by hand. Better yet, use a word processor.

Drafting Paper F	*Using present-tense verbs*
Assignment	Choose one of these assignments:
	❑ Think of someone who always annoys you or makes you angry. Describe what this person always does and why this behavior makes you angry.
	❑ Think of a person you know well (not yourself) who has an interesting job. Describe a typical day at work for this person, telling what he or she usually does and why you think this routine is interesting.
Get Ready	On a piece of scratch paper, free write on your chosen topic, first to narrow it to one specific example if necessary, and then to get ideas to use in developing your paper. Don't stop until you have plenty of ideas. Draw a line across the page when you have finished free writing.
	Read over your free writing, and decide on your main point. Write it in one complete sentence below the line.
	Plan your paragraphs by selecting enough supporting ideas from your free writing to make your main point interesting, clear, and convincing to a reader. Write your supporting ideas in a numbered list below your main point.
Draft	On another piece of scratch paper, write an introduction to your draft telling what your main point is.
	Then write at least one paragraph for each of your supporting ideas. Be sure to include enough examples, details, and facts to make your reader understand and believe each idea.
	Write your conclusion.
Revise	Revise your draft, using the four steps in revision listed on the inside front cover to make your paper better. Make sure that you have written at least four paragraphs, including an introduction and a conclusion.

Keep your draft of Paper F to use later.

Making Verbs Agree

6A	**Make present-tense verbs <u>agree</u> with their subjects.**

You sometimes hear teachers or students talking about singular and plural verbs. But remember that *singular* and *plural* are words that are used to refer to *one* or *more than one* of something; it's nouns (and pronouns) that can be counted like this. Verbs, just like the noncount nouns that you learned about in Module 5, refer to abstract ideas, and so it doesn't seem accurate to think that they can have singular or plural forms.

You'll find the whole concept of verb agreement less confusing if you remember that it's **subjects** (not verbs) that are singular or plural; what **verbs** need to do is **change form to agree** with their subjects.

Here in Module 6, you'll work on making **one-word verbs** agree with their subjects. In Modules 10 and 11, you'll work on making **helping verbs in verb phrases** agree with their subjects.

6A1	**Add <u>no ending</u> to make a present-tense verb agree with <u>a plural subject (or *I* or *you*)</u>.**

Many, even most, subjects are nouns. You learned in Module 5 how to tell whether a noun is plural: it needs an appropriate determiner, and an *S* ending. To check whether a subject is plural, you can try replacing it with *they* or *we*. Once you're sure that the subject is **plural**, you need to be sure to add **no ending** to the verb to make the verb agree with its subject.

> LEARN The girls learn things quickly.
> They learn things quickly.
> The subject *girls* is plural, so we can replace it with *they*. *Learn* has no ending to agree with these plural subjects.

> LEARN My friend and I learn things quickly.
> We learn things quickly.
> The subject *friend and I* is plural, so we can replace it with *we*. *Learn* has no ending to agree with these plural subjects.

The pronouns *I* and *you* may not seem to be plural, but for the purposes of verb agreement they are like plural subjects. So you should add no ending to make a present-tense verb agree with them.

> LEARN I learn things quickly.
> You learn things quickly.
> *Learn* has no ending to agree with *I* and with *you*.

Notice how confusing verb agreement is, if you think about verbs as being singular or plural. Again, you'll find the whole concept of verb agreement less confusing if you remember that it's **subjects** (not verbs) that are singular or plural; what **verbs** need to do is **change form to agree** with their subjects.

Exercise 6.2	Making verbs agree with plural subjects

① Box each subject. ② Fill in the present-tense form of the verb that agrees with the subject.

1. EAT   Americans _____ too much red meat.

2. COUNT   I _____ fat grams, not calories.

3. LOSE   You _____ weight by eating fruit.

4. KILL   Salt and animal fat _____ millions.

5. STUDY   We _____ food labels carefully.

6A2	Add an *S* ending to make a present-tense verb agree with a singular subject (but not *I* or *you*).

Again, you learned in Module 5 how to tell whether a noun is singular: it needs an appropriate determiner, and no ending. To check whether a subject is singular, you can try replacing it with *he, she,* or *it*. Once you're sure that the subject is **singular**, you need to be sure to add **an *S* ending** to the verb to make the verb agree with its subject.

> LEARN   My friend learns things quickly.
> She learns things quickly.
>> The subject *friend* is singular, so we can replace it with *she. Learns* has an S ending to agree with these singular subjects.

Again, notice how confusing verb agreement is, if you think about verbs as being singular or plural. You'll find the whole concept of verb agreement less confusing if you remember that it's **subjects** (not verbs) that are singular or plural; what **verbs** need to do is **change form to agree** with their subjects.

Exercise 6.3	Making verbs agree with singular subjects

① Box each subject. ② Fill in the present-tense form of the verb that agrees with the subject.

1. LIKE   Marietta _____ studying statistics.

               She _____ studying statistics.

2. APPOINT   The President _____ ambassadors.

               He _____ ambassadors.

3. HELP   A college diploma _____ you to get a job.

               It _____ you to get a job.

| Exercise 6.4 | Making verbs agree with contrasted subjects |

① Box each subject. ② Fill in the present-tense form of the verb that agrees with the subject.

1. LIKE

Marietta _____ studying statistics.

She _____ studying statistics.

Marietta and I _____ studying statistics.

We _____ studying statistics.

2. APPOINT

The President _____ ambassadors.

He _____ ambassadors.

The President and Vice President _____ ambassadors.

They _____ ambassadors.

3. HELP

A college diploma _____ you to get a job.

It _____ you to get a job.

College diplomas _____ you to get jobs.

They _____ you to get jobs.

| Exercise 6.5 | Making verbs agree with various subjects |

The verb in each sentence has two subjects. ① Circle each verb, and box both its subjects. ② Rewrite each sentence as two sentences, using each subject separately. ③ Mark your rewritten sentences in the same way. Follow this model:

A yellow [truck] and two [taxis] (park) here every day.
A yellow [truck] (parks) here every day. Two [taxis] (park) here every day.

1. The delivery men and the janitor use the service entrance.

_____

_____

2. *Jesse and his partner design toys.*

_____

_____

3. That Congressman and his supporters deny the charges.

_____

_____

4. Two planes and one train leave for Buffalo daily.

_____

_____

5. Harvey and I ask many questions in class.

_____

_____

Now we'll work on some special problems with verb agreement. These are verbs that don't behave in quite the way you'd expect, from the two rules you've just learned.

You learned in Module 5 that we need an *ES* ending rather than an *S* ending when the plural form of a noun is pronounced with an extra syllable, as in *watches* or *glasses*. In the same way, verbs that end with CH or SS or J sounds have an extra syllable when they agree with singular subjects. So add an *ES* ending rather than an *S* ending to make these kinds of verbs agree with singular subjects.

PASS   That car passes everything but the gas station.
Because *PASS* ends with a SS sound, *passes* has two syllables when it agrees with the singular subject *car*, so it needs an *ES* ending rather than an *S* ending.

You also learned that nouns ending in *SK* or *SP* or *ST* are **not** pronounced with an extra syllable in their plural form, as in *tests* or *gasps*, and so we add the normal *S* ending rather than an *ES* ending. In the same way, verbs ending in *SK* or *SP* or *ST* don't have an extra syllable when they agree with singular subjects. So add the normal *S* ending rather than an *ES* ending to make these kinds of verbs agree with singular subjects.

ASK   He asks too many questions.
Because *ASK* ends with *SK*, *asks* doesn't have an extra syllable when it agrees with the singular subject *he*, so it needs the normal *S* ending rather than an *ES* ending.

Exercise 6.6   Making more complicated verbs agree

① Box each subject. ② Say each sentence out loud to hear whether the required verb is pronounced with an extra syllable. Then fill in the present-tense form of the verb that agrees with the subject.

1. PASS   A safe driver never _____ without signaling first.

2. DRIVE   I never _____ in the passing lane.

3. HUSK   Graham always _____ the corn after the water boils.

4. EMPHASIZE   Southern customs _____ good manners and hospitality.

5. COAST   An incumbent official usually _____ to easy victory.

6. MARCH   Any big city mayor _____ in many parades.

7. MISS   This answer _____ the point of the question.

8. ASK   My English teacher _____ us to do a long writing assignment every week.

9. WAX   The museum never _____ its antique wooden furniture.

10. TEST   Going to college _____ your time-management skills.

You also learned that when a noun ends in a consonant + *Y*, we change the *Y* to *I* before adding the *ES* ending, as in *bodies*. In the same way, change the *Y* to *I* before adding an *ES* ending to make verbs ending in a consonant + *Y* agree with singular subjects.

    TRY   My neighbor tries to keep his yard neat.
              TRY ends in a consonant + *Y*, so the *Y* is changed to *I* in *tries*.

Remember that *Y* changes to *I* only after a **consonant**.

    PLAY   My son plays with his food at mealtime.
              PLAY ends in a **vowel** + *Y*, so the *Y* is not changed to *I* in *plays*.

Exercise 6.7   Making verbs with **Y** agree

① Box each subject. ② Fill in the present-tense form of the verb that agrees with the subject.

1. CRY   Someone always _____ at a wedding.

2. LAY   That chicken _____ brown eggs.

3. REMARRY   A widower almost always _____ within two years.

4. WORRY   That intersection _____ every parent in the neighborhood.

5. ANNOY   My sister often _____ me with her nosy remarks.

6. TERRIFY   The entrance examination _____ most students.

7. MARRY   Today young people usually _____ in their twenties.

Exercise 6.8   Making verbs agree in a paragraph

This paragraph contains base forms of verbs in capital letters. ① Box each subject. ② On scratch paper, rewrite the paragraph in the present tense, using one-word verbs only. ③ Mark another piece of paper Exercise 6.8, and copy your rewritten paragraph onto it. ④ Mark your rewritten paragraph as you have learned to.

Milagros LOVE sewing. She BUY beautiful fabric in a shop near where she LIVE. After she and her mother LAY out the pattern, Milagros CUT the dress out. Then she SEW it together carefully. She USE her iron as she FINISH each seam. Her brother and her mother HELP her with some of the work. For example, they ADJUST the hem as she TRY the new dress on, and they FIT the waist. Milagros SAY that she ENJOY sewing. She not only SAVE money by making her own clothes, but she always LOOK better than the other women in her office.

Three important and common verbs, *HAVE, DO,* and *GO,* have **irregular** forms, forms that you wouldn't expect, in the present-tense. If you simply add the normal *S* ending, you won't be able to write these verbs correctly.

verb	agrees with plural subject (or *I* or *you*)	agrees with singular subject (but not *I* or *you*)
HAVE	have	has
DO	do	does
GO	go	goes

HAVE is the simplest of these three verbs. As usual, there is no ending on the form that agrees with a plural subject. But use *has* (not some form like *haves*) to make it agree with a singular subject.

HAVE   My brothers have no children.
            I have no children.
            You have no children.
            HAVE has no ending to agree with a plural subject or *I* or *you.*

HAVE   My sister has three children.
            Has is the form that agrees with the singular subject *sister.*

Use *does* (not some form like *dos* or *dose*) to make the irregular verb *DO* agree with a singular subject.

DO   Those plasterers do neat and careful work.
            That plasterer does neat and careful work.
            Do agrees with the plural subject *plasterers. Does* agrees with the singular subject *plasterer.*

168

Use *goes* (not some form like *gos* or *gose*) to make the irregular verb *GO* agree with a singular subject.

GO These children go to this new school.
That child goes to that old school.
Go agrees with the plural subject *children*. Goes agrees with the singular subject *child*.

Exercise 6.9 Making irregular verbs agree

① Box each subject. ② Fill in the present-tense form of the verb that agrees with the subject.

1. HAVE Lolita _____ an expensive new pair of sunglasses.

2. DO Shaheed _____ his math problems carefully.

3. GO Marie _____ to visit her parents every summer.

4. HAVE These banks now _____ evening hours.

5. DO I _____ the best I can.

6. GO Latecia never _____ to the movies alone.

7. HAVE Coolidge always _____ the best answer.

8. DO Stein always _____ his own thing.

9. GO Some people never _____ to the movies at all.

10. HAVE The Harrises _____ 19 grandchildren.

11. DO While I _____ the shopping, she _____

GO the cooking, and our husbands _____ fishing.

Exercise 6.10 Fixing verb agreement errors in a paragraph

① Circle each verb, and box its subject. ② Correct each error in the space above the line.

Some frustrating laws seems to control our everyday lives. This list includes some of

the most familiar: ① **As soon as you mention something good, it go away.** As soon as you

speaks of something bad, it happens. One social scientist call this *The Unspeakable Law.*

② **The other line always move faster.** If you drives a car through toll gates or wait in

supermarket lines, you know that this law never fail. ③ **Bread always fall butter-side**

down. Another version of this law say that an object always collapse where it do the most damage. For example, your shopping bag rip just when you get to the middle of an intersection, and the glasses tumble off the tray as you reaches the middle of the new rug.

④ **Work always expand so that it fill up the time available.** If you have ten minutes for a job, you finish in ten minutes. However, if you has two hours, then it takes the whole two hours. ⑤ **The person with the gold makes the rules.** Most people learns this version of the Golden Rule before the one in the Bible. ⑥ **Nothing get better; it only get worse.** Some laws has exceptions—but never this last one.

This paragraph contained 20 errors. How many did you find? _____ If you didn't find all 20, try again before you check your work.

Editing Practice F.1	**Fixing verb agreement mistakes in your own writing**

1. Get your draft of Paper F.
2. Circle each verb, box its subject, and put a + over each connecting word.
3. Review Rules 6A-6A2.
4. Check that each verb agrees with its subject. Fix any mistakes with your green pen.
5. How many mistakes did you fix? _____ Your ability to find and fix these mistakes shows how much you've learned so far.

Keep your draft of Paper F to use again later.

Making Verbs Agree in More Complicated Sentences

Sometimes there are sentences where it's hard to tell whether the subject is singular or plural, or even what the subject is. Making verbs agree is especially difficult in sentences like these.

Subjects like *everyone* can be confusing, because they have general, plural meanings but are singular in form.

NEED   All people need oxygen.
        Everyone needs oxygen.

   Need has no ending to agree with the plural subject *people*. Even though *everyone* means about the same thing as *all people*, it's singular in form, so *needs* has an *S* ending to agree with it.

Here are six words that are **always singular** (but notice that *no one* is always two words):

everyone	anyone	no one
everybody	anybody	nobody

Write these six singular words here to help you remember them:

_____   _____   _____

_____   _____   _____

Exercise 6.11   Making verbs agree with confusing subjects

① Box each subject. ② Fill in the present-tense form of the verb that agrees with the subject.

1. TRY   Everyone _____ to take that course.

                   Most people _____ to take that course.

2. LIKE   Everybody _____ to win.

                   All of us _____ to win.

3. WANT   Few people _____ taxes to rise.

                   No one _____ taxes to rise.

4. APPRECIATE   Anybody _____ a sincere compliment.

                   We all _____ a sincere compliment.

5. ENJOY   Not many of us _____ working all the time.

                   Nobody _____ working all the time.

Exercise 6.12   Making verbs agree with various subjects

① Circle each verb. ② Fill in the subject that the verb agrees with.

1. child / children   The _____ seem quiet.

2. I / She   _____ always reads as much as possible.

3. shadow / shadows   The _____ fall at dusk.

4. You / She   _____ looks uncomfortable.

5. Jo and Amy / Jo   _____ seldom arrives on time.

6. Nobody / Few people   _____ pronounce the word *mischievous* correctly.

7. Everybody / People   _____ worries about inflation these days.

Whenever there is expansion after the subject, the word that is really the subject is probably far away from the verb, and another word is closer. But don't confuse expansion with the real subject. To find the subject, be sure to ask the question WHO? or WHAT? in front of the verb.

PLAY   The [children] on my block (play) games in the street.
                Block is next to the verb *play*. But *children* is the subject because it answers the question *WHO play games?*
                On my block is expansion telling more about the children. *Play* agrees with its plural subject *children*, not
                with *block*.

Sentences like these are especially confusing when the subject is a word like *one* or *some*. In these sentences, the expansion is an essential part of the meaning. Still, asking the question WHO? or WHAT? in front of the verb will tell you the real subject.

BORROW   [One] of my friends (borrows) my math textbook every Friday.
                One is the subject because it answers the question *WHO borrows my textbook?* *Of my friends* is expansion,
                even though it is an essential part of the meaning. *Borrows* agrees with its singular subject *one*, not *friends*.

Exercise 6.13	**Making verbs agree with expanded subjects**

① Box each subject. ② Fill in the present-tense form of the verb that agrees with the subject.

1. INTEREST   The discovery of those scientists _____ me.

                    The discoveries of that scientist _____ me.

2. INTIMIDATE   Women with confidence _____ some men.

                    A woman with confidence _____ some men.

3. WIN   The programs on this channel _____ awards every year.

                    One of these programs _____ an award every year.

4. PLAY   Four members of this orchestra _____ together
                    sometimes in a string quartet.

                    One member of this orchestra _____ timpani.

5. SEEM   An increase in income taxes _____ inevitable.

                    Income taxes for my family _____ to increase yearly.

6. ACT   Everybody in most families _____ irrational at one
                    time or another.

                    But nobody in this family ever _____ irrational.

7. UNLOCK   One of those keys _____ this door.

                    The keys on my keyring _____ every door but this one.

Y ou learned in Module 4 how to use the noun-expansion words *who, which,* and *that.* These words can be either singular or plural, depending on the nouns they refer to.

The children (who live here) always slam the door.
> The subject *who* is plural because it refers to *children. Live* agrees with its plural subject *who,* and *slam* agrees with its plural subject *children.*

The child (who lives here) always slams the door.
> The subject *who* is singular because it refers to *child. Lives* agrees with its singular subject *who,* and *slams* agrees with its singular subject *child.*

Exercise 6.14   Making verbs agree with *who* or *which*

These sentences contain base forms of verbs in capital letters. ① Box the subject of each verb. You may find it useful to put parentheses around expansion. ② Rewrite the sentence, making each verb agree with its subject. ③ Mark your rewritten sentence as you have learned to.

1.   This movie LAMPOON women who HARASS men.

     _____

2.   Machines which USE less fuel COST more.

     _____

3.   Voters usually PREFER a candidate who REJECT negative advertising.

     _____

4.   Anyone who LOVE this team HATE its owner.

     _____

5.   A magazine which EXPOSE a bad product DO the public a service.

     _____

I n a sentence with more than one verb, it's easy to lose track of which word is the subject. This can lead to verb agreement mistakes. Always make sure that every present-tense verb agrees with its subject.

A campaign worker calls people, solicits their votes, and takes them to the polls.
> All three verbs, *calls, solicits,* and *takes,* must agree with the singular subject *worker.*

Exercise 6.15   Making several verbs agree with one subject

① Write one sentence to answer each group of questions below. Use one-word verbs, not verb phrases with *does* or *do*. ② Mark your answer as you have learned to.

1. Does the new teacher worry too much? Does she work too hard?

   Yes, she _____

2. Do the trainees exercise in the morning? Do they study in the afternoon?

   Yes, they _____

3. Does Louise ask a lot of questions? Does she get into mischief? Does she keep her parents busy?

   Yes, she _____

4. Do children who get no love become angry? Do they rebel? Do they act out?

   Yes, they _____

5. Does a child who gets no love become angry? Does he rebel? Does he act out?

   Yes, he _____

Exercise 6.16   Making verbs agree in a paragraph

This paragraph is written with plural subjects. ① Circle each verb, and box its subject. You may find it useful to put parentheses around expansion. ② On scratch paper, rewrite the paragraph about Oscar only, making whatever other changes are necessary. Your paragraph will begin *Oscar, who says...* ③ Mark another piece of paper Exercise 6.16, and copy your rewritten paragraph onto it. ④ Mark your rewritten paragraph as you have learned to.

Andy and Oscar, who say that they want a quiet life in the fresh air, now live on a farm. They get up every morning at dawn. Before they have breakfast, they pick their way through the cow dung, open the smelly chicken coop, and hold their noses as they snatch the eggs. While they make a fire in their woodburning stove, they choke on the smoke. Then Andy and Oscar drive a deafening tractor out to the field. As they breathe in the blowing dust, they cough loudly and sneeze often. Until late in the evening, they do chores in the barn. Exhausted, they go to bed and dream of a sound-proofed office and an air-conditioned apartment.

Exercise 6.17   Making verbs agree in a paragraph

This paragraph is written in the past tense. ① Circle each verb, and box its subject. You may find it useful to put parentheses around expansion. ② On scratch paper, rewrite the paragraph in the present tense. Your paragraph will begin *When Lila goes...* ③ Mark another piece of paper Exercise 6.17, and copy your rewritten paragraph onto it. ④ Mark your rewritten paragraph as you have learned to.

When Lila went to Europe, she admired the wonderful subways there. The cleanliness of the European subways amazed her. Maintenance people polished the brass railings and washed down the walls. Gratefully, she sank into the soft seat which gave her such a comfortable ride. Excellent maps and clear signs on every wall guided her efficiently from one unfamiliar station to another. She remembered the sweltering cars, dirty stations, and confusing signs in the subways back home. Certainly, Lila never got homesick when she rode in European subway trains.

Rule 2F1 says:
To + the base form of a verb is an <u>infinitive</u>. An infinitive never changes to show different tenses, so it's not a verb.

    LIKE   My son likes to swim.
                    My son liked to swim.
                The forms of *likes* and *liked* are different, because they are verbs in the present and past tenses. But *to swim* is an infinitive, so it has the same form in both tenses..

Because an infinitive isn't a verb, you should never try to make it agree with a subject.

    LIKE   They like to swim.
                    He likes to swim.
                The forms of *like* and *likes* are different, because they must agree with different subjects. But *to swim* is an infinitive, so it has the same form with both subjects.

Exercise 6.18   Making verbs agree in sentences with infinitives

① Circle each verb, box its subject, and underline each infinitive. ② Rewrite each sentence in the present tense. ③ Mark your rewritten sentence in the same way.

1.   The committee wanted to require more liberal arts courses.

_____

2.   Three professors intended to retire.

_____

3.   Nobody wanted to go to the library.

_____

| Exercise 6.19 | Making verbs agree in a paragraph with infinitives |

This paragraph contains base forms of present-tense verbs and infinitives in capital letters. ① Box each subject, and underline each infinitive. ② On scratch paper, rewrite the paragraph in the present tense. ③ Mark another piece of paper Exercise 6.19, and copy your rewritten paragraph onto it. ④ Mark your rewritten paragraph as you have learned to, and underline each infinitive.

Somebody MAKE plans to BREAK most world records as soon as someone else SET them. When an athlete RUN the mile in under four minutes, his rival immediately START training to BEAT his time. When a woman SWIM around Manhattan in the summer, another HAVE to DO it in the winter. It SEEM heroic to TRY to BREAK records like these, but some other attempts MAKE no sense. We GRIEVE if someone DIE trying to FLY fast, but it LOOK silly for people to EAT or to DANCE themselves to death. In contests like these, foolish people often REFUSE to STOP. If they HAVE to KILL themselves to WIN, they KILL themselves. At that moment each contestant WANT to DO just one thing—to DANCE longer, or to EAT more, or to SCREAM louder than anyone else in the world.

| Exercise 6.20 | Fixing verb agreement errors in a paragraph |

① Circle each verb, and box its subject, and underline each infinitive. ② Correct each error in the space above the line.

To pay his bills, Ngo Nhu have to drive his taxi up to 16 hours a day. Even so, he hardly make enough to put nourishing food on the table for his wife and three small children. To get through his long day behind the wheel, he dream the American dream. As he creeps through the downtown traffic, he imagine relaxing with his family after supper in the backyard of their suburban home, the home he plans to buys some day. These thoughts keep him going until the restaurants and theaters close and the streets grows dark and empty. But when he get home after midnight, he finds his wife in bed and his children fast asleep.

So as each week drag on, Ngo Nhu become impatient with distant hopes and dreams. He try to make an extra buck by racing ahead of other taxis to picks up fares. As he drive faster and faster, his passengers cringe. When he switch lanes without signaling, nervous passengers often asks to get out. The cops chase him when he rush through stop signs, and

just one traffic ticket costs him a full day's pay.

When Ngo Nhu finally take a day off, however, life once more seem good and the

future seems bright. He plays with his children, talk to his wife about the week's

adventures, and study his manual of English verbs. Then the next morning, he drives away

at dawn, and the cycle of dreams and frustrations start all over again for Ngo Nhu.

This paragraph contained 20 errors. How many did you find? _____ If you didn't find all 20, try again
before you check your work.

Exercise 6.21	Fixing errors in verb agreement

① Circle each verb, and box its subject. ② Correct each error in the space above the line.

Recent medical research shows that our emotional reaction to life's ups and downs have

a profound effect on our health. The fifteen billion nerve cells in our brains constantly

change our hopes and fears into chemical substances which in turn either heals or harm our

bodies. Many people hears these facts but reject them. Depression run in their family, they

say. But researchers again have an answer: If people act cheerful, then they begins to feel

cheerful. When something unexpected wreck their plans, smart people looks for a hidden

advantage instead of moaning over it. When they gets a chance to say something positive,

they never hesitate to say it. Sensible individuals who see something beautiful takes time

out to enjoy it. When a small misfortune happen, they turns it over in their minds until they

find the funny side. (Everything do have a funny side.) This positive behavior produce

positive feelings. Most of the time we has the power to do what makes life more enjoyable,

to see the bright side, or at least to remember that sooner or later things will change. This

makes sense, and often mean the difference between sickness and health.

This paragraph contained 15 errors. How many did you find? _____ If you didn't find all 15, try again
before you check your work.

Editing Practice F.2   Fixing more verb agreement mistakes in your own writing
1. Get Paper F again.
2. Check again to make sure that each verb is circled, and its subject is boxed. If you find any more verbs and subjects, mark them with your green pen.
3. Check again to make sure that each verb agrees with its subject, and that you have not tried to make any infinitives agree. Fix any mistakes with your green pen.
4. How many more mistakes did you fix? _____ Your ability to find and fix these mistakes shows how much you've learned so far.

Keep your draft of Paper F to use again later.

The Irregular Verb *BE:* Present Tense

The verb *BE* is the most irregular verb in English. Its forms don't even look or sound like *BE*, except in the infinitive *to be* or in a few verb phrases like the future tense *will be*. But still, like other verbs, *BE* in the present tense must agree with its subject.

6B	Use *am* to make *BE* agree with *I* in the present tense. Use *is* to make *BE* agree with <u>a singular subject (but not *I* or *you*)</u> in the present tense. Use *are* to make *BE* agree with <u>a plural subject or *you*</u> in the present tense.

BE   I (am) at home.
           Am agrees with the subject *I*.

BE   She (is) at home.
           Is agrees with the singular subject *she*.

BE   The girls (are) at home.
           You (are) at home.
           Are agrees with the plural subject *girls*, and with the subject *you*.

Whether the subject *you* is singular or plural, use *are* to agree with it in the present tense.

BE   You (are) my friend.
           You both (are) my friends.
           Are agrees with both singular *you* and plural *you*.

| Exercise 6.22 | **Making BE agree in the present tense** |

This paragraph contains base forms of *BE* in capital letters. ① Box each subject. ② On scratch paper, rewrite the paragraph, using the present-tense form of *BE*. ③ Mark another piece of paper Exercise 6.22, and copy your rewritten paragraph onto it. ④ Mark your rewritten paragraph as you have learned to.

My wife and I BE trying to raise our children in a non-sexist way, but we BE unable to control the way in which other people talk to our four-year olds. The children BE twins, but Emma BE much more aggressive than her brother Dominick. The neighbors BE quick to praise Emma as "a little lady," but then they lift an eyebrow when she BE too boisterous. At the same time, they BE apt to say to Dominick, "You BE so quiet today! What BE wrong?" I BE not happy to see that sexual stereotyping BE still alive and well, at least on our block.

The verbs *am, is,* and *are* are often contracted. Contracted forms are more informal than uncontracted forms, but they're usually acceptable in writing. Be sure to use apostrophes to show where letters have been omitted.

Am can be contracted with its subject *I*.

BE — I am lucky.
BE — I'm lucky.
The apostrophe shows where the letter *A* has been omitted.

Because the apostrophe shows an omitted letter, it is never correct to write something like *I'am.*

BE — I' am lucky.
This contraction is incorrect.

Is and *are* can be contracted with their subjects, with *here, there,* and *where,* and with *not.*

BE — Carol is my sister.
Carol's my sister.

They are my friends.
They're my friends.
The apostrophes show where the letters *I* and *A* have been omitted.

BE — Here is your book.
Here's your book.

There is no reason for that behavior.
There's no reason for that behavior.
The apostrophes show where the letter *I* has been omitted.

179

BE   Lee (is) not my sister.
            Lee (isn)'t my sister.

            You (are) not my friends.
            You (aren)'t my friends.
The apostrophes show where the letter *O* has been omitted.

Exercise 6.23   Making contracted *BE* agree in the present tense

These sentences contain base forms of *BE* in capital letters. ① Box each subject. ② Rewrite each sentence, contracting the verb with the subject. ③ Mark your rewritten sentence as you have learned to.

1.   You BE rather short-tempered these days.

     _____

2.   I BE eager to hear from you.

     _____

3.   Nobody BE perfect.

     _____

4.   They BE members of the Latin Club.

     _____

5.   There BE a telephone call for you.

     _____

6.   Where BE the rent money?

     _____

7.   Here BE the man that I'm going to marry.

     _____

Exercise 6.24   Making various verbs agree

This paragraph contains base forms of present-tense verbs and infinitives in capital letters. Read it carefully to make sure that you understand it. ① Box each subject, and underline each infinitive. ② On scratch paper, rewrite the paragraph in the present tense. ③ Mark another piece of paper Exercise 6.24, and copy your rewritten paragraph onto it. ④ Mark your rewritten paragraph as you have learned to, and underline each infinitive.

Frustrated parents sometimes LIKE to IMAGINE that their children BE very

talented. Sometimes a father who WISH that he had been an actor WANT his son to BE a movie star, and so he TEACH the boy how to SING and to DANCE almost before he KNOW how to WALK or to TALK. A mother who wanted to DANCE THINK her daughter BE sure to BE another Pavlova, so she SEND the child to school to LEARN ballet before she BE able to READ. It BE true that every now and then a Macaulay Culkin TURN up and MAKE several million dollars in the movies before he BE ten years old; and once every four or five centuries a Mozart WRITE a symphony when he BE only nine. But much more often, these children BE remarkable only to their parents. When a so-called child prodigy GROW up, he usually never WANT to SEE a piano or to DANCE a step. He BECOME a plumber or a policeman, which BE just what he wanted to BE from the start.

Editing Practice F.3 *Fixing more verb agreement mistakes in your own writing*

1. Get your draft of Paper F again.
2. Check again to make sure that each verb (including *BE*) is circled, and its subject is boxed. If you find any more verbs and subjects, mark them with your green pen.
3. Review Rule 6B.
4. Check again to make sure that each verb agrees with its subject. Fix any mistakes with your green pen.
5. How many more mistakes did you fix? _____ Your ability to find and fix these mistakes shows how much you've learned so far..

Keep your draft of Paper F to use again later.

Exercise 6.25 **Fixing errors in both noun forms and verb agreement**

① Circle each verb, and box its subject. ② Correct each error in noun forms and in verb agreement in the space above the line.

All cat owner knows that domestic cats belongs to the same family of mammals as lions.

When a pet cat pounce on an insect or licks its paws and wash its face, it look just like a lion

in the zoo. But in one important way, cats and lion are completely different. Outdoors, in

pursuit of birds or mouses, a domestic cat act very independent. Aloof and solitary, it stalk

its victims alone. But lions, especially the females, tend to live and to hunt in groups. The

lions travel together and brings down their victims in a coordinated attack. They treat every

member of the group, even a cub, as an equal. If one of the young lion lag behind the group,

the others prod and push him. If one lion by accident hurt another as they scramble over a

carcass, the others lick her wounds and comforts her. In this cooperative behavior, lions is

not like domestic cats at all; in fact, they differ from all other member of the cat family.

This paragraph contained 17 errors. How many did you find? _____ If you didn't find all 17, try again before you check your work.

Writing Your Final Copy of Paper F

Use your final copy of Paper F to demonstrate what you've learned in Module 6 about making present-tense verbs agree with their subjects, and to show how well you're continuing to apply what you've learned previously.

Paper F	Using Present-tense Verbs
Edit for Previous Modules	Use your dictionary and the Rules Summaries for previous modules to: • Check your use of writing conventions. Fix any mistakes with your green pen. • Check the structure of each word-group. If any word-group doesn't have at least one verb, or has a verb without a subject, it is not a sentence. Put brackets [ ] around it. How many word-groups like this did you bracket? _____ • Check the structure of each word-group again. If any word-group doesn't have one simple sentence more than the number of connecting words, it is not a correct sentence. Put brackets [ ] around it. How many word-groups like this did you bracket? _____ • Check your use of nouns and pronouns. Fix any mistakes with your green pen.
Make Final Copy	Mark another piece of paper Paper F, and write the final copy of your paper on it, or print out a clean copy on your word processor. Be sure to include all your corrections. Mark your final copy as you did your draft.
Proofread	Read your final copy **out loud.** Correct any mistakes neatly by hand. If you used a word processor, enter your corrections, print out a corrected final copy, and mark it again.

Hand in your final copy of Paper F, and the rest of your exercises.

NAME _____

After you finish checking each exercise, fill in your number of mistakes.

7.1 _____	7.7 _____	7.12 _____	7.17 _____	7.22 _____
7.2 _____	7.8 _____	7.13 _____	7.18 _____	7.23 _____
7.3 _____	7.9 _____	7.14 _____	7.19 _____	7.24 _____
7.4 _____	7.10 _____	7.15 _____	7.20 _____	7.25 _____
7.5 _____	7.11 _____	7.16 _____	7.21 _____	7.26 _____
7.6 _____				

EXERCISES	INSTRUCTIONS	CHECKING	
❑ Complete	❑ Followed carefully	❑ Careful	❑ Green pen not used
❑ Incomplete	❑ Not careful enough	❑ Not careful enough	❑ Mistakes not corrected

PAPER G	EDITING PAPER G FOR THIS MODULE'S WORK	
❑ Doesn't follow the instructions; write a NEW Paper G.	❑ Careful	❑ Not careful enough
❑ Skips some instructions; COMPLETE everything.	EDITING PAPER G FOR PREVIOUS WORK	
❑ Too short; add MORE.	❑ Careful	❑ Not careful enough
	OVERALL EVALUATION OF PAPER G	
	❑ Excellent ❑ Good ❑ Acceptable ❑ Not acceptable	

COMMENTS

Rules Summary for Module 7

7A	Change the whole word to form the past tense of **irregular** verbs.
7B	Add a *D* or *ED* ending to form the past tense of **regular** verbs.
1	Make necessary **spelling** changes when writing past-tense verbs.
7C	Use *was* to make *BE* agree with **a singular subject or *I*** in the past tense. Use *were* to make *BE* agree with **a plural subject or *you*** in the past tense.

In Module 6 you learned about one-word verbs in the **present tense**. One-word verbs in the **past tense** may seem easier than those in the present tense because they don't have to agree with their subjects (except for the verb *BE*). However, past-tense verbs often cause problems in writing because many of the most common ones are **irregular**. Even the ones that are regular are hard to write correctly because it's easy to overlook or leave off their endings. This module will help you learn to write these verbs correctly.

Here in Module 7, you'll work on making **one-word verbs** show the past tense correctly. In Modules 10-11, you'll work on making **helping verbs in verb phrases** show the past tense.

Using Module 7 to Edit Your Own Writing

Use Paper G to discover how much you know already about using past-tense verbs. Later in this module, you'll be checking this paper by applying the rules of this module to what you have written.

You may write this paper by hand. Better yet, use a word processor.

Drafting Paper G	*Using past-tense verbs*
Assignment	Choose one of these assignments:
	❑ Think of a catastrophe that you read about, saw on TV, or experienced personally, a hurricane, flood, tornado, drought, or other natural disaster. Describe what happened, when and where it happened, and how it changed the lives of many people.
	❑ Think of something that happened when you were a child, an event that you can never forget. Describe what happened, telling why it was so important to you.
Get Ready	On a piece of scratch paper, free write on your chosen topic, first to narrow it to one specific example if necessary, and then to get ideas to use in developing your paper. Don't stop until you have plenty of ideas. Draw a line across the page when you have finished free writing.
	Read over your free writing, and decide on your main point. Write it in one complete sentence below the line.
	Plan your paragraphs by selecting enough supporting ideas from your free writing to make your main point interesting, clear, and convincing to a reader. Write your supporting ideas in a numbered list below your main point.
Draft	On another piece of scratch paper, write an introduction to your draft telling what your main point is.
	Then write at least one paragraph for each of your supporting ideas. Be sure to include enough examples, details, and facts to make your reader understand and believe each idea.
	Write your conclusion.

Revise	Revise your draft, using the four steps in revision listed on the inside front cover to make your paper better. Make sure that you have written at least four paragraphs, including an introduction and a conclusion.

Keep your draft of Paper G to use later.

Irregular Past-tense Verbs

7A	**Change the whole word to form the past tense of <u>irregular</u> verbs.**

Usually you can't predict what the past-tense form of an irregular verb will be, so if you don't already know it, you'll have to look it up in your dictionary. Follow the four steps below to practice this now.

1.   Get your dictionary. If you don't have it, don't go on until you do have it.

2.   Look up the irregular verb *SING*. Be sure to find the word with the label *v* for *verb*.

3.   How many other forms are listed? _____

   •   Usually three other forms are listed. *Sings* may be listed also, to remind you that verbs must agree with their subjects in the present tense.

4.   Write in the three other forms of *SING* (ignore *sings* if it's listed):

   SING   _____   _____   _____

   •   The 1st form *sing* (or *sings*) is used in the present tense.
   •   The 2nd form *sang* is used in the past tense.
   •   The 3rd form *sung* is the past participle.
   •   The 4th form *singing* is the *ING* form.

For some irregular verbs, the past-tense form and the past participle are the same.

BRING   I <u>brought</u>   I have <u>brought</u>
   BRING has the same past-tense and past participle forms.

For other irregular verbs, the past-tense form and the past participle are different.

SWIM   I <u>swam</u>   I have <u>swum</u>
   SWIM has different past-tense and past participle forms.

Except for the verb *BE* (which you will learn about later in this module), you don't need to worry about making past-tense verbs agree with their subjects. Past-tense verbs have just one form, whether the subject is singular or plural.

SWIM   [She] swam in the Pacific Ocean last year.
                 [We] swam in the Pacific Ocean last year.
          Swam is the correct past-tense form for both singular subjects like *she* and plural subjects like *we*.

Exercise 7.1	Practicing irregular past-tense verb forms

① Box the subject. ② Fill in the past-tense form of the given verb. For help, use your dictionary.

1.   GET   George Worsham, a Virginia farmer, _____ his tax bill on September 30, 1829.

2.   PAY   He _____ 40¢ per slave, 10¢ per horse, and 1¢ per two-wheeled carriage.

3.   BUY   In 1862, he _____ his grandson Henry a new horse for $120.

4.   BRING   Then Henry's mother _____ a box of cornbread to

     PUT   the verandah and _____ it in his knapsack.

5.   SAY   Henry _____ goodbye to his parents and

     RIDE   _____ away to join the First Virginia Cavalry.

6.   SEND   Three years later the Confederate States of America _____ Mr. Worsham $2965 in worthless currency for his dead horse, and nothing for his dead grandson.

7.   BEGIN   One by one, the freed black slaves then _____ to

     SELL   leave the farm, and Worsham _____ his livestock.

8.   SPEAK   On June 1, 1870, Worsham and his sons _____ to their

     TELL   lawyer and _____ him to file for bankruptcy on their behalf.

9.   GO   In 1873, Rebecca Worsham, George's granddaughter, _____

     TEACH   to a Young Ladies' Seminary in Kentucky and _____ Latin and Greek to support the family.

Remember to use your green pen to check each exercise as soon as you finish it. Write in any necessary corrections, and then write in your number of mistakes on the cover page.

Don't confuse the past participle of a verb with its past-tense form. Although you sometimes hear verbs used like this in speech, they aren't correct in writing.

                     x
SEE   [I] seen the Florida Keys last year.
            [I] saw the Florida Keys last year.
          Saw is the correct past-tense form of *SEE*.

Exercise 7.2   Avoiding common errors in irregular past-tense verbs

① Box the subject. ② Fill in the past-tense form of the given verb. For help, use your dictionary.

1. BEGIN   In 1861, the Civil War _____ with Confederate victories at Fort Sumter and Bull Run.

2. RUN   For many months after that, the timid Northern generals _____
   DO   away or _____ nothing.

3. COME   Early in 1862, Ulysses S. Grant _____ to President Lincoln's attention as the first Northern general to win a battle.

4. LEAD   He _____ his troops in the bloody but indecisive battles at Shiloh and Antietam.

5. SEE   Then, in the following year, Grant _____ a chance to win control of the Mississippi Valley.

6. DRINK   On July 4, 1863, he _____ a victory toast at Vicksburg,

   SING   and his troops _____ Yankee Doodle on the banks of the Mississippi.

7. SWING   After this triumph, the tide of the war _____ in favor of the North.

It may seem as though you need to memorize every irregular past-tense verb. But there are some patterns to their forms. The next exercise will help you learn those patterns.

Exercise 7.3   Discovering patterns in irregular verbs

Fill in the past-tense form of each verb. Then write in the letter (or letters) that each past-tense form is spelled with.

They buy. They _____.	They steal. They _____.
They bring. They _____.	They rise. They _____.
They catch. They _____.	They freeze. They _____.
They teach. They _____.	They choose. They _____.
Spell these verbs with A __ __ __ __ or with O __ __ __ __ in the past tense.	Spell these verbs with __ in the past tense.

They throw. They _____.	They say. They _____.
They know. They _____.	They lay. They _____.
They grow. They _____.	They pay. They _____.
Spell these verbs with __ __ in the past tense.	Spell these verbs with __ __ __ in the past tense.
They quit. They _____.	They ring. They _____.
They cut. They _____.	They swim. They _____.
They hit. They _____.	They begin. They _____.
They hurt. They _____.	They drink. They _____.
They put. They _____.	They sing. They _____.
These verbs have _____ change in the past tense.	Spell these verbs with __ in the past tense.
They send. They _____.	They keep. They _____.
They lose. They _____.	They feel. They _____.
They spend. They _____.	They leave. They _____.
They sleep. They _____.	Spell these verbs with __ in the past tense

Regular Past-tense Verbs

7B	Add a *D* or *ED* ending to form the past tense of <u>regular</u> verbs.

WALK   They walked to work during the strike.
LIVE   My friends lived in Greece last year.
      Walked and *lived* are the past-tense forms of the regular verbs *WALK* and *LIVE*.

Exercise 7.4   Practicing regular past-tense verbs

① Box the subject. ② Fill in the past-tense form of the given verb.

1. PRESENT   According to Joseph Smith, in 1829 an angel _____

     CALL   him with a book which he _____ *The Book of Mormon.*

2. INSPIRE   This book _____ him to found the Mormon Church.

3. PRACTICE   Because he and his followers _____ polygamy, an

     LYNCH   angry mob _____ him in 1844.

4. PASS   The leadership of the Church _____ to Brigham Young.

5. FOLLOW   Thousands of Mormon converts _____ Young to

     ESTABLISH   Salt Lake City, where they _____ a new community.

D on't get confused and add *ED* to make the past-tense form of an **irregular** verb. Whenever you're not sure of a past-tense form, use your dictionary.

✗   ✗

The band <u>beginned</u> to play as the team <u>ranned</u> onto the field.

The band <u>began</u> to play as the team <u>ran</u> onto the field.

Because *BEGIN* and *RUN* are irregular verbs, past-tense forms with *ED* are incorrect.

Exercise 7.5   Telling the difference between regular and irregular verbs

① Box the subject. ② Fill in the past-tense form of the given verbs.

1. PLANT   Gracia _____ a garden and

     GROW   _____ tomatoes.

2. STEAL   The shortstop _____ third base and

     SCORE   then _____ the winning run.

3. TEACH   Mr. Erickson _____ my high school Spanish class

     PASS   and _____ all his students with a B.

4. CATCH   The child _____ chicken pox and

     DEVELOP   _____ a high fever.

5. SIT   Everybody _____ in her seat and

     PRETEND   _____ to be working.

| 7B1 | Make necessary <u>spelling</u> changes when writing past-tense verbs. |

Rule 1J2 says:
**Change *Y* to *I* before adding *ED* if a word ends with a <u>consonant</u> + *Y*,
but never change *Y* to *I* if the word ends with a <u>vowel</u> + *Y*.**

FRY We <u>fried</u> the onions.
    FRY ends with a consonant + Y, so fried is spelled with I.

PLAY My son <u>played</u> with those little cars when he was younger.
    PLAY ends with a vowel + Y, so played is spelled with Y, not I.

| Exercise 7.6 | Applying spelling rules before adding *ED* |

① Box the subject. ② Fill in the past-tense form of the given verb.

1. RELY During the 1940s, American factories _____ on

  CARRY millions of women workers while their men _____
      arms in World War II.

2. ENJOY Most of these women _____ their earning power and

  BURY independence, but _____ these feelings when their
      husbands and sweethearts returned.

3. STAY Then throughout the 1950s, most wives _____ home

  PLAY and once again _____ a traditional role.

4. DELAY The post-war baby boom _____ feminism for an
      entire generation.

Don't confuse the **irregular** verbs *LAY, PAY,* and *SAY* with **regular** verbs ending with a vowel + *Y*. Never use the regular *ED* ending to make the past-tense forms of these irregular verbs.

     X
PAY I <u>payed</u> the bill.
    I <u>paid</u> the bill.
    Paid is the correct past-tense form of the irregular verb PAY.

LAY I <u>laid</u> the envelope down.
SAY I <u>said</u> nothing to her.
    Laid and said are the past-tense forms of the irregular verbs LAY and SAY.

Exercise 7.7   Practicing special past-tense forms

This paragraph contains base forms of verbs, in capital letters. Read it carefully to make sure that you understand it. ① Box each subject. ② Mark a piece of paper Exercise 7.7, and rewrite this paragraph onto it, using the appropriate **past-tense** form of the given verb. ③ Mark your rewritten paragraph as you have learned to.

After the bank COLLAPSE, the investigators LAY the entire blame on the bank

officials. They SAY that the officers RELY on inside information about stock investments

and DELAY paying interest on loans. As usual, the officers DENY the charges, but the

depositors PAY dearly for these illegal practices.

Rule 1G3 says:

If a verb ends with a single vowel + a consonant, double the consonant before adding *ED*.

> DROP   Matilda <u>dropped</u> her keys while opening the door.
> *DROP* ends with a single vowel + a consonant, so *dropped* is spelled with a double *P*.

Failing to double the consonant can cause a wrong-word mistake.

✗

> ROB   Bonnie and Clyde <u>robed</u> banks.
>   Bonnie and Clyde <u>robbed</u> banks.
> *Robed* is the past-tense form of the verb *ROBE*, not *ROB*. *ROB* ends with a single vowel + a consonant, so *robbed* is spelled with a double *B*.

Exercise 7.8   Practicing when to double the consonant before adding *ED*

① Box the subject. ② Fill in the past-tense form of the given verb.

1. HOPE   I _____ to get a B in my philosophy course last semester, but I didn't really expect to.

     HOP   Edmund _____ four miles last year to win a bet.

2. ROB   Somebody _____ the liquor store on the corner last week.

     ROBE   The graduates _____ in the hall before the ceremony.

3. RAP   Who _____ on my door a minute ago?

     RAPE   The Romans _____ the Sabines (that is, they carried them away).

4. PLAN   That group _____ the conference two years in advance.

     PLANE   The carpenter _____ the door so it would fit better.

5. STARE   We _____ at each other in disbelief.

    STAR   The film _____ William Hurt and Glenn Close.

Because *ED* endings are sometimes hard to pronounce and hard to hear, it can also be hard to see them written on the page, especially in paragraphs. As a result, *ED* endings are sometimes omitted. In proofreading a passage in the past tense, be especially careful to look for these endings.

Remember that an infinitive is not a verb. This means that an infinitive doesn't have a past-tense form. Sometimes students get confused and put *ED* endings on infinitives as well as past-tense verb forms. Be careful not to do this.

                               x
    HOPE   We hoped to visited Quebec last winter.
                   We hoped to visit Quebec last winter.
         The infinitive *to visit* doesn't have a past-tense form.

Exercise 7.9   Using appropriate *ED* endings

① Circle each verb, box its subject, and underline each infinitive. ② Underline each error, and correct it in the space above the line.

        As the storm battered the coast, the men on board the small fishing boat grasp the ropes

and furled their sails. Desperately, they flash distress signals to the shore. But the waves

surge savagely, overturned their boat, and threaten to drown them. All night, they clutch

the hull of their craft with aching fingers, and try to stay hopeful. At dawn, while the storm

still raged, helicopter pilots risk their lives when they hovered over the fishermen, drop

ladders, and pluck them out of the sea.

This passage contained nine errors. How many did you find?_____ If you didn't find all nine, try again before you check your work.

In the past-tense expression *used to*, the *D* ending is particularly hard to pronounce or to hear because it's followed by the letter *T*, which has the same sound. So it's easy to leave the *D* ending off. Be especially careful about this expression.

                               x
    USE   We use to go to the beach every summer.
                 We used to go to the beach every summer.
         Used is in the past tense, so it needs a *D* ending.

Exercise 7.10   Practicing *used to*

① Box the subject. ② Fill in the past-tense form of *USE* + the infinitive of the given verb.

1. DIE   Millions _____ _____ of smallpox.

2. HAVE   Some middle-income folks _____ _____ cooks and chauffeurs.

3. SAVE   Some retired Americans _____ _____ money by living abroad.

Exercise 7.11   Fixing other mistakes with *ED* endings

① Circle each verb, box its subject, and underline each infinitive. ② Correct each error in the space above the line.

Last week when I stepped out of the elevator in my apartment building, Sam the janitor warn me to be careful. He remind me about the rise in street crime during this past year. I just laughed as I pushed open the front door. When I reach the sidewalk, I stoped, buttoned up my coat, pulled on my gloves, and gather up all my packages again. It never occured to me to see if I had everything. I entered the bank on the corner and ask to apply for a credit card. The guard open the gate into the office area. I wented inside and picked up an application to fill out. But when I reach for my lavender purse to get a pen, nothing lavender appeared among my packages. I started to screamed. I kick the gate and yelled, "Somebody stealed my purse! Somebody rob me!" The guard told me to stopped for a minute and to try to think. I admitted to him, "Yes, maybe I lefted it on the street when I stopped and put my gloves on." In a panic, I dashed all the way home. Just inside the open door, Sam starred at me with my purse in his hand. He sayed, with a look of astonishment, "Some stranger spoted your purse behind the door and handed it to me." This week Sam switch the topic of his conversation from crime to the weather.

This paragraph contained 20 errors. How many did you find? _____ If you didn't find all 20, try again before you check your work.

Editing Practice G.1   *Fixing past-tense verb mistakes*

1. Get your draft of Paper G.
2. Circle each verb (either a one-word verb or a verb phrase), and box its subject.

3. Review Rules 7A-7B1.
4. Check to make sure that each past-tense verb is in the correct form and is correctly spelled. Fix any mistakes with your green pen.
5. How many mistakes did you fix? _____ Your ability to find and fix mistakes in your own writing shows how much you've learned so far.

Keep your draft of Paper G to use again later.

The Irregular Verb *BE:* Past Tense

BE is the only verb that must agree with its subject in the past tense as well as the present tense.

7C	**Use *was* to make *BE* agree with <u>a singular subject or *I*</u> in the past tense.** **Use *were* to make *BE* agree with <u>a plural subject or *you*</u> in the past tense.**

BE   One student was absent yesterday.
                    I was absent yesterday.
           Was agrees with the singular subject *student* and with *I*.

BE   The boys were absent yesterday.
                    You were absent yesterday.
           Were agrees with the plural subject *boys* and with *you*.

Whether the subject *you* is singular or plural, use *were* to agree with it in the past tense.

BE   You were my friend.
                    You both were my friends.
           Were agrees with both singular *you* and plural *you*.

Exercise 7.12   Understanding agreement with past-tense forms of *BE*

① Box the subject. ② Fill in the appropriate past-tense form of *BE*.

"Where _____ you when Kennedy was shot?" This

_____ a familiar question when I _____ a child, and the

answers _____ always interesting. We _____ at my son's

house last November 22ⁿᵈ, and a replay of the shocking events in Dallas in 1963

_____ on TV again. My small granddaughter suddenly looked up and

asked, "Who _____ Jack Kennedy?"

Exercise 7.13   Practicing agreement with past-tense forms of *BE*

Read this paragraph carefully to make sure that you understand it. ① Circle each verb, and box its subject. ② Mark a piece of paper Exercise 7.13, and rewrite this paragraph onto it, using the appropriate **past-tense** form of each verb. ③ Mark your rewritten paragraph as you have learned to.

> We are new at our jobs as bank tellers, so a counterfeit bill is hard for us to detect. But in this bank there are older tellers who have index fingers which are as sensitive as lie detectors. To their sharp eyes, a presidential face on a large bill is as familiar as their own. Presidents with crooked noses or bent ears are as obvious to them as the false smiles on the faces of thieves.

The past-tense verbs *was* and *were* can be contracted with *not*.

BE

He was not ready.
He wasn't ready.
They were not ready.
They weren't ready.

Apostrophes show where the letter *O* has been omitted.

Exercise 7.14   Contracting *BE* in the past tense

These sentences contain base forms of *BE*, in capital letters. ① Box each subject. ② Rewrite each sentence, contracting the appropriate past-tense form of *BE* with *not*. ③ Mark your rewritten sentence as you have learned to.

1.   We BE not sure of the answer.

   _____

2.   My mother BE not able to finish college.

   _____

3.   You BE not there when we called.

   _____

You already know that in sentences beginning with *here* and *there*, the subject follows the verb. So be especially careful to use the appropriate form of *BE* after these words.

BE   There were some interesting stories in the paper yesterday.
Were agrees with the plural subject stories.

BE   There (was) one [story] about narwhals in Alaska.
         Was agrees with the singular subject *story*.

Exercise 7.15	**Using the appropriate form of *BE* after *here* and *there***

These sentences contain base forms of *BE*, in capital letters. ① Box each subject. ② Rewrite each sentence, using the appropriate past-tense form of *BE*. ③ Mark your rewritten sentence as you have learned to.

1. There BE two terrible bus accidents in South America in 1991.

_____

2. There BE a huge celebration for the United States Bicentennial in 1976.

_____

3. There BE no cure for that disease before 1943.

_____

4. There BE just one person in the room then.

_____

Editing Practice G.2	**Fixing more past-tense verb mistakes**

1. Get your draft of Paper G again.
2. Check again to make sure that each verb is circled, and its subject is boxed. If you find any more verbs and subjects, mark them with your green pen.
3. Review Rule 7C.
4. Check to make sure that each past-tense form of *BE* agrees with its subject. Fix any mistakes with your green pen.
5. How many mistakes did you fix? _____ Your ability to find and fix mistakes in your own writing shows how much you've learned so far.

Keep your draft of Paper G to use again later.

Using Appropriate Tenses

In many sentences, there are **time words** that show what tense the sentence is in.

> Yesterday we (had) chicken curry for supper.
> Usually we (have) curry at least once a week.
> [We] (will have) vegetarian curry for supper tomorrow night.
>   The time words *yesterday, usually,* and *tomorrow night* show that these sentences are in the past, present, and future tenses.

Time words are sometimes entire pieces of expansion, with a connecting word, a verb, and a subject.

+
We ate dinner <u>as soon as Marcia got home from work</u>.
> The expansion *as soon as Marcia got home from work* shows that this sentence must be in the past tense.

In other sentences, there may not be any time words, but the verb shows the tense anyway.

I called her about the shopping trip.
He calls me to discuss his problems with his children.
She will call to tell us about her new pet cat.
> Even though there are no time words in these sentences, the verbs *called*, *calls*, and *will call* show that they are in the past, present, and future tenses.

Depending on the meaning, a sentence may even have different verbs in different tenses.

Although Tanya saw that TV show just <u>last night,</u> she will watch it again <u>tomorrow</u>.
> The time words *last night* show why *saw* is in the past tense. The time word *tomorrow* shows why *will watch* is in the future tense.

I am afraid that I will lose the watch that you gave me.
> *Am* is in the present tense because it is telling about right now. *Will lose* is in the future tense because it is telling about something that might happen in the future. *Gave* is in the past tense because it is telling about something that happened in the past.

Each verb must be in the tense that is appropriate to its meaning. This is usually easy to do in a sentence that has just one verb. But when sentences have more than one verb, you must be very careful to write each verb in its correct tense. Either the existing verbs or the time words (which may include verbs) will show what tense the other verbs should be in.

Exercise 7.16   Using appropriate tenses

① Underline the words that show what tense the missing verb should be in. ② Box the subject. ③ Fill in the appropriate present-tense or past-tense form of the given verb.

1. BUY   Before my brother moved to Chicago, he _____ a new car.

   Every time my brother makes a big change in his life, he _____ a new car.

2. BE   Whenever their parents disapprove of something, Maggie and Joan _____ eager to do it.

   Although their parents disapproved, Maggie and Joan _____ eager to become models.

3. DO   If a person is ambitious, she _____ the best job possible.

   Because Latrelle was ambitious, she always _____ her best work.

4. ASK   When Ping's husband comes home, she _____

    FEEL   him how he _____ .

                     When Ping's husband came home, she _____

                     him how he _____ .

5. STOP   Whenever she had time, Mrs. Franklin _____ and

    BUY   _____ a newspaper to read on her way to work.

                     Whenever she has time, Mrs. Franklin _____ and

                     _____ a newspaper to read on her way to work.

Exercise 7.17   Using the appropriate tense

① Underline the words that show what tense the missing verbs should be in. ② Box the subject. ③ Fill in the appropriate present-tense or past-tense form of the given verbs.

1. DROP   Last year, many people _____ their senile parents

    DRIVE   at the door of an emergency room and _____ away.

2. PASS   If Congress _____ that controversial bill, the President

    REACH   says that he will veto it when it _____ his desk.

3. FLY   Whenever I work at my computer, time _____ , and I

    LOSE   _____ myself in my work.

4. SHOP   A working mother often _____ for groceries on the way home,

    RUSH   and _____ to make supper before her husband arrives.

5. WASH   Then, while he _____ the dishes, she lies down on

    WATCH   the sofa and _____ TV.

6. HIDE   A deranged man _____ a hammer under his coat, and then

    CHIP   attacked Michaelangelo's famous statue of David and _____
                     its toe.

7. RING   When the doorbell _____ , Brenda looked to see who

    UNLOCK was there before she _____ the door.

8. ASK   A young child is hard to live with because she _____

    GET   questions constantly and _____ into a lot of mischief.

9. BE   There _____ several drugs which prolong the lives of

    FIND   AIDS victims, but until doctors _____ a cure, the
                 disease will continue to spread.

10. SING   Before the game started, Roseanne _____ "The Star-

    CAUSE   Spangled Banner" off key and almost _____ a riot.

Exercise 7.18   Using the appropriate tense

① Write one sentence to answer each group of questions, using the appropriate present-tense or past-tense verbs. ② Mark your answer as you have learned to.

1. Did Olaf stand up? Did he start an argument? Did he stalk away?

    Yes, he _____

2. Does Colette worry about money? Does she shop very carefully? Does she pay all her bills?

    Yes, she _____

    _____

3. Does Consuelo attend school? Does she keep house for her family? Does she study every weekend?

    Yes, she _____

    _____

4. Did the phone ring? Did it stop? Did it begin ringing again?

    Yes, it _____

5. Do I wake up at 9am? Do I have breakfast? Do I listen to the morning news? Do I go back to bed?

    Yes, I _____

    _____

6. Did the preacher pray? Did he read from the Bible? Did he lead a hymn? Did he say the benediction?

    Yes, he _____

    _____

One reason that the verb BE is especially difficult is that you must make it agree with its subject at the same time that you're using the appropriate tense consistently.

| Exercise 7.19 | Making *BE* agree in the appropriate tense |

① Underline the words that show what tense the missing verb should be in. ② Box the subject. ③ Fill in the appropriate present-tense or past-tense form of *BE*.

1. Doctors tell us that the pressures of modern life _____ a threat to health.

2. Before the Revolution began, the principal religion of the Chinese people _____ Confucianism.

3. Because the point of many of his jokes _____ basically cruel, I dislike Professor Keys.

4. The loudspeaker announced that nobody _____ a clear winner in yesterday's competition.

5. The mayor claims that the number of violent crimes in our city _____ relatively low.

6. Several books from that set _____ on the table before the moderator arrived.

7. When I registered, not one of the delegates to this convention _____ in the hall.

8. I _____ furious with him about the way he's acting.

You already know that, depending on the meaning, a sentence may have different verbs in different tenses.

I remember the day when I received the good news about my mother.
Remember is a present-tense verb because I'm remembering now in the present. *Received* is a past-tense verb because I received the good news in the past.

| Exercise 7.20 | Using appropriate tenses of *BE* |

① Underline the words that show what tense the missing verb should be in. ② Box the subject. ③ Fill in the appropriate present-tense or past-tense form of *BE*.

1. Julian wonders why he _____ so shy when he was a child.

2. My grandparents seldom talk about the olden days, when they _____ young.

3. I sometimes forget that my little girl _____ all grown up now.

4. Do you remember the time last year when we _____ almost late for the plane?

Exercise 7.21	Using appropriate tenses of *BE*

This paragraph contains base forms of *BE* in capital letters. Read it carefully to make sure that you understand it. You may find it helpful to underline any words that show what tense each verb should be in. ① Box each subject. ② Mark a piece of paper Exercise 7.21, and rewrite this paragraph onto it, using the appropriate tense of each verb. ③ Mark your rewritten paragraph as you have learned to.

When I BE a small boy, my friends BE always eager to hear my grandfather's war stories. This BE Chapter One in his collection of stories: "Who BE I? Well, sonny, my name BE Bill Williams, and I BE 99 years old. In World War I, I BE a fighter pilot. The Red Baron and I BE up there, stalking each other in the clouds. Fragments of shrapnel BE all around me, but I BE not one bit scared. Here BE an old photograph of me in my uniform. I BE 19 years old at the time. Those campaign ribbons on my chest BE my pride and joy then, and they still BE now. And here on this table BE some more souvenirs—a couple of old brass artillery shells that now BE lamps. It BE hard to believe, but these shells BE once in a German cannon. And now here they BE, looking pretty in my living room. I BE one high flyer in the Great War, child, and I still BE."

Editing Practice G.3	*Checking past-tense verbs again*

1. Get your draft of Paper G again.
2. Check again to make sure that each verb is circled, and its subject is boxed. If you find any more verbs and subjects, mark them with your green pen.
3. Check again to make sure that each past-tense form is correct. If you find any more mistakes, fix them with your green pen..
4. Check again to make sure that each past-tense form of *BE* agrees with its subject. If you find any more mistakes, fix them with your green pen.
5. How many more mistakes did you fix? _____ Your ability to find and fix mistakes in your own writing shows how much you've learned so far.

Keep your draft of Paper G to use again later.

The following exercises review everything you've learned about present-tense and past-tense verbs in Modules 6-7.

Exercise 7.22	Review: Fixing errors in verb agreement

① Circle each verb, box its subject, and underline each infinitive. ② Correct each error in the space above the line.

Aunt Mattie, like many people over sixty, think that all her young relatives need

to knows how great the good old days was—before TV, when she and her sisters was growing

up. Every Sunday, when my brother Jake watch her coming up the block, he frowns, and mutters that trouble was on the way. She always rush into our kitchen with a big hello, but then she act like a lady preacher. There is a thousand things she like to criticize. While we eat dinner, Auntie M. tries to gets our attention, and if she don't, she thumps the table, demands silence, and begin to preach a sermon against modern times. She says it's a scandal that girls these days is wearing sexy jeans and that boys are kissing girls they don't even know. And there is those boom boxes all over the place! When she was a girl, she declare, things was a lot different. She say life was better when times was harder. And then she asks what I am doing with all the money that I earns. We tries to be polite, but she really test our patience. Jake usually jumps up and leave the room at some point long before Aunt Mattie's final amen. The next time she wants to visit, we are ready to tell her that we has to goes out!

This paragraph contained 25 errors. How many did you find? _____ If you didn't find all 25, try again before you check your work.

Exercise 7.23   Review: Using past-tense verbs

Read this paragraph carefully to make sure that you understand it. ① Circle each verb, and box its subject. ② Mark a piece of paper Exercise 7.23, and rewrite this paragraph onto it, using the **past-tense** form of each verb. ③ Mark your rewritten paragraph as you have learned to.

I am not a suspicious person, but I know that something is wrong. Whenever I leave the house, someone follows me. I never see him, but I know that he is there. I hear the sound of feet behind me when I walk. As I stop to glance into shop windows, I catch a glimpse of someone who stands off to one side, but when I turn around, he is not there. I feel his presence in crowds. As I choose a magazine, he looks over my shoulder. As I buy toothpaste or pay for my groceries, he passes near and counts my change. As I hurry home, I feel his eyes on my back. I go out less and less. He watches me through my windows. When the phone rings, I never answer. I sleep very little. My friends think that I am paranoid, but I wonder if they are in league with him.

Exercise 7.24   Review: Using regular past-tense verbs

This paragraph contains only regular past-tense verbs. ① Circle each verb, box its subject, and underline each infinitive. ② Correct each error in the space above the line.

The 14 leading cars carry tents and equipment, and the next seven transported the animals. In the fading light of June 22, 1918, the crew hitch the four sleeping cars to the end of the train. The flagman signaled to the engineer, and the Hagenbeck-Wallace Circus clatter out of Michigan City. In the wooden sleepers, 300 circus people chatted and play cards, or climbed into their bunks and dream of the next day's opening performance in Hammond, Indiana.

Near the town of Ivanhoe, the circus train pulled into a side track while the crew try to fix an overheated brake box. The Pullman cars extended out onto the main track, so Ernest Trimm, the flagman, propped up emergency flares and check to make sure that the signal lights were flashing warnings. Suddenly, an unscheduled troop train thunder down the track, hurtling toward the circus cars. Asleep at the throttle, Engineer Alonso Sargent never slow down. As the oncoming train pass through the yellow caution lights, Trimm waved his lantern frantically and then hurl it through the engineer's window. But the speeding locomotive rip past the red stop lights and plowed into the fragile wooden sleeping cars, crushing and killing most of the performers. Gas lights started fires in the wreckage, and the animals bellowed in terror as the flames lick toward them. Trapped in their cages, some burn to death. Their roars terrify the townspeople, and hysterical reports traveled from house to house. According to so-called eyewitnesses, lions and tigers jumped from the train and roam the streets.

On the evening after the wreck, though, the circus open on schedule. Performers and acts from all over the country rush to Indiana and substituted for the victims of the crash. For years afterwards, the people of Ivanhoe use to sit around on summer evenings, talking about that terrible night when one exhausted man destroy almost an entire circus.

This passage contained 20 errors. How many did you find? _____ If you didn't find all 20, try again before you check your work.

Exercise 7.25   Review: Using past-tense verbs

This paragraph contains base forms of verbs in capital letters. Read it carefully to make sure that you understand it. ① Box each subject, and underline each infinitive. ② Mark a piece of paper Exercise 7.25, and rewrite this paragraph onto it, using the appropriate past-tense or infinitive form. ③ Mark your rewritten paragraph as you have learned to.

        In the Middle Ages, marriage customs USE to BE strange and cruel, especially for women. While brides BE still in their cradles, their parents USE to ARRANGE their weddings. Sometimes a girl never SEE her husband until they MEET at the altar rail, and all too often this meeting TURN out to BE quite a shock. But no matter how she FEEL about him, the marriage contract MAKE it clear that he HAVE to HAVE an heir. If the wife FAIL to DELIVER a child within a year or two, her husband often USE to GET an annulment, and then he MARRY someone else. The man BE free to TAKE a mistress, but if his wife even LOOK at another man, he BEAT her. Some women THINK that it BE better not to MARRY at all, and CHOOSE to ENTER the convent instead.

Exercise 7.26   Review: Fixing errors in present- and past-tense verbs and infinitives

① Circle each verb, box its subject, and underline each infinitive. ② Correct each error in the space above the line.

        My grandmother grew up in the Depression of the 1930s, when it costed just eight cents to buy a loaf of bread. Even with such low prices, her parents was too poor to put a good meal on the table every day. She and her family seen some really hard times. Since almost everybody were in the same boat, though, they laugh off their troubles, and waited for the economy to recovered. They and their neighbors was right to believe what President Roosevelt always said on his weekly radio broadcasts, that prosperity was just around the corner. Compared to the Great Depression, recent years seem prosperous to most people. Parts of the economy is thriving, and one of my own neighbors have two BMWs and a vacation home. But the lives of many working people today aren't much different from my grandmother's. For example, my nephew, a recent high school graduate, is having a hard time finding a decent job, and not one of his friends own a car. There is people in the middle, like me and my husband. We pay our bills and drive an old station wagon, but our

dream of owning our own home get dimmer and dimmer. Our future seem just as likely to

get worse as it is to get better, as America move into the 21st century.

This passage contained 14 errors in verbs, verb phrases, and infinitives. How many did you find? _____
If you didn't find all 14, try again before you check your work.

Writing Your Final Copy of Paper G

Use your final copy of Paper G to demonstrate what you've learned in Module 7 about using past-tense verbs, and to show how well you're continuing to apply what you've learned previously.

Paper G	Using past-tense verbs
Edit **for Previous Modules**	Use your dictionary and the Rules Summaries for previous modules to: • Check your use of writing conventions. Fix any mistakes with your green pen. • Check the structure of each word-group. If any word-group doesn't have at least one verb, or has a verb without a subject, it is not a sentence. Put brackets [ ] around it. How many word-groups like this did you bracket? _____ • Check the structure of each word-group again. If any word-group doesn't have one simple sentence more than the number of connecting words, it is not a correct sentence. Put brackets [ ] around it. How many word-groups like this did you bracket? _____ • Check your use of nouns and pronouns. Fix any mistakes with your green pen. • Check your use of present-tense verbs. Fix any mistakes with your green pen.
Make Final Copy	Mark another piece of paper Paper G, and write the final copy of your paper on it, or print out a clean copy on your word processor. Be sure to include all your corrections. Mark your final copy as you did your draft.
Proofread	Read your final copy **out loud.** Correct any mistakes neatly by hand. If you used a word processor, enter your corrections, print out a corrected final copy, and mark it again..

Hand in your final copy of Paper G, and the rest of your exercises.

8 Recognizing and Fixing Run-ons

NAME _____

After you finish checking each exercise, fill in your number of mistakes.

8.1 _____	8.4 _____	8.7 _____	8.10 _____	8.13 _____
8.2 _____	8.5 _____	8.8 _____	8.11 _____	8.14 _____
8.3 _____	8.6 _____	8.9 _____	8.12 _____	8.15 _____

EXERCISES
❑ Complete
❑ Incomplete

INSTRUCTIONS
❑ Followed carefully
❑ Not careful enough

CHECKING
❑ Careful
❑ Not careful enough
❑ Green pen not used
❑ Mistakes not corrected

PAPER H
❑ Doesn't follow the instructions; write a NEW Paper H.
❑ Skips some instructions; COMPLETE everything.
❑ Too short; add MORE.

EDITING PAPER H FOR PREVIOUS WORK
❑ Careful   ❑ Not careful enough
EDITING PAPER H FOR THIS MODULE'S WORK
❑ Careful   ❑ Not careful enough
OVERALL EVALUATION OF PAPER H
❑ Excellent   ❑ Good   ❑ Acceptable   ❑ Not acceptable

COMMENTS

Rules Summary for Module 8

8A	A word-group with too few connecting words (or too many simple sentences) is a **run-on**.
8B	Don't confuse **transition words** with **connecting words**.

Run-ons look like this:

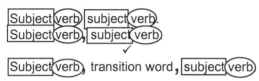

8C	Fix some run-ons by rewriting them as separate sentences.
8D	Fix most run-ons by connecting the sentences with either a **joining word** (to create a compound sentence) or an **expansion word** (to create a complex sentence).
8E	Fix some run-ons with transition words by writing them as separate sentences. Use a **period before** the transition word and a **comma after** it.
8F	Fix many run-ons with transition words by using a **semi-colon before** the transition word and a **comma after** it.

Correct sentences look like this:

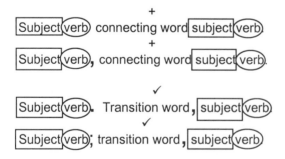

B y applying what you already know about sentences, you can now not only recognize word-groups that are not correct sentences but also learn to rewrite them correctly. These word-groups are usually either **run-ons** (two or more simple sentences run together without the necessary connecting words) or **fragments** (words between a capital letter and a period that lack something they need to be a sentence). In Module 7, you'll learn how to avoid and fix run-ons, and you'll also learn how to write better sentences by using appropriate connecting and transition words.

Rule 3C says:
The number of simple sentences contained in a compound or complex sentence always should be one more than the number of connecting words.

This compound sentence contains two simple sentences and one connecting word.

This complex sentence contains two simple sentences and one connecting word.

If you have one simple sentence, then there can be no connecting words, or else the sentence won't be correct.

Neither of these simple sentences has a connecting word.

If you have two simple sentences, then there should be one connecting word, or else the sentence won't be correct. If you don't have a connecting word with two simple sentences, then there is no connection between them. This is what we call a **run-on**.

This run-on contains two simple sentences and no connecting words.

Putting a comma between the two simple sentences of a run-on doesn't make it correct.

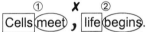

Even though there is a comma here, this is still a run-on. There are still two simple sentences and no connecting words.

Using Module 8 to Edit Your Own Writing

Use Paper H to discover how much you know already about using past-tense verbs. Later in this module, you'll be checking this paper by applying the rules of this module to what you have written.

You may write this paper by hand. Better yet, use a word processor.

Drafting Paper H	*Writing correct sentences*
Assignment	Choose one of these assignments:
	❑ Think of someone who is important to you, and explain why that person is important.
	❑ Think of a personal problem you once had, and explain how it was solved.
Get Ready	On a piece of scratch paper, free write on your chosen topic, first to narrow it to one specific example if necessary, and then to get ideas to use in developing your paper. Don't stop until you have plenty of ideas. Draw a line across the page when you have finished free writing.
	Read over your free writing, and decide on your main point. Write it in one complete sentence below the line.
	Plan your paragraphs by selecting enough supporting ideas from your free writing to make your main point interesting, clear, and convincing to a reader. Write your supporting ideas in a numbered list below your main point.
Draft	On another piece of scratch paper, write an introduction to your draft telling what your main point is.
	Then write at least one paragraph for each of your supporting ideas. Be sure to include enough examples, details, and facts to make your reader understand and believe each idea.
	Write your conclusion.
Revise	Revise your draft, using the four steps in revision listed on the inside front cover to make your paper better. Make sure that you have written at least four paragraphs, including an introduction and a conclusion.

Keep your draft of Paper H to use later.

Recognizing Run-ons

8A	**A word-group with too few connecting words (or too many simple sentences) is a <u>run-on</u>.**

Circle each verb, box its subject, and put a + over each connecting word:

The climate in Cuernavaca is wonderful the sun always shines.

How many simple sentences did you find in this word-group? _____

How many connecting words did you find in this word-group? _____

The number of simple sentences should be one more than the number of connecting words. Is it? _____

In this word-group, the number of simple sentences is two more than the number of connecting words, rather than one more. So this word-group has too few connecting words (or too many simple sentences). This is a **run-on**:

The [climate] in Cuernavaca (is) wonderful the [sun] always (shines)

Now circle each verb, and box its subject, in the following word-group. Put a + over each connecting word:

The climate in Cuernavaca is wonderful **,** the sun always shines.

How many simple sentences did you find in this word-group? _____

How many connecting words did you find in this word-group? _____

The number of simple sentences should be one more than the number of connecting words. Is it? _____

In this word-group, even though there is a comma, the number of simple sentences is still two more than the number of connecting words, rather than one more. So this word-group still has too few connecting words (or too many simple sentences). This is still a **run-on**:

The [climate] in Cuernavaca (is) wonderful **,** the [sun] always (shines)

The kind of run-on where a comma is used is sometimes called a **comma splice** or a **comma fault**. This word-group is incorrect. You can't use a comma to join two simple sentences; only a connecting word can do that. And you can't use a comma to separate two simple sentences; only a period (or a question mark or exclamation mark) can do that. A comma just shows a pause.

Run-ons often occur when a new sentence begins with a **pronoun** like one of these:

I you he, she, it	we they	this that

This happens because the writer is adding another idea onto the first sentence. But you need either a new sentence or a connecting word if the new idea is another simple sentence.

Exercise 8.1   Distinguishing between sentences and run-ons

① Circle each verb (either a one-word verb or a verb phrase), box its subject, and put a + over each connecting word. ② Fill in how many simple sentences and connecting words you found, and check off whether the word-group is a sentence or a run-on.

1. The TV station canceled its regular programs, it was having a fund-raising drive.

   _____ simple sentence(s) with _____ connecting word(s) is a ❑ sentence ❑ run-on.

   The TV station canceled its regular programs because it was having a fund-raising drive.

   _____ simple sentence(s) with _____ connecting word(s) is a ❑ sentence ❑ run-on.

2. Some volunteers were answering phone calls, and others were praising the station.

   _____ simple sentence(s) with _____ connecting word(s) is a ❑ sentence ❑ run-on.

   Some volunteers were answering phone calls, others were praising the station.

   _____ simple sentence(s) with _____ connecting word(s) is a ❑ sentence ❑ run-on.

3. An actor asked for large contributions, he had starred in some popular programs.

   _____ simple sentence(s) with _____ connecting word(s) is a ❑ sentence ❑ run-on.

   An actor who had starred in some popular programs asked for large contributions.

   _____ simple sentence(s) with _____ connecting word(s) is a ❑ sentence ❑ run-on.

4. As telephones rang, he looked into the camera, he pleaded for funds.

   _____ simple sentence(s) with _____ connecting word(s) is a ❑ sentence ❑ run-on.

   As telephones rang, he looked into the camera and pleaded for funds.

   _____ simple sentence(s) with _____ connecting word(s) is a ❑ sentence ❑ run-on.

Remember to use your green pen to check each exercise as soon as you finish it. Write in any necessary corrections, and then write your number of mistakes on the cover page.

You probably had no problem distinguishing between sentences and run-ons in Exercise 8.1. However, when you're reading whole paragraphs, especially paragraphs of your own writing, it's much harder to recognize a run-on. Follow the three steps below to improve your chances of recognizing run-ons:

1. Read the entire paragraph to make sure that you understand its meaning.

2. Without thinking again about meaning, find each word-group that starts with a capital letter and ends with a period or question mark.

3. Look for simple sentences and connecting words within this word-group. If the word-group has too few connecting words (or too many sentences), then it is a run-on.

Use this three-step process in doing the following exercise.

Exercise 8.2	Distinguishing between sentences and run-ons

① Circle each verb, box its subject, and put a + over each connecting word. ② If the word-group is a sentence, write in *SENTENCE*. If it's a run-on, write in *RUN-ON*.

¹ In big cities, taxi driving has changed in recent years.

1 _____

² For one thing, it has become so dangerous that women rarely drive cabs any more, most cabbies are now men. ³ For another,

2 _____

25 years ago most taxi drivers spoke fluent English, today many taxi drivers are immigrants who speak English poorly.

3 _____

⁴ When passengers ask to go to Broad Street, they sometimes end up at Broadway. ⁵ In New York City, taxi drivers must

4 _____

take classes at the Taxi Driver Institute, it teaches geography, American manners, and traffic rules to its immigrant students.

5 _____

⁶ In just a few weeks, they can learn Taxi English, it's a language with only 177 words and phrases.

6 _____

Understanding Transition Words

Transition words are words like *then, also, finally, however, nevertheless, moreover,* and *therefore*. Transition words show the relationship between two sentences, but they **are not connecting words**. As the **transit system** carries passengers from one station to another, **transition words** carry you from the meaning of one sentence to the meaning of the next without actually connecting the two sentences. Like a local bus, you must stop and start again when you use a transition word.

8B	Don't confuse <u>transition words</u> with <u>connecting words</u>.

Transition words are most often used as the first word in a sentence, showing the relationship between that sentence and the previous one.

Lochinvar (was) the most handsome knight at King Arthur's court. However, he (was) not rich.
The transition word *however* is the first word in the second sentence, telling something unexpected about Lochinvar.

213

Because transition words have meanings that are similar to connecting words, they are sometimes confused with them. This confusion causes run-ons.

$+$

Lochinvar was the most handsome knight at King Arthur's court, but he was not rich.
The joining word *but* connects these two related simple sentences into a correct compound sentence.

✗

Lochinvar was the most handsome knight at King Arthur's court, however, he was not rich.
This run-on was caused by confusing *however* with the joining word *but*. Even though it may mean the same thing as *but*, *however* is a **transition word**, and can't connect sentences.

Exercise 8.3   **Recognizing run-ons caused by transition words**

① Circle each verb, box its subject, put a + over each connecting word, and put a ✓ over each transition word. ② If the word-group is a sentence, write in *SENTENCE*. If it's a run-on, write in *RUN-ON*.

¹ Many African Americans became educated and prosperous during the later decades of the 19th century.   1 _____

² However, around 1900 the "Jim Crow" segregation laws were passed, then the social and economic fortunes of all blacks rapidly declined. ³ Under the Jim Crow laws, not even the most   2 _____ gifted blacks were admitted to the better schools, also, they were prohibited from owning property, even if they had more than enough money to buy it. ⁴ They were turned away from   3 _____ restaurants and hotels and forced to sit in the backs of buses and trolleys, moreover, their dignity as human beings was wounded even more deeply by "Whites Only" signs on restrooms, water fountains, playgrounds, and other public facilities. ⁵ Finally,   4 _____ these laws were removed from the books in the 1950s and 1960s after civil disturbances erupted from coast to coast.   5 _____

⁶ Nevertheless, the Jim Crow laws caused psychological and economic scars which are still obvious everywhere in American society.   6 _____

This paragraph contained three connecting words. How many did you find? _____ This paragraph also contained six transition words. How many did you find? _____ If you didn't find all nine, try again before you check your work.

Editing Practice H.1   **Recognizing run-ons**

1. Get your draft of Paper H.
2. Circle each verb (either a one-word verb or a verb phrase), box its subject, put a + over each connecting word, and put a ✓ over each transition word.

3. Review Rules 8A-8B.
4. In the margin, next to each sentence, write the number of simple sentences and connecting words in that sentence, like this: *2 - 1.*
5. If you find any run-ons, put brackets [ ] around them. How many run-ons did you find? _____ Your ability to find these run-ons shows how much you've learned so far.

Keep your draft of Paper H to use again later.

So far in Module 8, you have learned to **recognize** run-ons (two or more simple sentences run together without the necessary connecting words). Now we'll work on learning how to **fix** these run-ons, and how to **write better sentences** by using appropriate connecting and transition words.

Fixing Run-ons I

8C	Fix some run-ons by rewriting them as separate sentences.

The noise goes on for days, it ruins my 4th of July.
This word-group has too few connecting words, so it's a run-on.

The noise goes on for days . It ruins my 4th of July.
The run-on has been fixed by rewriting it as two separate sentences.

Exercise 8.4   Fixing run-ons by rewriting them as separate sentences

① Circle each verb, and box its subject. ② Fix the run-on by rewriting it as separate sentences. ③ Mark your rewritten sentences as you have learned to.

1. Owning a house is a lot of trouble, there are too many expensive problems.

2. Mrs. Kim rents an old house, sometimes something breaks.

3. However, it never costs her anything, she just calls the owner, he fixes everything.

Fixing Run-ons II

Although rewriting a run-on as two or more separate sentences always makes it correct, there's often a better way to fix this kind of mistake. When two or more sentences are written together as a run-on, it's usually because the writer sees a connection between the ideas in them but hasn't used a connecting word to express this connection.

8D	Fix most run-ons by connecting the sentences with either a <u>joining word</u> (to create a compound sentence) or an <u>expansion word</u> (to create a complex sentence).

Let's work first on using **joining words** to fix run-ons.

Rule 3A says:
The joining words *and*, *but*, *or*, and *so* make compound sentences by connecting two or more related simple sentences.

You learned in Module 3 always to use a comma in front of the connecting word in a compound sentence.

You also learned in Module 3 that the joining word *and* joins two ideas that are **similar**, while the joining word *but* joins two ideas that are **contrasted**.

X
Japanese cars used to be very popular, American cars now sell better.
This word-group has too few connecting words (or too many sentences), so it's a run-on.

+
Japanese cars used to be very popular **,** but American cars now sell better.
The run-on has been fixed with the joining word *but*, which shows a contrast between the two parts of the compound sentence. Notice the comma in front of the connecting word.

Exercise 8.5
Using joining words to fix run-ons

① Circle each verb, and box its subject. ② Fix each run-on by connecting the two sentences into a compound sentence, using one of the joining words *and*, *but*, or *so*. Make sure that your compound sentence makes sense. ③ Mark your compound sentence as you have learned to: circle each verb, box its subject, and put a + over each connecting word.

1. The snow was already eight inches deep it was still falling.

   _____

2. Two feet of snow were predicted by morning, people were told to stay home.

   _____

3.   Rajendra worried about leaving the house, he wanted to rent a video.

_____

4.   He decided to go anyway, he started up his car.

_____

5.   He got out of the garage he made it only halfway down the driveway.

_____

6.   His car slid onto his neighbor's lawn, it hit a big oak tree.

_____

7.   Rajendra's trip was very expensive, he never did get to see that video.

_____

Y ou learned in Module 3 how to use **expansion words** to connect related simple sentences by turning one sentence into expansion of the other.

x

The climate in Cuernavaca is wonderful, the sun always shines.
>   This word-group has too few connecting words, so it's a run-on. The ideas in the two sentences are connected; the second sentence is the reason for the first.

+

The climate in Cuernavaca is wonderful because the sun always shines.
>   The run-on has been fixed by connecting the two sentences with the connecting word *because*. This turns the second sentence into expansion that tells **why** the climate is wonderful.

Exercise 8.6	Using expansion words to fix run-ons

① Circle each verb, and box its subject. ② Fix each run-on by connecting the two simple sentences into one complex sentence, using the most appropriate expansion word from the list at the right. Make sure that your complex sentence makes sense. Check off each word as you use it, and use each word only once. ③ Mark your complex sentence as you have learned to: circle each verb, box its subject, put a + over each connecting word, and put parentheses around expansion.

❑ because
❑ even though
❑ until
❑ when

1.   Sandra was nervous, she was supposed to sing a solo in church in a week.

_____

2.   She decided to keep practicing, she could sing her solo perfectly.

_____

3. Sunday arrived, she felt pretty confident.

    _____

4. The organist made many mistakes, Sandra sang beautifully anyway.

    _____

When the second sentence in a run-on begins with a pronoun like *I, you, he, she, it, we,* or *they,* the two sentences in the run-on can usually be connected by using one of the noun-expansion words *who, which,* or *that.* Remember that sometimes the expansion contains **information which <u>is</u> needed** to answer the question *WHICH?* about the noun. In this case, **commas should <u>not</u> be used** around the expansion. At other times, the expansion contains **extra information which is <u>not</u> needed** to answer the question *WHICH?* about the noun. In this case, **commas <u>should</u> be used** around the expansion.

> Yesterday they demolished a building, it had collapsed last year.
> The arrow shows that the pronoun *it* refers to the *building.*

> Yesterday they demolished a building which had collapsed last year.
> The run-on has been fixed with the noun-expansion word *which,* which has turned the second sentence into expansion telling more about the *building.* Because this expansion is needed to tell *which building,* commas are not used.

> Yesterday they demolished a building (which had collapsed last year).
> The parentheses around the expansion *which had collapsed last year* help us to understand the structure of the sentence.

Exercise 8.7	**Using noun-expansion words to fix run-ons**

① Circle each verb, and box its subject. ② Draw an arrow between the two related words. ③ Fix each run-on by connecting the two sentences into a complex sentence, using one of the noun-expansion words *who* or *which,* and using commas if needed. ④ Mark your complex sentence as you have learned to: circle each verb, box its subject, put a + over each connecting word, and put parentheses around expansion.

1. Jerome dropped the rock, it landed on his foot.

    _____

2. We rushed him to the doctor, she said his foot was broken.

    _____

3. She put on a cast, he'd have to wear it for a month.

    _____

4. Jerome always exercised by swimming, he could no longer do it.

    _____

5. The lack of exercise was not good for Jerome, he had always had a weight problem.

    _____

6. Finally the doctor removed the cast she had put it on a month earlier.

    _____

7. Jerome could no longer fit into the swimsuit he had worn it before the accident.

    _____

Remember that this kind of connecting word must be put next to the word it refers to. When the expansion tells more about the subject of the sentence, it comes in the middle of the sentence.

The building has been reconstructed, it had collapsed last year.
    The arrow shows that the pronoun *it* refers to the *building*.

The building which had collapsed last year has been reconstructed.
    The run-on has been fixed with the noun-expansion word *which*, which has turned the second sentence into expansion telling more about the *building*. Because this expansion is needed to tell *which building*, commas are not used.

Putting parentheses around the expansion helps you to see the structure of a complicated sentence like this.

The building (which had collapsed last year) has been reconstructed.
    The parentheses around the expansion *which had collapsed last year* help us to understand the structure of the sentence.

Exercise 8.8	Using noun-expansion words to fix run-ons

① Circle each verb, and box its subject. ② Draw an arrow between the two related words. ③ Fix each run-on by connecting the two sentences into a complex sentence, using one of the noun-expansion words *who* or *which*, and using commas if needed. ④ Mark your complex sentence as you have learned to.

1. That car refused to start again this morning, it was repaired just yesterday.

    _____

2. The battery seemed to be dead, it was just replaced.

    _____

3. The mechanic sent out a tow truck, he repaired my car yesterday.

_____

4. Now the alternator needs replacing, it keeps the battery charged.

_____

5. These constant repair bills are driving me crazy, I have to pay them.

_____

Exercise 8.9 — Fixing run-ons in various ways

① Circle each verb, and box its subject. ② Draw arrows between the related words. ③ On scratch paper, fix each run-on by connecting the simple sentences with the given words. Use commas if needed. Make sure your fixed sentences make sense. ④ Mark another piece of paper Exercise 8.9, and copy your fixed sentences onto it as a paragraph. Mark your paragraph as you have learned to.

1. although — Albert Einstein was perhaps the greatest scientist of all time, he was a very simple human being.

2. who — To his teachers, he seemed a normal child, he grasped things rather slowly.

3. after / because — He became a renowned physicist, his colleagues at Princeton smiled in disbelief when he asked them to pause and repeat their statements, his mind understood new things so slowly.

4. before — He joined the Institute for Advanced Study, he was told to name his own salary.

5. because — The director had to plead with him to accept more money, he asked for such an impossibly small amount.

6. when / which — Famous scientists and world leaders visited him, he greeted them wearing an old sweater, baggy pants, and a pair of sandals, he wore them on all occasions.

7. when / while — Some children came knocking at his door one Christmas Eve, he followed them through the streets of Princeton, he accompanied their carols on his violin.

There should be seven sentences in your corrected paragraph. How many did you write? _____ If you didn't write seven, try again before you check your work.

Exercise 8.10 — Fixing run-ons in various ways

① Circle each verb, box its subject, and put a + over each connecting word. ② Fix each run-on as instructed. ③ Mark your corrected sentences as you have learned to.

1. For the best coffee, you should buy whole coffee beans, they will stay fresh longer than ground coffee.

   As two sentences: _____

   _____

   As one sentence, using *because:* _____

   _____

   As one sentence, using *which:* _____

   _____

2. You should also store them in the freezer, they will stay fresh even longer.

   As two sentences: _____

   _____

   As one sentence, using *so that:* _____

   _____

   As one sentence, using *where:* _____

   _____

3. Then you should grind the beans fresh every morning, this process takes time, it produces the best-tasting coffee.

   As three sentences: _____

   _____

   As two sentences, using *but* in the second sentence: _____

   _____

   As two sentences, using *although* in the second sentence:_____

   _____

4. Finally, you should always use cold water, this will give you the best-tasting coffee.

   As two sentences: _____

   _____

   As one sentence, using *because:* _____

   _____

As one sentence, using *which:* _____

_____

| **Editing Practice H.2** | **Fixing run-ons** |

1. Get your draft of Paper H again.
2. Review Rules 8C-8D.
3. How many run-ons did you find in Editing Practice H.1? _____
4. Draw a line across the page, and below it rewrite each run-on, fixing it by rewriting it as separate sentences, or by connecting the separate sentences with a joining or (preferably) an expansion word into a compound or a complex sentence. Your ability to fix run-ons shows how much you've learned so far.
5. If you found fewer than five run-ons, look back at Paper H, and find some related short, simple sentences. Use connecting words to turn these simple sentences into compound or complex sentences. Change your sentences as necessary so that they sound natural. Write your new sentences below the line, making sure that you have at least five corrected or new sentences.
6. Number these corrected or new sentences in the margin, and mark each one as you have learned to.

Keep your draft of Paper H to use again later.

Fixing Run-ons III

| **8E** | Fix some run-ons with transition words by writing them as separate sentences. Use a <u>period before</u> the transition word and a <u>comma after</u> it. |

x

Lohengrin was the richest knight at King Arthur's court, however, Gwendolyn refused him anyway.

> This run-on was caused by using the transition word *however* as if it were a connecting word.

✓

Lohengrin was the richest knight at King Arthur's court **.** However **,** Gwendolyn refused him anyway.

> The run-on has been fixed by writing it as two sentences, using a period before the transition word *however* and a comma after it.

| **Exercise 8.11** | **Fixing run-ons with transition words** |

Here again is the paragraph you worked on in Exercise 8.3.

> Many African Americans became educated and prosperous during the later
>
> decades of the 19th century. However, around 1900 the "Jim Crow" segregation laws
>
> were passed, then the social and economic fortunes of all blacks rapidly declined. Under

the Jim Crow laws, not even the most gifted blacks were admitted to the better schools, also, they were prohibited from owning property, even if they had more than enough money to buy it. They were turned away from restaurants and hotels and were forced to sit in the backs of buses and trolleys, moreover, their dignity as human beings was wounded even more deeply by "Whites Only" signs on restrooms, water fountains, playgrounds, and other public facilities. Finally, these laws were removed from the books in the 1950s and 1960s after civil disturbances erupted from coast to coast. Nevertheless, the Jim Crow laws caused psychological and economic scars which are still obvious everywhere in American society.

① Mark a piece of paper Exercise 8.11, and rewrite this paragraph onto it, fixing each run-on by writing it as two sentences. You may find it helpful to look back at your answers for Exercise 8.3. ② Mark your rewritten paragraph as you have learned to: circle each verb, box its subject, put a + over each connecting word, and put a ✓ over each transition word.

There should be nine sentences in your rewritten paragraph. How many did you write? _____ If you didn't write nine, try again before you check your work.

8F	**Fix many run-ons with transition words by using a <u>semi-colon before</u> the transition word and a <u>comma after</u> it.**

A transition word shows the relationship between two sentences. And using a semi-colon rather than a period between two sentences suggests that they belong together somehow. So a semi-colon is often the best kind of punctuation to use when you have two closely related sentences and a transition word. But don't forget to put a comma after the transition word.

X
Lohengrin was the richest knight **,** however **,** Gwendolyn refused him anyway.
This run-on was caused by using the transition word *however* as if it were a connecting word.

✓
Lohengrin was the richest knight **.** However **,** Gwendolyn refused him anyway.
Writing a run-on as two sentences is one way to fix it.

✓
Lohengrin was the richest knight **;** however **,** Gwendolyn refused him anyway.
Using a semi-colon is usually a better way to fix a run-on with a transition word.

A semi-colon is either a special kind of period, or a special kind of comma. Which do you think it is?

_____

If a semi-colon were a comma, then the third sentence above would be just like the first sentence, which is a run-on. But the third sentence is correct, just like the second sentence. So **a semi-colon is a special kind of period**. It is the kind of period which is often used between closely related simple sentences with a transition word.

Exercise 8.12	Fixing run-ons with transition words

Here again is the paragraph you worked on in Exercises 8.3 and 8.11.

Many African Americans became educated and prosperous during the later decades of the 19th century. However, around 1900 the "Jim Crow" segregation laws were passed, then the social and economic fortunes of all blacks rapidly declined. Under the Jim Crow laws, not even the most gifted blacks were admitted to the better schools, also, they were prohibited from owning property, even if they had more than enough money to buy it. They were turned away from restaurants and hotels and forced to sit in the backs of buses and trolleys, moreover, their dignity as human beings was wounded even more deeply by "Whites Only" signs on restrooms, water fountains, playgrounds, and other public facilities. Finally, these laws were removed from the books in the 1950s and 1960s after civil disturbances erupted from coast to coast. Nevertheless, the Jim Crow laws caused psychological and economic scars which are still obvious everywhere in American society.

① Mark a piece of paper Exercise 8.12, and rewrite this paragraph onto it one more time, fixing each run-on by writing it with a semi-colon before the transition word, and a comma after it. ② Mark your rewritten paragraph as you have learned to.

There should be six sentences in your rewritten paragraph. How many did you write? _____ If you didn't write six, try again before you check your work.

Here are some of the most common transition words and phrases. Refer to this list when you are trying not only to fix run-ons, but also to make your meaning clearer by showing the relationship between one sentence and the next.

Meaning	Transition words and phrases	Connecting words
shows the order of events or ideas	then, next, first, second, finally, in conclusion, at the same time	and, after, as, as soon as, before, once, until, when, whenever, while
adds more information	also, furthermore, in addition, moreover	and
shows a contrast or a condition	however, nevertheless, on the other hand	but, although, even though, if, though, unless, whereas, whether
shows a cause or an effect	therefore, as a result, consequently, hence	because, for, since, so, so that

illustrates a point	for example, for instance	
emphasizes a point	indeed, in fact, as a matter of fact	

Exercise 8.13   Using transition words and connecting words

① Circle each verb, and box its subject. ② Rewrite the two sentences as one sentence, using the given connecting or transition word. When you use a transition word, use a semi-colon before it and a comma after it. Make sure that your sentences make sense. ③ Mark your rewritten sentences as you have learned to.

1. Americans seem very health-conscious. Most of us eat diets full of sugar and fat anyway.

   but _____

   although _____

   _____

   nevertheless _____

   _____

2. We know that fast food restaurants are unhealthy. We often go there for supper.

   however _____

   _____

   but _____

   _____

   although _____

   _____

3. We eat greasy hamburgers and french fries. We drink sugar-laden soda pop.

   and _____

   _____

   while _____

   _____

   moreover _____

   _____

4. We talk about losing weight. We continue to eat junk food.

    but _____

    _____

    nevertheless _____

    _____

    although _____

    _____

Editing Practice H.3   *Fixing run-ons again*

1. Get your draft of Paper H again.
2. Review Rules 8E-8F.
3. How many corrected or new sentences did you write below the line in Editing Practice H.2? _____
4. Draw another line across the page, and below it rewrite each corrected or new sentence which has an expansion word, using a transition word that means the same thing in place of the expansion word. Use the chart on page 224 above for help. Use a semi-colon before and a comma after each transition word. Your ability to use transition words shows how much you've learned so far.
5. Number these rewritten sentences in the margin, and mark each one as you have learned to.

Keep your draft of Paper H to use again later.

Exercise 8.14   **Review: Fixing run-ons**

Here again is the paragraph you worked on in Exercise 8.2.

> In big cities, taxi driving has changed in recent years. For one thing, it has become so dangerous that women rarely drive cabs any more, most cabbies are now men. For another, 25 years ago most taxi drivers spoke fluent English, today many taxi drivers are immigrants who speak English poorly. When passengers ask to go to Broad Street, they sometimes end up at Broadway. In New York City, taxi drivers must take classes at the Taxi Driver Institute, it teaches geography, American manners, and traffic rules to its immigrant students. In just a few weeks, they can learn Taxi English, it's a language with only 177 words and phrases.

① Mark a piece of paper Exercise 8.14, and rewrite this paragraph onto it, fixing each run-on by writing it as one sentence, using expansion words or transition words. You may find it helpful to look back at your answers for Exercise 8.2. Use the chart on page 224 above for help. ② Mark your rewritten paragraph as you have learned to.

There should be six sentences in your rewritten paragraph. How many did you write? _____ If you didn't write six, try again before you check your work.

Exercise 8.15	Fixing run-ons in a paragraph

This paragraph is punctuated with commas only. Some of the commas are correct, but many others are not. ① Circle each verb, box its subject, and put a + over each connecting word, a ✓ over each transition word, and an ✗ over each comma that is incorrect. ② On scratch paper, rewrite the paragraph, fixing the run-ons by changing each incorrect comma to either a period or a semi-colon, and using capital letters where they are needed. Make sure that your sentences make sense. ④ Mark another piece of paper Exercise 8.15, and copy your rewritten paragraph onto it. ⑤ Mark your rewritten paragraph as you have learned to.

Our ancestors died of many diseases which the modern world knows little about, like bubonic plague and smallpox, in the Middle Ages, bubonic plague killed thousands, in fact, the populations of entire cities died of this scourge, which recurred every few generations, in despair, because they knew that there were no cures, doctors told the officials to lock the city gates, people shuddered when anyone mentioned its gruesome name, indeed, they even nicknamed it "Black Death," up to the 18th century, smallpox was another killer, even if the victims recovered, the pockmarks which it left on their faces disfigured them for life, this disease was particularly dreadful for women, however, modern medicine has discovered vaccines, sanitation, and antibiotics, so that smallpox, like bubonic plague, has become merely a memory, moreover, past successes in eliminating these diseases encourage researchers who now are seeking cures for AIDS and cancer.

Writing Your Final Copy of Paper H

Use your final copy of Paper H to demonstrate what you've learned in Module 8 about recognizing and fixing run-ons, and to show how well you're continuing to apply what you've learned previously.

Paper H	*Writing correct sentences*
Edit for Previous Modules	Use your dictionary and the Rules Summaries for previous modules to: <ul><li>Check your use of writing conventions. Fix any mistakes with your green pen.</li><li>Check the structure of each word-group. If any word-group doesn't have at least one verb, or has a verb without a subject, it is not a sentence. Put brackets [ ] around it. How many word-groups like this did you bracket? ____</li><li>Check your use of nouns and pronouns. Fix any mistakes with your green pen.</li><li>Check your use of present-tense verbs. Fix any mistakes with your green pen.</li></ul>

- Check your use of past-tense verbs. Fix any mistakes with your green pen.

Make Final Copy   Mark another piece of paper Paper H, and write the final copy of your paper on it, or print out a clean copy on your word processor. Be sure to include all your corrections. Mark your final copy as you did your draft.

Proofread   Read your final copy **out loud.** Correct any mistakes neatly by hand. If you used a word processor, enter your corrections, print out a corrected final copy, and mark it again.

Hand in your final copy of Paper H, and the rest of your exercises.

9 Recognizing and Fixing Fragments

NAME _____

After you finish checking each exercise, fill in your number of mistakes.

9.1 _____	9.5 _____	9.9 _____	9.12 _____	9.15 _____
9.2 _____	9.6 _____	9.10 _____	9.13 _____	9.16 _____
9.3 _____	9.7 _____	9.11 _____	9.14 _____	9.17 _____
9.4 _____	9.8 _____			

EXERCISES	INSTRUCTIONS	CHECKING	
❑ Complete	❑ Followed carefully	❑ Careful	❑ Green pen not used
❑ Incomplete	❑ Not careful enough	❑ Not careful enough	❑ Mistakes not corrected

PAPER J
❑ Doesn't follow the instructions; write a NEW Paper J.
❑ Skips some instructions; COMPLETE everything.
❑ Too short; add MORE.

EDITING PAPER J FOR THIS MODULE'S WORK
❑ Careful   ❑ Not careful enough
EDITING PAPER J FOR PREVIOUS WORK
❑ Careful   ❑ Not careful enough
OVERALL EVALUATION OF PAPER J
❑ Excellent   ❑ Good   ❑ Acceptable   ❑ Not acceptable

COMMENTS

Rules Summary for Module 9

9A	A word-group that has no verb, or has a verb without a subject, is a **fragment**.
9B	Fix some fragments by **rewriting** them with an appropriate verb or subject or both.
9C	Fix other fragments by **connecting** them to a sentence.

Fragments without verbs, or with verbs but no subjects, have many forms. Some look like this:

Expansion.
(Verb) expansion

9D	A word-group with too many connecting words (or too few simple sentences) is a **fragment**.
9E	Fix most fragments with too many connecting words by **connecting** them to an appropriate simple sentence.

Fragments with too many connecting words have many forms. Some look like this:

$$+$$
(Connecting word subject (verb)).
$$+$$
Noun (connecting word subject (verb)).

n incorrect sentence is usually either a **run-on** (two or more simple sentences run together without the necessary connecting words) or a **fragment** (a word-group that doesn't have something it needs to be a sentence). You learned in Module 8 how to recognize and fix run-ons. Here in Module 9, you'll learn how to recognize and fix fragments.

Rule 2A says:
Every sentence must have a verb and a subject.

These simple sentences are correct because each has both a verb and a subject.

Creating life.

This word-group is not a sentence because it doesn't have a verb.

And then creates life.

Even though this word-group has a verb, this is not a sentence because it doesn't have a subject.

Using Module 9 to Edit Your Own Writing

Use Paper J to discover how much you know already about writing correct sentences. Later in this module, you'll be checking this paper by applying the rules of this module to what you have written.

You may write this paper by hand. Better yet, use a word processor.

Drafting Paper J	*Writing correct sentences*
Assignment	Choose one of these assignments:
	☐ Think of a social problem (like violence, drugs, poverty, malnutrition, alcoholism, etc.). Describe what causes the problem, how it has affected you and others, and what can be done about it.
	☐ Think of a controversial issue (like drug laws or the death penalty). Describe your position on this issue, giving several reasons why you feel as you do.
Get Ready	On a piece of scratch paper, free write on your chosen topic, first to narrow it to one specific example if necessary, and then to get ideas to use in developing your paper. Don't stop until you have plenty of ideas. Draw a line across the page when you have finished free writing.
	Read over your free writing, and decide on your main point. Write it in one complete sentence below the line.
	Plan your paragraphs by selecting enough supporting ideas from your free writing to make your main point interesting, clear, and convincing to a reader. Write your supporting ideas in a numbered list below your main point.
Draft	On another piece of scratch paper, write an introduction to your draft telling what your main point is.
	Then write at least one paragraph for each of your supporting ideas. Be sure to include enough examples, details, and facts to make your reader understand and believe each idea.

Write your conclusion.

Revise   Revise your draft, using the four steps in revision listed on the inside front cover to make your paper better. Make sure that you have written at least four paragraphs, including an introduction and a conclusion.

Keep your draft of Paper J to use later.

Recognizing Fragments

9A	**A word-group that has no verb, or has a verb without a subject, is a <u>fragment</u>.**

Exercise 9.1	**Distinguishing between sentences and fragments**

① Circle each verb (either a one-word verb or a verb phrase), and box its subject. ② Check off whether the word-group has or doesn't have both a verb and a subject, and whether it is a sentence or a fragment.

1. Information from books, magazines, and the Internet.

   This ❏ has ❏ doesn't have both a verb and a subject, so it is a ❏ sentence ❏ fragment.

   Students get information from books, magazines, and the Internet.

   This ❏ has ❏ doesn't have both a verb and a subject, so it is a ❏ sentence ❏ fragment.

2. Students can access the Internet from computers at school.

   This ❏ has ❏ doesn't have both a verb and a subject, so it is a ❏ sentence ❏ fragment.

   Or from computers at home.

   This ❏ has ❏ doesn't have both a verb and a subject, so it is a ❏ sentence ❏ fragment.

3. Books and magazines may be lost or checked out from the library.

   This ❏ has ❏ doesn't have both a verb and a subject, so it is a ❏ sentence ❏ fragment.

   But are always available on the Internet.

   This ❏ has ❏ doesn't have both a verb and a subject, so it is a ❏ sentence ❏ fragment.

4.   Information available 24 hours a day.

This ❏ has ❏ doesn't have both a verb and a subject, so it is a ❏ sentence ❏ fragment.

Information is available 24 hours a day.

This ❏ has ❏ doesn't have both a verb and a subject, so it is a ❏ sentence ❏ fragment.

Sometimes too much information.

This ❏ has ❏ doesn't have both a verb and a subject, so it is a ❏ sentence ❏ fragment.

Remember to use your green pen to check each exercise as soon as you finish it. Write in any necessary corrections, and then write your number of mistakes on the cover page.

You probably had no problem distinguishing between sentences and fragments in Exercise 9.1. However, when you're reading whole paragraphs, especially paragraphs of your own writing, it's much harder to recognize a fragment. Follow the three steps below to improve your chances of recognizing fragments:

1.   Read the entire paragraph to make sure that you understand its meaning.

2.   Without thinking again about meaning, find each word-group that starts with a capital letter and ends with a period or question mark.

3.   Look for a verb and then for its subject within this word-group. If you can't find both a verb and its subject, then the word-group is a fragment.

Use this three-step process in doing the following exercises.

Exercise 9.2	Recognizing fragments

① Circle each verb, and box its subject. ② If the word-group is a sentence, write in *SENTENCE*. If it's a fragment, write in *FRAGMENT*.

[1] Lawrence used to eat at a local diner.

1 _____

[2] Really enjoyed the great tasting food.

2 _____

[3] Also of course the low prices. [4] Then he read a

3 _____

Health Department report on the kitchen.

4 _____

[5] Roaches, greasy pots, and a filthy refrigerator, all

5 _____

frighteningly obvious. [6] It was hard to believe.

6 _____

[7] But better not to take chances with his health.

7 _____

[8] He found another place to have lunch.

8 _____

Exercise 9.3	More practice in recognizing fragments

① Circle each verb, and box its subject. ② If the word-group is a sentence, write in *SENTENCE*. If it's a fragment, write in *FRAGMENT*.

[1] In the 17th century, religious persecution was spreading in England, France, Holland, and other European countries. [2] To escape this persecution, religious groups emigrating to the New World. [3] Puritans to worship in their simple churches in the New England countryside. [4] Quakers gathered in their meeting-houses in Pennsylvania. [5] Later on, Irish Catholics began sailing for Boston and Baltimore. [6] Each group, alone in its new location, rejoiced in its freedom to practice its faith openly. [7] But after a few decades sometimes refused to extend the same tolerance to newcomers of different religions. [8] By the end of the century, religious persecution becoming nearly as intense in the New World as in the Old.

1 _____
2 _____
3 _____
4 _____
5 _____
6 _____
7 _____
8 _____

Editing Practice J.1	Recognizing fragments

1. Get your draft of Paper J.
2. Circle each verb (either a one-word verb or a verb phrase), box its subject, put a + over each connecting word, and put a ✓ over each transition word.
3. Review Rule 9A.
4. If you find any fragments, put brackets [ ] around them. How many fragments did you find? _____ Your ability to find these fragments shows how much you've learned so far.

Keep your draft of Paper J to use again later.

Fixing Fragments

9B	Fix some fragments by <u>rewriting</u> them with an appropriate verb or subject or both.

✗ Hugh Grant, the actor, an overnight sensation.
This is a fragment, because it has no verb.

Hugh Grant, the actor, became an overnight sensation.
The fragment has been fixed by adding the verb *became*.

Exercise 9.4   **Fixing fragments**

Here again is the paragraph you worked on in Exercise 9.2.

> Lawrence used to eat at a local diner. Really enjoyed the great tasting food. Also of course the low prices. Then he read a Health Department report on the kitchen. Roaches, greasy pots, and a filthy refrigerator, all frighteningly obvious. It was hard to believe. But better not to take chances with his health. He found another place to have lunch.

① Mark a piece of paper Exercise 9.4, and rewrite this paragraph onto it, fixing each fragment by adding an appropriate verb or subject (or both). You may find it helpful to look back at your answers for Exercise 9.2. ② Mark your rewritten paragraph as you have learned to: circle each verb, box its subject, and put a + over each connecting word.

You already know that infinitives (like *to go*) and *ING* words by themselves (like *going*) are not verbs. But changing infinitives and *ING* words into verbs is often a good way to fix fragments without verbs.

> ✗ John in trade school <u>to learn</u> carpentry.
>   This word-group is a fragment because it has no verb.

> John is learning carpentry in trade school.
> John learns carpentry in trade school.
>   These word-groups are correct sentences.

> ✗ I going back home to Bangladesh this summer.
>   This word-group is a fragment because it has no verb.

> I am going back home to Bangladesh this summer.
>   This word-group is a correct sentence.

Exercise 9.5   **Fixing fragments**

Here again is the paragraph you worked on in Exercise 9.3.

> In the 17th century, religious persecution was spreading in England, France, Holland, and other European countries. To escape this persecution, religious groups emigrating to the New World. Puritans to worship in their simple churches in the New England countryside. Quakers gathered in their meeting-houses in Pennsylvania. Later on, Irish Catholics began sailing for Boston and Baltimore. Each group, alone in its new location, rejoiced in its freedom to practice its faith openly. But after a few decades sometimes refused to extend the same tolerance to newcomers of different religions. By the end of the century, religious persecution becoming nearly as intense in the New World as in the Old.

① Mark a piece of paper Exercise 9.5, and rewrite this paragraph onto it, fixing each fragment by adding an appropriate verb or subject (or both). You may find it helpful to look back at your answers for Exercise 9.3. ② Mark your rewritten paragraph as you have learned to.

9C	Fix other fragments by <u>connecting</u> them to a sentence.

Hugh Grant became famous overnight. ✗ And then was arrested
> The second word-group is a fragment because the verb phrase *was arrested* has no subject. It can be fixed by connecting it to the first sentence.

Hugh Grant became famous overnight and then was arrested
> The fragment has been fixed by connecting it to the first sentence.

Exercise 9.6 — Fixing fragments

Read this paragraph carefully to make sure that you understand it. ① Circle each verb, and box its subject. ② Mark a piece of paper Exercise 9.6, and rewrite this paragraph onto it, fixing each fragment by connecting it to an appropriate sentence. ③ Mark your rewritten paragraph as you have learned to.

Some athletes need more than athletic skills to succeed. Especially a black man like Jackie Robinson. He was a superb athlete. Starring in football, basketball, track, and baseball in college. He had been playing baseball for many years. But not of course in the Major Leagues. The racism of many players and owners had limited him to the Negro Leagues. In 1957, however, Branch Rickey, owner of the Brooklyn Dodgers, chose Robinson to break the color barrier. By integrating his team. Robinson could hit, throw, and catch as well as (or better than) most white players. And was a gentleman as well. With a quiet but strong self-control. He needed all his inner strength to resist the taunts of hostile fans and other players. He ignored their curses and threats. And concentrated on proving himself to the world. In just his second year, he was named to the All-Star team. And in his third year became the Most Valuable Player. Jackie Robinson earned the respect of players and fans throughout the country. For both his dignity and his athleticism. He was the right man to integrate Major League baseball. And in 1962 the Baseball Hall of Fame.

Editing Practice J.2 — Fixing fragments

1. Get your draft of Paper J again.
2. Review Rules 9B–9C.
3. How many fragments did you find in Editing Practice J.1? _____
4. Draw a line across the page, and below it rewrite each fragment, fixing it either by adding an appropriate verb or subject (or both), by changing words, or by connecting it to an appropriate sentence. Your ability to fix fragments shows how much you've learned so far.

5. Number these corrected sentences in the margin, and mark each one as you have learned to.

Keep your draft of Paper J to use again later.

Fixing Fragments Caused by Expansion Words

So far you have worked on word-groups that are fragments because they don't have both a verb and a subject. Now let's work on a more complicated sentence problem, word-groups that are fragments even though they do have both a verb and a subject.

Rule 3C says:
The number of simple sentences contained in a compound or complex sentence always should be one more than the number of connecting words.

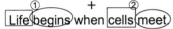

> This sentence is correct because it contains two simple sentences and one connecting word.

If you have one simple sentence, then you must have no connecting words, or else the sentence won't be correct.

> Each of these simple sentences is correct because neither one has a connecting word.

9D	**A word-group with too many connecting words (or too few simple sentences) is a <u>fragment</u>.**

Whenever you have a connecting word with just one simple sentence, then there is nothing for the connecting word to connect the simple sentence to. This is another kind of **fragment**. In fact, this is actually a piece of expansion.

Circle each verb, box its subject, and put a + over each connecting word:

>   If the alarm clock rings.

How many simple sentences did you find? _____

How many connecting words did you find? _____

The number of simple sentences should be one more than the number of connecting words. Is it? _____

In this word-group, the number of simple sentences is the same as the number of connecting words, rather than one more. So this word-group has too many connecting words (or too few simple sentences). This is a **fragment**, actually just a piece of expansion (so we can put parentheses around it):

+

✗ (If the alarm ⬚clock⬚ (rings).)

Now we must modify the three-step process for recognizing fragments that you learned earlier:

1.   Read the entire paragraph to make sure that you understand its meaning.

2.   Without thinking again about meaning, find each word-group that starts with a capital letter and ends with a period or question mark.

3.   Look for a verb and its subject, and look for connecting words, within this word-group. If you can't find a verb with a subject, or if there are too many connecting words, then the word-group is a fragment.

Use this revised three-step process in doing the following exercises.

| **Exercise 9.7** | **Distinguishing between sentences and fragments** |

① Circle each verb, box its subject, and put a + over each connecting word. ② Fill in how many simple sentences and connecting words you found, and check off whether the word-group is a sentence or a fragment.

1.   Although the meeting started late.

 _____ simple sentence(s) with _____ connecting word(s) is a ❑ sentence ❑ fragment.

 Although the meeting started late, it ended early.

 _____ simple sentence(s) with _____ connecting word(s) is a ❑ sentence ❑ fragment.

2.   Because nobody from the Elections Committee attended.

 _____ simple sentence(s) with _____ connecting word(s) is a ❑ sentence ❑ fragment.

 Because nobody from the Elections Committee attended, the meeting ended early.

 _____ simple sentence(s) with _____ connecting word(s) is a ❑ sentence ❑ fragment.

3.   If we don't have an election next week.

 _____ simple sentence(s) with _____ connecting word(s) is a ❑ sentence ❑ fragment.

 We won't be able to meet legally if we don't have an election next week.

 _____ simple sentence(s) with _____ connecting word(s) is a ❑ sentence ❑ fragment.

9E	Fix most fragments with too many connecting words by connecting them to an appropriate simple sentence.

Look back at Exercise 9.7. Notice that the fragments consist of pieces of expansion, while the sentences consist of those same pieces of expansion connected to other sentences. This is how to fix most fragments like these.

✗ When his mother calls

This word-group contains one simple sentence and one connecting word. The expansion word *when* has turned the sentence into expansion.

Lamont comes in immediately when his mother calls.

This sentence is correct because it contains two simple sentences and one connecting word. The number of simple sentences is one more than the number of connecting words.

Exercise 9.8	Fixing fragments

① Circle each verb, box its subject, and put a + over each connecting word. ② Fix each fragment by connecting it to the sentence. ③ Mark your rewritten sentence as you have learned to.

1. Everyone will be able to hear. If the audio system operates properly.

2. However, the audience was getting rowdy. Because they couldn't hear anything.

3. When the audio system gets fixed. Things should calm down.

Fragments can contain even more than one simple sentence. This often makes them seem harder. But marking them in the same way will help you to understand them.

✗ If supper isn't ready as soon as Lamont comes in.

This word-group contains two simple sentences and two connecting words. It has too many connecting words (or too few sentences), so it's a fragment.

Exercise 9.9   Fixing longer fragments

① Circle each verb, box its subject, and put a + over each connecting word. ② Fix each fragment by connecting it to the sentence. ③ Mark your rewritten sentence as you have learned to.

1. Before Bertha arrived. They turned off the lights. Because they wanted to surprise her.

   _____

   _____

2. When Bertha walked in the door and they shouted "Surprise!" She was frightened. So that she dropped her purse.

   _____

   _____

3. The clasp broke. So that everything fell out on the floor, and a small bottle of perfume broke.

   _____

   _____

4. After they cleaned up the mess. Everyone just laughed. Because the presents included a new purse and some perfume.

   _____

   _____

Exercise 9.10   Fixing fragments in a paragraph

Read this paragraph carefully to make sure that you understand it. ① Circle each verb, box its subject, and put a + over each connecting word. ② Mark a piece of paper Exercise 9.10, and rewrite this paragraph onto it, fixing each fragment by connecting it to an appropriate sentence. ③ Mark your rewritten paragraph as you have learned to.

        When the brutal emperor Caligula ruled Rome. He had complete power to do anything. No matter how inhuman. On the hottest days, he often removed the canopies at the outdoor theater. He then refused to let anyone leave. So that the spectators collapsed from sunstroke. When Caligula was sick once, a friend promised to commit suicide. If the gods spared the emperor's life. Later after Caligula got well. He compelled his friend to keep that promise. He forced important administrators to trot beside his chariot. Because he enjoyed making them look ridiculous. When two officials failed to announce his birthday. He removed them from office. And sent them into exile. If he liked the looks of a woman, he took her home with him. Even if she was unwilling. Until he died at the hands of an assassin. Caligula continued to brutalize others. Because

other people's suffering was, for him, the best entertainment.

There should be nine sentences in your corrected paragraph. How many did you write? _____ If you didn't write nine, try again before you check your work.

Fixing Fragments Caused by Noun-expansion Words

Like *when, because, if,* and similar expansion words, a **noun-expansion word** must also connect two sentences, turning one of them into expansion. Any expansion that is not connected to a **sentence** is a fragment (because the word-group has too many connecting words). Putting parentheses around the expansion may help to make the structure of the word-group clearer.

✗ (Which was on sale).
> This word-group contains one simple sentence and one connecting word. It has too many connecting words (or too few sentences), so it's a fragment. Parentheses help to show that *which was on sale* is expansion, which must be connected to a sentence.

✗ The encyclopedia (which was on sale).
> *Which was on sale* tells *which* encyclopedia, but *encyclopedia* is not in a sentence. This word-group still has too many connecting words, and still is not connected to a sentence, so it's still a fragment.

Exercise 9.11 — Recognizing noun-expansion fragments

① Circle each verb, box its subject, and put a + over each connecting word. You may find it useful to put parentheses around expansion. ② Check off whether the expansion is or isn't connected to a sentence, and whether the word-group is a sentence or a fragment.

1. VCRs which are hard to program.

   The expansion ❑ is ❑ isn't connected to a sentence, so this is a ❑ sentence ❑ fragment.

   Most people own VCRs which are hard to program.

   The expansion ❑ is ❑ isn't connected to a sentence, so this is a ❑ sentence ❑ fragment.

2. The time, which constantly blinks 12:00.

   The expansion ❑ is ❑ isn't connected to a sentence, so this is a ❑ sentence ❑ fragment.

   Often they can't set the time, which constantly blinks 12:00.

   The expansion ❑ is ❑ isn't connected to a sentence, so this is a ❑ sentence ❑ fragment.

3. They can't even record programs which they are watching on TV.

    The expansion ❏ is ❏ isn't connected to a sentence, so this is a ❏ sentence ❏ fragment.

    Programs which they are watching on TV.

    The expansion ❏ is ❏ isn't connected to a sentence, so this is a ❏ sentence ❏ fragment.

4. People who invent VCRs which are easier to use.

    The expansion ❏ is ❏ isn't connected to a sentence, so this is a ❏ sentence ❏ fragment.

    People who invent VCRs which are easier to use will make a lot of money.

    The expansion ❏ is ❏ isn't connected to a sentence, so this is a ❏ sentence ❏ fragment.

Remember that sometimes the expansion contains **information which <u>is</u> needed** to answer the question *WHICH?* about the noun. In this case, **commas should <u>not</u> be used** around the expansion. At other times, the expansion contains **extra information which is <u>not</u> needed** to answer the question *WHICH?* about the noun. In this case, **commas <u>should</u> be used** around the expansion.

$$\overset{\textcircled{2}}{} \qquad\qquad\qquad + \ \ \textcircled{2}$$
Effie bought the encyclopedia (which was on sale).
This sentence contains two simple sentences and one connecting word. The expansion is needed to tell *which encyclopedia*, so commas should not be used.

Exercise 9.12   Fixing noun-expansion fragments

① Circle each verb, box its subject, and put a + over each connecting word. ② Fix each fragment by connecting it to the other sentence, using commas if needed. ③ Mark your rewritten sentence in the same way.

1. There once was a Greek mathematician. Who was named Zeno.

    _____

2. He thought of a paradox. Which has puzzled people ever since.

    _____

3. Somebody who wants to cross a room. He has to cross half the room first.

    _____

4. Then he has to cross half of the half. That is remaining.

    _____

5. No matter how far he goes, there still remains half of the distance. Which he has yet to cross.

    _____

6.   How can he ever get to the wall? Which always remains half of some distance away?

_____

| **Exercise 9.13** | **Recognizing noun-expansion fragments** |

① Circle each verb, box its subject, and put a + over each connecting word. ② If the word-group is a sentence, write in *SENTENCE*. If it's a fragment, write in *FRAGMENT*.

[1] Animals have elaborate communication systems which resemble human speech. [2] And which some people describe as language. [3] Certainly most animals communicate fear and sexual desire through movement and sounds. [4] Like the songs that birds sing. [5] Sounds like these do have some of the qualities of human speech. [6] Each melody which we hear signals food, danger, or a sense of territory. [7] Furthermore, tapes of the sounds that dolphins make. [8] These tapes reveal vibrations like the pulses of Navy sonar equipment. [9] Some scientists consider them to be the equivalent of human speech. [10] Also, the complicated dances which bees perform. [11] These dances tell other bees about sources of nectar. [12] Now scientists are studying animals which seem to be able to learn actual human language. [13] A woman who invented a signal system like the finger talk of the deaf. [14] Later she taught it to a chimpanzee which now has a vocabulary of over 100 words. [15] However, not even this smart monkey uses language like that of humans. [16] Language that expresses general and original ideas.

1 _____
2 _____
3 _____
4 _____
5 _____
6 _____
7 _____
8 _____
9 _____
10 _____
11 _____
12 _____
13 _____
14 _____
15 _____
16 _____

| **Exercise 9.14** | **Fixing noun-expansion fragments** |

Look back at the paragraph you worked on in Exercise 9.13. ① Mark a piece of paper Exercise 9.14, and rewrite this paragraph onto it, fixing each fragment, either by connecting it to an appropriate sentence, or by adding, removing, or changing words, and using commas if needed. You may find it helpful to look back at your answers for Exercise 9.13. ② Mark your rewritten paragraph as you have learned to.

Exercise 9.15 — Recognizing various fragments

① Circle each verb, box its subject, and put a + over each connecting word. ② If the word-group is a sentence, write in *SENTENCE*. If it's a fragment, write in *FRAGMENT*.

¹Black ice is a beautiful phenomenon which occurs only rarely. ²Even for people who grow up or live in the country. ³Because it demands three unusual weather conditions which have to come together in a special way. ⁴The first, a period of subfreezing temperature which lasts long enough to create at least six inches of solid ice. ⁵Second, black ice requires a windless atmosphere which leaves the surface of the ice as smooth as glass. ⁶With the slightest breezes, little ripples which ruin the clear transparency that reveals the lake's black depths. ⁷The third condition is the most difficult, because just a half inch of snow will destroy the surface. ⁸By leaving a residue even if it is shoveled. ⁹Sometimes, though, when several freezing, windless, snowless days occur in a row, the miracle happens. ¹⁰Then skaters who fly over the invisible surface. ¹¹And have the sensation of gliding on air.

1 _____
2 _____
3 _____
4 _____
5 _____
6 _____
7 _____
8 _____
9 _____
10 _____
11 _____

Exercise 9.16 — Fixing various fragments

Look back at the paragraph you worked on in Exercise 9.15. ① Mark a piece of paper Exercise 9.16, and rewrite this paragraph onto it, fixing each fragment, either by connecting it to an appropriate sentence, or by adding, removing, or changing words, and using commas if needed. You may find it helpful to look back at your answers for Exercise 9.15. ② Mark your rewritten paragraph as you have learned to.

Exercise 9.17 — Fixing various fragments

Read this paragraph carefully to make sure that you understand it. ① Circle each verb, box its subject, and put a + over each connecting word. ② Mark a piece of paper Exercise 9.17, and rewrite this paragraph onto it, fixing each fragment by connecting it to an appropriate sentence, and using commas if needed. ③ Mark your rewritten paragraph as you have learned to.

In 1935 Charles Richter, an American scientist, developed a scale. That uses numbers to measure the intensity of earthquakes. Few people feel an earthquake that's rated number 1 unless they're very sensitive to faint tremors. Most people do notice a number 2. Even though nothing seems to move. Almost everyone sees and feels the effects of a number 3 earthquake. Which makes hanging objects swing. Beginning with number 4, an earthquake makes sounds. Dishes rattle. Glasses clink. Sometimes they even tumble from the shelf. A number 5 earthquake is frightening. Because it's strong enough to break windows and to crack walls. A number 6 injures people. And can even kill them when loose bricks and weak chimneys come crashing down. A number 7 turns whole buildings into rubble. Which can bury everyone. Who is inside. A number 8 shakes the earth strongly. So that even hills move. Although more violent earthquakes are theoretically possible, none that was stronger than a number 8 has ever been recorded.

There should be 13 sentences in your corrected paragraph. How many did you write?_____ If you didn't write 13, try again before you check your work.

Editing Practice J.3	*Fixing more fragments*

1. Get your draft of Paper J again.
2. Check again to make sure that you have circled each verb, boxed its subject, put a + over each connecting word, and put a ✓ over each transition word.
3. In the margin, next to each sentence, write the number of simple sentences and connecting words in that sentence, like this: *2 - 1.*
4. If you find any more fragments, put brackets [ ] around them. How many more fragments did you find?
   ____
5. Review Rules 9D-9E.
6. Draw another line across the page, and below it rewrite each additional fragment, fixing it either by rewriting it, or by connecting it to an appropriate sentence. Your ability to fix fragments shows how much you've learned so far.
7. Number these additional corrected sentences in the margin, and mark each one as you have learned to.

Writing Your Final Copy of Paper J

Use your final copy of Paper J to demonstrate what you've learned in Modules 8 and 9 about recognizing and fixing run-ons and fragments, and to show how well you're continuing to apply what you've learned previously.

Paper J	*Writing correct sentences*
Edit for Previous Modules	Use your dictionary and the Rules Summaries for previous modules to:

  • Check your use of writing conventions. Fix any mistakes with your green pen.

  • Check your use of nouns and pronouns. Fix any mistakes with your green pen.

  • Check your use of present-tense verbs. Fix any mistakes with your green pen.

  • Check your use of past-tense verbs. Fix any mistakes with your green pen.

- Check the structure of each word-group to find any run-ons. Fix any mistakes with your green pen, either by rewriting them as two sentences, or by connecting them with joining or expansion or transition words, being sure to punctuate them correctly. How many run-ons did you find and correct? _____

Make Final Copy   Mark another piece of paper Paper J, and write the final copy of your paper on it, or print out a clean copy on your word processor. Be sure to include all your corrections. Mark your final copy as you did your draft.

Proofread   Read your final copy **out loud.** Correct any mistakes neatly by hand. If you used a word processor, enter your corrections, print out a corrected final copy, and mark it again..

Hand in your final copy of Paper J, and the rest of your exercises.

NAME _____

After you finish checking each exercise, fill in your number of mistakes.

10.1 _____	10.7 _____	10.13 _____	10.19 _____	10.24 _____
10.2 _____	10.8 _____	10.14 _____	10.20 _____	10.25 _____
10.3 _____	10.9 _____	10.15 _____	10.21 _____	10.26 _____
10.4 _____	10.10 _____	10.16 _____	10.22 _____	10.27 _____
10.5 _____	10.11 _____	10.17 _____	10.23 _____	10.28 _____
10.6 _____	10.12 _____	10.18 _____		

EXERCISES	INSTRUCTIONS	CHECKING	
❑ Complete	❑ Followed carefully	❑ Careful	❑ Green pen not used
❑ Incomplete	❑ Not careful enough	❑ Not careful enough	❑ Mistakes not corrected

PAPER K
❑ Doesn't follow the instructions; write a NEW Paper K.
❑ Skips some instructions; COMPLETE everything.
❑ Too short; add MORE.

EDITING PAPER K FOR THIS MODULE'S WORK
❑ Careful   ❑ Not careful enough
EDITING PAPER K FOR PREVIOUS WORK
❑ Careful   ❑ Not careful enough
OVERALL EVALUATION OF PAPER K
❑ Excellent   ❑ Good   ❑ Acceptable   ❑ Not acceptable

COMMENTS

Rules Summary for Module 10

10A	With modal helping verbs, use the **base form** of the main verb.
1	Modal helping verbs never change to show different tenses.
2	Modal helping verbs never change to agree with their subjects.
10B	With the helping verb *DO*, use the **base form** of the main verb.
10C1	Present-tense verb phrases with *HAVE* tell about something that began in the past, and is still true or is still happening.
2	Past-tense verb phrases with *HAVE* tell about something that was true or happened in the past, **before** something else happened.
3	With the helping verb *HAVE*, use the **past participle** of the main verb. To form the past participle of most **irregular** verbs, change the whole word.
4	To form the past participle of **regular** verbs, add a *D* or *ED* ending.
5	Make necessary **spelling** changes when writing past participles.

Y ou have already learned some basic facts about verb phrases, beginning in Module 3:

- Verbs can be **one word** or more than one word, a **verb phrase**.
- A verb phrase has two parts: a **helping verb**, and a **main verb**.
- The helping verb shows the **tense** of the verb phrase.
- The helping verb, like a one-word verb, must **agree** with its subject in the present tense.
- The main verb tells the **general meaning** of the verb phrase.

You probably use verb phrases in your writing even more often than you use one-word verbs. In the next two modules, you will learn how to form various verb phrases and when to use them to express certain meanings and various time relationships. Here in Module 10, you will work on three common kinds of verb phrases:

- verb phrases with ten special helping verbs called **modals**, to express certain special meanings
- verb phrases with the **helping verb** *DO*, to make negatives, to ask questions, and to emphasize
- verb phrases with the **helping verb** *HAVE*, to make a special kind of past-tense form

Using Module 10 to Edit Your Own Writing

Use **Paper K** to discover how much you know already about using verb phrases. Later in this module, you'll be checking this paper by applying the rules of this module to what you have written.

You may write this paper by hand. Better yet, use a word processor.

Drafting Paper K	*Using verb phrases*
Assignment	Choose one of these assignments:

    ❑ Think of a talented person you know who has a particular ambition, but is getting little or no help from parents, friends, teachers, and others who should be helping. Write the story of this person's striving, including one paragraph for each of these three kinds of information:
- what those who should be helping this person don't do now and have never done in the past
- what this person has accomplished in life so far despite the failure of others to help
- what you think others can, should, and may do to make a difference

    ❑ Think of an elderly woman you know who has raised a family and who now lives alone on a limited income. Write the story of this person's present life, including one paragraph for each of these three kinds of information:
- what her three sons and one daughter had done for their mother before they got married, but don't do any longer
- what her neighbors, friends, and community agencies like Meals on Wheels and the Visiting Nurse Service have done in the past for this woman, but don't do on any regular basis
- what her children and social agencies could, might, and should do as she becomes increasingly helpless

| **Get Ready** | On a piece of scratch paper, free write on your chosen topic, first to narrow it |

to one specific example if necessary, and then to get ideas to use in developing your paper. Don't stop until you have plenty of ideas. Draw a line across the page when you have finished free writing.

Read over your free writing, and decide on your main point. Write it in one complete sentence below the line.

Review the three kinds of information that you will have to include, listed above. Plan your paragraphs by selecting enough supporting ideas from your free writing to provide the required information, and to make your main point interesting, clear, and convincing to a reader. Write your supporting ideas in a numbered list below your main point.

Draft

On another piece of scratch paper, write an introduction to your draft telling what your main point is.

Then write one paragraph for each of the three kinds of information. Be sure to include enough examples, details, and facts to make your reader understand and believe each idea.

Write your conclusion.

Special Instructions

In paragraph #2, use at least six verb phrases with the helping verbs *DO* and *HAVE*. In paragraph #3, use at least six verb phrases with the helping verbs *DO* and *HAVE*. In paragraph #4, use at least six verb phrases with three or more different helping verbs from this group: *will, can, may, must, would, could, might*, and *should*. Underline each verb phrase as you use it.

Revise

Revise your draft, using the four steps in revision listed on the inside front cover to make your paper better. Make sure that you have written exactly five paragraphs, including an introduction, one paragraph for each of the three kinds of information, and a conclusion.

Keep your draft of Paper K to use later.

Verb Phrases with Modal Helping Verbs

Probably the most common helping verb is *will*, which is used for the future tense. *Will* is one of a group of ten special helping verbs called **modals**. These modal helping verbs are used to suggest certain subtle and sometimes confusing meanings.

This diagram shows the general meanings of the ten modal helping verbs:

		general meaning
will	would	future
can	could	ability
may	might	possibility
shall ought to	should	obligation
must		necessity

ATTEND   [They] (will attend) that concert tomorrow.
This sentence says that attendance will occur in the future.

[They] (can attend) that concert tomorrow.
This sentence says that they are able to attend it.

[They] (may attend) that concert tomorrow.
This sentence says that it is possible that they will attend it.

[They] (should attend) that concert tomorrow.
This sentence says that they are obliged to attend it.

[They] (must attend) that concert tomorrow.
This sentence says that it is necessary that they attend it.

The differences in meaning among the modal helping verbs are often very subtle. But the diagram above should help you understand in general how to use these helping verbs.

Verb phrases are frequently interrupted by expansion. Be careful not to circle expansion when you're marking the parts of a sentence.

[I] (will) always (remember) you.
[We] (must) not (forget) each other.
The verb phrases *will remember* and *must forget* are interrupted by *always* and *not*.

Exercise 10.1 — Recognizing modal helping verbs

Circle each verb phrase, and box its subject.

1. SEE   You will see us tomorrow.

2. ACCEPT   Alvin may not accept your nomination.

3. PAINT   I might not paint my house until spring.

4. MEET   You simply must meet Mr. Fowler.

5. REMEMBER   We shall always remember this occasion.

6. FIND   Denise never could find that committee list.

7. FINISH   Can Felix ever finish his homework on time?

8. FORGET   She would never forget your birthday.

9. LEAVE   You should not leave the scissors on that table.

Remember to use your green pen to check each exercise as soon as you finish it. Write in any necessary corrections, and then write your number of mistakes on the cover page.

10A	With modal helping verbs, use the <u>base form</u> of the main verb.

ATTEND   They might attend that concert tomorrow.
Attend is the base form of the main verb *ATTEND*. It would be wrong to use *attends* or *attending* or *attended* in this verb phrase.

Exercise 10.2	Using base forms of main verbs

These sentences contain base forms of main verbs in capital letters. ① Rewrite each sentence, using the appropriate form of the given main verb. ② Mark your rewritten sentence as you have learned to.

1. Your brother can BORROW my motorcycle.

    _____

2. He must RETURN it by Friday.

    _____

3. He should REPLACE the gas he uses.

    _____

Modal helping verbs are different from every other verb in two important ways:

10A1	Modal helping verbs never change to show different tenses.
10A2	Modal helping verbs never change to agree with their subjects.

Modal helping verbs do not have present-tense or past-tense forms. But some of these helping verbs are used as if they had different tenses:

usually used with present-tense verbs	usually used with past-tense verbs
will	would
can	could
may	might

I think that he can do it if he tries.
These verbs all suggest the present tense.

I thought that he could do it if he tried.
These verbs all suggest the past tense.

Exercise 10.3   Using modal helping verbs in different tenses

① Underline the words that show what tense the missing verb should be in. ② Fill in the appropriate modal helping verb. Follow this model:

may / might   They said last year that they _might_ go back home.

                They say this year that they _may_ go back home.

1. will / would   By this afternoon we _____ be ready to go.

                We promised an hour ago that we _____ be ready to go by 3:00.

2. may / might   I think now that I _____ do it.

                Yesterday I thought that I _____ do it.

3. can / could   Last year, students _____ not major in business at that school.

                This year, they _____ major in business or computers.

You learned in Module 6 that present-tense verbs must agree with their subjects. But modal helping verbs don't have different tenses. This is why they don't change to agree with their subjects.

ATTEND   She may attend that concert tomorrow.
               They may attend that concert tomorrow.
       The helping verb *may* is used with both the singular subject *she* and the plural subject *they*.

Exercise 10.4   Writing modal verb phrases

These sentences contain base forms of verbs in capital letters. ① Rewrite each sentence, using the appropriate verb phrase. ② Mark your rewritten sentence as you have learned to.

1.   They WOULD APPRECIATE a card.

_____

     She WOULD APPRECIATE a card.

_____

2.   Alice MIGHT NEED more time.

_____

     Alice and Ray MIGHT NEED more time.

_____

3.   You CAN COMPLETE this form quickly.

_____

     He CAN COMPLETE this form quickly.

_____

Sometimes you hear the modal helping verbs *will* and *would* left out in speech. But be careful never to do this in writing.

BE	✗ I be home for Christmas.
HAVE	✗ I rather have Linda for my teacher.

These sentences are incorrect because the helping verbs have been left out.

BE	I will be home for Christmas. I'll be home for Christmas.
HAVE	I would rather have Linda for my teacher. I'd rather have Linda for my teacher.

These sentences are correct.

The helping verb *will* is usually used to suggest the future. The helping verb *would* is usually used to suggest a desire or preference, often with words like *rather* or *prefer*.

Exercise 10.5   Inserting missing modal helping verbs

① Rewrite each sentence, correcting it by including the missing helping verb *will* or *would*. ② Rewrite each sentence a second time, contracting the verb phrase. ③ Mark your rewritten sentences as you have learned to. Follow this model:

She rather go shopping.
She would rather go shopping.
She'd rather go shopping.

1. She prefer not to talk about that.

_____

_____

2. He be there before midnight.

_____

_____

3. They rather fight than switch.

_____

_____

4. I be home soon.

_____

_____

Editing Practice K.1	*Fixing modal helping verbs*

1. Get your draft of Paper K.
2. In paragraph #4, circle each verb (either a one-word verb or a verb phrase), and box its subject.
3. Review Rules 10A-10A2.
4. In paragraph #4, check each verb phrase with a modal helping verb to make sure that it is correct: that its helping verb does not change to agree with its subject, and its main verb is a base form. Fix any mistakes with your green pen.
5. How many mistakes did you fix? _____ Your ability to find and fix mistakes in your own writing shows how much you've learned so far.

Keep your draft of Paper K to use again later.

Verb Phrases with *DO*

Verb phrases with the helping verb *DO* are probably the second most common verb phrases. You use them in three kinds of sentences:

- to make a statement negative
- to ask a question that can be answered *yes* or *no*
- to make a statement emphatic

Like a one-word verb, the helping verb *DO* changes to show different tenses, and must agree with its subject in the present tense.

DO
> Vincent does a good job.
> Vincent and Keisha do a good job.
> Keisha did a good job.
>
> *Does, do*, and *did* are one-word verbs that show different tenses and (in the present tense) agree with different subjects.

LIKE
> Vincent really does like rap music.
> Vincent and Keisha really do like rap music.
> Keisha really did like rap music.
>
> *Does, do*, and *did* are helping verbs that show different tenses and (in the present tense) agree with different subjects. *Like* is the main verb.

Exercise 10.6	Distinguishing between one-word and helping verb *DO*

Circle each verb (either a one-word verb or a verb phrase), and box its subject.

1. Aurelia usually does very nice work.

    Of course, Kristie sometimes does earn higher job ratings.

2. First I did the dishes.

    I always do try to finish all my chores before watching TV.

3. Those two skaters do perform beautifully together.

    They do the spins in perfect unison.

Exercise 10.7	Making the helping verb *DO* agree in the present tense

These sentences contain base forms of the helping verb *DO* in capital letters. ① Rewrite each sentence, using the appropriate present-tense form of *DO*. ② Mark your rewritten sentence as you have learned to.

1. Rena really DO like Hiroshi.

Both Rena and her sister really DO like Hiroshi.

_____

2. These stereos DO certainly need a few repairs.

_____

That stereo DO certainly need a few repairs.

_____

3. Yes, I DO have a nasty temper.

_____

Yes, she DO have a nasty temper.

_____

The word *not* always interrupts a negative verb phrase.

LIKE   Vincent does not like country music.
            Does like is a verb phrase, interrupted by *not*.

Exercise 10.8 — Recognizing negative verb phrases with *DO*

Circle each verb phrase, and box its subject. Do not circle any interrupting words.

1. Today Delma does not have enough money to buy lunch.

2. Her sisters do not have lunch money either.

3. They did not have lunch money all week.

In questions that can be answered *yes* or *no,* the subject always interrupts the verb phrase.

LIKE   Does Vincent like classical music?
            Does like is a verb phrase, interrupted by the subject *Vincent.*

Exercise 10.9 — Recognizing verb phrases in questions

Circle each verb phrase, and box its subject. Do not circle any interrupting words.

1. Does she want me to call her back?

2. Did you really need a receipt?

3. Do their parents ever return their calls?

In emphatic sentences, an emphatic word sometimes interrupts the verb phrase.

LIKE   Vincent really does like rap music.
Ramona does not really like rap music.
Does like is an emphatic verb phrase, interrupted by *really* in the second sentence.

Exercise 10.10 — Recognizing emphatic verb phrases

Circle each verb phrase, and box its subject. Do not circle any interrupting words.

1. She does always want you to call her back immediately.

2. You do really need your receipt to get that refund.

3. Their parents never did return that call.

10B — With the helping verb *DO*, use the <u>base form</u> of the main verb.

SING   Ophelia really does sing well.
Sing is the base form of the main verb *SING*. It would be wrong to use *sings* or some other form in this verb phrase.

You already know that helping verbs in verb phrases change to show tense and agreement (except for modal helping verbs). Main verbs never change to show tense and agreement. With the helping verb *DO*, main verbs must always be in the base form.

SING   Ophelia does not sing in the chorus.
Ophelia and Ethel do not sing in the chorus.
Ethel never did sing in the chorus.
The helping verbs *does* and *do* show the present tense, and agree with different subjects. The helping verb *did* shows the past tense. The main verb *sing* never changes.

Exercise 10.11 — Writing verb phrases with *DO* in the appropriate tense

These sentences contain base forms of verbs in capital letters. ① Underline the words that show what tense the other verbs should be in. ② Rewrite the sentence, using the appropriate verb phrase. ③ Mark your rewritten sentence as you have learned to. Follow this model:

Mario DO not ever VISIT us <u>while Manuel is away</u>.
Mario does not ever visit us while Manuel is away.
Mario DO not VISIT us last year <u>while Manuel was away</u>.
Mario did not visit us last year while Manuel was away.

1. Joyce and John DO not ENJOY their trip last year.

   _____

   Joyce DO ENJOY traveling when John stays home.

   _____

2. When we bought these chairs, they DO not NEED repairs.

   _____

   Even now one of them still DO not NEED repairs.

   _____

3. DO those stores OFFER senior discounts last week?

   _____

   DO those stores still OFFER discounts on unpopular items?

   _____

The helping verb *DO* is often contracted with *not* in a negative verb phrase.

   LIKE   Vincent doesn't like that new band.
              Does like is a verb phrase, interrupted by the contraction *n't*.

Exercise 10.12   Writing negative sentences with contractions

① Circle each verb, and box its subject. ② Rewrite each sentence, making it negative, and contracting *not* with the helping verb *DO*. Be careful not to change the tense of the sentence. ③ Mark your rewritten sentence as you have learned to. Do not circle any interrupting words. Follow this model:

   Her husband traveled a lot.
   Her husband doesn't travel a lot.

1. Those new shirts look good on you.

   _____

2. This typewriter works well.

   _____

3. That teacher tried to help.

   _____

Exercise 10.13 — Writing negative contractions

Read this paragraph carefully to make sure that you understand it. ① Circle each verb, and box its subject. ② Mark a piece of paper Exercise 10.13, and rewrite this paragraph onto it, making each sentence negative and contracting *not* with the helping verb *DO*. Your paragraph will begin *Marjorie doesn't always...* ③ Mark your rewritten paragraph as you have learned to.

Marjorie always impresses me with her skill at tennis. She certainly understands how to keep her opponents off balance. Her drop shots, for example, often catch them off guard. And after a drop shot, she hits long. Her serves usually land deep in the court, and her opponents find it hard to return them. Her friends want her as a partner and fear her as an opponent. All in all, Marjorie's skill on the tennis court really overwhelms me.

Exercise 10.14 — Writing negative questions with contractions

① Circle each verb, and box its subject. ② Rewrite each sentence as a negative question, contracting *not* with the helping verb *DO*. ③ Mark your rewritten sentence in the same way. Follow this model:

Her husband travels a lot.
Doesn't her husband travel a lot?

1. Those new shirts look good on you.

_____

2. This typewriter worked well.

_____

3. That teacher tries to help.

_____

Editing Practice K.2 — Fixing verb phrases with DO

1. Get your draft of Paper K again.
2. In paragraphs #2-#3, circle each verb (either a one-word verb or a verb phrase), and box its subject.
3. Review Rule 10B.
4. In paragraphs #2-#4, check each verb phrase with *DO* to make sure that it is correct: that its helping verb is in the correct tense and (in the present tense) agrees with its subject, and its main verb is a base form. Fix any mistakes with your green pen.
5. How many more mistakes did you fix? _____ Your ability to find and fix mistakes in your own writing shows how much you've learned so far.

Keep your draft of Paper K to use again later.

Verb Phrases with *HAVE*

Verb phrases with the helping verb *HAVE* are also very common. You use them to show two special kinds of past tenses.

Like a one-word verb, the helping verb *HAVE* changes to show different tenses, and must agree with its subject in the present tense.

HAVE

> Priscilla has a new car.
> Priscilla and Susan have new cars.
> Priscilla had a new car.

Has, have, and *had* are one-word verbs that show different tenses and (in the present tense) agree with different subjects.

BUY

> Priscilla has bought a new car.
> Priscilla and Susan have bought new cars.
> Priscilla had bought a new car before she moved away.

Has, have, and *had* are helping verbs that show different tenses, and (in the present tense) agree with different subjects. *Bought* is the main verb.

Exercise 10.15   Distinguishing between one-word and helping verb *HAVE*

Circle each verb (either a one-word verb or a verb phrase), and box its subject.

1.   Someone has my notebook.

Someone has taken my notebook by mistake.

2.   No one had the answer.

No one had answered the last question before the end of the hour.

3.   Many cities have financial problems.

Many cities have grown smaller in population recently.

Exercise 10.16   Making the helping verb *HAVE* agree in the present tense

These sentences contain base forms of the helping verb *HAVE* in capital letters. ① Rewrite each sentence, using the appropriate present-tense form of *HAVE*. ② Mark your rewritten sentence as you have learned to.

1.   Poland HAVE begun to trade with the West.

_____

Poland and Czechoslovakia HAVE begun to trade with the West.

_____

2.   Pavel HAVE beaten the computer at chess seven times.

_____

Most of the time the computer HAVE beaten me at chess.

_____

3.   My brother HAVE had to borrow money.

_____

I HAVE had to borrow money.

_____

In Module 9, you learned that one-word verbs in the past tense tell about something that happened once in the past, but is now finished. Verb phrases with *HAVE* are a more complicated kind of past-tense verb.

LEAVE   Last night Honoria left early.
           The one-word verb *left* tells us that Honoria did something last night.

LEAVE   Honoria often has left our parties early.
           Honoria had left before I arrived.
           The verb phrases *has left* and *had left* express a more complicated relationship to the past than the simple one-word verb *left*.

10C1	**Present-tense** verb phrases with *HAVE* tell about something that began in the past, and is still true or is still happening.

Present-tense verb phrases with *HAVE* are usually used with time words like *since* a time or *for* a period of time. Time words like these emphasize that what you're talking about began sometime in the past, and is still true or is still happening now. This is sometimes called the **present perfect** tense.

BE   Since 1995, the stock market has been bullish.
           For the past few months, the stock market has been bullish.
           The present-tense verb phrase *has been* shows that the stock market's bullish behavior began in the past and is still true or is still happening in the present.

10C2	**Past-tense** verb phrases with *HAVE* tell about something that was true or happened in the past, <u>before</u> something else happened.

Past-tense verb phrases with *HAVE* are usually used with time words like *before* a time in the past, or *until* a time in the past. Time words like these emphasize that what you're talking about began in the past, and was still true or was still happening, but then something else happened. This is sometimes called the **past perfect** tense.

Time words in sentences like these are often pieces of expansion, with a connecting word, a verb, and a subject.

> BE   Until the war started, jobs had been scarce.
> The past-tense verb phrase *had been* shows that jobs were scarce during the period before the war began.

> RECOVER   Before the war ended, the economy had recovered.
> The past-tense verb phrase *had recovered* shows that the economy recovered during the period when the war was still occurring.

Exercise 10.17   Using verb phrases with *HAVE* in the appropriate tense

These sentences contain base forms of the helping verb *HAVE* in capital letters. ① Underline the words that show what tense the verb phrase should be in. ② Rewrite the sentence, using the appropriate tense of *HAVE*. ③ Mark your rewritten sentence as you have learned to.

1.   Before the 1995 Oklahoma City bombing, many people HAVE defended complete freedom of speech.

_____

      Since the bombing, those same people HAVE been less ready to defend it.

_____

2.   This town HAVE had almost no commercial development up until the Civil War.

_____

      But it HAVE become famous for its antique shops since then.

_____

3.   Just before that big storm last winter, Jonas HAVE put a new roof on his house.

_____

      He HAVE had a much dryer house for the last year.

_____

4.   Since 1998, I HAVE sold women's shoes.

_____

      Up until 1997, I HAVE hoped to be a professional basketball player.

_____

5.   Sampson HAVE been a suspect in this murder case until Gelman was arrested.

_____

Sampson HAVE been a suspect in three murder cases for the last seven years.

_____

10C3	**With the helping verb *HAVE*, use the <u>past participle</u> of the main verb.** **To form the past participle of most <u>irregular</u> verbs, change the whole word.**

GO   We have gone to the movies twice this week already.
Gone is the past participle of the irregular verb *GO.*

Usually you can't predict what the past participle of an irregular verb will be, so if you don't already know it, you'll have to look it up in your dictionary. Follow the four steps below to practice this now.

1.   Get your dictionary. If you don't have it, don't go on until you do have it.

2.   Look up the irregular verb *SING.* Be sure to find the word with the label *v* for *verb.*

3.   How many other forms are listed? _____

•   Usually three other forms are listed. *Sings* may be listed also, to remind you that verbs must agree with their subjects in the present tense.

4.   Write in the three other forms of *SING* (ignore *sings* if it's listed):

SING   _____   _____   _____

•   The 1st form *sing* (or *sings*) is used in the present tense.
•   The 2nd form *sang* is used in the past tense.
•   The 3rd form *sung* is the past participle.
•   The 4th form *singing* is the *ING* form.

You learned in **Module 9** that, for some irregular verbs, the past-tense form and the past participle are the same.

BRING   I <u>brought</u>   I have <u>brought</u>
BRING has the same past-tense and past participle forms.

For other irregular verbs, the past-tense form and the past participle are different.

SWIM   I <u>swam</u>   I have <u>swum</u>
SWIM has different past-tense and past participle forms.

Exercise 10.18   Comparing past-tense forms to past participles

① Get your dictionary. ② Look up each verb, and write in the past-tense form and the past participle.

	past-tense form	past participle
1. SEE	_____	_____
2. GO	_____	_____
3. BUY	_____	_____
4. PAY	_____	_____
5. HAVE	_____	_____
6. BE	_____	_____

Exercise 10.19   Writing verb phrases with irregular main verbs

These sentences contain base forms of verbs in capital letters. ① Underline the words that show what tense the verb phrase should be in. ② Rewrite each sentence, using the appropriate verb phrase. ③ Mark your rewritten sentence as you have learned to. Follow this model:

<u>Before 1970</u>, American manufacturers HAVE SELL more cars than anyone else.
Before 1970, American manufacturers had sold more cars than anyone else.

1. By the end of the 1970s, though, sales of American cars HAVE GO down.

    _____

2. Before we knew it, Japan HAVE TAKE the lead.

    _____

3. By the end of the 1980s, prices HAVE RISE, and profits HAVE SHRINK.

    _____

4. Up until 1990, American companies HAVE CHOOSE to ignore the problem.

    _____

5. Lately, however, we HAVE HAVE to change our old ways.

    _____

6.   Consequently, the trade outlook for the USA HAVE BE more encouraging recently.

_____

7.   But at this time, Congress still HAVE not DO enough about this problem.

_____

10C4	To form the past participle of <u>regular</u> verbs, add a *D* or *ED* ending.

WALK   I walked to work today.
             I have walked to work every day this week.
             Walked is both the past-tense form and the past participle of the regular verb *WALK*.

Exercise 10.20	**Using verb phrases with regular main verbs**

These sentences contain base forms of verbs in capital letters. ① Underline the words that show what tense the verb phrase should be in. ② Rewrite each sentence, using the appropriate verb phrase. ③ Mark your rewritten sentence as you have learned to.

1.   Up until the 1950s, infant mortality HAVE INCREASE slowly.

_____

2.   But since then, doctors HAVE LEARN how to save premature babies.

_____

3.   For the last 50 years, modern medicine HAVE PREVENT many childhood diseases.

_____

Exercise 10.21	**Fixing errors in past participles of regular verbs**

① Circle each verb phrase, and box its subject. ② Correct each error in the space above the line.

        Over the centuries, *triskaidekaphobia,* the fear of the number 13, has terrorize many

people, and has cause them to act in strange ways. In all ages and in all countries, people

have refuse to hold celebrations on the 13th of the month, and in some societies, they have

drown children born on this evil day. Recently, architects have learn to deal with

triskaidekaphobia by giving the number 14 to the floor after 12. In this way, also, hospitals have trick patients into accepting beds on the 13th floor. Yet despite this superstition, for two

centuries Americans have saluted a flag with 13 stripes, and immigrants have flock from all

over the world to pledge allegiance to it.

This paragraph contained seven errors. How many did you find? _____ If you didn't find all seven, try again before you check your work.

10C5	**Make necessary <u>spelling</u> changes when writing past participles.**

Rule 1G2 says:
**Change *Y* to *I* before adding *ED* if a word ends with a <u>consonant</u> + *Y*,
but never change *Y* to *I* if the word ends with a <u>vowel</u> + *Y*.**

Rule 1G3 says:
If a word ends with a single vowel + a consonant, double the consonant before adding *ED*.

Exercise 10.22	**Using verb phrases with spelling changes**

This paragraph contains base forms of verbs in capital letters. Read it carefully to make sure that you understand it. ① Mark a piece of paper Exercise 10.22, and rewrite this paragraph onto it, using the appropriate **present-tense** verb phrases. ③ Mark your rewritten paragraph as you have learned to.

This winter, some serious accidents HAVE OCCUR in my apartment building.
Several elderly tenants HAVE SLIP on icy sidewalks. They HAVE APPLY to the landlord
for compensation. Because he HAVE DENY any responsibility, the tenants organization
HAVE PLAN a protest meeting for next week.

Be careful not to confuse the simple one-word present tense (used for something that is usually true or usually happens) and present-tense verb phrases with *HAVE* (used to tell about something that began in the past, and is still true or is still happening, and used usually with time words like *since* a time or *for* a period of time).

Exercise 10.23	**Using the appropriate present-tense form of a verb**

These sentences contain base forms of verbs in capital letters. ① Write each sentence with the appropriate one-word present-tense verb or verb phrase with *HAVE*. ② Mark your rewritten sentences as you have learned to, and underline the time words in the sentence with the verb phrase. Follow this model:

Dorothea BE a social worker in Glen River Junction.
Dorothea is a social worker in Glen River Junction.
Dorothea BE a social worker since 1995.
Dorothea has been a social worker since 1995.

1.   Dr. Deer SPECIALIZE in treating hantavirus disease.

Dr. Deer SPECIALIZE in this disease for eight years.

_____

2.   In recent decades, attitudes toward sex CHANGE radically.

_____

Sexual behavior sometimes CHANGE more slowly than attitudes.

_____

3.   The high rate of crime in the USA sometimes DISCOURAGE tourism.

_____

The murder of several tourists DISCOURAGE tourism in Florida since 1997.

_____

4.   Our newly widowed friend BE in a state of shock.

_____

Since his wife's death, our friend BE in a state of shock.

_____

Be especially careful not to confuse the simple one-word past tense (used for something that happened once in the past, but is now finished) and past-tense verb phrases with *HAVE* (used to tell about something that was true or happened in the past, before something else happened).

WATCH   Last night we watched two movies.
            Watched is in the correct tense to tell about something that happened once in the past.

                                  ✗
WATCH   Last night we had watched two movies.
            The past-tense verb phrase *had watched* is not correct to tell about something that happened once in the past.

WATCH   Last night we had watched two movies already before she arrived.
            Had watched is used correctly to tell about something that happened in the past before something else.

Exercise 10.24	Using the appropriate past-tense form of a verb

These sentences contain base forms of verbs in capital letters. ① Write each sentence with the appropriate one-word past-tense verb or verb phrase with *HAVE*. ② Mark your rewritten sentences as you have learned to, and underline the time words in the sentence with the verb phrase. Follow this model:

Last Saturday we GO to the mall.
Last Saturday we went to the mall.
We already GO there twice earlier that week.
We already had gone there twice earlier that week.

1. In the early 1990s, we SEE sudden changes in Eastern Europe.

    _____

    Until then, we SEE nothing to warn us about this turn of events.

    _____

2. In 1990, the two Germanys once more BECOME one nation.

    _____

    Before that, several Communist countries BECOME democracies.

    _____

3. The people of Vienna BURY Beethoven with pomp and ceremony.

    _____

    Several decades earlier, they BURY Mozart in a pauper's grave.

    _____

4. In his first year in office, President Clinton RAISE taxes.

    _____

    But three years earlier, President Bush RAISE them even more.

    _____

5. Until the invention of synthetic fibers, housewives SPEND many hours ironing.

    _____

    My grandmother SPEND every Tuesday ironing back in the 1950s.

    _____

6. Before the cold weather, my daughter's health BE fine.

    _____

But she BE quite ill in January.

_____

| **Editing Practice K.3** | **Fixing verb phrases with HAVE** |

1. Get your draft of Paper K again.
2. Review Rules 10C1-10C5.
3. In paragraphs #2-4, check each verb phrase with *HAVE* to make sure that it is correct: that its helping verb is in the correct tense and (in the present tense) agrees with its subject, and that its main verb is a past participle and is correctly spelled. Fix any mistakes with your green pen.
4. How many more mistakes did you fix? _____ Your ability to find and fix mistakes in your own writing shows how much you've learned so far.

Keep your draft of Paper K to use again later.

Remember that, whether a sentence has time words or not, each verb must be in the tense that is appropriate to its meaning. Because the meanings of present-tense and past-tense verb phrases with *HAVE* are subtle, you must be especially careful when using them with other verbs.

> The house where we <u>have lived</u> for 30 years <u>belongs</u> to my uncle.
>> This sentence means that we are still living there, and that it still belongs to my uncle.

> The house where we <u>had lived</u> for 30 years <u>belongs</u> to my uncle now.
>> This sentence means that we aren't living there any longer.

> The house where we <u>have lived</u> for 30 years <u>belonged</u> to my uncle once.
>> This sentence means that it doesn't belong to my uncle any longer.

> The house where we <u>had lived</u> for 30 years <u>belonged</u> to my uncle then.
>> This sentence means that we aren't living there any longer, and that it doesn't belong to my uncle any longer.

| **Exercise 10.25** | **Using appropriate tenses of verb phrases with HAVE** |

① Underline the words that show what tense the verb phrase should be in. ② Rewrite each sentence, using a verb phrase with *HAVE* in the appropriate tense. ③ Mark your rewritten sentence as you have learned to, and underline the time words in the sentence with the verb phrase. Follow this model:

> Dillard BE my favorite uncle <u>until he got married</u>.
> *Dillard had been my favorite uncle until he got married.*
> Campbell BE my favorite uncle <u>since last year</u>.
> *Campbell has been my favorite uncle since last year.*

1. Pilar LIKE Rafael for six months.

_____

Pilar LIKE Tomas until she saw him with Emilia.

_____

2. Ruby and Dee BE friends for years; they live next door to one another.

    _____

    Ruby and Vikki BE best friends until Vikki married Ruby's brother.

    _____

3. Stavros TAKE the bus to work every day this week.

    _____

    Stavros TAKE his bicycle to work, until somebody stole it.

    _____

4. My sister BAKE three sweet potato pies so far this week.

    _____

    My sister already BAKE two apple pies before we arrived at her house last night.

    _____

Exercise 10.26	**Using verb phrases with *HAVE***

Read this paragraph carefully to make sure that you understand it. ① Circle each verb, and box its subject. ② Mark a piece of paper Exercise 10.26, and rewrite this paragraph onto it, using present-tense verb phrases with the helping verb *HAVE*. Your paragraph will begin *For the past three months, Heinrich Schlegel, the retired school headmaster, has visited...* ③ Mark your rewritten paragraph as you have learned to.

Every morning at 10am, Heinrich Schlegel, the retired school headmaster, visits the west bank of the blue Danube. His neighbors notice that Hilde Hindenberg, the banker's widow, goes to the same spot at almost the same hour. Behind their shuttered windows these nosy neighbors whisper about the secret meetings. But all this gossip is nonsense. Whenever these two go to the embankment, they sit about three meters apart. The widow closes her eyes for a snooze. The headmaster waits for her first snore before he rolls up his pants to the knee for a sunbath. Then he buries his head in a book, while she snores gently on. If he feels the slightest interest in her plump form, he certainly never gives any sign of it.

Exercise 10.27 — Using various tenses appropriately

① Circle each verb, and box its subject. ② Rewrite each sentence, using the given time words, and changing each verb as appropriate. ③ Mark your rewritten sentences in the same way. Follow this model:

Now, Charles acts on Broadway.
Last year, *Charles acted on Broadway.*
For the past year, *Charles has acted on Broadway.*
Until he broke his arm, *Charles had acted on Broadway.*

1. Every day, Minnie drives to work.

   Last week, _____

   For the past month, _____

   Until she wrecked her car, _____

2. This year, Pedro is the store manager.

   Last year, _____

   For the last five years, _____

   Before the store was closed, _____

3. Noreen reads romance magazines and writes in her diary.

   Last month, _____

   For the last six months, _____

   Until she eloped, _____

Exercise 10.28 — Using appropriate tenses

① Circle each verb, and box its subject. ② Rewrite the paragraph, using the given time words, and changing each verb as appropriate. ③ Mark your rewritten paragraphs in the same way.

Every day Charlene makes her rounds as a traffic patrol officer. She checks parking meters, and she writes tickets for violators. Drivers often are angry with her. But Charlene never relents, for she is proud of her reputation as a heartless meter maid.

1. Last week, _____

_____

_____

_____

_____

2. For the last six months, _____

_____

_____

_____

_____

3. Until a driver attacked her, _____

_____

_____

_____

_____

_____

_____

Editing Practice K.4	*Fixing various verb phrases*

1. Get your draft of Paper K again.
2. Check again to make sure that you have circled each verb, and boxed its subject. If you find any more verbs or subjects, mark them with your green pen.
3. Check again to make sure that each verb phrase is correct: that its helping verb is in the correct tense and (in the present tense) agrees with its subject, and that its main verb is in the correct form and is correctly spelled. Fix any mistakes with your green pen.
4. How many more mistakes did you fix? _____ Your ability to find and fix mistakes in your own writing shows how much you've learned so far.

Writing Your Final Copy of Paper K

Use your final copy of Paper K to demonstrate what you've learned in Module 10 about verb phrases, and to show how well you're continuing to apply what you've learned previously.

Paper K	*Using verb phrases*
Edit **for Previous Modules**	Use your dictionary and the Rules Summaries for previous modules to: • Check your use of writing conventions. Fix any mistakes with your green pen. • Check your use of nouns and pronouns. Fix any mistakes with your green pen. • Check your use of present-tense verbs. Fix any mistakes with your green pen. • Check your use of past-tense verbs. Fix any mistakes with your green pen. • Check the structure of each word-group to find any run-ons. Fix any mistakes with your green pen, either by rewriting them as two sentences, or by connecting them with joining or expansion or transition words, being sure to punctuate them correctly. How many run-ons did you find and correct? _____ • Check the structure of each word-group to find any fragments. Fix any mistakes with your green pen, either by connecting them to an appropriate sentence, or by adding, removing, or changing words. How many fragments did you find and correct? _____
Make Final Copy	Mark another piece of paper Paper K, and write the final copy of your paper on it, or print out a clean copy on your word processor. Be sure to include all your corrections. Mark your final copy as you did your draft.
Proofread	Read your final copy **out loud**. Correct any mistakes neatly by hand. If you used a word processor, enter your corrections, print out a corrected final copy, and mark it again.

Hand in your corrected Paper K, and the rest of your exercises.

11 Mastering Verb Phrases II

NAME _____

After you finish checking each exercise, fill in your number of mistakes.

11.1 _____	11.6 _____	11.11 _____	11.16 _____	11.21 _____
11.2 _____	11.7 _____	11.12 _____	11.17 _____	11.22 _____
11.3 _____	11.8 _____	11.13 _____	11.18 _____	11.23 _____
11.4 _____	11.9 _____	11.14 _____	11.19 _____	
11.5 _____	11.10 _____	11.15 _____	11.20 _____	

EXERCISES
- ❑ Complete
- ❑ Incomplete

INSTRUCTIONS
- ❑ Followed carefully
- ❑ Not careful enough

CHECKING
- ❑ Careful
- ❑ Not careful enough
- ❑ Green pen not used
- ❑ Mistakes not corrected

PAPER L
- ❑ Doesn't follow the instructions; write a NEW Paper L.
- ❑ Skips some instructions; COMPLETE everything.
- ❑ Too short; add MORE.

EDITING PAPER L FOR THIS MODULE'S WORK
- ❑ Careful
- ❑ Not careful enough

EDITING PAPER L FOR PREVIOUS WORK
- ❑ Careful
- ❑ Not careful enough

OVERALL EVALUATION OF PAPER L
- ❑ Excellent ❑ Good ❑ Acceptable ❑ Not acceptable

COMMENTS

Rules Summary for Module 11

11A	Use the helping verb *BE* and the *ING* form of the main verb to tell about something happening **over a period of time**.
1	Make necessary **spelling** changes when writing *ING* forms of main verbs.
11B	Use the helping verb *BE* and the past participle of the main verb in a **passive** sentence.

In Module 10, you learned how to form and use verb phrases with modal helping verbs, with the helping verb *DO*, and with the helping verb *HAVE*. Here in Module 11, you'll learn how to form and use two different kinds of verb phrases with the helping verb *BE*:

- verb phrases used in active sentences
- verb phrases used in passive sentences

Verb Phrases with *BE*

Like *DO* and *HAVE*, *BE* can be either a one-word verb or a helping verb in a verb phrase. Like a one-word verb, the helping verb *BE* changes to show different tenses, and must agree with its subject in both the past and present tenses.

BE
    Shelley is happy.
    Shelley and Carmen are happy.
    Was Shelley happy?
    Were Shelley and Carmen happy?
      Is, are, was, and *were* are one-word verbs, and the sentences are about **being**.

SING
    Shelley is singing a folk song.
    Shelley and Carmen are singing a folk song.
    Was Shelley singing a folk song?
    Were Shelley and Carmen singing a folk song?
      Is, are, was, and *were* are helping verbs, and *singing* is the main verb. The sentences are about **singing**.

Exercise 11.1	Distinguishing between one-word and helping verb *BE*

Circle each verb (either a one-word verb or a verb phrase), and box its subject.

1. Charlotte is an excellent pianist.

   Charlotte is playing the piano in the studio.

2. I am ready to leave.

   I am going to the store.

3. It was snowing last night.

   The temperature was below freezing.

Remember to use your green pen to check each exercise as soon as you finish it. Write in any necessary corrections, and then write your number of mistakes on the cover page.

Using Module 11 to Edit Your Own Writing

Use Paper L to discover how much you know already about using verb phrases with the helping verb *BE*. Later in this module, you'll be checking this paper by applying the rules of this module to what you have written.

You may write this paper by hand. Better yet, use a word processor.

Drafting Paper L	*Using verb phrases with BE*
Assignment	Think of the activities of your siblings or friends and yourself at three different times of your lives: ① at some time in the past, ② now, and ③ ten years in the future. Describe two different kinds of activities: in the past, not just what you were doing but also what was done to you; in the present, not just what you are doing but also what is done to you; in the future, not just what you will do, but also what will be done to you. Write one paragraph for each period of time. Then in your conclusion, discuss briefly what these differing activities show about the experience of growing up.
Get Ready	On a piece of scratch paper, free write on this topic to get ideas to use in developing your paper. Don't stop until you have plenty of ideas. Draw a line across the page when you have finished free writing.
	Read over your free writing, and decide on your main point. Write it in one complete sentence below the line.
	Review the two different kinds of activities above, and the three different times of life during which they have happened, are happening, and will happen. Plan your paragraphs by selecting enough supporting ideas from your free writing to provide the required information, and to make your main point interesting, clear, and convincing to a reader. Write your supporting ideas in a numbered list below your main point.
Draft	On another piece of scratch paper, write an introduction to your draft telling what your main point is.
	Then write one paragraph for each of the three different times of life. Be sure to include enough examples, details, and facts to make your reader understand and believe each idea.
	Write your conclusion.
Special Instructions	Use at least three verb phrases with each of the helping verbs *am, is, are, was, were,* and *will be* in verb phrases like *was told, are working,* and *will be dropped.* You should have a total of at least 18 verb phrases with the helping verb *BE*.
Revise	Revise your draft, using the four steps in revision listed on the inside front cover to make your paper better. Make sure that you have written exactly five paragraphs, including an introduction, one paragraph for each of the three times of life, and a conclusion.

Keep your draft of Paper L to use later.

Exercise 11.2	Making the helping verb *BE* agree in the present tense

These sentences contain base forms of the helping verb *BE* in capital letters. ① Rewrite each sentence, using the appropriate present-tense form of *BE*. ② Mark your rewritten sentence as you have learned to.

1. Right now I BE planning to move to California.

2. My children BE grumbling because they must make new friends.

3. My husband BE trying to help them adjust.

Exercise 11.3	Making the helping verb *BE* agree in the past tense

These sentences contain base forms of the helping verb *BE* in capital letters. ① Rewrite each sentence, using the appropriate past-tense form of *BE*. ② Mark your rewritten sentence as you have learned to.

1. As crime and poverty rose in Russia, Boris Yeltsin's popularity BE slipping.

2. I BE expecting a promotion when I was fired.

3. BE you making more money on your last job?

Verb Phrases with *BE* in Active Sentences

A sentence is **active** when the subject is doing the action of the verb. Most sentences are active.

EAT
Eva eats apples.
Eva ate an apple.
Eva will eat an apple.
Eva is eating an apple.
Eva has eaten an apple.
These sentences have various meanings, but they are all active because Eva is doing the eating.

In Module 6 you learned that one-word present-tense verbs tell what usually happens or is generally true, but don't usually tell what is happening right now.

In Module 7 you learned that one-word past-tense verbs tell what happened at some time in the past, but don't usually tell what was happening over a period of time in the past.

And in Module 10 you learned that verb phrases with *WILL* tell what is going to happen at some time in the future, but don't usually tell what will be happening over a period of time in the future.

When you want to tell what happens over a period of time, whether in the past, present, or future, you use verb phrases with various tenses of the helping verb *BE* and the *ING* form of the main verb.

11A	**Use the helping verb *BE* and the *ING* form of the main verb to tell about something happening <u>over a period of time</u>.**

BAKE

> Freddy was baking a cake last night.
> Freddy is baking a cake right now.
> Freddy will be baking a cake tomorrow night.
> These verb phrases tell what happens over a period of time, in the past, present, and future.

The differences between one-word verbs and these kinds of verb phrases with *BE* are subtle. Usually the verb phrase emphasizes that the action **is or was taking place over a period of time**. That is why these kinds of verb phrases are sometimes called **continuous** or **progressive** verbs.

These sentences use present-tense verbs:

BAKE

> Freddy is baking a cake right now.
> Freddy bakes a cake every week.
> The verb phrase *is baking* emphasizes that he is doing it right now. The one-word verb *bakes* means that he usually does it, but says nothing about what he is doing right now.

These sentences use past-tense verbs:

BAKE

> Freddy was baking a cake last night.
> Freddy baked a cake last night.
> The verb phrase *was baking* emphasizes that the baking took place over a period of time last night. The one-word verb *baked* simply means that he did it once in the past.

These sentences use future-tense verbs:

BAKE

> Freddy will be baking a cake tomorrow night.
> Freddy will bake a cake tomorrow night.
> The verb phrase *will be baking* emphasizes that the baking will take place over a period of time tomorrow night. The verb phrase *will bake* simply means that he will do it once in the future.

11A1	**Make necessary <u>spelling</u> changes when writing *ING* forms of main verbs.**

The *ING* form of many verbs simply adds an *ING* ending to the verb. But spelling changes are necessary for some verbs.

Rule 1G3 says:
If a verb ends with a single vowel + a consonant, double the consonant before adding *ING*.

Rule 1G4 says:
If a verb ends with a consonant + *E*, drop the *E* before adding *ING*.
Never drop *Y* before adding *ING*.

Exercise 11.4	Spelling the main verb correctly

These sentences contain base forms of main verbs in capital letters. ① Rewrite each sentence, using the appropriate *ING* form of the given main verb. ② Mark your rewritten sentence as you have learned to.

1. For a change, my husband is COOK dinner tonight.

   _____

2. During the blackout, the defendant was ROB the store.

   _____

3. Those clerks are FILE our computer output.

   _____

4. I am MEET her for lunch today.

   _____

5. Bertram is PLAN to go to Trinidad this winter.

   _____

6. Itzak was TAKE notes during the lecture.

   _____

We use **present-tense** verb phrases with *BE* to tell what is happening over a period of time right now, often while something else is happening. Time words in sentences like these are often pieces of expansion, with a connecting word, a verb, and a subject.

BAKE   Freddy is baking a cake right now as I am talking to you.
            This sentence tells what is happening right now.

Exercise 11.5 — Using present-tense verb phrases with *BE*

These sentences contain base forms of verbs in capital letters. ① Underline the words that show what tense the verb phrase should be in. ② Rewrite the sentence, using the present-tense form of *BE,* and the appropriate form of the given main verb. ③ Mark your rewritten sentence as you have learned to. Follow this model:

> We BE LOSE time <u>because you're on the telephone with your sister.</u>
> *We are losing time because you're on the telephone with your sister.*

1. I BE WORK for a computer software company now.

   _____

2. Those departments BE CUT employees so that they can save money.

   _____

3. Irina BE TRY to start her own business because she wants more money.

   _____

4. Today I BE BE very careful not to annoy you.

   _____

We use **past-tense** verb phrases with *BE* to tell about something that was happening over a period of time in the past, often at the same time that something else happened. Time words in sentences like these are often pieces of expansion, with a connecting word, a verb, and a subject.

BAKE   Freddy was baking a cake <u>when the phone rang</u>.
This sentence tells what was happening in the past when something else happened.

Exercise 11.6 — Using past-tense verb phrases with *BE*

These sentences contain base forms of verbs in capital letters. ① Underline the words that show what tense the verb phrase should be in. ② Rewrite the sentence, using the past-tense form of *BE,* and the appropriate form of the given main verb. ③ Mark your rewritten sentence as you have learned to.

1. Until recently, unemployment BE DECLINE.

   _____

2. Just before the explosion occurred, I BE HURRY to catch the bus.

   _____

3. After the sales increased, they BE HOPE for a raise.

   _____

4.   Last night I BE BE very careful not to annoy you.

_____

We use **future-tense** verb phrases with *BE* to tell about something that will be happening over a period of time in the future. These verb phrases always use the double helping verb *will be,* where *will* shows the future and *be* (with the *ING* form of the main verb) shows that it will happen over a period of time. Time words in sentences like these are often pieces of expansion, with a connecting word, a verb, and a subject.

BAKE   Freddy will be baking a cake <u>as soon as he finishes the salad</u>.
This sentence tells what will be happening over a period of time in the future.

Exercise 11.7   Using future-tense verb phrases with *BE*

These sentences contain base forms of verbs in capital letters. ① Underline the words that show what tense the verb phrase should be in. ② Rewrite the sentence, using the future-tense form of *BE*, and the appropriate form of the given main verb. ③ Mark your rewritten sentence as you have learned to.

1.   By next month, unemployment BE DECLINE.

_____

2.   I BE LEAVE for Dallas as soon as the letter arrives.

_____

3.   They BE ATTEND that concert tomorrow night.

_____

4.   I BE WATCH that game as soon as the TV set is repaired.

_____

Remember that, whether a sentence has time words or not, each verb must be in the tense that is appropriate to its meaning. Because the meanings of verb phrases with *BE* are often subtle, you must be especially careful when using them with other verbs.

Exercise 11.8   Using verb phrases with *BE* in various tenses

These sentences contain base forms of verbs in capital letters. ① Underline the words that show what tense the verb phrase should be in. ② Rewrite the sentence, using the appropriate tense of *BE*, and the appropriate form of the given main verb. ③ Mark your rewritten sentence as you have learned to.

1.   I BE HURRY when I twisted my ankle.

_____

2.   My two sisters BE PLAN to go skating yesterday.

_____

3.   We BE TRY right now to finish this job.

   _____

4.   They BE PAY too much for car insurance last year.

   _____

5.   Linda BE WRITE some e-mail when the phone rang.

   _____

6.   Next year these companies BE GO out of business.

   _____

7.   I BE WORK in the supermarket last year, but now I BE SELL computers.

   _____

The helping verb is usually not repeated if there is a second main verb in the sentence. Sentences like these have two verbs and one subject.

> The engine was vibrating and was making strange noises.
>   This sentence is correct but seems slightly unnatural.

> The engine was vibrating and making strange noises.
>   This sentence is more natural. Was is understood as the helping verb for the second main verb making.

Exercise 11.9   Recognizing verb phrases when the helping verb is understood

Circle each verb phrase, and box its subject.

1.   My friend Jewel is studying Spanish and hoping to make a career as a bilingual secretary.

2.   The oncoming drivers were slowing their cars and staring at the accident.

3.   The chickens were pecking at my legs and clucking furiously.

4.   That raging blizzard is moving down from northern Canada and burying the upper Midwest in snow.

Exercise 11.10   Understanding where the helping verb may be omitted

① Circle each verb phrase, and box its subject. ② Cross out any helping verb which may be omitted.

1.   Those volunteers are answering the phones and are accepting donations.

2.   The cheerleaders were screaming and were leaping into the air as the crowd was filling the bleachers.

3.   The student government is preparing petitions, is collecting signatures, and is organizing a campaign for

   a new day care center on campus.

The following exercises review everything that you have learned about verbs so far.

Exercise 11.11	Fixing errors in verbs and verb phrases

① Circle each verb (either a one-word verb or a verb phrase), and box its subject. ② Correct each error in the space above the line.

1. Extremes of heat and cold from one day to the next are occuring regularly now.

2. We're experienceing higher sea levels and hotter winds every year. But is these events due to normal climate variation?

3. People around the world is ever more anxiously asking the big question: Is global warming really happening, or is the signs of a warming trend merely accidental?

4. Climate scientists have measure climate variation over many centuries, and are finally reach firm conclusions: The symptoms of global warming is multiplying too rapidly to be normal.

5. Heat-trapping gases from increased manufacturing activity are preventing solar heat from escaping into space and is raising the global temperature a fraction of a degree each year, so that during the next 100 years the earth's temperature will be riseing between 1.5 and 6 degrees Fahrenheit.

6. If the human race do nothing to prevent this disaster, it's eventually going to become extinct.

Exercise 11.12	Fixing errors in verbs and verb phrases

① Circle each verb, and box its subject. ② Correct each error in the space above the line.

These days, baby toys is selling briskly, and toy manufacturing is big business. In the past, toys for infants was mostly simple plastic rattles and terry-cloth balls. Now toy makers is constantly trying to come up with new gimmicks that will appeal to parents. In fact, they've turn for inspiration to research on babies, even on unborn babies. Investigators has recently discover that soft music is able to soothe not only a pregnant woman but also her unborn child. So an ingenious manufacturer is now selling "Babyphones," lightweight stereo speakers that an expectant mother wear around her waist. A cassette player hook onto her pocket or purse. If the fetus starts kicking, the mother switch on the "womb tunes" (as the maker call these tapes). What else do the fetus hear besides violins or guitars? One favorite be a home-made tape of Mom and Dad singing lullabies. Then, to help the newborn baby to make the transition from the familiar womb to the scary outside world, toy makers has thought up yet another helpful invention. For nine months a baby has listen to the sounds of its mother's body and the beat of her heart. After birth, the parents is able to buy a tape player to put in the baby's bed, where it play the same comforting rhythms. Toy manufacturers is also publicizing the discovery that babies enjoys the high contrast of black and white. Now zebras, pandas, and other black-and-white animals is making big bucks for them. They're also promoteing black-and-white mobiles to hang on the crib. In this age of the consumer, the manufacturers exploits the idea that nobody be too young for an expensive toy.

This paragraph contained 22 errors. How many did you find? _____ If you didn't find all 22, try again before you check your work.

Editing Practice L.1	***Fixing verb phrases in active sentences***

1. Get your draft of Paper L.
2. Circle each verb (either a one-word verb or a verb phrase), box its subject, and put a + over each connecting word.
3. Review Rules 11A-11A1.
4. Read over paragraphs #2-#5 to find verb phrases in active sentences. How many did you find? _____ If you don't have at least nine, draw a line across the page, and below it write more active sentences with verb phrases.
5. Check to make sure that each verb phrase (including those in the new sentences below the line) is correct: that its helping verb is in the correct tense and agrees with its subject, and that its main verb is an *ING* form and is correctly spelled. Fix any mistakes with your green pen.
6. How many mistakes did you fix? _____ Your ability to find and fix mistakes in your own writing shows how much you've learned so far.

Keep your draft of Paper L to use again later.

In Module 10 you learned one use of past participles, as main verbs in verb phrases with *HAVE*. Now you'll learn another way that past participles are used, as main verbs in passive sentences.

Verb Phrases with *BE* in Passive Sentences

Sentences may be either active or passive. A sentence is **passive** when the subject is not doing the action of the verb, but rather the **action is happening to the subject**. Usually a group of words with *by* tells who is doing or was doing the action. Passive sentences always have verb phrases.

EAT The apple was eaten by Eva.
The eating happened to the apple in this passive sentence. *By Eva* tells who did the eating.

Sometimes there is no group of words with *by* to tell exactly who is doing or was doing the action, but usually the meaning is obvious anyway.

EAT The apple was eaten before the banana.
The eating happened to the apple in this passive sentence, even though we aren't told exactly who did it.

Exercise 11.13   Distinguishing between active and passive sentences

① Circle each verb phrase, and box its subject. ② Check off whether the subject is doing the action, and whether the sentence is active or passive. Follow this model:

This man was driving that truck.
The subject ☒ is ☐ is not doing the action, so the sentence is ☒ active ☐ passive.
That truck was driven by this man.
The subject ☐ is ☒ is not doing the action, so the sentence is ☐ active ☒ passive.
That man was driven to the store by his friend.
The subject ☐ is ☒ is not doing the action, so the sentence is ☐ active ☒ passive.

1. Dr. Hermann will teach the business seminar.

The subject ☐ is ☐ is not doing the action, so the sentence is ☐ active ☐ passive.

The business seminar will be taught by Dr. Hermann.

The subject ☐ is ☐ is not doing the action, so the sentence is ☐ active ☐ passive.

Dr. Hermann is admired by the students in his seminar.

The subject ☐ is ☐ is not doing the action, so the sentence is ☐ active ☐ passive.

2. A small committee planned the conference.

The subject ☐ is ☐ is not doing the action, so the sentence is ☐ active ☐ passive.

The conference was planned by a small committee.

The subject ☐ is ☐ is not doing the action, so the sentence is ☐ active ☐ passive.

A small committee was appointed to plan the conference.

The subject ☐ is ☐ is not doing the action, so the sentence is ☐ active ☐ passive.

3. The shortstop was throwing the ball.

    The subject ❑ is   ❑ is not doing the action, so the sentence is ❑ active   ❑ passive.

    The ball was thrown too late.

    The subject ❑ is   ❑ is not doing the action, so the sentence is ❑ active   ❑ passive.

    The shortstop was thrown out of the game for fighting.

    The subject ❑ is   ❑ is not doing the action, so the sentence is ❑ active   ❑ passive.

Verb phrases in passive sentences can be in various tenses. The helping verb shows the tense.

> CHECK   Usually, our luggage is checked by an immigration official.
> Yesterday, our luggage was checked by an immigration official.
> Tomorrow, our luggage will be checked by an immigration official.
> Present-, past-, and future-tense forms of the helping verb *BE* are used with the past participle of *CHECK* in these passive sentences.

You already know that *BE*, whether it is a one-word verb or the helping verb in a verb phrase, must agree with its subject in both the present and past tenses.

> DESIGN   Those dresses are designed by Perry Ellis.
> Those dresses were designed by Perry Ellis.
> *Are* and *were* agree with the plural subject *dresses* in these passive sentences.

Exercise 11.14   Using present-tense and past-tense passive sentences

These sentences contain base forms of the helping verb *BE* in capital letters. ① Underline the words that show what tense the verb phrase should be in. ② Rewrite each sentence, using the appropriate form of *BE*. ③ Mark your rewritten sentence as you have learned to.

1. Somebody BE injured almost every day in this playground.

    _____

2. Benita BE promoted twice last year.

    _____

3. The arsonists BE sentenced last month after a short trial.

    _____

4. They BE now locked up in a maximum security prison.

    _____

5.   Even now, I BE still surprised at the speedy verdict.

11B	Use the helping verb *BE* and the past participle of the main verb in a <u>passive</u> sentence.

The main verb in a passive sentence can be either regular or irregular. Be careful to use the correct past participle form.

TAG   Our luggage was tagged by the baggage clerk.
Tagged is the past participle of the regular verb *TAG*.

FLING   Our luggage was flung down the chute.
Flung is the past participle of the irregular verb *FLING*.

Exercise 11.15 | **Writing passive sentences**

These sentences contain base forms of main verbs in capital letters. ① Rewrite each sentence, using the appropriate form of the given main verb. ② Mark your rewritten sentence as you have learned to.

1.   Every day the same routine tasks are PERFORM by dozens of workers.

2.   Fortunes are LOSE on Wall Street every day.

3.   That old trunk is USE as a coffee table now.

4.   Usually, sardines are CATCH in nets.

5.   Emily was ANNOY by that remark yesterday.

6.   Last week, his windshield was BREAK by a rock.

Exercise 11.16 — Writing passive sentences

These sentences contain base forms of verbs in capital letters. ① Underline the words that show what tense the verb phrase should be in. ② Rewrite each sentence, using the appropriate verb phrase. ③ Mark your rewritten sentence as you have learned to.

1.   When I was a child, I BE FASCINATE by complicated puzzles.

———————————————————————————————————————

I BE still FASCINATE by puzzles that are hard to solve.

———————————————————————————————————————

2.   These days teenagers BE often INFLUENCE by peer pressure.

———————————————————————————————————————

In the past, teenagers BE INFLUENCE most by their families.

———————————————————————————————————————

3.   This opera BE SING by Richard Tucker in 1960.

———————————————————————————————————————

Today it BE often SING by Roberto Alagna.

———————————————————————————————————————

4.   The author of *Alice in Wonderland* BE once SUSPECT of child molestation.

———————————————————————————————————————

He BE CONSIDER innocent by modern scholars.

———————————————————————————————————————

Sometimes the helping verb *GET* is used instead of *BE* in a passive sentence. *GET* is more informal than *BE* but is usually acceptable in writing.

SNATCH   Many purses are snatched in crowded stores during the holidays.
                  Many purses get snatched in crowded stores during the holidays.
          These two passive sentences both mean the same thing.

Exercise 11.17 — Writing passive sentences with *BE* and *GET*

These sentences contain base forms of verb phrases, in capital letters. ① Underline the words that show what tense the verb phrase should be in. ② Rewrite the sentence, using the appropriate verb phrase. ③ Mark your rewritten sentences as you have learned to.

1. Last night, Ali BE ROB in front of his own house.

    _____

    Last night, Ali GET ROB in front of his own house.

    _____

2. Miss Holder BE PAY much less than she deserves these days.

    _____

    Miss Holder GET PAY much less than she deserves these days.

    _____

3. Basil and Vera BE DIVORCE just two months after they BE MARRY last year.

    _____

    Basil and Vera GET DIVORCE just two months after they GET MARRY last year.

    _____

Exercise 11.18	Writing active and passive sentences

This paragraph contains base forms of verbs in capital letters. Read it carefully to make sure that you understand it. ① Mark a piece of paper Exercise 11.18, and rewrite this paragraph onto it, using the appropriate one-word verbs or verb phrases. ② Mark your rewritten paragraph as you have learned to.

> In every culture, people BE FORBID to perform certain acts which BE CALL
> *taboos*. Some modern taboos BE not always CONSIDER evil in the past. In ancient
> Egypt, royal siblings often GET MARRY to each other. American Indian warriors USE to
> eat the hearts of enemies that they HAVE KILL, to show respect for their courage. Now
> both incest and cannibalism HAVE BECOME almost universal taboos. We BE HORRIFY
> by incest. And if anyone EAT human flesh today, that person BE CONDEMN as a
> monster. In 1972 a famous plane crash in the Andes ILLUSTRATE how strongly this
> taboo BE FEEL in modern times. Although some survivors KEEP themselves alive by
> eating the bodies of the passengers who HAVE PERISH in the crash, the taboo against
> cannibalism BE too strong for most of them. Instead they CHOOSE to die of starvation.

Editing Practice L.2	*Fixing verb phrases in passive sentences*

1. Get your draft of Paper L again.
2. Check to make sure that you have circled each verb (either a one-word verb or a verb phrase), boxed its subject, and put a + over each connecting word. If you find any more verbs or subjects, mark them with your green pen.

3. Review Rule 11B.
4. Read over paragraphs #2-#5 to find verb phrases in passive sentences. How many did you find? _____ If you don't have at least nine, draw another line across the page, and below it write more passive sentences with verb phrases.
5. Check to make sure that each verb phrase (including those in the new sentences below the line) is correct: that its helping verb is in the correct tense and agrees with its subject, and that its main verb is a past participle and is correctly spelled. Fix any mistakes with your green pen.
6. How many mistakes did you fix? _____ Your ability to find and fix mistakes in your own writing shows how much you've learned so far.

Keep your draft of Paper L to use again later.

The following exercises review everything that you have learned about verbs so far.

Exercise 11.19	Fixing errors in past-tense verbs and past participles

① Circle each verb, and box its subject. ② Correct each error in the space above the line.

In 1981, President Reagan chosed the renowned doctor, C. Everett Koop, as Surgeon

General of the United States, not because he were famous, but because he had openly oppose

abortion. But once the Senate had confirm his appointment, this conservative doctor

astonish everyone. The President had ask him to write a report showing that abortion was

harmful to women's health. Koop believe that abortion was morally wrong, but, when he

study the evidence, he seen that it failed to prove that abortion necessarily caused physical

or psychological damage to women. So he explain to the President that he, as an honest and

competent scientist, could not write this report. Then he turn his attention to smoking and

AIDS. The Administration had not express much interest in these problems, but, according

to Koop, they was health hazards which the Surgeon General's office could and should do

something about. Within a few years, his warnings on cigarette packages had catched the

attention of every smoker, and many had kick the habit. Next, his report on AIDS show that

for the first time someone in the government had taken the deadly virus seriously. He

strongly encourage early sex education and the use of condoms. The Administration was

angry, and the liberals was happy. Both said that he had change. Koop answered mildly

that he had not budge from his original position on any issue. By the time he leave office in

1989, many of his early opponents had turned into supporters, and some of his former

supporters claim that he had betray them. In TV interviews after his retirement, Dr. Koop

insisted that his views had never altered. The problem, he said, was that nobody had bother

to learn what his convictions really was in the first place.

This paragraph contained 25 errors. How many did you find? _____ If you didn't find all 25, try again
before you check your work.

Exercise 11.20	Using a variety of verbs and verb phrases

① Circle each verb, and box its subject. ② Mark a piece of paper Exercise 11.20, and rewrite this
paragraph onto it, using the present tense, and making whatever other changes are necessary. Your
paragraph will begin *Geraldine wants to ...* ③ Mark your rewritten paragraph as you have learned to.

Geraldine wanted to lose weight. She planned exactly what food she would buy,

and how much of it. She had even memorized the layout of the supermarket, because

she knew that if she could stay away from the ice cream and candy, she would lose five

pounds in one week. She said that she was going to stick to her diet until she could get

into every outfit which was hanging in her closet, especially those velvet slacks which she

hadn't been able to wear for years. But, of course, Geraldine had made these plans

before. Her friends didn't think that she would actually lose a pound.

Exercise 11.21	Using negative verb phrases

① Circle each verb, and box its subject. ② Mark a piece of paper Exercise 11.21, and rewrite this
paragraph onto it in the negative, contracting *not* with every verb. Your paragraph will begin *Mickey
hasn't been...* ③ Mark your rewritten paragraph as you have learned to.

Mickey has been a very satisfactory dog. As a puppy, he knew when to stay on

his training paper. As a one-year-old, he would chew his plastic bone and could abstain

from the upholstery. At two, he could tell the difference between friend and foe, and

growled or wagged his tail appropriately. So the mailman and meter reader especially

cherish this canine. Now at three, Mickey is the most popular dog on the block. He can

fetch the newspaper. He will heel on command. And he even knows when to leave

people in peace. His owner often brags about him. To her, Mickey is the perfect pet.

You should mention his name, because she will beam with delight.

| **Exercise 11.22** | **Correcting various errors in verbs and verb phrases** |

① Circle each verb, and box its subject. ② Correct each error in the space above the line.

Since my wife and I begun to do crossword puzzles together, we have bought a lot of

reference books, including a new edition of *The Guinness Book of World Records*. This book

has certainly help us with our puzzles, but it have also been a source of fascinating

information. It don't just tell about recent sports records. Each edition try to include every

amazing and amusing feat of the human race. Here are some we will always remember: ①

Although Strombo the Maniac has establish the longest official record of 65 hours for lying

on a bed of nails, that record was totally demolish by Silki the Fakir, who done the same

thing for 101 days—but only his followers saw him do it. ② Lightning has strucked one

living man seven times—Roy Sullivan, a Shenandoah park ranger. His body was hit in five

different places, and twice his head was burn bald. ③ Steve Weldon of Texas has ate the

longest meal in the shortest time: 100 yards of spaghetti in 28 seconds. ④ By the time he

died in 597 AD, St. Simon Stylites had chalk up the all-time pole-sitting record: 45 years on

top of a stone pillar. ⑤ And what book has selled the most copies in the past 25 years? *The*

Guinness Book of World Records, of course!

This paragraph contained 13 errors. How many did you find? _____ If you didn't find all 13, try again
before you check your work.

| **Exercise 11.23** | **Correcting various verb errors** |

① Circle each verb, and box its subject. ② Correct each error in the space above the line.

My mother has often tried to tell me that crime don't pay. But then, my mother have

never run for office. I have never told her about what happen when I was a sophomore in

high school. I had campaign hard to be class president, and election day had finally arrive.

Just before the vote was taking, our teacher remind us, "You shouldn't vote for yourself.

Each student must writes down somebody else's name on the ballot." But I was scare that I

might lose the election by one vote. I knew that I should not have did it, but when the slips was passed around, I voted for myself. I has never forgotten the moment when the votes

was all counted, and our teacher said, "There are 31 votes for Mary Williams and one vote

for Ted Collins." As soon as the teacher announce the results, Ted jumped up to say that I

had not cast my vote for him. But then he sat down even more quickly. It tooked me a day

to figure out that Ted had voted for himself, too. He could not accuse me without accusing

himself. So even if I did committed a crime, on that occasion I wasn't punish. In fact, I was

praise for voting for my opponent.

This paragraph contained 18 errors. How many did you find? _____ If you didn't find all 18, try again
before you check your work.

Editing Practice L.3	*Fixing various verb phrases*

1. Get your draft of Paper L again.
2. Check again to make sure that you have circled each verb (either a one-word verb or a verb phrase),
   boxed its subject, and put a + over each connecting word If you find any more verbs or subjects, mark
   them with your green pen.
3. Check again to make sure that each present-tense verb agrees with its subject, that each past-tense verb
   is in the correct form, and that each verb phrase is correct: that its helping verb is in the correct tense
   and (if necessary) agrees with its subject, and that its main verb is in the correct form and is correctly
   spelled. Fix any mistakes with your green pen.
4. How many more mistakes did you fix? _____ Your ability to find and fix mistakes in your own writing
   shows how much you've learned so far.

Writing Your Final Copy of Paper L

Use your final copy of Paper L to demonstrate what you've learned in Module 11 about verb phrases with
the helping verb *BE*, and to show how well you're continuing to apply what you've learned previously.

Paper L	*Using verb phrases with BE*

Edit for Previous Modules

Use your dictionary and the Rules Summaries for previous modules to:

- Check your use of writing conventions. Fix any mistakes with your green
  pen.

- Check your use of nouns and pronouns. Fix any mistakes with your green
  pen.

- Check your use of present-tense verbs. Fix any mistakes with your green
  pen.

- Check your use of past-tense verbs. Fix any mistakes with your green pen.

- Check the structure of each word-group to find any run-ons. Fix any mistakes with your green pen, either by rewriting them as two sentences, or by connecting them with joining or expansion or transition words, being sure to punctuate them correctly. How many run-ons did you find and correct? _____

- Check the structure of each word-group to find any fragments. Fix any mistakes with your green pen, either by connecting them to an appropriate sentence, or by adding, removing, or changing words. How many fragments did you find and correct? _____

Make Final Copy   Mark another piece of paper Paper L, and write the final copy of your paper on it, or print out a clean copy on your word processor. Be sure to include all your corrections. Mark your final copy as you did your draft.

Proofread   Read your final copy **out loud.** Correct any mistakes neatly by hand. If you used a word processor, enter your corrections, print out a corrected final copy, and mark it again.

Hand in your final copy of Paper L, and the rest of your exercises.

Mastering Expansion

NAME _____

After you finish checking each exercise, fill in your number of mistakes.

12.1 _____	12.7 _____	12.13 _____	12.19 _____	12.25 _____
12.2 _____	12.8 _____	12.14 _____	12.20 _____	12.26 _____
12.3 _____	12.9 _____	12.15 _____	12.21 _____	12.27 _____
12.4 _____	12.10 _____	12.16 _____	12.22 _____	12.28 _____
12.5 _____	12.11 _____	12.17 _____	12.23 _____	12.29 _____
12.6 _____	12.12 _____	12.18 _____	12.24 _____	

EXERCISES
❑ Complete
❑ Incomplete

INSTRUCTIONS
❑ Followed carefully
❑ Not careful enough

CHECKING
❑ Careful   ❑ Green pen not used
❑ Not careful enough   ❑ Mistakes not corrected

PAPER M
❑ Doesn't follow the instructions; write a NEW Paper M.
❑ Skips some instructions; COMPLETE everything.
❑ Too short; add MORE.

EDITING PAPER M FOR THIS MODULE'S WORK
❑ Careful   ❑ Not careful enough
EDITING PAPER M FOR PREVIOUS WORK
❑ Careful   ❑ Not careful enough
OVERALL EVALUATION OF PAPER M
❑ Excellent   ❑ Good   ❑ Acceptable   ❑ Not acceptable

COMMENTS

Rules Summary for Module 12

12A	To make a noun possessive, do this: If the noun is **plural and has an *S* ending already**, add an **apostrophe only** after the *S* ending. Otherwise, add an **apostrophe + *S***.
12B	Don't confuse possessive **nouns** with possessive **pronouns**.
12C	Don't confuse apostrophes in **possessives** with apostrophes in **contractions**.
12D	Don't confuse **plural** nouns with **possessive** nouns.
12E	Use **adjectives** to expand nouns. Use **adverbs** to expand verbs, adjectives, and other adverbs.
12F	To make **comparisons** with adjectives and adverbs, use the appropriate comparative and superlative forms.
12G	For clearer sentences, place noun expansion **right next to** the noun or pronoun it expands.
12H	For more effective sentences, make their parts **parallel**.

In previous modules, you have been focusing mostly on these three of the four basic parts of the written sentence: **verbs**, their **subjects**, and **connecting words**. In this final module, you will learn more about the fourth part, **expansion**. You have already learned about the most complicated kind of expansion, which contains a verb and its subject, and is created by expansion words like *when, because,* and *if,* and *who, which,* and *that.* However, there are several more rules about expansion that you need to learn and practice in order to avoid confusing your readers. Now that you have mastered the overall framework of sentence construction, it will be easier for you to learn and use these additional rules relating to expansion.

In this module, you will learn how to do each of the following correctly:

- use **possessive forms** to expand nouns
- use **adjective forms** to expand nouns, and **adverb forms** to expand verbs, adjectives, and other adverbs
- use **-ING and -ED forms** to expand nouns
- arrange these forms and other parts of a sentence as **parallel parts**

In school grammar the various forms of expansion (including those mentioned above) are called **modifiers.**

Using Module 12 to Edit Your Own Writing

Use Paper M to discover how much you know already about using expansion. Later in this module, you'll be checking this paper by applying the rules of this module to what you have written.

You may write this paper by hand. Better yet, use a word processor.

Paper M	*Using expansion*
Assignment	Think of some one you know personally, or someone you have learned about through reading or television, who formerly led an extremely active life but now is older and less active. Describe this person's life, telling both what this person did and what happened to him or her, both during active life and in old age.
Get Ready	On a piece of scratch paper, free write on this topic, first to narrow it to one specific example if necessary, and then to get ideas to use in developing your paper. Don't stop until you have plenty of ideas. Draw a line across the page when you have finished free writing.
	Read over your free writing, and decide on your main point. Write it in one complete sentence below the line.
	Plan your paragraphs by selecting enough supporting ideas from your free writing to make your main point interesting, clear, and convincing to a reader. Write your supporting ideas in a numbered list below your main point.

Draft	On another piece of scratch paper, write an introduction to your draft telling what your main point is.
	Then write at least one paragraph for each of your supporting ideas. Be sure to include enough examples, details, and facts to make your reader understand and believe each idea.
	Write your conclusion.
Revise	Use the four steps in revision listed on the inside front cover to make your paper better. Make sure that you have written at least four paragraphs, including an introduction and a conclusion.

Keep your draft of Paper M to use later.

Using Possessive Forms

A possessive form is the kind of expansion that tells more about another noun. Most possessive forms show **ownership** or **possession**.

> That is a <u>book belonging to Gillian</u>.
> That is <u>Gillian's book</u>.
>> The possessive form *Gillian's* means that Gillian owns the book.

> That is a <u>book belonging to me</u>.
> That is <u>my book</u>.
>> The possessive form *my* means that I own the book.

The concept of possession can be expressed in many ways. Using a possessive form is usually the clearest, simplest, and most natural.

> That is a <u>book which is owned by Gillian</u>.
> That is a <u>book which belongs to Gillian</u>.
> That is a <u>book belonging to Gillian</u>.
> That is <u>Gillian's book</u>.
>> These sentences all mean the same thing. But the last sentence, using the possessive form *Gillian's*, is the most natural one.

We also use possessive forms to show other relationships.

> We are reading <u>plays written by Shakespeare</u>.
> We are reading <u>Shakespeare's plays</u>.
>> The possessive form *Shakespeare's* means that Shakespeare wrote the plays.

> That store sells <u>clothing designed for children</u>.
> That store sells <u>children's clothing</u>.
>> The possessive form *children's* means that the clothing is intended for children.

They did <u>hard work lasting for two days</u> on that project.
They did <u>two days' hard work</u> on that project.
>The possessive form *days'* means that the hard work filled up two days.

Like any other noun, a possessive noun may have expansion. This expansion is part of the entire possessive phrase.

That store sells <u>expensive clothing designed for young children</u>.
That store sells <u>young children's expensive clothing</u>.
>*Expensive* tells more about the *clothing*, and *young* tells more about the *children*.

Exercise 12.1	Recognizing possessive forms and their meanings

① Underline the entire possessive phrase. ② Fill in the blank. Follow this model:

<u>Her father's taxi</u> finally arrived. The taxi had been called for *her father* .

1. We sent a thank-you note to my grandfather's friends.

   They were friends of _____

2. The new government's policy was announced at a press conference.

   The policy had been formulated by _____

3. An old union motto is, "Work one day for one day's pay."

   The pay was for _____

4. The theater company's next play is going to be Shakespeare's *Othello*.

   The next play will be given by _____

   Othello was written by _____

Possessive Noun Forms

12A	To make a noun possessive, do this: If the noun is <u>plural and has an S ending already</u>, add an <u>apostrophe only</u> after the S ending. Otherwise, add an <u>apostrophe + S</u>.

When a plural noun that already has an *S* ending is made possessive, no sound is added. That's why we write the possessive form with an apostrophe only.

They did <u>two days'</u> work on that project.
> *Days* is plural and already has an *S* ending, so we make it possessive by adding an apostrophe only after the *S* ending. The possessive form sounds the same as the plural form.

When a plural noun without an *S* ending, or a singular noun, is made possessive, the apostrophe + *S* ending adds a ZZZ or SSS sound.

That store sells <u>children's</u> clothing.
> *Children* is plural but doesn't have an *S* ending, so we make it possessive by adding an apostrophe + an *S* ending, which adds a ZZZ sound.

We are reading <u>Shakespeare's</u> plays.
> *Shakespeare* is singular, so we make it possessive by adding an apostrophe + an *S* ending, which adds a ZZZ sound.

We can visualize the rule with this diagram:

Form of the noun	How to make it possessive	What its ending sounds like
plural with *S* ending already	add apostrophe only, after the *S* ending	no sound is added
anything else	add apostrophe + *S* ending	ZZZ or SSS sound is added

Exercise 12.2 — Understanding and writing possessive nouns

① Underline and fill in the noun that can be written in the possessive form. ② After studying the diagram above, check off how to make this noun possessive. ③ Rewrite the phrase, using a possessive noun. Underline the possessive noun. ④ Then check off what sound this ending has. Follow this model:

the wrong answer given by <u>Bob</u>
The noun that can be written in the possessive form is <u>*Bob*</u>.
To make it possessive, add ☐ apostrophe only ☒ apostrophe + *S* ending
<u>*Bob's wrong answer*</u>
This ending has ☐ no sound added ☒ ZZZ or SSS added

1. the silk scarves belonging to Jennifer
The noun that can be written in the possessive form is _____
To make it possessive, add ☐ apostrophe only ☐ apostrophe + *S* ending

_____
This ending has ☐ no sound added ☐ ZZZ or SSS added

2. the shiny equipment used by some cooks
The noun that can be written in the possessive form is _____
To make it possessive, add ☐ apostrophe only ☐ apostrophe + *S* ending

_____
This ending has ☐ no sound added ☐ ZZZ or SSS added

3. razor blades intended for men
    The noun that can be written in the possessive form is _____
    To make it possessive, add   ❑ apostrophe only   ❑ apostrophe + *S* ending

    _____

    This ending has   ❑ no sound added   ❑ ZZZ or SSS added

4. the lyric poems written by Robert Frost
    The noun that can be written in the possessive form is _____
    To make it possessive, add   ❑ apostrophe only   ❑ apostrophe + *S* ending

    _____

    This ending has   ❑ no sound added   ❑ ZZZ or SSS added

5. cocktail dresses designed for women
    The noun that can be written in the possessive form is _____
    To make it possessive, add   ❑ apostrophe only   ❑ apostrophe + *S* ending

    _____

    This ending has   ❑ no sound added   ❑ ZZZ or SSS added

6. a frustrating delay of three days
    The noun that can be written in the possessive form is _____
    To make it possessive, add   ❑ apostrophe only   ❑ apostrophe + *S* ending

    _____

    This ending has   ❑ no sound added   ❑ ZZZ or SSS added

Exercise 12.3   Distinguishing between singular and plural possessive nouns

Rewrite each phrase, using a possessive noun. Say each answer out loud as you write it, listening carefully to the sound of the ending. Underline the possessive noun. Follow this model:

> the new car owned by my sister
> *my sister's* new car
> the new car owned by my sisters
> *my sisters'* new car

1. the dirty tools belonging to my brother

    _____ dirty tools

    the dirty tools belonging to my brothers

    _____ dirty tools

2. the expanding career of one woman

    _____ expanding career

    the expanding careers of many women

    _____ expanding careers

3. the strong opinion expressed by one person

    _____ strong opinion

    the strong opinions expressed by many people

    _____ strong opinions

4. The heavy responsibilities given to a man

    _____ heavy responsibilities

    the heavy responsibilities given to men

    _____ heavy responsibilities

Even when **a singular** noun already ends with *S* or *Z*, the rule tells us to add an apostrophe + an *S* ending for the possessive form, just as we would for any other possessive form. This ZZZ sound of the possessive ending adds an extra syllable.

> Here is <u>Lois's</u> expensive book.
>> *Lois* is singular, so we make it possessive by adding an apostrophe + an *S* ending. The ZZZ sound of the ending adds an extra syllable.

You already know that when a singular noun ends with *Y*, you need to change the *Y* to *I* for the plural form. But **never change *Y* to *I* for a possessive form**. The rule tells us to add an apostrophe + an *S* ending, just as we would for any other possessive form. This possessive ending adds a ZZZ sound.

> That <u>city's</u> residents are almost all minorities.
>> *City* is singular, so we make it possessive by adding an apostrophe + an *S* ending, without changing the *Y* to *I*. The ending adds a ZZZ sound.

Exercise 12.4	Writing more complicated possessive nouns

Rewrite the phrase, using a possessive noun. Say each answer out loud as you write it, listening carefully to the sound of the ending. Underline the possessive noun. Follow this model:

> the broken windshield of the bus
> *the bus's broken windshield*

1. the multimedia computer used by Tess

    _____

2. the new pen bought by Harry

    _____

3. hard assignments given to one class

    _____

304

4.   the brand new house belonging to that family

_____

5.   the profound teachings of Jesus

_____

Exercise 12.5 | **Writing possessive nouns in a paragraph**

Read this paragraph carefully to make sure that you understand it. ① Mark a piece of paper Exercise 12.5, and rewrite this paragraph onto it, changing the underlined phrases into possessive nouns. Say each sentence out loud as you write it, listening carefully to the sound of the ending. Your paragraph will begin *Our grandparents' big old house* was... ② Underline every change in your rewritten paragraph.

The big old house owned by our grandparents was crowded. In the recreation room, the stereo belonging to Tasha was blaring rap music while the cousins checked out the new dance steps of each other. In the kitchen, the wonderful aroma of the roast turkey wafted from the oven belonging to Grandma while the yam casserole made by Uncle Joe and the mince pies made by Aunt Betty were displayed for the approval of the assembled guests. In the living room, the photo albums belonging to our grandparents were being passed around, to the amusement of everyone. "Look at the miniskirts of our aunts! Get a load of the haircut on Joe!" From the den, where the television belonging to Granddad was tuned to a football game, came the occasional roar of voices of men. The Thanksgiving reunion of the family was in full swing.

Editing Practice M.1 | *Checking possessive noun forms*

1.   Get your draft of Paper M.
2.   Underline each possessive noun. How many did you underline? _____ If you didn't find at least six, draw a line across the page, and below it write more sentences for your paper, each with at least one possessive noun.
3.   Review Rule 12A.
4.   Check to make sure that each possessive noun is correct. Fix any mistakes with your green pen.
5.   How many mistakes did you fix? _____ Your ability to find and fix mistakes in your own writing shows how much you've learned so far.

Keep your draft of Paper M to use again later.

Possessive Pronoun Forms

12B	**Don't confuse possessive <u>nouns</u> with possessive <u>pronouns</u>.**

Possessive **nouns** have apostrophes, but possessive **pronouns never** have apostrophes.

There are two different possessive pronoun forms. Use the first form before a noun, and the second form by itself, without a noun, often at the end of the sentence.

pronouns	possessive pronouns	
I	my	mine
you	your	yours
he	his	his
she	her	hers
it	its	its
we	our	ours
they	their	theirs

If this is <u>Maria's</u> pen and that is <u>her</u> dictionary, then the notebook is also <u>hers</u>.
> The possessive noun *Maria's* has an apostrophe. The possessive pronouns *her* and *hers* do not.
> *Her* is used before the noun *dictionary*, and *hers* is used by itself, without a noun.

Never write the possessive pronoun *mine* with an *S* ending. Although it sometimes occurs in speech, *mines* is incorrect in writing.

X
That seat is <u>mines</u>.
> The possessive pronoun *mines* is incorrect.

That seat is <u>mine</u>.
> The possessive pronoun *mine* is correct.

Exercise 12.6	Fixing incorrect possessive forms

Underline each incorrect possessive form, and correct it in the space above the line.

1. Valerie says that her sister's cooking is better than her's and even better than mine.

2. My familie's friends are staying at my brother house.

3. The jury asked it's foreman to request a copy of the judge's instructions.

4. Sid's brother and sister-in-law were each married for the second time, and they always joked that

    their children were "his, her's and our's."

Avoiding Other Problems with Apostrophes

Rule 1F says:
Use an apostrophe to show where letters have been omitted in contractions.

<u>Here's</u> Geeta's dictionary.
> *Here's* is a contraction for *Here is*. *Geeta's* is the possessive form of *Geeta*.

| **12C** | **Don't confuse apostrophes in <u>possessives</u> with apostrophes in <u>contractions</u>.** |

| **Exercise 12.7** | **Fixing errors in possessive forms and contractions** |

Underline each error, and correct it in the space above the line.

1. Whos the person who wanted to borrow Melvins notebook?

2. We havent seen any apartment as attractive as ours, except perhaps your's.

3. Its been predicted that the finance committee will deliver its report only after the Senates last meeting of

   the year.

| **Exercise 12.8** | **Fixing errors in possessive forms and contractions** |

Underline each error, and correct it in the space above the line.

Its becoming almost a habit: The University raises its tuition nearly every year, and

when it does, its certain that a small group of students will protest against the

administrations decision. They lock themselves into the Presidents office and hang banners

out the windows. News reporters come to interview the strikers leaders. After a weeks

delay and negotiation, the administrators call the police. They always say that the decision

hasnt been easy, but that the students whove gone on strike are interfering with other

students right to an education.

| **12D** | **Don't confuse <u>plural</u> nouns with <u>possessive</u> nouns.** |

Use apostrophes to make nouns possessive. **Never** use them to make nouns plural.

X
<u>Luanne's</u> two <u>sister's</u> moved to Phoenix.
   An apostrophe is correct in the possessive form *Luanne's*. It is incorrect in the plural form *sisters*.

<u>Luanne's</u> two <u>sisters</u> moved to Phoenix.
   Sisters is the correct noun plural form.

Module 12: *Mastering Expansion*

| **Exercise 12.9** | **Distinguishing between possessive and plural forms** |

These sentences contain base forms of nouns in capital letters. ① Rewrite each sentence, using the appropriate plural possessive and plural noun forms. ② Underline every change in your rewritten sentences. Follow this model:

> They ignored their PARENT WARNING.
> *They ignored their parents' warnings.*

1. Both APPLICANT ACCEPTANCE arrived yesterday.

     _____

2. TEACHER SALARY were raised last year.

     _____

3. Those STORE CUSTOMER all objected to the loss of parking.

     _____

| **Exercise 12.10** | **Writing plural and possessive forms** |

This paragraph contains base forms of nouns in capital letters. Read it carefully to make sure that you understand it. ① Mark a piece of paper Exercise 12.10, and rewrite this paragraph onto it, using the appropriate singular or plural possessive and noun forms. Your paragraph will begin *My twin sisters' babies were...* ② Underline every change in your rewritten paragraph.

My twin SISTER BABY were born just three WEEK apart, so the CHILD grew up together. ROSA little girl and CHITA little boy were both healthy INFANT, but their MOTHER often wondered why the CHILD PERSONALITY were so very different. ROBERTO temperament was sunny, but his cousin ESTELLA TANTRUM became famous in the family. Still, the two CHILD got along very well together. Perhaps OPPOSITE attract. At any rate, they never fought over each OTHER TOY, and they happily shared their COOKY and TREAT. In fact, their RELATIVE always called them "the junior TWIN."

| ***Editing Practice M.2*** | ***Checking apostrophes and possessive pronouns*** |

1. Get your draft of Paper M again.
2. Check again to make sure that each possessive noun is underlined. If you find any more possessive nouns, mark them with your green pen.
3. Underline each other word with an apostrophe.
4. Review Rules 12B-12D.
5. Check each word that you underlined to make sure that it is correct, by asking these questions:
    *   Is this word a possessive pronoun? If so, it should not have an apostrophe.

- Is this word a contraction? If so, does the apostrophe follow Rule 1F by showing where letters have been omitted?
- Is this word a plural noun that is not possessive? If so, it should not have an apostrophe.

6. Fix any mistakes with your green pen.
7. Check to make sure that each word without an apostrophe really should not have one. If a word is a contraction or a possessive noun but doesn't have an apostrophe, fix it with your green pen.
8. How many mistakes did you fix? _____ Your ability to find and fix mistakes in your own writing shows how much you've learned so far.

Keep your draft of Paper M to use again later.

Using Adjectives and Adverbs

Expansion with Adjectives and Adverbs

Adjectives and adverbs are another common form of expansion.

| 12E | Use <u>adjectives</u> to expand nouns. Use <u>adverbs</u> to expand verbs, adjectives, and other adverbs. |

An **adjective** is expansion that tells more about a **noun**.

The <u>quick</u> <u>brown</u> fox jumped over the <u>lazy</u> dog.
> *Quick* and *brown* are adjectives telling more about the noun *fox*. *Lazy* is an adjective telling more about the noun *dog*.

An **adverb** is expansion that tells more about a **verb**, or an **adjective**, or another **adverb**.

<u>Yesterday</u> the fox jumped <u>very</u> <u>quickly</u> over that <u>exceptionally</u> lazy dog.
> *Yesterday* and *quickly* are adverbs telling more about the verb *jumped*. *Very* is an adverb telling more about the adverb *quickly*, and *exceptionally* is an adverb telling more about the adjective *lazy*.

Using an adjective as if it were an adverb is probably the most common mistake in using these forms.

✗
That teacher talks too <u>soft</u>.
> In this sentence, the adjective *soft* is incorrect because it's used to tell more about the verb *TALK*.

✗
It's <u>real</u> hard to hear him.
> In this sentence, the adjective *real* is incorrect because it's used to tell more about another adjective *hard*.

To correct mistakes like these, turn the adjectives into adverbs. Almost all adjectives can be turned into adverbs by adding the ending *LY*.

That teacher talks too <u>softly</u>.
It's <u>really</u> hard to hear him.
> These sentences are correct. *Softly* is an adverb telling more about the verb *TALK*, and *really* is an adverb telling more about the adjective *hard*. Both answer the question *HOW?* about the words they expand.

To turn adjectives ending in Y (like *sleepy, easy,* and *lucky*) into adverbs, change the Y to I before adding the LY ending (*sleepily, easily,* and *luckily*).

There are some adverbs that do **not** have LY endings. Many of these tell *HOW MUCH?*, like *quite, almost, very,* and *somewhat*

Another common mistake in using these forms is **using adverbs instead of adjectives**, in sentences like these:

> *X*
> These flowers look <u>beautifully</u> in this vase.
> > The adverb *beautifully* is incorrect because it's used like an adjective to tell more about the noun *flowers*.

> *X*
> This medicine tastes <u>bitterly</u>.
> > The adverb *bitterly* is incorrect because it's used like an adjective to tell more about the noun *medicine*.

An adjective should be used after verbs that express sense impressions, like *BE, SEEM, BECOME, FEEL, SMELL, LOOK, SOUND,* and *TASTE*, because it refers back to the subject.

> These flowers look <u>beautiful</u> in this vase.
> > This sentence is correct because the adjective *beautiful* tells more about the noun *flowers*.

> This medicine tastes <u>bitter</u>.
> > This sentence is correct because the adjective *bitter* tells more about the noun *medicine*.

> These cookies smell <u>sweet</u>. Smiling <u>sweetly</u>, she offered me one.
> This dress seems <u>perfect</u>. It fits me <u>perfectly</u>.
> > These sentences are all correct because the adjectives tell more about the nouns, and the adverbs tell more about the verbs or verb forms.

Two particularly confusing words are *well* and *good*. *Good* is always an adjective, but *well* is an adjective only when it is used to mean "in good health."

> The <u>good</u> news is that you're almost a <u>well</u> man.
> > In this sentence, *good* and *well* are both used as adjectives to tell more about the nouns *news* and *man*.

However, *well* is also used as the irregular adverb form of the adjective *good*.

> *X*
> Spencer is playing <u>good</u> today.
> Spencer is playing <u>well</u> today.
> > Only the second sentence is correct. The adverb *well*, not the adjective *good*, is used to tell more about the verb *is playing*.

Exercise 12.11	Using adjectives and adverbs

This paragraph contains base forms of adjectives and adverbs in capital letters. Read it carefully to make sure that you understand it. ① Decide whether each base form should be an adjective or an adverb. ② Mark a piece of paper Exercise 12.11, and rewrite this paragraph onto it, changing the base forms into the appropriate adjective and adverb forms. Your paragraph will begin *Some movies can make boring lawsuits seem really...* ③ Underline every change in your rewritten paragraph.

> Some movies can make BORING lawsuits seem REAL INTERESTING. A PARTICULAR GOOD example is *Erin Brockovich,* directed BRILLIANT by Steven Soderbergh. In this TRUE story, an UNTRAINED LEGAL secretary METICULOUS assembles bits and pieces of CAREFUL CONCEALED evidence which ULTIMATE exposes the CRIMINAL NEGLIGENT behavior of a gas company. It becomes OBVIOUS, as the plot GRADUAL unfolds, that Soderbergh has done GOOD in choosing Julia Roberts as the star. To achieve his BEST effects, the director leans HEAVY on both her COMEDIC and DRAMATIC talents. INSTANT, as the movie begins, she challenges her viewers to reconsider what's REAL IMPORTANT to them as they drift THOUGHTLESS through life. In her role as Erin, Roberts dresses TASTELESS, talks OBSCENE, and behaves CRUDE and SOMETIMES even DISGUSTING, and yet SIMULTANEOUS she remains dedicated to an UNQUESTIONABLE NOBLE cause. Only Julia Roberts could have turned a movie about sifting through MUSTY files into both a MORAL challenge and a VAST ENTERTAINING experience.

Placement of Adverbs in Sentences

In another way also, adverbs work differently from adjectives.

> Yesterday the fox jumped quickly over that dog.
>> The adverbs *yesterday* and *quickly* answer the questions *WHEN?* and *HOW?* about the verb *jumped.*

These adverbs, like other pieces of expansion that tell more about verbs, can move around in a sentence to any position that sounds natural.

> The fox quickly jumped over that dog yesterday.
> Quickly yesterday, the fox jumped over that dog.
>> The adverbs *yesterday* and *quickly* are moved to different positions in this sentence. Moving the adverbs may change the emphasis in a sentence but doesn't usually change its basic meaning.

However, special adverbs like *only, nearly, almost,* and similar words telling *HOW MUCH?* or *HOW MANY?* about other adjectives, can cause confusion if they are misplaced in a sentence. These words should always go right before the word they tell more about.

x

Joey almost (grew) a foot last year.

Almost means *not quite* or *nearly*, so this sentence seems to mean that Joey didn't quite grow. Actually what the writer means is that Joey did grow but not quite a foot. So *almost* belongs before *a foot*, not before *grew*.

Joey (grew) almost a foot last year.

This sentence is clear.

Exercise 12.12 — Moving adverbs to make sentences clear

① Mark with an *x* any adverb whose placement makes the sentence confusing. ② On a piece of scratch paper, move the adverb around to make the sentence clearer. Read your rewritten sentence out loud to see whether the adverb sounds natural in its new position, and whether the sentence is clearer. If you are not a native speaker of English, read them to someone who is. ③ After you have decided on an appropriate place for the expansion, rewrite the sentence so that it is clear, and put parentheses around the expansion.

1. The union members almost cast 300 votes in favor of the strike.

   _____

2. Actually, they only needed 174 to approve the strike proposal.

   _____

3. When they finally got a new contract, they nearly achieved all their goals.

   _____

Using Adjectives and Adverbs in Comparisons

12F — **To make <u>comparisons</u> with adjectives and adverbs, use the appropriate comparative and superlative forms.**

In comparing adjectives and adverbs, there are three degrees of comparison, **positive** (used when dealing with only one noun), **comparative** (used when dealing with two nouns), and **superlative** (used when dealing with three or more nouns). Use this diagram to learn the forms that show these comparisons. Notice that *the* is used before each superlative adjective to show that the noun it expands is alone in its class: *the sharpest knife of all, the most magnificent house in the city.*

	positive	comparative	superlative
shorter adjectives	sharp cloudy few some	sharper cloudier fewer more	the sharpest the cloudiest the fewest the most
longer adjectives	magnificent	more magnificent less magnificent	the most magnificent the least magnificent
irregular adjectives	good bad little	better worse less	the best the worst the least
most adverbs	magnificently	more magnificently less magnificently	most magnificently least magnificently
irregular adverbs	badly well little	worse better less	worst best least

You learned in Module 5 to use *few* with **count** nouns and *little* with **noncount** nouns:

> There are a <u>few</u> cookies here and a <u>little</u> milk.
> There are <u>few</u> cookies left and very <u>little</u> milk.
>> Cookies **can** be counted, so *few* is correct. Milk **can't** be counted so *little* is correct.

In the same way, we use the comparative form *fewer* with count nouns and the comparative form *less* with noncount nouns:

> There are <u>fewer</u> cookies here, and even <u>less</u> milk.
>> *Fewer* is correct because cookies **can** be counted. *Less* is correct because milk **can't** be counted.

Using *less* instead of *fewer* is a very common mistake.

> *X*
> There are <u>less</u> cookies here than there were a minute ago.
>> *Less* here is incorrect because cookies **can** be counted. The correct adjective is *fewer*.

One other common error is adding the *ER* and *EST* ending unnecessarily, resulting in mistakes like these:

>   *X*   *X*
> Yesterday the weather got <u>worser</u>, but today is <u>the worstest</u> day so far.
>   *X*   *X*
> Tomorrow will be a <u>less cloudier</u> day but <u>the most coldest</u> so far.
>> These comparative and superlative forms are incorrect.

> Yesterday the weather got <u>worse</u>, but today is the <u>worst</u> day so far.
> Tomorrow will be a <u>less cloudy</u> day but <u>the coldest</u> so far.
>> These comparative and superlative forms are correct.

313

| Exercise 12.13 | Using positive, comparative, and superlative forms |

This paragraph tells the story of Viola's marriage to Caspar. It contains base forms of adjectives and adverbs in capital letters. Read it carefully to make sure that you understand it. ① Decide whether each base form should be an adjective or an adverb. ② Mark a piece of paper Exercise 12.13, and rewrite this paragraph onto it, changing the base forms into the appropriate adjective and adverb forms. ③ Underline every change in your rewritten paragraph.

Viola always looked BEAUTIFUL, with LONG, LUSTROUS hair and BRIGHT, WHITE teeth. She dressed ATTRACTIVE and moved GRACEFUL. She enjoyed living EXTRAVAGANT, so she looked CAREFUL for a SMART man who was becoming rich QUICK. She behaved STUPID by picking Caspar, who had LITTLE charm and FEW brains. After six months in a FASHIONABLE part of town, Caspar began to trade stocks RECKLESS and made a BAD decision. After moving into a DUMPY neighborhood, the couple had LITTLE to look forward to and MUCH to regret.

| Exercise 12.14 | Using positive, comparative, and superlative forms |

Here is the same paragraph you worked on in Exercise 12.13, now telling the story of Katherine's marriage to Brad, and comparing this couple to Viola and Caspar. ① Mark a piece of paper Exercise 12.14, and rewrite this paragraph onto it, changing the base forms into the appropriate **comparative** adjective and adverb forms. Your paragraph will begin *Katherine always looked <u>more beautiful</u> than Viola....* ② Underline every change in your rewritten paragraph.

Katherine always looked BEAUTIFUL than Viola, with LONG, LUSTROUS hair and BRIGHT, WHITE teeth. She dressed ATTRACTIVE and moved GRACEFUL. She enjoyed living EXTRAVAGANT, so she looked CAREFUL for a SMART man who was becoming rich QUICK than Caspar was. She behaved STUPID than Viola by picking Brad, who had LITTLE charm and FEW brains than Caspar. After six months in a FASHIONABLE part of town, Brad began to trade stocks RECKLESS than Caspar and made a BAD decision. After moving into a DUMPY neighborhood, the couple had LITTLE to look forward to than Viola and Caspar and MUCH to regret.

| Exercise 12.15 | Using positive, comparative, and superlative forms |

Here again is the same paragraph you worked on in Exercises 12.13-14, now telling the story of Diane's marriage to Duncan, and comparing this third couple to the two previous ones, Viola and Caspar, and Katherine and Brad. ① Mark a piece of paper Exercise 12.15, and rewrite this paragraph onto it, changing the base forms into the appropriate **superlative** adjective and adverb forms. Your paragraph will begin *Diane always looked <u>the most beautiful</u> of the three women...* ② Underline every change in your rewritten paragraph.

Diane always looked BEAUTIFUL of the three women, with LONG, LUSTROUS hair and BRIGHT, WHITE teeth. She dressed ATTRACTIVE and moved GRACEFUL.

She enjoyed living EXTRAVAGANT, so she looked CAREFUL for a SMART man who was becoming rich QUICK of the three men. She behaved STUPID of the three women by picking Duncan, who had LITTLE charm and FEW brains of the three men. After six months in a FASHIONABLE part of town, Duncan began to trade stocks RECKLESS of the three men and made a BAD decision. After moving into a DUMPY neighborhood, the couple had LITTLE to look forward to of the three couples and MUCH to regret.

Editing Practice M.3   **Checking adjectives and adverbs**

1. Get your draft of Paper M again.
2. Underline each adjective and adverb.
3. Review Rules 12E-12F.
4. Check to make sure that each adjective and adverb is correct. Fix any mistakes with your green pen.
5. How many mistakes did you fix? _____ Your ability to find and fix mistakes in your own writing shows how much you've learned so far.

Keep your draft of Paper M to use again later.

Using Other Expansion

Placement of Noun and Verb Expansion

As you already know, incorrect placement of expansion can cause confusion. Whether it's a single word, or a phrase, or a longer piece of expansion beginning with *who, which,* or *that,* **noun expansion** must go **next to** the noun it expands, or the sentence may be confusing. **Verb expansion** can usually be moved around within a sentence, but it must be placed where it does not make the sentence confusing.

 In school grammar, this kind of problem is called a **misplaced modifier**.

12G	For clearer sentences, place noun expansion <u>right next to</u> the noun or pronoun it expands.

One-word noun expansion goes **before** the noun it expands, while expansion created by the noun-expansion words *who, which,* or *that* always goes **after** the noun it expands.

Ben studied the (restaurant) bill, (which was enormous).
>   These two pieces of expansion, both telling more about the *bill*, are placed correctly, and the sentence is clear.

You already worked on the problem of sentences with misplaced *who, which,* and *that* expansion on page 118 in Module 4. Now check your understanding of this problem. First put parentheses around the *who* expansion in this confusing sentence. Then rewrite the sentence by moving the expansion so that the intended meaning is clear.

The officer arrested the thief who had earned four medals for bravery.

_____

The problem is that the expansion *who had earned four medals for bravery* tells about the *officer*, not about the *thief*. Placing the expansion after *officer* makes the sentence clear:

The officer (who had earned four medals for bravery) arrested the thief.

Misplacing **verb expansion** that begins with a preposition can further confuse a sentence, especially when the sentence also has noun expansion.

This morning Manuel began repairs to Juana's new car ✗ (in his body shop), (which had been hit by an old van).
>   *In his body shop* is verb expansion telling WHERE Manuel began repairs. When it is placed right after *car*, it gets in the way of the noun expansion *which had been hit by an old van*. So the sentence is confusing.

The verb expansion *in his body shop*, like all verb expansion, can be moved around in the sentence. Here are four possible places to put it. Read each sentence out loud to see which sounds most natural:

(In his body shop) this morning Manuel began repairs to Juana's new car.
This morning (in his body shop) Manuel began repairs to Juana's new car.
This morning Manuel (in his body shop) began repairs to Juana's new car.
This morning Manuel began repairs (in his body shop) to Juana's new car.

If you are a native speaker of English, all but the third of these sentences probably sounded pretty natural. Notice that in the third sentence, the expansion *in his body shop* is placed right after the noun Manuel. This re-creates the confusion in the original sentence: putting verb expansion after a noun.

Now that we have found some suitable places for the verb expansion, we can write the original sentence more clearly, putting both pieces of expansion in appropriate places:

(In his body shop) this morning Manuel began repairs to Juana's new car, (which had been hit by an old van).
This morning (in his body shop) Manuel began repairs to Juana's new car, (which had been hit by an old van).
This morning Manuel began repairs (in his body shop) to Juana's new car, (which had been hit by an old van).
>   None of these sentences is confusing.

Exercise 12.16	Moving expansion to make sentences clear

① Put parentheses around expansion. ② Mark with an ✗ any piece of expansion whose placement makes the sentence confusing. Remember that more than one piece of expansion may be misplaced. ③ On a piece of scratch paper, move the expansion around to make the sentence clearer. Read your rewritten sentence out loud to see whether the expansion sounds natural in its new position, and whether the sentence is clearer. If you are not a native speaker of English, read them to someone who is. ④ After you have decided on an appropriate place for the expansion, rewrite the sentence so that it is clear, and put parentheses around the expansion.

1. Jane served samosas at her open house, which her guests ate greedily.

    _____

2. All the guests wanted the recipe, who were vegetarians.

    _____

3. Later Jane realized that the open house hadn't been a success, which she had almost spent a fortune on.

    _____

Noun Expansion with *ING* Words

Another kind of expansion begins with an *ING* word. In **Module 2**, you learned that an *ING* word by itself is not a verb, but that an *ING* word can be the main verb in a verb phrase after the helping verb *BE*.

> <u>Hoping</u> for a silver medal, Viviane <u>was running</u> as fast as she could.
> > *Hoping* is not a verb but is part of expansion telling more about *Viviane*. *Was running* is a verb phrase.

In school grammar, an *ING* word is called a **present participle**.

Two short, choppy sentences can often be combined into a single more expressive and more compact sentence by using *ING* expansion.

> Viviane was hoping for a silver medal. She was running as fast as she could.
> (Hoping for a silver medal), Viviane was running as fast as she could.
> > The two short sentences have been combined into one more effective one.

When one sentence is turned into *ING* expansion of an appropriate noun or pronoun in another sentence, this expansion is placed sometimes before the word it expands and sometimes after it.

> (Hoping for a silver medal), Viviane was running her best time ever.
> Viviane, (hoping for a silver medal), was running her best time ever.
> > Both sentences are correct.

ING expansion can be used even in sentences which are in the past tense.

> She hoped for silver. She won gold.
> <u>Hoping for silver</u>, she won gold.

> She held up her trophy. It glinted in the sun
> She held up her trophy, <u>glinting in the sun.</u>
>> One sentence in each pair of past-tense sentences has been turned into *ING* expansion of a noun or pronoun in the other. The expansion is placed sometimes before the word it expands, sometimes after it.

Putting *ING* expansion, like other kinds of expansion, in the wrong place can sometimes cause unclear sentences.

> That SUV scratched my car, ✗ (pulling out too quickly).
>> Which vehicle pulled out too quickly? This sentence is not clear, because the expansion *pulling out too quickly* is placed next to *my car.*

> That SUV, (pulling out too quickly), scratched my car.
>> Putting the expansion in the right place makes it clear that the SUV was the offending vehicle.

In general, then, because *ING* expansion is like expansion created by noun-expansion words, it should be placed right next to the noun it tells more about, as in the second example above.

Another similarity between *ING* expansion and expansion created by noun-expansion words is how they should be punctuated.

You learned on page 119 in Module 4 that expansion sometimes contains **information which is needed** to answer the question *WHICH?* about a noun. In this case, **commas should <u>not</u> be used** around the expansion. At other times, expansion contains **extra information which is <u>not</u> needed** to answer the question *WHICH?* about a noun. In this case, **commas <u>should</u> be used** around the expansion.

> That SUV**,** pulling out too quickly**,** scratched my car.
>> The words *that sports utility vehicle* are sufficient to identify the car, so *pulling out too quickly* is additional information which is not needed; therefore, commas **are** used around the expansion.

> The vehicle pulling out too quickly scratched my car.
>> The words *the vehicle* are not sufficient to identify the car, so *pulling out too quickly* is needed to identify it exactly; therefore, commas **are not** used around the expansion.

Exercise 12.17	**Punctuating *ING* expansion to make sentences clear**

① Put parentheses around *ING* expansion. ② Insert commas where they are needed.

1. In his first draft of the Declaration of Independence, a man owning two hundred slaves wrote a paragraph denouncing slavery.

2. Benjamin Franklin fearing that the patriots from the southern colonies would refuse to sign the Declaration crossed out this paragraph.

3. Thomas Jefferson, the author of the document, claimed that the blacks living under his paternal care could not survive in a hostile white world.

4. Modern historians reviewing Jefferson's words and behavior wonder about his sincerity.

Exercise 12.18	Moving *ING* expansion to make sentences clear

① Put parentheses around *ING* expansion. ② Mark with an ✗ any piece of expansion whose placement makes the sentence confusing. ③ On a piece of scratch paper, move the expansion around to make the sentence clearer. Read your rewritten sentence out loud to see whether the expansion sounds natural in its new position, and whether the sentence is clearer. If you are not a native speaker of English, read them to someone who is. ④ After you have decided on an appropriate place for the expansion, rewrite the sentence so that it is clear, and put parentheses around the expansion.

1. A man left a bloody footprint at the crime scene, wearing a special brand of shoes.

_____

2. Some photos were exhibited to the jury, showing the defendant in this expensive footgear.

_____

3. The defense lawyer spoke to the judge, vehemently dismissing the photos as fakes.

_____

There is one important difference between *ING* expansion and expansion caused by noun-expansion words like *who* and *which*. *ING* expansion, because it doesn't have a noun-expansion word, can go **before a noun**. In this case, it must be followed by a comma:

> Marcella, (who was tying her shoelaces), felt a pain in her back.
> Marcella, (tying her shoelaces), felt a pain in her back.
> (Tying her shoelaces), Marcella felt a pain in her back.
> > These sentences are all correct.

Here are three exceptions to the general principle that *ING* expansion can go either before or after the noun it tells more about:

1. When the *ING* expansion contains information which is needed to answer the question *WHICH?* about a noun, it must go after the noun. In this case, commas should not be used:

> ✗ (Attending Marcella), the doctor gave her a painkiller.
> The doctor (attending Marcella) gave her a painkiller.
> > Only the second sentence is correct.

2. When the noun to be expanded is not the subject of the sentence, the *ING* expansion must go after it:

> ✗ (Crying with pain), the medicine helped Marcella.
> The medicine, ✗ (crying with pain), helped Marcella.
> The medicine helped, ✗ (crying with pain), Marcella.
> The medicine helped Marcella, (crying with pain).
> > Only the last sentence is correct.

3. Sometimes *ING* expansion tells more about a pronoun rather than a noun. In this case, when the pronoun is a subject, the *ING* expansion goes before it, at the beginning of the sentence, and is followed by a comma:

> She, ✗ (crying with pain), waited for the medicine to take effect.
> (Crying with pain), she waited for the medicine to take effect.
> > Only the second sentence is correct.

This diagram summarizes what you've learned about the placement and punctuation of *ING* expansion:

ING expansion	placement	commas
needed to tell *WHICH?* About a noun	after the noun	should not be used
tells more about a noun which is not the subject of the sentence	after the noun	should not be used if the expansion is needed to tell *WHICH?* about the noun; otherwise, should be used
tells more about a pronoun at the beginning of the sentence	before the pronoun	should be used
otherwise	either before or after the noun	should be used

Exercise 12.19   Using *ING* expansion in clear sentences

① Rewrite the two sentences as one sentence, turning the **second** sentence into *ING* expansion of the appropriate noun in the first sentence, and punctuating your sentence correctly. ② Put parentheses around the *ING* expansion.

1. Miss Solgars flirted with her boss.
   She was hoping for a promotion.

   _____

   _____

   _____

2. She was happy to find his very positive performance evaluation.
   It was lying on top of his desk.

   _____

   _____

   _____

3. Christopher recognized the picture.
   He was entering the room.

   _____

   _____

4. Christopher recognized the picture.
   It was hanging on the wall.

   _____

   _____

5. The foul ball hit a spectator.
   It was soaring into the last row.

   _____

   _____

6. The foul ball hit a spectator.
   She was sitting in the last row.

   _____

   _____

Exercise 12.20	Using *ING* expansion of pronouns in clear sentences

① Rewrite the two sentences as one sentence, turning the second sentence into *ING* expansion of the appropriate pronoun in the first sentence, and punctuating your sentence correctly. ② Put parentheses around the *ING* expansion in your rewritten sentence.

1. We are building unmanned space vehicles.
   We hope to save not just billions but trillions.

   _____

   _____

   _____

2. They travel light and on the cheap.
   They operate without expensive life-support systems.

   _____

   _____

3. They perform elaborate experiments on distant planets.
    They respond to commands from Mission Control at Houston.

    _____

    _____

4. They beam brilliant pictures back to Earth.
    They contain tiny but powerful cameras.

    _____

    _____

Noun Expansion with Past Participles

As you learned in Module 11, the past participles of all **regular** verbs end in *ED*. Like *ING* words, *ED* words and other past participles can be used as expansion to tell more about nouns.

Remember that you can find the past participle of all **irregular** verbs in the dictionary.

> I threw away the <u>broken</u> bottle and the <u>chipped</u> plate.
>> *Broken* and *chipped* are the past participles of the irregular verb *BREAK* and the regular verb *CHIP*. Here they are used as expansion to tell more about the nouns *bottle* and *plate*.

Exercise 12.21   Writing past participles as expansion

① Fill in the past participle of the given main verb. ② Then rewrite the two sentences as one sentence, using the past participle as expansion. ③ Put parentheses around the expansion in your rewritten sentence. Follow this model:

TERRIFY   The child hid in the doorway. She was *terrified* .
              The (terrified) child hid in the doorway.

1. ICE   The tea was delicious. It was _____

              _____

2. COVER   The bridge is a landmark. It was _____

              _____

3. DEPRESS   The patient took tranquilizers. He was _____

              _____

4. USE   Leroy repaired the stereo. It was _____

              _____

5.   PREJUDICE   The banker refused to lend me money. He was _____

_____

Like *ING* expansion, if noun expansion beginning with a past participle is misplaced in a sentence, it can make the sentence unclear:

> The history teacher, (embarrassed by her mistake), apologized to her students.
>
> Who was embarrassed? _____
>
> The history teacher apologized to her students, (embarrassed by her mistake).
>
> Who was embarrassed? _____

The only difference between these two sentences is the placement of the expansion. But these two sentences have completely different meanings. If the intended meaning is that the teacher was embarrassed, then putting the expansion *embarrassed by her mistake* next to the noun *students* will make the sentence unclear and confusing.

Because the past participles of regular verbs like *EMBARRASS* always have a *D* or *ED* ending, and this ending is often hard to pronounce and hard to hear, it's sometimes omitted in writing. However, this ending is important because it shows that **something has happened to** the noun. Be especially careful not to leave off this *D* or *ED* ending.

> The judge was prejudiced by that defendant's appearance.
> .   *Prejudiced is the past participle of the verb PREJUDICE.*
>
> **✗**
> The judge, (prejudice by his appearance), gave him the maximum sentence.
>   *The expansion is incorrect because prejudice is not the past participle of the verb PREJUDICE.*
>
> The judge, (prejudiced by his appearance), gave him the maximum sentence.
> The (prejudiced) judge gave him the maximum sentence.
>   *These two sentences are correct. The past participle prejudiced tells what has happened to the judge.*

The rules about punctuating and placing *ING* expansion also apply to expansion beginning with a past participle. Review these rules on page 320 above, and then apply them to past-participle expansion in doing the following exercises.

Exercise 12.22	Using past-participle expansion in clear sentences

① Rewrite the two sentences as one sentence, turning the second sentence into past-participle expansion of a noun in the first sentence, and punctuating your sentence correctly. ② Put parentheses around the past-participle expansion in your rewritten sentence.

1.   Diana abruptly hung up on Nancy.
     Diana was enraged by her question about Charlie.

_____

_____

2.   Diana talked to her neighbor, Betty Windsor.
     Diana was irritated by Nancy's insensitivity.

_____

_____

3.   Betty tried to calm down her friend.
     Diana was so easily irked by a simple inquiry.

_____

_____

Exercise 12.23   Using past-participle expansion of pronouns in clear sentences

① Rewrite the two sentences as one sentence, turning the second sentence into past-participle expansion of a pronoun in the first sentence, and punctuating your sentence correctly. ② Put parentheses around the past-participle expansion in your rewritten sentence.

1.   He made an appointment with her.
     He was puzzled by his grade.

_____

_____

2.   She hesitated to see him.
     She had been assaulted recently by a disgruntled student.

_____

_____

3.   However, they actually enjoyed their chat.
     They were surprised by each other's quiet reasonableness.

_____

_____

Exercise 12.24   Moving past-participle expansion to make sentences clear

These sentences are about the British author George Eliot. Read them carefully to make sure that you understand them. ① Put parentheses around past-participle expansion. ② Mark with an ✗ any piece of expansion whose placement makes the sentence confusing. ③ On a piece of scratch paper, move the expansion around to make the sentence clearer. Read your rewritten sentence out loud to see whether the expansion sounds natural in its new position, and whether the sentence is clearer. If you are not a native speaker of English, read them to someone who is. ④ After you have decided on an appropriate place for the expansion, rewrite the sentence so that it is clear, and put parentheses around the expansion.

1. Condensed into six brief episodes for TV, thousands watched the dramatization of Mary Ann Evans's Victorian novel *Middlemarch*.

_____

_____

2. Described by her contemporaries as a homely, horse-faced woman, George Henry Lewes was deeply in love with *Middlemarch's* supremely ugly but superbly gifted author.

_____

_____

_____

3. The pen-name George Eliot protected the feminine identity of this writer, suggested by her lover's first name.

_____

_____

4. Lewes lived until he died with this talented writer, still married to his despised wife, but forbidden by a quirk of the law to divorce her.

_____

_____

Exercise 12.25   Moving expansion to make sentences clear

Read these sentences carefully to make sure that you understand them. ① Put parentheses around expansion. ② Mark with an *X* any piece of expansion whose placement makes the sentence confusing. ③ On a piece of scratch paper, move the expansion around to make the sentence clearer. Read your rewritten sentence out loud to see whether the expansion sounds natural in its new position, and whether the sentence is clearer. If you are not a native speaker of English, read them to someone who is. ④ After you have decided on an appropriate place for the expansion, rewrite the sentence so that it is clear, and put parentheses around the expansion.

1. Abandoned on the bar room counter, Uncle Boris picked up this morning's newspaper, eager to know the latest horse-racing results.

_____

_____

_____

2. Immediately a huge headline informed him that his most recent stock investment had plummeted on the financial page, which he read in disbelief.

_____

_____

3. Then he noticed the obituary of a favorite drinking companion, still turning the pages in search of the sports news.

_____

_____

4. Discovering that his horse had indeed won at the bottom of the last page, my poor uncle remembered that he'd forgotten to place his bet, who boasts that he never forgets anything.

_____

_____

_____

To use *ING* expansion and past participle expansion correctly and effectively, focus on these general guidelines:

* Use expansion beginning with **present participles** (*ING* words) to tell what a noun **is or was doing**.

* Use expansion beginning with **past participles** (often *ED* words) to tell what **has happened** to a noun.

> Nixon gave the V for victory sign.
> He was <u>disgraced</u>.
>> The past participle tells what **has happened** to Nixon.
>
> But he was still <u>smiling</u>.
>> The *ING* word tells what he **was doing**.
>
> (<u>Disgraced</u> but still <u>smiling</u>), Nixon gave the V for victory sign.
>> *Disgraced* tells what happened to Nixon; *smiling* tells what Nixon was doing.

Exercise 12.26	**Using *ING* and *ED* expansion in paragraphs**

Read these sentences carefully to make sure that you understand them. ① On scratch paper, rewrite each group of sentences by using the ideas in the other sentences to expand nouns in the **first** sentence: change any sentence telling what a noun is doing into *ING* expansion, and change any sentence telling what has happened to a noun into past-participle expansion. Make sure that your sentences make sense. ② Mark another piece of paper Exercise 12.26, and copy your rewritten sentences onto it as a paragraph. Your paragraph will begin *Some animal lovers, carried away by...* ③ Put parentheses around the expansion in your rewritten sentence.

1. Some animal lovers seem to ignore the best interests of both beasts and humans.
    The animal lovers are carried away by their enthusiasm for animal rights.

2. For example, some deer and a community of Long Island home-owners have become a menace to
    each other.
    The deer are white-tailed.
    The deer are now multiplying into the hundreds.
    The deer and home-owners are trapped together on a small peninsula a few miles wide.

3. Angry residents stare bitterly at their gardens.
    The residents are bitten by deer ticks.
    The ticks are carrying Lyme disease.
    The residents' gardens are devastated.
    The residents' gardens are devoured by deer.
    The deer are starving.

4. Nevertheless, animal activists lobby against all attempts to control the deer population in this
    community.
    The animal activists are driven by an irrational zeal.
    The animal activists are living in distant, deer-free towns.

5. These animal lovers continue to oppose any laws.
    The animal lovers are dedicated.
    The animal lovers are relentlessly reminding us that the woods and plains once belonged to these
    animals.
    The laws are favoring the rights of humans over animals.

Dangling Expansion

Some confused sentences are harder to make clear than any of those above. These are sentences with noun expansion that doesn't expand **any** noun in the sentence. This kind of noun expansion is described as **dangling**, or just hanging in the air, not attached to anything in the sentence.

> ✗ (Sitting on my porch), a hawk flew overhead.
>> The expansion *sitting on my porch* doesn't tell more about *hawk* or any other noun, so we don't know who was sitting. The expansion dangles.

To make clear who was doing the sitting, you must change the sentence. Here are two possible ways to change it:

> (While I was sitting on my porch), a hawk flew overhead.
>> In this sentence, a subject, verb, and connecting word have been added to the *ING* expansion to tell who was sitting.

> (Sitting on my porch), I saw a hawk flying overhead.
>> In this sentence, a subject and verb have been added to the sentence to tell who was sitting.

327

Exercise 12.27   Fixing dangling expansion to make sentences clear

These sentences are all about Dorothy. ① Put parentheses around expansion. ② Mark with an **X** any dangling expansion. ③ Answer the question about the meaning of the sentence. ④ Using one of the models above, rewrite the sentence, fixing the dangling expansion, and punctuating your sentence correctly. Put parentheses around expansion in your rewritten sentence.

1. Dorothy's dinner turns cold watching TV.

    Who is watching TV? _____

    _____

2. Ignored by her friends, Dorothy's life is lonely.

    Who is ignored by her friends? _____

    _____

3. Dorothy's health is poor, never going out or getting any exercise.

    Who never goes out or gets any exercise? _____

    _____

4. Contacted recently by her granddaughter, Dorothy's future may be brighter.

    Who was contacted recently by her granddaughter? _____

    _____

Editing Practice M.4   *Checking ING and past participle expansion*

1. Get your draft of Paper M again.
2. Underline each example of *ING* expansion. How many did you underline? _____ If you didn't find at least three, draw another line across the page, and below it either write more sentences with *ING* expansion, or rewrite existing sentences so that they have *ING* expansion.
3. Underline each example of past participle expansion. How many did you underline? _____ If you didn't find at least three, either write more sentences with past participle expansion below the line, or rewrite existing sentences so that they have past participle expansion.
4. Review Rule 12G.
5. Check to make sure that each example of *ING* and past participle expansion is correct, and is not misplaced. Fix any mistakes with your green pen.
6. How many mistakes did you fix? _____ Your ability to find and fix mistakes in your own writing shows how much you've learned so far.

Keep your draft of Paper M to use again later.

Using parallel parts

12H	**For more effective sentences, make their parts <u>parallel</u>.**

You already know that words like *and, or,* and *but* are used to join sentence parts of equal importance. To emphasize their equal importance, the parts of a sentence joined by these words should have the same structures. Such structures are called **parallel**. Parallel parts are particularly important in series and in comparisons:

> I like <u>skating</u>, <u>skiing</u>, and <u>riding</u> horses.
>> In this series, the parallel parts *skating, skiing,* and *riding* make this sentence easy to read and understand.

Non-parallel forms distract the reader from the meaning of a sentence:

> ✗
> I like <u>skating</u>, <u>skiing</u>, and <u>to ride</u> horses.
>> In this series, the word *and* is a signal to the reader that the *ING* words *skating* and *skiing* will be followed by another *ING* word (like *riding*). The infinitive *to ride* is not parallel, and distracts the reader from the meaning.

In a comparison, as in a series, what is being compared should also be in parallel form:

> ✗
> I like <u>skating</u> better than <u>to ski</u>.
>> *Better than* signals a comparison, requiring parallel forms. But *skating* and *to ski* are not parallel forms.

> I like <u>skating</u> better than <u>skiing</u>.
>> The parallel forms *skating* and *skiing* make this sentence easy to read and understand.

To write sentences with parallel parts, watch for joining words like *and* and *or* which join words in a series, and also for words like *than* which express comparisons. The parts being joined or compared should be parallel.

Exercise 12.28	**Making the appropriate parts of sentences parallel**

① Underline each item in a series or a comparison. ② In the space above the line, correct any part that is not in parallel form.

1. For Clara, getting ready to retire was a great experience, mentally, physically, and for her emotions.

2. It was a pleasure to clear out her desk, to turn in her office keys, and saying goodbye to her workaholic friends.

3. As for her other co-workers—the hypocrites, the ones who tell lies, and the snobs—she would just send them dazzling postcards from her new home.

4. To her surprise, her grumpy boss stopped for a moment, smiled, and even was shaking her hand.

5. Of course, she still had to decide whether to drive to her new home, to take the bus, or she could go on the train.

6. As for her dilapidated car, it needed a new transmission, a complete tune-up, and four tires had to be replaced.

7. Maybe it would save money in the long run to buy a new car rather than repairing that old one.

8. One thing she had already decided: Walking on the beach is more fun than to answer phones or entering data into the company's computer.

9. Clara looked forward to Monday morning when she would turn off the lights, collect her bags, and then leaving for her new life.

Exercise 12.29	Writing sentences with parallel parts

This sentence tells what I do:

I read books, listen to CDs, watch videos, and play computer games.

Use the ideas in this sentence to complete each sentence below, following the structure of the given beginning. Your first sentence will begin *Tomorrow I will read books, will listen to…*

1. Tomorrow I will read books, _____

   _____

2. Yesterday I read my books, _____

   _____

3. I have read your books, _____

   _____

4. I have books to read, _____

   _____

5. I will need some exercise after reading Audrey's books, _____

   _____

6.   These have all enriched my life: the books that I've read, _____

_____

_____

7.   I rarely go out because I have so many books to read, _____

_____

_____

Editing Practice M.5	***Checking parallel parts***

1.   Get your draft of Paper M again.
2.   Review Rule 12H.
3.   Check to make sure that you haven't made any mistakes with parts that should be parallel. Fix any mistakes with your green pen.
4.   How many mistakes did you fix? _____ Your ability to find and fix mistakes in your own writing shows how much you've learned so far.

Writing Your Final Copy of Paper M

Use your final copy of Paper M to demonstrate what you've learned in Module 12 about using expansion, and to show how well you're continuing to apply what you've learned previously.

Paper M	**Using expansion**

Edit for Previous Modules

Use your dictionary and the Rules Summaries for previous modules to:

- Check your use of writing conventions. Fix any mistakes with your green pen.

- Check your use of nouns and pronouns. Fix any mistakes with your green pen.

- Check your use of present-tense verbs. Fix any mistakes with your green pen.

- Check your use of past-tense verbs. Fix any mistakes with your green pen.

- Check the structure of each word-group to find any run-ons. Fix any mistakes with your green pen, either by rewriting them as two sentences, or by connecting them with joining or expansion or transition words, being sure to punctuate them correctly. How many run-ons did you find and correct? _____

- Check the structure of each word-group to find any fragments. Fix any mistakes with your green pen, either by connecting them to an appropriate sentence, or by adding, removing, or changing words. How many fragments did you find and correct? _____

- Check your use of verb phrases. Fix any mistakes with your green pen.

Make Final Copy   Mark another piece of paper Paper M, and write the final copy of your paper on it, or print out a clean copy on your word processor. Be sure to include all your corrections.

Proofread   Read your final copy **out loud.** Correct any mistakes neatly by hand. If you used a word processor, enter your corrections, and print out a corrected final copy.

Hand in your final copy of **Paper M**, and the rest of your exercises.

Answers

Exercise 0.1

1. A girl with three younger **brothers** often has a difficult childhood.
2. In the early evening, the fireworks factory was rocked by a **powerful** explosion.
3. When his mother walked in with a tiny bundle in her arms, Gerald rushed up to get a good look at his new baby **sister**.
4. The **best** way to prepare this sauce is to beat it vigorously for three minutes.
5. Victor, an experienced **electrician** from Czechoslovakia, wants to join the local electricians' **union**.

Exercise 0.2 The three mistakes that you cannot hear, but must actually see, are the word *sail*, the incorrect capital letter *P* in *Property*, and the missing capital letter *W* in *whatever*.

Buying property is ~~is~~ **even** riskier than buying used **cars**. For example, a store **by** the library in ~~in~~ my neighborhood is going to **be** put up for **sale** soon. The owner, Hank Dawson, **may** try to get **$90,000** for **it**, but the value of the **property** is actually much less than that. A building inspector **was** in the basement recently and saw termites. He checked the beams and found **they** were completely rotten and ready to collapse. Buyers, beware! **Whatever** claims Dawson makes about that building, you can bet **your** bottom dollar they're **not** true.

Exercise 0.3

From the 1920s through the 1950s, cigarette smoking was considered **a** harmless and even glamorous habit. Stars of **the** silver screen, wearing tuxedos and evening gowns, lighted **each** other's cigarettes in night club scenes. Film detectives chain-smoked as **they** solved their cases. The children in many pictures sneaked **their** first puffs behind the garage. **But** modern audiences watching old movies on TV find these scenes disturbing.

Exercise 0.4

From the 1920s through the 1950s, cigarette smoking was **considered** a harmless and even glamorous habit. Stars of the silver screen, **wearing** tuxedos and evening gowns, lighted each other's **cigarettes** in night club scenes. Film detectives chain-smoked as they **solved** their cases. The children in many pictures **sneaked** their first puffs behind the garage. But modern audiences **watching** old movies on TV find these scenes disturbing.

Exercise 0.5

From the 1920s through the 1950s, cigarette smoking was considered a harmless and even glamorous habit. Stars of the **silver** screen, wearing tuxedos and evening gowns, lighted each other's cigarettes in night club scenes. **Film** detectives chain-smoked as they solved their cases. The **children** in many pictures sneaked their **first** puffs behind the garage. But **modern** audiences watching old movies on TV find these scenes **disturbing**.

Section 1: *Practicing the Writing Process*

Editing Silvia's final copy for correctness

Because of all the new information about the Roosevelts that has been published during the past ten years, the American public has begun to realize that the marriage of President Franklin Delano Roosevelt to his cousin Eleanor was **extraordinary**, particularly as a marriage that began early in the 20th century.
spelling

When people look at the early photographs of the couple, they marvel that these two got married in the first place. They wonder how the handsome, charming young Franklin and the serious, shy, and not very attractive Eleanor could have fallen in love with each other. Their attraction to each other, however, is not as strange as it seems. In that period of his life, the future President felt a need for the sincerity and moral strength he found in Eleanor. As for her, with very little love and not much fun when growing up, she was flattered by his boundless charm and delighted by his **sociability**. These and other strongly contrasting qualities always made them a kind of odd but striking couple.
spelling

It appears, however, that the first sixteen years of this couple's marriage **were** no different from most marriages of that period. In their early years together, Eleanor loved being a wife and mother, and bore and raised six children while Franklin pursued his career in the Navy and in politics. Then Eleanor discovered her husband's affair with her own social **secretary**. He begged her not to to divorce him, because at that time a divorce would have ended his political career. **S**he agreed, but only because she believed so strongly in his gift for politics and in his future as great President. From this time on, she felt free to spend her time and her enormous energies in pursuing a new career as an agitator for social change and human rights. The shy and insecure Eleanor was **transformed** into a different kind of partner, capable of helping her husband in new and important ways.
subject-verb agreement
spelling
run-on sentence
verb forms

When Franklin became **paralyzed** by polio from the waist down, the Roosevelt marriage progressed into its final and most remarkable phase, which lasted the rest of their lives together. During his campaigns for high office and his four terms as President, his wife became his eyes and ears all over the country. She went where his lifeless legs could not take him. **S**he shared what she learned from her **journeys**, and in this way gave him a better understanding of complicated national issues. Without her, he might not have been able to solve the enormous problems of the Depression. In the years after Pearl **Harbor**, when the President was frantically busy
spelling
run-on sentence
spelling
capital letter

334

with the world war now raging on two fronts, the First Lady **traveled** hundreds of thousands of miles to gather facts about social and economic conditions in rural and urban America. Whenever she returned to the White House, she succeeded in getting her husband to pay attention again to domestic affairs and to continue the reforms he had begun before the war.

spelling

Both Franklin and Eleanor, as husband and wife, had the power to rise above each other's flaws, to recognize the other's remarkable gifts, and even to go on loving each other for their best qualities. The result was an extraordinary marriage, of benefit not only to themselves but to many Americans for years to come.

Proofreading Silvia's final copy

Because of all the new information about the Roosevelts that has been published during the past ten years, the American public has begun to realize that the marriage of President Franklin Delano Roosevelt to his cousin Eleanor was extraordinary, particularly as a marriage that began early in the 20th century.

When people look at the early photographs of the couple, they marvel that these two got married in the first place. They wonder how the handsome, charming young Franklin and the serious, shy, and not very attractive Eleanor could have fallen in love with each other. Their attraction to each other, however, is not as strange as it seems. In that period of his life, the future President felt a need for the sincerity and moral strength he found in Eleanor. As for her, with very little love and not much fun when growing up, she was flattered by his boundless charm and delighted by his sociability. These and other strongly contrasting qualities always made them a kind of odd but striking couple.

It appears, however, that the first sixteen years of this couple's marriage were no different from most marriages of that period. In their early years together, Eleanor loved being a wife and mother, and bore and raised six children while Franklin pursued his career in the Navy and in politics. Then Eleanor discovered her husband's affair with her own social secretary. He begged her not **to** ~~to~~ divorce him, because at that time a divorce would have ended his political career. She agreed, but only because she believed so strongly in his gift for politics and in his future as **a** great President. From this time on, she felt free to spend her time and her enormous energies in pursuing a new career as an agitator for social change and human rights. The shy and insecure Eleanor was transformed into a different

repeated word

omitted word

kind of partner, capable of helping her husband in new and important ways.

When Franklin became paralyzed by polio from the waist down, the Roosevelt marriage progressed into its final and most remarkable phase, which lasted the rest of their lives together. During his campaigns for high office and his four terms as President, his wife became his eyes and ears all over the country. She went where his lifeless legs could not take him. She shared what she learned from her journeys, and in this way gave him a better understanding of complicated national issues. Without her, he might not have been able to solve the enormous problems of the Depression. In the years after Pearl Harbor, when the President was frantically busy with the world war now raging on two fronts, the First Lady traveled hundreds of thousands of miles to gather facts about social and economic conditions in rural and urban America. Whenever she returned to the White House, she succeeded in getting her husband to pay attention again to domestic affairs and to continue the reforms he had begun before the war.

Both Franklin and Eleanor, as husband and wife, had the power to rise above each other's flaws, to recognize the other's remarkable gifts, and even to go on loving each other for their best qualities. The result was an extraordinary marriage, of benefit not only to themselves but to many Americans for years to come.

Module 1: *Mastering Writing Conventions*

Tombstone Inscription

Here lyeth the body of William Vogwell the Elder buried November 3, 1683 AD.

Exercise 1.1

Anglo-Saxon, an old Germanic language, ranks first among many languages that contributed to our modern English vocabulary. This language, spoken by early inhabitants of England, gave us words like <u>cow</u>, <u>pig</u>, <u>plow</u>, <u>walk</u> — common words associated with outdoor life and the activities of farmers and workers.

The second most important source of modern English words is Norman French. This language, brought to England by a conquering army, gave us words like <u>beef</u>, <u>pork</u>, <u>study</u>, <u>dance</u> — more refined words associated with life indoors and the pastimes of a ruling class.

Exercise 1.2

1. **When Roberto** goes to college, he will study psychology and **Spanish**.
2. **Has** your mother made an appointment with the doctor?
3. **Today I** went to see **Dr. Alston**.

4. **My** youngest uncle is an engineer for the **Sperry Corporation**.
5. **The** house where **Aunt Sally** was born is on **Narcissus Street**.

Exercise 1.3

1. St. Mary's is the only **church** in the **neighborhood** that has a **raffle** every Friday night.
2. Our math **professor** owns stock in the **railroad** which the Metropolitan Transit Authority took over.
3. The local **high school** improved its **curriculum** by offering new courses in **geography** and requiring four years of Spanish or another **foreign language**.

Exercise 1.4

1. **Is** it time to go **?**
2. **Did** he ask if it was time to go **?**
3. **He** asked if it was time to go **.**
4. **They** couldn't decide whether to write the letter **.**
5. **Did Loretta** write the letter **?**

Exercise 1.5

1. it**'s**
2. doe**sn't**
3. i**sn't**
4. **I'm**
5. d**on't**
6. w**on't**

Exercise 1.6

It's amazing how much **we're** able to learn about the so-called good old days from old mail order catalogues. **Here's** a sampling of their ads between 1912 and 1932:
Model H Motor Car, $348: "**We'll** refund every penny if it **won't** go 15 miles an hour."
Baby Grand Piano, $118: "**She's** a beauty. Delivery? **It's** free!"
Two-piece Bathing Suits, $1.63: "**They're** the latest—backless and skirtless." And a model says, "**Where's** your courage? **I'm** wearing one. **It's** the cat's pajamas."
Bargains? **You're** wrong. A person **who's** making five dollars an hour today **wouldn't** have made five dollars a day when these ads were printed.

Exercise 1.7

If **you're** on a diet, **it's** likely that **you're** counting calories. However, nutritionists are now saying that calories **aren't** necessarily bad for a person **who's** trying to lose weight. **They've** discovered that carbohydrates like potatoes, bread, and cereals have lots of calories, but **they're** full of nutrition, so they **don't** add pounds quickly. On the other hand, fats like butter **aren't** nutritious at all, so **it's** easy to gain weight by eating them. Even worse, most people **don't** realize how much fat **they're** getting in cheese, meat, and ready-made foods. So if **you're** dieting, **you'd** do well to remember this: **Fat's** what makes you fat.

Exercise 1.8

1. Jeremiah overcame procrastination by repeating to himself**,** **"**Anything worth doing is worth doing badly**."**
2. **"**Any man's death diminishes me**,"** wrote the poet John Donne.
3. The new student muttered**,** **"**I must be in the wrong class**,"** as she picked up her books and bolted out the door.

Exercise 1.9

1. The old saying tells us, "**When** in Rome, do as the Romans do."
2. According to Murphy's law, "**If** anything can go wrong, it will."
3. The proverb says, "**Practice** makes perfect," but athletes advise us, "**Only** perfect practice makes perfect."

Exercise 1.10

1. In **December** the student **government** will present **a Christmas** show to raise funds for the trip to **South** America.
2. Between Battery **Park and** Greenwich Village, most of the **streets** in **New York City** have names instead of numbers.
3. Dr. Farley's new address is 15722 Princess St., River Falls, MN 55203. [This sentence is correct.]

Exercise 1.11

1. I read only **three** chapters of the book Mrs. Duff lent me, **and** then I lost it.
2. The **professor** in my **government** class assigned **133 pages** of homework for **Tuesday**.
3. When I was **six years** old, we moved to a quiet **street** in **Philadelphia**.
4. **Ninety** people began to picket in front of 10 Downing St., London, on March 9, 1997.
5. She told me to take **one** teaspoonful of cough medicine every four **hours** for the next 48 hours.

Exercise 1.12 Your dictionary's meanings may be slightly different.

1. Everyday means **commonplace, usual**.
   a. **Every day** most people do their jobs and care for their families.
   b. These **everyday** activities require commitment, even dedication.
2. Nobody means **no person, no one**.
   a. The court declared Judge Crater dead even though **no body** was ever found.
   b. Jane had nothing and **nobody** to call her own.
3. Sometimes means **occasionally, now and then**.
   a. For criticizing your parents, **some times** are better than others.
   b. You are **sometimes** exasperating.

Exercise 1.13

Health care costs so much nowadays that people worry **a lot** about taking care of **themselves**. **In fact**, everyday expenses are so heavy now that almost **nobody** (**myself** included) has any money put **aside** for health emergencies. **However**, I had a high fever **today** and decided that maybe I should see my doctor, who gave me an **antibiotic**. She said I **may be all right** by **tomorrow**. I certainly hope so, for I **do not** want to miss **another** day at work.

Exercise 1.14

In our **history** class last week, I gave a report on the Golden Gate **Bridge** in California. I'd heard **a lot** about this bridge, but I **wasn't** really sure of all my facts. **When** I said the **bridge** was one of the **seven** wonders of the world, our **professor** asked me what the other wonders were. ＿ **In fact**, I didn't know, but I guessed the Rocky **Mountains**. No one else in the class even tried to guess. Our teacher laughed **and** said he'd give us a hint. **Every** single one of the seven wonders, he said, was built by man, and each was built at least 2,100 **years** ago. After a while, **someone** guessed **one** right answer, those huge stone pyramids in **Egypt**. But **nobody** could name even one of the other six wonders. Can you **?**

Exercise 1.15

1.	f **ie** ld	line **1**
2.	c **ei** ling	line **2**
3.	**ei** ght	line **3**
4.	rec **ei** pt	line **2**
5.	fr **ie** nd	line **1**
6.	v **ie** w	line **1**
7.	v **ei** ns	line **3**

Exercise 1.16

Do you **believe** in magic? When people play the lottery or enter a sweepstakes, they always **believe** in their hearts that they're going to win. It's hard to conceive that the odds against winning a sweepstakes are millions to one. Did you ever have a **friend** who won a big state lottery? Probably not. But most of us have friends and neighbors who consistently play their lucky number and lose. These people might not spend a dime without a receipt, and they would be outraged if a **thief** took **their** hard-earned dollars. However, again and again they **deceive** themselves and squander money that never can be **retrieved**, all on a brief fantasy of magical gains. (Do you believe that you have a lucky number?)

Exercise 1.17

1.	pla**ys**	pla**yed**
2.	marr**ies**	marr**ied**
3.	enjo**ys**	enjo**yed**
4.	repl**ies**	repl**ied**
5.	terrif**ies**	terrif**ied**
6.	x-ra**ys**	x-ra**yed**

Exercise 1.18

1. grin**ning**
2. rain**ed**
3. star**ring**
4. matter**ed**
5. repel**lent**
6. repeal**ing**
7. shop**ped**
8. swim**mer**
9. prefer**red**

10. cover**ed**

Exercise 1.19

1. The choir members were **robing** in the church vestry.
   That gang has been **robbing** shops in this neighborhood.
2. **Planning** next year's schedule is the chairman's responsibility.
   The carpenter is **planing** the boards.
3. For Americans, **staring** at strangers seems very impolite.
   Many actors with **starring** roles on TV never work in movies.

Exercise 1.20

1.	carr**ies**	carr**ied**	carr**ying**
2.	worr**ies**	worr**ied**	worr**ying**
3.	tr**ies**	tr**ied**	tr**ying**
4.	repl**ies**	repl**ied**	repl**ying**
5.	stud**ies**	stud**ied**	stud**ying**

Exercise 1.21

Reading, '**riting**, and '**rithmetic** have been called the three Rs of education, the basics that every child should have **studied** and **mastered** by the end of elementary school. Now some educators are **saying** that the new basics will be **reading**, **writing**, and **computing**. But the computer should not be **identified** only with **studying** arithmetic and numbers. For example, word **processing** is much more than just **typing**. Young children have **tried using** a word processor before they have even **studied** the alphabet, and their teachers are **saying** that **writing** on the computer has **helped** them to read sooner and with more **understanding**. A special computer language called *LOGO* **applies reasoning** skills by **having** children draw pictures on the screen. Some people are **worried** that children will become too dependent on machines, but the ones who are **worrying** the most are usually not the ones who have **tried** to teach in this new way.

Exercise 1.22

The **automobile** has changed the landscape and the way we live **dramatically** in less than a hundred years. **Cities** once were built on rivers, with stores clustered on Main Street. Now suburban **shopping** malls and parking lots sprawl for miles along the highways, and it's not **unusual** for families to own two or even three cars. Scientists who are **studying** the **environment** know that car **exhaust** fumes are a major cause of smog and acid rain. They even **believe** that our reliance on the internal **combustion** engine may be **contributing** to global warming. Yet many Americans still take **their** right to drive for granted, and the **average** person thinks commuting to work by car is far better than **riding** on the mass transit system.

Exercise 1.23

The first **and** most basic **writing** convention is the direction of words on the **page**. If you **don't** read **anything** but English or some other **European** language, it probably hasn't **occurred** to you that words **may be** arranged in more than **one** way. But at the dawn of **history**, writing from **right** to left apparently seemed natural for many people. **In fact Hebrew** still runs from right to left, **and** Japanese runs from top to bottom.

The second basic **writing** convention, standard spelling, followed the invention of the **printing press** in the 15th **century**. Handwritten books were scarce and **didn't** circulate very far. **When** local writers spelled words the way they pronounced them, **their** local readers had no **problem**. But printed books traveled to distant neighborhoods, so a standard spelling was gradually developed. By 1775, when **Dr.** Samuel **Johnson** published the first dictionary in **English**, there was usually just one accepted way to spell a word, even though readers were **pronouncing** it in **two** or **three** different ways.

The third basic writing convention, the use of **punctuation** marks, **wasn't** followed **consistently** until about **250 years** ago. For centuries dots were used in random ways, and commas **weren't** used **at all**. **Writers** gradually started to use dots as periods or full stops, showing readers where to pause. However, only in modern times were **commas** introduced, to indicate the difference between **brief** pauses and longer ones.

Exercise 1.24

1.   **SP   WW**
    Thier class was to large for the room.
2.   **SP   WW**
    This television progam has been condemned for it's sex and violence.
3.   **WW   SP**
    Whose the owner of that vechile?
4.   **WW   SP**
    Their is no possible chance of wacthing the fireworks tonight.
5.   **WW SP**
    Marisol likes mathematics more then writting.

Exercise 1.25

1.   Sharon liked studying current events better **than** history.
2.   **Then** she signed up for an archeology course.
3.   Her class took a field trip to the Indian pueblos at Santa Clara and Taos in New Mexico; **then**, they visited Mesa Verde National Monument.
4.   Now Sharon is thinking of majoring in Native American history rather **than** continuing her studies in journalism.

Exercise 1.26

1.   The celebrated orator Edward Everett spoke **to** the crowd at Gettysburg.
2.   He spoke for **two** hours.
3.   Abraham Lincoln spoke, **too**.
4.   A photographer stood up **to** take Lincoln's picture.
5.   By the time he had focused his camera, he was already **too** late.
6.   After less than **two** minutes, Lincoln sat down.
7.   It was **too** late **to** capture a great moment of history, the Gettysburg Address.

Exercise 1.27

1.   **It's** important to check the air pressure in your car's tires every week.
2.   And **it's** a good idea to have your car serviced every 5,000 miles.
3.   You should change **its** oil and oil filter.
4.   Every 10,000 miles, your car should have **its** tires rotated.
5.   Your car will last longer if **it's** not neglected.

Exercise 1.28

1. Even if you don't believe in astrology, **you're** unusual if you don't know what sign of the Zodiac you were born under.
2. Astrologers say that **your** sign in the stars influences **your** character and attitudes.
3. For example, if **you're** a Leo, **your** temperament is domineering, like a lion's.
4. And if **you're** a Gemini (born under the sign of the twins), **your** friends will notice that you have contradictory traits.
5. To tell the truth, doesn't **your** sign of the Zodiac fit you?

Exercise 1.29

1. Throughout the United States **there** are many young people who dream of a future in professional sports.
2. **They're** interested in athletics, not **their** studies.
3. **Their** minds are on news stories about huge salaries made by professional athletes.
4. So every day **they're** out practicing instead of studying in the library.
5. But **there** are few stories about college players who don't make the pros, or about high-paid athletes who lose all **their** money to bad investments.
6. Students should be aware that **there** are few things more important than **their** college degrees.

Exercise 1.30

1. When you spend more **than** you earn, **then** it's time to take out a loan; I'd rather owe money **than** do without.
2. Ramon goes **to** the school gym **to** swim because the health club is **too** expensive. **Two** of his friends go there, **too**.
3. **It's** strange but true that an insect will often eat **its** mate, or even **its** offspring.
4. When **you're** anxious, **your** blood pressure sometimes rises.
5. **There** are millions of men who support equal rights for women, and if the Equal Rights Amendment comes up for a vote again, **they're** going to be **there** at the polls to cast **their** votes for it.

Exercise 1.31

If **you're** not in the habit of writing down **your** ideas and then proofreading what is written there on the page, **it's** hard for you to see that, although some contractions and possessive pronouns sound exactly alike, **they're** very different. People who don't write much may not use apostrophes at all, because they don't realize their importance. **They're** simply not aware that every contraction must have its apostrophe to be correct. On the other hand, **there** are writers who treat apostrophes like confetti. They scatter them around in **their** writing like decorations. But **they're** guilty of confusing **their** readers even more than the writers who leave apostrophes out entirely. If **you're** ambitious to become a clear and correct writer, it's important for you to learn the following apostrophe rule and **its** application: "**There** is a group of words called possessive pronouns, which mean *belonging to*. These words are never written with apostrophes. When you use an apostrophe with a pronoun, **it's** always a contraction. Contractions can also be written as two words."

Exercise 1.32

1. Where's **your** textbook? **You're** sure to need it today.
2. This show has lost **its** popularity, and so **it's** time to take it off the air.

3. Diane struggled **to** the bus stop. She was carrying **two** big boxes, and had a full shopping bag, **too**. This luggage was almost **too** heavy for her to handle.
4. The passengers are picking up **their** luggage in the airport. Two friends are meeting them **there** to drive them home. **They're** all eager to get going.

Exercise 1.33

It's an interesting fact that many people are much better at speaking **than** at writing. **There** are some people who can start a riot just by shouting to an angry crowd. But **too** few of these born orators are able to write a two-line letter to the newspaper which **its** editor wouldn't find **too** awkward and ungrammatical to publish. Then there are those who would rather spend $200 on telephone calls **than** $2 on stamps. When they pick up a telephone, **they're** chattering away in an instant. And yet when they pick up a pencil, it's likely that they'll chew it for 20 minutes before **they're** able to write a single word. You may be an excellent speaker, but unless **you're** able to write your ideas correctly and clearly, **you're** going to have problems.

Exercise 1.34 Your dictionary's meanings may be slightly different.

1. *Passed* is the past-tense form of the verb **pass**.
    Past means **beyond**.
    Just **past** Rosie's bar, we **passed** a big accident.
2. *Know* means **to possess knowledge, be aware**.
    No means **not any**.
    We **know** that you have **no** time to see us.
3. *Here* means **at or to this place**.
    Hear means **to learn by listening**.
    Here comes Joseph to **hear** the latest gossip.
4. *Whose* is a possessive form meaning "belonging to **who (or whom)**."
    Who's is a contraction for **who is**.
    Who's the student **whose** papers are on the table?
5. *Find* means **to discover after searching**.
    Fine means **very well**.
    Harold felt **fine** after he was able to **find** the money.

Exercise 1.35

You hear **a lot** about "the wonders of the world," but only a few people know that this phrase originally **referred** to seven wonders in the ancient world. Hardly anybody nowadays can name these monuments of early civilization. **There** is a good reason for this. Just one of these wonders is still standing, the huge stone pyramids in Egypt. A few people also **know** about the second wonder, the magnificent terraced gardens which a king of **Babylon** built to please his wife. The **third** wonder, a seated statue of Zeus in a temple at Olympia in **Greece**, was made of ivory **and** gold, with precious jewels in **its** eyes. (If this huge statue could have stood up, it would have hit **its** head on the **ceiling**.) Some fragments of the **fourth** wonder, a **temple** dedicated to the goddess Diana, were found in **Turkey** about a hundred **years** ago. Earthquakes destroyed all **three** of the other wonders: a beautiful tomb built for King Mausolus in Turkey, an enormous lighthouse near the coast of Egypt (huge fragments of which were **dragged** from the sea only a few years ago), and a giant statue of Apollo at Rhodes in Greece. The colossal statue at Rhodes must have been more spectacular **than** the Statue of Liberty. According to an old legend, it stood in the middle of a harbor with its legs spread **apart**, while ships **passed** between them.

Answers

Module 2: *Understanding Simple Sentences*

Exercise 2.1

1. In the course of history, great armies, led by ambitious generals, sometimes battled for supremacy over weaker countries.
2. These weaker countries, poorly armed and with meager resources, often collapsed before the superior forces of their attackers.
3. Then vast empires, like the Greek, the Roman, and more recently the British, arose as rulers of the earth for centuries.

Exercise 2.2

1. Every morning the warden talks to the prison inmates.
   Yesterday morning the warden talked to the prison inmates.
2. Usually he announces the day's activities.
   Yesterday he announced the day's activities.
3. Often he reminds them about their behavior.
   Recently he reminded them about their behavior.

Exercise 2.3

1. This music soothes my frazzled nerves.
   This music will soothe my frazzled nerves.
2. The instruments convey a peaceful feeling.
   The instruments will convey a peaceful feeling.
3. The song tells of quiet relaxation.
   The song will tell of quiet relaxation.

Exercise 2.4

1. At dawn the birds chirped loudly.
   At dawn the birds chirp loudly.
2. They disturbed my sleep.
   They disturb my sleep.
3. But I rolled over for another short snooze.
   But I roll over for another short snooze.

Exercise 2.5

1. These horses are sprinters. They gallop at top speed.
   These horses were sprinters. They galloped at top speed.
2. They streak across the finish line. Their owners are jubilant.
   They streaked across the finish line. Their owners were jubilant.
3. Sometimes their trainers seem anxious. These mounts are worth millions.
   Sometimes their trainers seemed anxious. These mounts were worth millions.

Exercise 2.6

   This year Jane and Walter are intern doctors at Central Hospital. Medical facts fill their brains, but they have little medical experience, and they are

344

sometimes on duty for 36 hours without a break. Just as they tumble into their beds, their beepers sound so with bleary eyes, Jane and Walter stagger back to the intensive care unit. Their patients pray hard that they commit no mistakes. But the hospital's staff checks everything that Jane and Walter do The resident doctor reviews their prescriptions carefully, and the nurse watches closely as their fingers fumble with the intravenous tubes.

Last year Jane and Walter were intern doctors at Central Hospital. Medical facts filled their brains, but they had little medical experience, and they were sometimes on duty for 36 hours without a break. Just as they tumbled into their beds, their beepers sounded, so with bleary eyes, Jane and Walter staggered back to the intensive care unit. Their patients prayed hard that they committed no mistakes. But the hospital's staff checked everything that Jane and Walter did The resident doctor reviewed their prescriptions carefully, and the nurse watched closely as their fingers fumbled with the intravenous tubes.

Exercise 2.7

John Kennedy became President in 1961 and died from an assassin's bullet in 1963. He started the Peace Corps, and thousands joined The Peace Corps volunteers traveled to many countries, improved medical conditions, taught better farming practices, and served as ambassadors for the USA. People around the world were grateful for the help of the Peace Corps and mourned Kennedy's death.

Exercise 2.8

Some gifted people encountered incredible obstacles, lost hope, and ended their careers. Vincent Van Gogh, the Dutch artist, painted hundreds of masterpieces, sold only one, cut off his ear and finally shot himself. Others, though, pursued their goals, succeeded, and gained greater fame. Ludwig van Beethoven, the German composer, lost his hearing, kept working, and then wrote some of his greatest musical masterpieces. Sarah Bernhardt, the great actress, went lame in 1905, lost a leg to gangrene in 1914, but then became famous all over the world before her death in 1923.

Exercise 2.9

1. Marvin needs a new battery for his car.
2. He parks his car alongside the store.
3. He is inside for only a minute.
4. That eager policeman gives him a parking ticket.
5. Marvin's new battery is very expensive.

Exercise 2.10

1. Time passes.
    Time passes slowly for little children.
    Time passes quickly for old folks.

2. Bridges sway.
   Well-built suspension bridges always sway a little in high winds.
   Poorly built bridges sometimes sway dangerously in hurricanes.
3. People complained.
   Those grouchy people in the next apartment always complained about our parties.
   The frightened people in this building never complained to the police about the drug pushers.

Exercise 2.11

1. The leader of the hike arrived without a map.
2. The river between the hikers and the mountains blocked their path.
3. However, the trail along the north side of the river led them to a shallow place.
4. The hikers, with their shoes in their hands, crossed over dry and safe.
5. The hike from the campground to the mountains was a success.

Exercise 2.12

1. Sometimes styles of architecture from the distant past become popular again in later centuries.
2. During the 18th and 19th centuries, imitations of ancient Greek and Roman architecture appeared everywhere in European and American homes.
3. Wealthy settlers in the South often built homes in the Greek style with triangular roofs and three-story classical columns.
4. Some residents of New England preferred Italian villas with Renaissance features, or Gothic Revival houses.
5. Frequently architects will use a wide variety of features from different periods, like pointed Gothic windows, Greek columns, and French mansard roofs, all in the same building.
6. Even for a student of architecture, identification of the main style in a house sometimes is quite difficult.

Exercise 2.13

1. Here are some quarters for the toll.
2. There goes their car through the tollgate ahead of us.
3. Here is a twenty-dollar bill for gas.

Exercise 2.14

My aunt and uncle gave us a sofa for our new house. The dog and the cat ripped the fabric on one side with their sharp claws. My mother and sister made a slipcover and hid the damage with it.

Exercise 2.15

Between 1970 and 1995, angry environmentalists and concerned legislators together campaigned vigorously against waste and pollution. Today many earth-watchers still complain and worry about the condition of the air and the water. On Earth Day, gloomy prophets loudly foretell the End. Influential newspapers and telecasts around the nation echo their pessimistic statements. Yet humans today breathe healthier air and drink purer water than their grandparents or great-grandparents. Unbiased scientists report a one-third reduction in smog since 1972. By comparison with the 1960s, our rivers, lakes, and oceans are now twice as safe. However, environmentalists and other concerned citizens have good reasons for their fears. The next Congress probably will repeal many federal environmental regulations, will cut funding for environmental protection, and thus will reverse the current trend toward a cleaner planet.

Exercise 2.16

1. The customers are impatient.
   They are becoming more impatient by the minute.
2. That man has some defective clothing for the Returns clerk.
   He has been in line for an hour already.
3. The woman with the baby is furious.
   Her baby is crying loudly.
1. Over in the stockroom, the Returns clerk does nothing about the angry customers.
   But he does look forward to closing time.

Exercise 2.17

These days, Americans are reconsidering their use of alcoholic beverages. People of all ages, anxious about their health, are drinking less. In restaurants, they are ordering white wine or nonalcoholic beer. Equally important, attitudes are changing. Intoxicated people no longer seem so funny. Comedians crack fewer jokes about the antics of drunks. In more and more states the police are arresting drunk drivers, and the authorities are giving them stiff fines. Some judges are sending them to prison. Abuse of alcohol is recognized as a threat to health, to life, and to society.

Exercise 2.18

1. My lawyer will call soon.
   She will be calling about the lawsuit.
2. She will prepare the legal forms today.
   She might have prepared them already this morning.
3. Our case will be heard within two months.
   However, it should have been heard before that bad publicity.

Exercise 2.19

The mailman will be here in half an hour. However, he should have been here already by now. The extra mail for Christmas does slow him down. Also, the snowy weather has made travel difficult. Still, he has been late with his deliveries every day this week. Maybe he should start earlier in the mornings. In addition, he could spend less time in the Donut Shop. He might lose a little weight that way.

Exercise 2.20

1. Khalil's a clown in the Europa Circus.
2. He wasn't at work today and isn't at home now.
3. We're not sure of his whereabouts.
4. Maybe it's just another one of his jokes.

Exercise 2.21

Your brother's been in a car accident. He's not badly hurt, fortunately. He's being taken to Central Hospital. They'll take good care of him there.

347

They've got the best Emergency Room around. The police are still investigating the accident. They're arresting the other driver. She's been charged with drunk driving. She's on probation from a previous accident. She'd better get a good lawyer. She'll need one. Right now we're going to the hospital. We'll pick you up in 15 minutes.

Exercise 2.22

1. Elaine is hoping to become a successful actress.
2. To achieve fame has become her one goal in life.
3. To improve her chances for success, she plans to move from Kansas to Los Angeles.

Exercise 2.23

1. Elaine likes living in Los Angeles.
2. However, she hates competing with hundreds of others for one job.
3. After trying out for dozens of roles without success, she is getting depressed.
4. Moving back to Kansas starts seeming like a good idea.

Exercise 2.24

1. A. Long disputes are very frustrating.
   B. My friend Mi-long disputes our plans for February.
   Disputes is the verb in sentence **B**.
2. A. We visit Canada to go skiing every year in February.
   B. Our last visit was a catastrophe for Mi-long.
   Visit is the verb in sentence **A**.
3. A. She lost her wallet somewhere on the slopes.
   B. The lost wallet contained over $400 in cash.
   Lost is the verb in sentence **A**.

Exercise 2.25

Near the Italian town of Modena, a blood-red car rockets around a twisting track and quickly soars to 120 miles an hour. The driver pumps the brakes and careens into a hairpin turn. Skidding briefly, he turns the steering wheel sharply to regain his hold on the road. He roars around the track a few more times and screeches to a stop. The driver steps out grinning. This Ferrari passes.

Enzo Ferrari began producing his racing cars in 1929. His trademark was a prancing black horse, the insignia of the flying ace, Francesco Baracca. Ferrari cars started to win racing championships during the next decade. In 1945 Ferrari designed his first 12-cylinder model for everyday use. He developed a system of checks and controls to produce perfect parts and hired daring engineers to create shovel-nosed hoods and swooping fenders. The result was a powerful and almost indestructible machine. It was also stunningly beautiful. In every country around the globe, car buffs and drag racers rushed to buy it even at extravagant prices.

The next Ferrari to come out of Modena is likely to cost more than $300,000, and to have a speed of over 200 miles an hour. The Ferrari factory will produce no more than a few thousand of these cars. Consequently, they're sure to vanish from the dealerships within days of their arrival. Then they'll spend their lives cruising over roads at 55 miles an hour — about one-fourth of their capacity. Still, the proud owners of these aristocrats of the road will continue to smile, and to smile again, at the turning heads and staring eyes of envious drivers everywhere.

Exercise 2.26

Moving day is often a nightmare. [Especially for people with large families and lots of belongings.] To keep things under control, the parents have to make long check-off lists and remember a hundred details. [Like not to pack every cup and spoon.] After all, everybody needs to eat breakfast, even on moving day. Still nothing seems to go right. [The movers arriving at dawn, immediately snatching every chair in sight, and leaving the children and old folks with nothing to sit on.] The weather, of course, is always terrible. Essential tools disappear, Boxes break [The dog barking in wild excitement.] [The children weeping for the loss of old friends.] Anxious to get going, the moving van driver revs up the motor. [And takes off without warning, leaving two closets still full of odds and ends.] Finally, at the end of the exhausting day, the movers arrange the heavy furniture in the living room. [And only then remember to roll out the rug.]

How many word-groups have no verbs? **5**
How many verbs have no subjects? **2**
How many word-groups did you bracket? **7**

Module 3: *Understanding More Complicated Sentences I*

Exercise 3.1

1.   +
    Friday was payday, so we went out last night.
2.   +
    I went to the movies, and my brother went to a concert.
3.   +
    The movie was terrible, but the concert was outstanding.
4.   +
    I'll go to a concert next week, or I'll stay home.

Exercise 3.2

1. A. Mahinder was born in India but now lives in Los Angeles.
    B.   +
       His family emigrated in 1990, but he didn't come here until last year.
       Sentence **B** is a compound sentence.
2. A.   +
       He had been attending college in New Delhi, and he was living with his uncle.
    B. He was studying electronics and wanted to work with computers.
       Sentence **A** is a compound sentence.
3. A. Mahinder had excellent grades but wasn't very good at writing.
    B.   +
       He applied for a job at Air India, but they wouldn't hire him.
       Sentence **B** is a compound sentence.
4. A. Then he moved to Los Angeles and joined his family's business.

B.
+
Now he manages a printing shop, so he never has to write anything.
Sentence **B** is a compound sentence.

Exercise 3.3

Frequently Henry has bored his friends by telling and retelling the story of his first driving lesson. As a once-told tale, it's actually rather amusing. Henry arrived for his lesson
+
and found his instructor dozing at the wheel. Sleepily he moved over, and Henry took his place in the driver's seat. His instructor then smiled encouragingly and pointed to the ignition key and the accelerator. Henry hesitantly turned the key and stepped on the gas.
+
The motor started to run, and he looked at his instructor with amazement. Next, the instructor taught him how to shift gears. Henry shifted into "Drive" and held on tight to the
+
wheel. The car jerked and then it slowly edged forward. Henry looked anxiously ahead. A truck and a car with a "Wide Load" sign were creeping toward him at 20 miles an hour.
+
Quickly he slammed on the brakes, and his instructor almost went through the windshield.
+
Telling Henry to stop, the instructor began to open the car door. Henry tried to obey, but he stepped on the accelerator instead of the brake. Henry had a new instructor for his next lesson.

Exercise 3.4

1.
+
Ching-si wants to be a stock broker, but she doesn't speak English very well yet.

2.
+
She knows a lot about economics, so she's optimistic about her future.

3.
+
She has a great personality, but many people can't understand her speech.

4.
+
Her parents want her to go to college to learn English better, or maybe she can study at a language school.

Exercise 3.5

1.
+
In the prosperous 1960s, gasoline was plentiful and cheap, so the big, gas-guzzling American cars were popular.

2.
+
By the 1970s, gas prices had soared, but American cars still had very low gas mileage.

3.
+
In the 1980s, Detroit needed to start making more economical cars, or imported cars would put them out of business.

4.
+
In recent years, American cars have offered good values, and they have regained their earlier popularity.

Exercise 3.6

1.
+

I asked my brother (if he would go with me to the drugstore).

2.
+

He wanted to know (when I was going to leave).

3.
+

I left without him (because he was watching soap operas on TV).

Exercise 3.7

1.
+

Jacques will gain weight (if he doesn't exercise).
If he doesn't exercise tells under what **condition** Jacques will gain weight.

2.
+

(When he moved to Seattle), therefore, he bought a bicycle.
When he moved to Seattle tells **when** he bought the bicycle.

3.
+

He's getting fat anyway (because it rains too much to ride the bike very often).
Because it rains too much to ride the bike very often tells **why** he's getting fat.

4.
+

Now he always drives (when he needs to go someplace).
When he needs to go someplace tells **when** he drives.

5.
+

Jacques wants to move soon (because he worries about getting too fat).
Because he worries about getting too fat tells **why** he wants to move.

Exercise 3.8

1.
+

I wanted to visit the Grand Canyon (after I saw that show about it on TV).

2.
+

I bought some books about geology (so that I could learn more about it).

3.
+

I got more and more excited about going (while I was reading the books).

4.
+

However, I need to save some more money (before I'll be able to go).

5.
+

I should have enough by next month (unless my bills this month are too high).

Exercise 3.9

1. A. Mustafa is going to buy a telephone answering machine after lunch.
   B.
   +

   He decided this (after he missed a call about a new job).
   Sentence **B** is a complex sentence.

2. A. He has been trying to get another job since last Christmas.
   B.
   +

   He has been unhappy (since he began working nights and weekends).
   Sentence **B** is a complex sentence.

3.   A.
                                       +

Often he doesn't get home (until his children leave for school).

  B. Then he just goes to sleep until dinnertime.

      Sentence **A** is a complex sentence.

Exercise 3.10

      +

(If Sangeeta can save enough money), she will soon be able to buy a car.
                       +

She needs it badly (because now she has to work evenings and weekends).
 +

(Since her job is in an isolated neighborhood), she is nervous about taking

public transportation to work at night. (Although her friend, Mustafa,
                                         +

has been traveling with her), he will probably quit his job soon. (If he can get
a good job), he wants to work in the daytime. However, Sangeeta prefers

working nights, (because she makes more money that way).

Exercise 3.11

1.   +

    (If she can't buy a car), Sangeeta may have to quit her job.

2.   +

    (As soon as Mustafa quits), she will have to travel alone on the bus.

3.   +

    (Because few people are on the bus late at night), the trip makes her very nervous.

Exercise 3.12

1.   +

    The newspapers are criticizing the merchants (because they oppose the boycott).

2.   +

    (If the boycott continues), some merchants will lay off workers or even go out of business.

3.   +

    (After a teenager was falsely accused of shoplifting), the local block association asked the residents
to shop elsewhere.

Exercise 3.13 Words in italics and square brackets *[like this]* show possible alternative answers.

1.   +

    Maria Callas stood out among opera singers (because she was slender and attractive).
      +

    [(Because she was slender and attractive), Maria Callas stood out among opera singers.]

2.   +

    Her performances had great passion, (so that audiences around the world adored her).

3.   +

    She lived only for her art (until she met the billionaire shipowner Aristotle Onassis).
     +

    [(Until she met the billionaire shipowner Aristotle Onassis), she lived only for her art).]

4.
$+$
Her public remained faithful for a while, (although her vocal powers were declining).
$+$
[(Although her vocal powers were declining), her public remained faithful for a while.]

5.
$+$
Callas fell apart completely (once Onassis ditched her for Jackie Kennedy).
$+$
[(Once Onassis ditched her for Jackie Kennedy), Callas fell apart completely.]

Exercise 3.14

People and information continue to hurtle through space at higher and higher speeds.
$+$
(When John Adams traveled from Boston to Williamsburg in the 1770s), he was on the road
$+$
for more than a week. Today the trip takes 90 minutes by plane. (After Andrew Jackson
$+$
was elected President in 1828,) a month went by (before some voters heard the news). Today
$+$
most people know the new President's name (before the polls close). However, one notable
exception to this law of progress is the daily mail. The pony express delivered mail in the
19th century faster than some modern mail trucks. Back in the 1940s, the postman came to
$+$ $+$
my great-grandmother's house twice a day (unless there was a big snowstorm). (When she
mailed a letter in the late afternoon), it usually arrived the next morning at a friend's house 50
$+$
miles away. (If her friend wrote back that morning), Great-Grandma sometimes got her reply
the same day. This service used to cost just six cents. Today I pay over $11 for Express Mail,
$+$ $+$
and it sometimes can take several days to arrive anyway. In fact, (although it runs up my
$+$
phone bill), I often fax a letter or send e-mail (because the mails are so undependable). Today's
postal service seems to be an example of progress in reverse.

Exercise 3.15

1.
$+$ $+$
Saving money is hard (when inflation is high), (because everything costs a lot).
This entire sentence contains **3** simple sentences and **2** connecting words.

2.
$+$ $+$
Interest rates on savings are also high (when inflation is high), (so that savings
$+$
can grow quickly) (if you can manage to save).
This entire sentence contains **4** simple sentences and **3** connecting words.

3.
$+$
(Because economics seems hard and boring), many people don't understand the
$+$
importance of saving, (so that their financial situation gets worse rather than better).
This entire sentence contains **3** simple sentences and **2** connecting words.

4.   +
(If you can save money), you will be protecting yourself against rising prices, and you will have a more comfortable life in the future.
This entire sentence contains **3** simple sentences and **2** connecting words.

Exercise 3.16

1.   +
(Because they enjoyed so much wealth and power), the English royal families often behaved outrageously, their subjects from time to time simply had to kill or to exile them.
How many simple sentences does this word-group contain? **3**
How many connecting words does it have? **1**
This word group ❑ is ☒ is not a correct sentence.

2.   +
(After Henry VIII divorced his first wife and beheaded the second, burying the third, and beheading the fourth).
How many simple sentences does this word-group contain? **1**
How many connecting words does it have? **1**
This word group ❑ is ☒ is not a correct sentence.

3. The Stuart kings, the descendants of Mary Queen of Scots, one of them by the name of Charles I getting his head chopped off, and another by the name of James II fleeing to Ireland and eventually to France.
How many simple sentences does this word-group contain? **0**
How many connecting words does it have? **0**
This word group ❑ is ☒ is not a correct sentence.

4.   +
Queen Victoria seemed to be a model of propriety, but her son Albert, later to be Edward VII, was notorious for his exploits with women.
How many simple sentences does this word-group contain? **2**
How many connecting words does it have? **1**
This word group ☒ is ❑ is not a correct sentence.

5.   +
Perhaps the most celebrated episode relating to the English monarchy in the 20th century (when Edward VIII renounced his throne to marry an American divorcee).
How many simple sentences does this word-group contain? **1**
How many connecting words does it have? **1**
This word group ❑ is ☒ is not a correct sentence.

6.   +   +
(When in 1992 two of her sons' marriages broke up and her main home was almost destroyed by fire), Queen Elizabeth II pronounced that year an *annus horribilis*.
How many simple sentences does this word-group contain? **3**
How many connecting words does it have? **2**
This word group ☒ is ❑ is not a correct sentence.

Exercise 3.17

Robert E. Lee, as Commander-in-Chief of the Confederate Army of Northern Virginia, made only one serious mistake in his otherwise brilliant military career. However, that mistake was a disastrous one. [A failure of judgment resulting in the deaths of thousands].
    For the first two years of the American Civil War, Lee had taken enormous risks against
                        +
overwhelming odds, but consistently his tactics had triumphed over the caution of the Union

generals. Hence, with high hopes in the summer of 1863, |he (led)|his devoted troops into Pennsylvania to crush the blundering Army of the Potomac. **[** Clashing at Gettysburg, |rebels| and |Yankees| (fought) fiercely for two long days, |thousands| (were killed) and many |more| (were)

+   +

(wounded) on both sides **]**. **[** (Although, (when |night| (fell) on the second day), neither |side| (could) (claim) victory) **]**. **[** Nevertheless, at that point the federal |troops| (had) one distinct advantage, |they|

+

(had fled) to high ground, where |they| (ranged) their batteries along the ridge overlooking Lee's encampment **]**.

+

    [On the third day, (after the Confederate |commander| (had devised) one plan after another to surprise and outwit the federals, only to find his plans foiled by their unanticipated counterattacks along a five-mile battle front) **]**. In the late afternoon, a desperate |Lee| (ordered) his officers to lead their surviving troops in parade formation across a mile-wide open field in direct line with Union cannon and rifles at the ready. According to Lee's plan, in a flanking movement, his |troops| (would converge) on a clump of trees on the far side of the field. **[** Then (storm) up an embankment and (slaughter) and (rout) the enemy in hand to hand

+

combat **]**. (Since |they| (had) total confidence in the wisdom of their commander), his |soldiers|

+

(marched) forward obediently, with drums beating and battle flags flying. **[** (Until enemy |fire| (cut) them down like blades of grass and (turned) the field into a bloody carpet of the dead and dying) **]**. Afterwards this incredibly daring but foredoomed |assault| (was known) as Pickett's

+

Charge. **[** (Because the main |division| participating in the attack (happened) to be under the

+

command of General Pickett) **]**. Later still, (when the |war| (was) over), |historians| (pronounced) this ghastly blunder the turning point of the Civil War.

How many word-groups have no verbs? **1**
How many verbs have no subjects? **3**
How many word-groups have too many connecting words? **4**
How many word-groups have too few connecting words? **2**
How many word-groups did you bracket? **8**

Module 4: Understanding More Complicated Sentences II

Exercise 4.1

1.   Last week, |Raj| (bought) a new television set. |He| (is watching) it now.

+

    Last week, |Raj| (bought) a new television set (which |he| (is watching) now).

2. |Raj| (avoids) certain programs. His |wife| (dislikes) them.

+

    |Raj| (avoids) certain programs (that his |wife| (dislikes)).

3.   Still, |he| always (watches) *Baywatch*. |He| (enjoys) it very much.

+

    Still, |he| always (watches) *Baywatch*, (which |he| (enjoys) very much).

355

Exercise 4.2

1.
                                                    +
   Retirees want long-term health care (that many of them can't afford).
2.
                                                              +
   Therefore, they pay close attention to legislation (which their elected representatives are considering).
3.
                                              +
   They write their Senators frequent letters (which the Senators read carefully).
4.
                                        +
   The Senators will vote for programs (that their constituents want).
5.
                                              +
   In turn, the retirees will cast their own votes, (which the Senators want just as much).

Exercise 4.3

1. I met a woman. She knew you in high school.
              +
   I met a woman (who knew you in high school).
2. She still remembers the basketball team. It won the state championship.
                                      +
   She still remembers the basketball team (that won the state championship).
3. You were dating Shawn. He was the center on that team.
              +
   You were dating Shawn, (who was the center on that team).
4. She is now married to Shawn. He is a high school teacher.
                        +
   She is now married to Shawn, (who is a high school teacher).
5. They live in an apartment. It is right around the corner.
                        +
   They live in an apartment (which is right around the corner).

Exercise 4.4

1.
                        +
   This car is the one (**which** cost $13,000 three years ago).
2.
                        +
   My uncle is the salesman (**who** sold it to me).
3.
                              +
   Now I need to replace the tires (**which** came with the car).
4.
                                          +
   My uncle introduced me to his brother-in-law, (**who** sells tires cheap).

Exercise 4.5

1.
                  +
   I have a sister (who is now afraid of dogs).
2.
                                    +
   Years ago, we had a pet cocker spaniel (which used to sleep on my sister's bed).
3.
                              +
   One night she had a nightmare (which awoke her from a deep sleep.

4.
Her sudden movement startled the sleeping dog, (which instinctively bit her arm).

5.
Now she won't even visit our parents, (who still have dogs).

Exercise 4.6

1. Concerts are very popular. They feature Irish music.

   Concerts (which feature Irish music) are very popular.

2. Aly Bain is a well-known Irish fiddler. He plays with The Boys of the Lough.

   Aly Bain, (who plays with The Boys of the Lough), is a well-known Irish fiddler.

3. Phil Cunningham often plays with Aly. He writes songs and plays the accordian.

   Phil Cunningham, (who writes songs and plays the accordian), often plays with Aly.

4. A concert is at Music Hall tomorrow. It features them.

   A concert (which features them) is at Music Hall tomorrow.

Exercise 4.7

1. The airport (which recently opened in Denver) is very modern.

2. Passengers (who use the terminal) praise the baggage-handling system.

3. This system, (which moves bags on conveyer belts), is now working well.

4. Last year, though, Dan Stoddard, (who used the airport on its first day), lost all his bags.

5. The bags (which he lost that day) have never been found.

Exercise 4.8

1. The surgeon saved a young girl's life. He had developed the new procedure.
   The expansion ☒ is ☐ is not needed to tell *which*, so commas ☐ should ☒ should not be used.

   The surgeon (who had developed the new procedure) saved a young girl's life.

2. This young girl had a rare heart malformation. She came from Ecuador.
   The expansion ☐ is ☒ is not needed to tell *which*, so commas ☒ should ☐ should not be used.

   This young girl, (who came from Ecuador), had a rare heart malformation.

3. Her heart was ready to fail. It was too weak to pump effectively.
   The expansion ☐ is ☒ is not needed to tell *which*, so commas ☒ should ☐ should not be used.

   Her heart, (which was too weak to pump effectively), was ready to fail.

4. The operation cost $30,000. It saved her life.
   The expansion ☒ is ☐ is not needed to tell *which*, so commas ☐ should ☒ should not be used.

   The operation (which saved her life) cost $30,000.

Answers

5. The local newspaper raised all the needed money. It told the girl's story on page 1.
   The expansion ❑ is ☒ is not needed to tell *which*, so commas ☒ should ❑ should not be used.

   The local newspaper, (which told the girl's story on page 1), raised all the needed money.

Exercise 4.9

1. Antonio Vivaldi, (who lived in 17th century Italy), wrote music (which still moves audiences).

2. He worked for years at an orphanage (which housed girls) (who sang and played instruments).

3. The girls (who performed in Vivaldi's orchestra) must have been excellent musicians to play his
   music, (which still demands great skill).

4. Vivaldi's *Gloria,* (which contains some of his most beautiful music), was performed
   last night by some local girls (who didn't do such a good job with it).

Exercise 4.10

1. Some people believe that environment and heredity influence behavior equally.
   The noun clause beginning with *that* answers the question **WHAT** *do some people believe?*

   However, according to recent research, the genes (that we inherit) are the strongest factor in
   shaping our character and personality.
   The expansion beginning with *that* answers the question **WHICH** *genes?*

2. Psychiatrists have found that the behavior of identical twins often turns out the same despite great
   differences in their life experiences.
   The noun clause beginning with *that* answers the question **WHAT** *have psychiatrists found?*

   The studies (that psychiatrists have published recently on this subject) are therefore very
   discouraging to parents.
   The expansion beginning with *that* answers the question **WHICH** *studies?*

3. Studies (that gather data on identical twins) show that home environment and education make little
   difference in human development.
   The expansion beginning with *that* answers the question **WHICH** *studies?*
   The noun clause beginning with *that* answers the question **WHAT** *do the studies show?*

Exercise 4.11

1. My boss says **that** I have to work overtime.

2. But the extra money (**that** I earn from overtime) just isn't worth it.

3. I know **that** I need to spend more time with my family.

4.
　　Last night I decided to tell my husband **that** I'm looking for a different job.

5.
　　He was happy about the decision (**that** I had made).

Exercise 4.12

　　Michaelangelo was a 16th century sculptor (who also painted). His huge paintings on the Sistine Chapel ceiling are in all art history books, but his marble statues are even more famous. (Because marble was plentiful in the hills not far from Florence), he always used this beautiful stone. (While he was planning his statues), he seemed to hear voices (which came from within the blocks of marble). One day he was painting a prince's portrait, (which he wanted to finish before sunset), (when his helpers carried in a large chunk of marble). (After they left), Michaelangelo continued to paint, but he sensed the presence of an invisible person in the room. (When he turned and saw the marble), he understood (As he touched the rough surface), Michaelangelo felt a figure (which moved in the marble). It was Moses the prophet, (who was waiting for Michaelangelo to set him free). The prince (who had ordered the painting) would have to wait, (because at this moment a more important person was giving Michaelangelo orders).

Exercise 4.13

　　Cockroaches are perhaps the most durable form of life on earth. They do well in cathedrals, in grass huts, and in swanky duplex apartments. [Or any other place in the world (which is habitable by humans)]. Roaches will eat almost anything. [Including leather, glue, paper, and even the starch in bookbinding]. [(So that office storerooms and public libraries are among their preferred residences)]. They're able to live 50 days without food and 14 days without water. In fact, after years of eating huge doses of supermarket roach-poisons, some populations of roaches become immune to them. [And pass this immunity on to their descendants]. [(Who then go on to die of advanced old age)]. Exterminators praise the effectiveness of some powerful anti-roach chemicals, like hydroprene, (which renders juvenile roaches sterile). [And amidinolhydrazone (which roaches are not likely to recognize as poison) (because it acts so slowly)]. [Nevertheless, according to cynical apartment dwellers, (if nuclear war comes)), all life on earth will probably become extinct — with one exception, cockroaches will survive and will thrive on nuclear waste and radioactive dust].

How many word-groups have no verbs? **1**
How many verbs have no subjects? **1**
How many word-groups have too many connecting words? **4**
How many word-groups have too few connecting words? **1**
How many word-groups did you bracket? **7**

Module 5: *Using Nouns and Pronouns*

Exercise 5.1

1. A. The Brinkers skate to work.
   B. Hans lost a skate.
      Skate is a noun in sentence **B**.
2. A. They always laugh at him.
   B. But he'll have the last laugh.
      Laugh is a noun in sentence **B**.
3. A. She knelt and picked a rose.
   B. She rose from her knees and gave it to me.
      Rose is a noun in sentence **A.**
4. A. Mark is swimming in the championship meet.
   B. Swimming in this championship will make him famous.
      Swimming is a noun in sentence **B**.
5. A. He was sleeping on the bank of the river.
   B. I usually bank at Acme Savings & Loan.
   C. A bank shot is the hardest one in billiards.
      Bank is a noun in sentence **A**.

Exercise 5.2

1.   S
   one fork

   P
   many forks

2.   P
   seven speeches

   S
   a speech

3.   S
   a task

   P
   some tasks

4.   P
   three apples

   S
   an apple

Exercise 5.3

1.   S   P
   A tree may have 17,000 leaves.

2.   P   S
   Sixty-three persons crowded into one room.

3.   P   P
   Both ideas were discussed for seven hours.

Exercise 5.4

1.   S   P
   Each suitcase was searched by several guards.
2.   P   P
   Some neighbors donated many cakes.
3.   S   P
   Every delivery was delayed for days.
4.   P   P
   Some neighborhoods allow no businesses.
5.   P   P
   Most cars now have airbags.

Exercise 5.5

1.   P   S
   These tools are needed for that job.
2.   S   P
   This boy liked those games.
3.   S   P
   The worker paid the fees.
4.   S   P
   I bought this book and these magazines.
5.   S   P
   She owns that car and those bicycles.
6.   S   P
   I have the pen and the pencils right here.

Exercise 5.6

1.   S   P
   I ate a broiled pork chop and three ripe peaches yesterday.
2.   P   S
   I gave her twelve yellow mums and one beautiful red rose.
3.   P   S
   Some talented housewives made this prizewinning quilt.

Exercise 5.7

   1. those speeding **trucks**
   2. some delivery **vans**
   3. a few passionate **kisses**
   4. these dirty **dishes**
   5. three exciting **races**
   6. many loud **gasps**
   7. those bad **risks**
   8. the bird **nests**
   9. six ripe **tomatoes**
   10. their loud **radios**

Exercise 5.8 Remember that plural nouns can often be written with different plural determiners, or even with no determiner. Stars ** show where different plural determiners can be used. Check to make sure that both the determiner and the noun in your answer are plural.

1. **Those** battered old **chairs** sold for ***several* dollars**.
2. ***All*** young **participants** received **these** framed **certificates**.
3. **These** powerful **computers** beat ***some*** leading chess **champions** in ***a few* games**.
4. ***Some*** spiteful **reviewers** forced **these** fine **shows** to close.
5. **Those** new-born **pandas** died in ****** American **zoos**.
6. ***Two*** local TV **stations** televised the X-rated **films**.
7. ***Many*** silver **spoons** disappeared along with **those** uninvited **guests**.
8. ***Some*** true **artists** must have designed **these** beautiful **gardens**.
9. **Those teenagers** spent ***several* hours** at ***some* discos** yesterday.

Exercise 5.9

1. some crying **babies**
2. six sharp **knives**
3. most religious **beliefs**
4. those fond **memories**
5. both my cousins' **wives**

Exercise 5.10

1. four big **feet**
2. several athletic **men**
3. three happy **children**
4. two loose **teeth**
5. both elderly **women**
6. all the news **media**

Exercise 5.11

1. The young **women** wrote ***some*** mystery **stories**.
2. **Those** stylish **men** liked **these** plaid wool **scarves**.
3. ***Two*** clever **girls** fixed **these** broken **shelves**.
4. **These** naughty **children** broke **those** expensive **dishes**.
5. The new **secretaries** made _ extra **copies** for the **bosses** upstairs.

Exercise 5.12

1. Leora broke one of her mother's favorite **dishes**.
   The handle of the **dish** broke off.
2. Another of those awful **tests** was given yesterday.
   Part of that **test** gave me a lot of trouble.
3. One of the **questions** was especially tricky.
   The first word of the **question** puzzled me.
4. Every one of those **knives** needs sharpening.
   The blade of the **knife** rusted in the rain.
5. We won one of those portable **radios** as a prize.
   Almost immediately, the tuning knob of the **radio** broke.

Exercise 5.13

All **Austrians** are fascinated by **elaborate** timepieces. In Vienna, many **streets** have two or three shops that sell fancy **watches** of all shapes and sizes, plus clocks made of gold, silver, porcelain, and many other precious **materials**. In the Clock Museum are two astronomical **clocks**, each as big as a room, and several **timepieces** so tiny that you can't read the **numbers** on their faces without a magnifying glass. The most famous Viennese timepiece is the Anker Clock. Three **floors** above the street, twelve life-sized **statues** of Austrian **national** heroes march across its enormous face. When **this** clock strikes the hour, **melodies** by many Viennese musical geniuses salute these historical **figures**.

Exercise 5.14

Both **parents** of the newborn quadruplets were returning home from the hospital. For the first 24 **hours**, two of their four tiny **babies** had struggled for their **lives**. Although still in incubators, now they all seemed to be doing well. So at this moment the parents were worrying more about the many huge **bills** that were piling up. The mother was asking herself why she had taken those fertility **pills**. And where, they both wondered, would they get the cash for all the **things** on their shopping list — diapers, **blankets**, **shirts**, pins, **bottles**, and countless other basic **items**? Approaching the front door, the couple saw that all the **lights** were shining in the three rooms of their small house. At first, they were afraid that burglars had been there, but as they looked around inside, their **eyes** widened with surprise. In the living room were all their **neighbors**. On the floor were four **boxes**, each filled with baby clothes, **toys**, and medical **supplies**. Among other **things** were four pairs of **booties**, matching sweaters and caps in four different **colors**, and even four little **hairbrushes**. When they picked up a big brown envelope, their **neighbors** all shouted at once, "Open it!" More than fifty **checks** fell out on the table. For a couple of months, anyway, their **worries** about money were over.

Exercise 5.15

1. many ideas
   much information
2. much equipment
   many typewriters
3. many slices
   much bread
4. many accidents
   much luck
5. little leisure
   few hobbies
6. few cries
   little crying
7. little traffic
   few cars
8. few assignments
   little homework

Exercise 5.16

1. Sophia has no **interest** in spelunking.
    Sophia has so many **interests** that she hardly has time to sleep.
2. Most of the **time** it's better to keep your temper.
    How many **times** must I tell you not to do that?
3. **Experience** may be the best teacher.
    We usually can learn the most from our bad **experiences**.
4. Many of his **writings** have been translated into Polish.
    He likes **writing** at night.
5. All of the **lights** had gone out.
    But the room was filled with the **light** of the moon.

Exercise 5.17

1. Neither of the **apartments** was big enough for a family of four.
2. A lot of the **steel** for the new building had rusted.
3. Each of the **women** thought that her child was the most intelligent one in the class.
4. How much of the **information** was useful for your paper?
5. That is one of the best **comedies** the drama club has ever staged.
6. Two quarts of whole **milk** daily is no longer recommended, even for adolescent boys.
7. Our teacher gave at least two assignments of **homework** every week.
8. Happy coincidences are examples of good **luck**.
9. The roofs of the **houses** were blown off in the storm.
10. We bought a big bunch of **celery**.

Exercise 5.18

Joe and Gloria often switched work-**roles** before they had their first two **children**. About three **times** a month, Gloria used to bring home several of her **friends** from work, and Joe would prepare fancy **meals** for them. He specialized in **dishes** they could get their **teeth** into. One night he served thick French onion soup to his two **guests**. As he mixed their **drinks**, he gave them some **advice** about cooking: "When I sliced these **onions**, I used the sharpest of all my **knives**. Always cut the cheese into small pieces. Three **dashes** of **salt** should be enough for a quart of soup. Keep many different **spices** on your **shelves**." The women said that his soup was one of the best **feasts** they had ever eaten. Gloria gave her husband two big **kisses** as a reward, and after dinner she helped him clean up the mess. The other two **women** went home and told their **men** to make onion soup for them. The next night angry stomping, several loud **crashes**, and excited **cries** were heard in the kitchens of these **ladies**. Later they told Gloria that onion soup had turned their happy marriages into complete **wrecks**.

Exercise 5.19

1. **These women** sold **their guitars**.
2. **Those farmers** needed advice about **their problems**.
3. The **lawyers** won **their cases**.
4. **Those boys** asked for hockey equipment for **their birthdays**.
5. The constant gossiping of **these neighbors** annoyed **those children**.
6. *Some* **students** tried to steal the final **exams** from **those** sealed **boxes**.

Exercise 5.20 Stars ** mark where different <u>singular</u> determiners can be used. Check to make sure that both the determiner and the noun in your answer are singular.

1. **That child** caught ***a* butterfly** with ***her* net**.
2. **This woman** earned **her** master's **degree**.
3. Because **his wife** had gone camping, **that man** ate out a lot.
4. **This car** stalled in traffic, and **its driver** couldn't start **it**.
5. **That choir** needed some new music for **its** radio **program**.
6. **The new tenant** built some furniture for ***his*** apartment.

Exercise 5.21

1. For his first twelve years, a little <u>boy</u> is learning how to understand what is said to <u>him</u>, to do what **he** can see others doing, and to make sense out of **his** world. If love surrounds **him**, **he is** likely to be loving in return. If <u>he</u> never sees anything but violence, <u>he</u> may grow up to think and act violently.
2. These days a young <u>woman</u> has many opportunities open to <u>her</u>. **She** can get married and become a housewife, or seek a career. Or <u>she</u> can do both. However, **she** must realize the difficulties of being a good mother to <u>her</u> children and getting ahead on <u>her</u> job at the same time.
3. Responsible <u>teachers</u> make an effort to interest, as well as to instruct, **their** students. **They** may take the children on trips, or **they** may plan class projects. For example, they can help their students to hold a science fair or to raise a family of gerbils. **They** obviously must keep order in class, but the classroom should also be a place where their students have fun. If they can succeed in this, both **they** and **their** students will look forward to school every day.

Exercise 5.22

Some rich local **citizens** recently bought ***several*** beautiful old **houses**. **They** fixed **them** up as ** **museums** and opened **them** to the public. ***A few*** **teachers** took **their** fourth grade **classes** to visit **these mansions**. **They** asked the **guides** to give **them** some information about the **families** who once lived there. The **guides** told **them** and **their classes** all about the **men** and the **women** who had built **these houses** long ago.

Exercise 5.23

One* child** wanted to know more about the ornate furniture. It included ***a tiny carved **desk**, ***one*** huge **bed**, ***a* cradle** made of jet black wood, and ***a*** grandfather **clock** which still kept perfect time. ***One* boy** thought **he** heard ghostly whispering in the locked **closet**. Later on, in **his** English **class, that student** made up ***a*** spooky **story** about the **ghost** who still sat at **that** fancy **desk**, and rocked **that** black **cradle**, and slept in **that** big **bed**.

Exercise 5.24

1. The invitations were addressed to Elizabeth and **me**.
2. Julia Roberts starred in *Erin Brockovich*, in which Albert Finney and **she** won a case against polluters.
3. My mother and **I** talk on the telephone at least once a week.
4. A large fence ran along the property line between **us** and the Mercados.
5. Leave the package with the receptionist or **me**.
6. Just between you and **me**, Harriet and **he** get on my nerves.
7. She and I consider him and his wife to be our best friends.

Exercise 5.25

1. The young defendant decided to fire his lawyer and represent **himself** at the hearing.
2. The members of the criminal justice system are **themselves** responsible for this entire fiasco.
3. What their worst enemies wouldn't do, these young criminals did to **themselves**.
4. The judge reviewed the facts with the lawyer and **me**.
5. After the trial, we asked **ourselves**, "Was justice served?"
6. The boys' parents and **I** were determined to appeal the verdict.

Exercise 5.26

1. <u>People</u> don't function well under pressure, because then **they** don't feel like doing anything at all.
2. The counselor taught <u>the students</u> to have confidence in **themselves**.
3. When <u>we</u> grow up, **we** often see **our** parents differently.

Exercise 5.27

1.
    A good cook always keeps <u>her</u> knives handy.
2.
    A writer often chooses themes from <u>his</u> own life.
3.
    When a professor does research for an outside agency, <u>he</u> should inform the University about <u>his</u> activities.

Exercise 5.28

1. <u>Young people</u> ought to choose **their** first employment carefully, because **they** will most likely continue in the same general line of work in which **they** started.
2. In heavy traffic, <u>bicycle riders</u> should not go through red lights. **They** may cause accidents by surprising drivers or pedestrians who don't expect to see **them** in the intersection. Such reckless **cyclists** may endanger **themselves**, as well as others.

Exercise 5.29

   Taxpayers who receive orders to report to the Internal Revenue Service with **their** tax records may feel that the government is out to get **them**. I received such a summons last summer. I called a friend who is an accountant, and **she** [*or **he**] told me not to worry. Then I called another friend, but **she** [*or **he**] just congratulated **herself** [*or **himself**] that the problem wasn't **hers** [*or **his**]. So I went through my files and put **them** in order. At the big gray IRS building the following Tuesday, **I** waited for half an hour until a clerk called **my** name. Then the clerk told me to follow **him** [*or **her**]. My auditor was a severe woman who greeted me with a frown. Somehow, when a woman is in a position of authority, **she** can seem even more intimidating than a man would be. I sat down, reached for my papers, and dropped **them** all over the floor. When I recovered, the auditor started checking my return. Two hours later, she said, "Your tax return is fine." By then **she** and I felt like old friends. Mrs. Harris had learned things about **me** and my life that nobody else knew. She said that I had done a fine job on my tax return, better than most taxpayers do preparing it by **themselves**. I realized with relief that if I ever had to deal with officials at the IRS again, I wouldn't be afraid of **them**.

* These pronouns are dependent on the actual gender, male or female, of the accountant, friend, and clerk.

Exercise 5.30

According to a *New York Times* report, the typical black serviceman is upbeat about **his** career in the Army. He finds that the pay is better and that he enjoys more job satisfaction than **he** would as **a** civilian **employee**. Although there is still some discrimination, the chances are good that **he** can eventually win promotion. However, on the downside, **he** will sometimes have trouble getting a white subordinate to obey him. Also, he may have to prove **himself** not only equal to all his white **counterparts**, but superior to them. Overall, however, a black **serviceman** generally feels **he** would have succeeded no better, and in some instances not as well, in civilian life.

Exercise 5.31

Female officers, also interviewed by *New York Times* reporters, were somewhat negative about life in the armed forces. They said their biggest problems centered on getting **their** male superiors or subordinates to accept them as soldiers or sailors or **Marines** with the same rights and duties as their male counterparts. Most of these **women** complained that getting the men under **them** to follow **their** orders was often difficult. Black service women asserted that they were often treated unfairly, not because they were black, but because they were **women**. Some of the women interviewed protested vehemently against the laws which still exclude **them** from certain combat operations, and consequently from some senior command positions and higher pay.

Module 6: *Making Present-tense Verbs Agree*

Exercise 6.1

Every day some very fast planes leave Heathrow Airport in London. They arrive in New York only three hours later. The seats cost a lot. But some business people need to meet deadlines. So they take these planes to save time. They complete their business in New York quickly. Often they return home the same day.

Every day a very fast plane leaves Heathrow Airport in London. It arrives in New York only three hours later. A seat costs a lot. But Colin Walker needs to meet deadlines. So he takes this plane to save time. He completes his business in New York quickly. Often he returns home the same day.

Exercise 6.2
1. Americans **eat** too much red meat.
2. I **count** fat grams, not calories.
3. You **lose** weight by eating fruit.
4. Salt and animal fat **kill** millions.
5. We **study** food labels carefully.

Exercise 6.3

1. Marietta **likes** studying statistics.
   She **likes** studying statistics.
2. The President **appoints** ambassadors.
   He **appoints** ambassadors.
3. A college diploma **helps** you to get a job.
   It **helps** you to get a job.

Exercise 6.4

1. Marietta **likes** studying statistics.
   She **likes** studying statistics.
   Marietta and I **like** studying statistics.
   We **like** studying statistics.
2. The President **appoints** ambassadors.
   He **appoints** ambassadors.
   The President and Vice President **appoint** ambassadors.
   They **appoint** ambassadors.
3. A college diploma **helps** you to get a job.
   It **helps** you to get a job.
   College diplomas **help** you to get jobs.
   They **help** you to get jobs.

Exercise 6.5

1. The delivery men and the janitor use the service entrance.
   The delivery men use the service entrance.
   The janitor uses the service entrance.
2. Jesse and his partner design toys.
   Jesse designs toys.
   His partner designs toys.
3. That Congressman and his supporters deny the charges.
   That Congressman denies the charges.
   His supporters deny the charges.
4. Two planes and one train leave for Buffalo daily.
   Two planes leave for Buffalo daily.
   One train leaves for Buffalo daily.
5. Harvey and I ask many questions in class.
   Harvey asks many questions in class.
   I ask many questions in class.

Exercise 6.6

1. A safe driver never **passes** without signaling first.
2. I never **drive** in the passing lane.
3. Graham always **husks** the corn after the water boils.
4. Southern customs **emphasize** good manners and hospitality.
5. An incumbent official usually **coasts** to easy victory.
6. Any big city mayor **marches** in many parades.
7. This answer **misses** the point of the question.
8. My English teacher **asks** us to do a long writing assignment every week.
9. The museum never **waxes** its antique wooden furniture.
10. Going to college **tests** your time-management skills.

Exercise 6.7

1. Someone always **cries** at a wedding.
2. That chicken **lays** brown eggs.

3. A widower almost always **remarries** within two years.
4. That intersection **worries** every parent in the neighborhood.
5. My sister often **annoys** me with her nosy remarks.
6. The entrance examination **terrifies** most students.
7. Today young people usually **marry** in their twenties.

Exercise 6.8

Milagros loves sewing. She buys beautiful fabric in a shop near where she lives. After she and her mother lay out the pattern, Milagros cuts the dress out. Then she sews it together carefully. She uses her iron as she finishes each seam. Her brother and her mother help her with some of the work. For example, they adjust the hem as she tries the new dress on, and they fit the waist. Milagros says that she enjoys sewing. She not only saves money by making her own clothes, but she always looks better than the other women in her office.

Exercise 6.9

1. Lolita **has** an expensive new pair of sunglasses.
2. Shaheed **does** his math problems carefully.
3. Marie **goes** to visit her parents every summer.
4. These banks now **have** evening hours.
5. I **do** the best I can.
6. Latecia never **goes** to the movies alone.
7. Coolidge always **has** the best answer.
8. Stein always **does** his own thing.
9. Some people never **go** to the movies at all.
10. The Harrises **have** 19 grandchildren.
11. While I **do** the shopping, she **does** the cooking, and our husbands **go** fishing.

Exercise 6.10

Some frustrating laws seem to control our everyday lives. This list includes some of the most familiar: ① As soon as you mention something good, it goes away. As soon as you speak of something bad, it happens. One social scientist calls this *The Unspeakable Law.* ② The other line always moves faster. If you drive a car through toll gates or wait in supermarket lines, you know that this law never fails. ③ Bread always falls butter-side down. Another version of this law says that an object always collapses where it does the most damage. For example, your shopping bag rips just when you get to the middle of an intersection, and the glasses tumble off the tray as you reach the middle of the new rug. ④ Work always expands so that it fills up the time available. If you have ten minutes for a job, it takes ten minutes. However, if you have two hours, then it takes the whole two hours. ⑤ The person with the gold makes the rules. Most people learn this version of the Golden Rule before the one in the Bible. ⑥ Nothing gets better; it only gets worse. Some laws have exceptions — but never this last one.

Exercise 6.11

1. Everyone **tries** to take that course.
   Most people **try** to take that course.
2. Everybody **likes** to win.
   All of us **like** to win.
3. Few people **want** taxes to rise.
   No one **wants** taxes to rise.
4. Anybody **appreciates** a sincere compliment.
   We all **appreciate** a sincere compliment.
5. Not many of us **enjoy** working all the time.
   Nobody **enjoys** working all the time.

Exercise 6.12

1. The **children** seem quiet.
2. **She** always reads as much as possible.
3. The **shadows** fall at dusk.
4. **She** looks uncomfortable.
5. **Jo** seldom arrives on time.
6. **Few people** pronounce the word *mischievous* correctly.
7. **Everybody** worries about inflation these days.

Exercise 6.13

1. The discovery of those scientists **interests** me.
   The discoveries of that scientist **interest** me.
2. Women with confidence **intimidate** some men.
   A woman with confidence **intimidates** some men.
3. The programs on this channel **win** awards every year.
   One of these programs **wins** an award every year.
4. Four members of this orchestra **play** together sometimes in a string quartet.
   One member of this orchestra **plays** timpani.
5. An increase in income taxes **seems** inevitable.
   Income taxes for my family **seem** to increase yearly.
6. Everybody in most families **acts** irrational at one time or another.
   But nobody in this family ever **acts** irrational.
7. One of those keys **unlocks** this door.
   The keys on my keyring **unlock** every door but this one.

Exercise 6.14 Parentheses are optional but help make the structure of the sentence clearer.

1. This movie lampoons women (who harass men).
2. Machines (which use less fuel) cost more.
3. Voters usually prefer a candidate (who rejects negative advertising).
4. Anyone (who loves this team) hates its owner.
5. A magazine (which exposes a bad product) does the public a service.

Exercise 6.15

1. Yes, she **worries** too much and **works** too hard.
2. Yes, they **exercise** in the morning and **study** in the afternoon.
3. Yes, she **asks** a lot of questions, **gets** into mischief, and **keeps** her parents busy.
4. Yes, they **become** angry, **rebel**, and **act** out.
5. Yes, he **becomes** angry, **rebels**, and **acts** out.

Exercise 6.16

Oscar, who **says** that **he wants** a quiet life in the fresh air, now **lives** on a farm. **He gets** up every morning at dawn. Before **he has** breakfast, **he picks** his way through the cow dung, **opens** the smelly chicken coop, and **holds** his **nose** as **he snatches** the eggs. While **he makes** a fire in **his** woodburning stove, **he chokes** on the smoke. Then **Oscar drives** a deafening tractor out to the field. As **he breathes** in the blowing dust, **he coughs** loudly and **sneezes** often. Until late in the evening, **he does** chores in the barn. Exhausted, **he goes** to bed and **dreams** of a sound-proofed office and an air-conditioned apartment.

Exercise 6.17

When Lila **goes** to Europe, **she admires** the wonderful subways there. The **cleanliness** of the European subways **amazes** her. Maintenance **people polish** the brass railings and **wash** down the walls. Gratefully, **she sinks** into the soft seat **which gives** her such a comfortable ride. Excellent **maps** and clear **signs** on every wall **guide** her efficiently from one unfamiliar station to another. **She remembers** the sweltering cars, dirty **stations**, and confusing signs in the subways back home. Certainly, Lila never **gets** homesick when **she rides** in European subway trains.

Exercise 6.18

1. The **committee wants** to require more liberal arts courses.
2. Three **professors intend** to retire.
3. **Nobody wants** to go to the library.

Exercise 6.19

Somebody makes plans to **break** most world records as soon as **someone** else **sets** them. When an **athlete runs** the mile in under four minutes, his **rival** immediately **starts** training to **beat** his time. When a **woman swims** around Manhattan in the summer, **another has** to **do** it in the winter. **It seems** heroic to **try** to **break** records like these, but some other **attempts make** no sense. **We grieve** if **someone dies** trying to **fly** fast, but **it looks** silly for people to **eat** or to **dance** themselves to death. In contests like these, foolish **people** often **refuse** to **stop**. If **people have** to **kill** themselves to **win**, **they kill** themselves. At that moment each **contestant wants** to **do** just one thing — to **dance** longer, or to **eat** more, or to **scream** louder than anyone else in the world.

Exercise 6.20

To pay his bills, **Ngo Nhu has** to drive his taxi up to 16 hours a day. Even so, **he** hardly **makes** enough to put nourishing food on the table for his wife and three small children. To get through his long day behind the wheel, **he dreams** the American dream. As **he creeps** through the downtown traffic, **he imagines** relaxing with his family after supper in the backyard of their suburban home, the home **he plans** to **buy** some day. These **thoughts** keep him going until the restaurants and theaters close and the streets grow dark and empty. But when he gets home after midnight, he finds his wife in bed and his children fast asleep.

So as each week **drags** on, Ngo Nhu becomes impatient with distant hopes and dreams. He tries to make an extra buck by racing ahead of other taxis to **pick** up fares. As he drives faster and faster, his passengers cringe. When he switches lanes without signaling, nervous passengers often ask to get out. The cops chase him when he rushes through stop signs, and just one traffic ticket costs him a full day's pay.

When Ngo Nhu finally takes a day off, however, life once more seems good and the future seems bright. He plays with his children, talks to his wife about the week's adventures, and studies his manual of English verbs. Then the next morning, he drives away at dawn, and the cycle of dreams and frustrations starts all over again for Ngo Nhu.

Exercise 6.21

Recent medical research shows that our emotional reaction to life's ups and downs has a profound effect on our health. The fifteen billion nerve cells in our brains constantly change our hopes and fears into chemical substances which in turn either heal or harm our bodies. Many people hear these facts but reject them. Depression runs in their family, they say. But researchers again have an answer: If people act cheerful, then they begin to feel cheerful. When something unexpected wrecks their plans, smart people look for a hidden advantage instead of moaning over it. When they get a chance to say something positive, they never hesitate to say it. Sensible individuals who see something beautiful take time out to enjoy it. When a small misfortune happens, they turn it over in their minds until they find the funny side. (Everything does have a funny side.) This positive behavior produces positive feelings. Most of the time we have the power to do what makes life more enjoyable, to see the bright side, or at least to remember that sooner or later things will change. This makes sense, and often means the difference between sickness and health.

Exercise 6.22

My wife and I are trying to raise our children in a non-sexist way, but we are unable to control the way in which other people talk to our four-year olds. The children are twins, but Emma is much more aggressive than her brother Dominick. The neighbors are quick to praise Emma as "a little lady," but then they lift an eyebrow when she is too boisterous. At the same time, they are apt to say to Dominick, "You are so quiet today! What is wrong?" I am not happy to see that sexual stereotyping is still alive and well, at least on our block.

Exercise 6.23

1. You 're rather short-tempered these days.
2. I 'm eager to hear from you.
3. Nobody 's perfect.
4. They 're members of the Latin Club.
5. There 's a telephone call for you.
6. Where 's the rent money?
7. Here 's the man that I 'm going to marry.

Exercise 6.24

Frustrated parents sometimes like to **imagine** that their children are very talented. Sometimes a father who wishes that he had been an actor wants his son to **be** a movie star, and so he teaches the boy how to **sing** and to **dance** almost before he knows how to **walk** or to **talk**. A mother who wanted to **dance** thinks her daughter is sure to **be** another Pavlova, so she sends the child to school to **learn** ballet before she is able to **read**. It is true that every now and then a Macaulay Culkin turns up and makes several million dollars in the movies before he is ten years old; and once every four or five centuries a Mozart writes a symphony when he is only nine. But much more often, these children are remarkable only to their parents. When a so-called child prodigy grows up, he usually never wants to **see** a piano or to **dance** a step. He becomes a plumber or a policeman, which is just what he wanted to **be** from the start.

Exercise 6.25

All cat owners know that domestic cats belong to the same family of mammals as lions. When a pet cat pounces on an insect or licks its paws and washes its face, it looks just like a lion in the zoo. But in one important way, cats and **lions** are completely different. Outdoors, in pursuit of birds or **mice**, a domestic cat acts very independent. Aloof and solitary, it stalks its victims alone. But lions, especially the females, tend to live and to hunt in groups. The lions travel together and bring down their victims in a coordinated attack. They treat every member of the group, even a cub, as an equal. If one of the young **lions** lags behind the group, the others prod and push him. If one lion by accident hurts another as they scramble over a carcass, the others lick her wounds and comfort her. In this cooperative behavior, lions are not like domestic cats at all; in fact, they differ from all other **members** of the cat family.

Module 7: *Mastering Past-tense Verbs*

Exercise 7.1

1. George Worsham, a Virginia farmer, **got** his tax bill on September 30, 1829.
2. He **paid** 40¢ per slave, 10¢ per horse, and 1¢ per two-wheeled carriage.
3. In 1862, he **bought** his grandson Henry a new horse for $120.
4. Then Henry's mother **brought** a box of cornbread to the verandah and **put** it in his knapsack.
5. Henry **said** goodbye to his parents and **rode** away to join the First Virginia Cavalry.
6. Three years later the Confederate States of America **sent** Mr. Worsham $2965 in worthless currency for his dead horse, and nothing for his dead grandson.
7. One by one, the freed black slaves then **began** to leave the farm, and Worsham **sold** his livestock.
8. On June 1, 1870, Worsham and his sons **spoke** to their lawyer and **told** him to file for bankruptcy on their behalf.
9. In 1873, Rebecca Worsham, George's granddaughter, **went** to a Young Ladies' Seminary in Kentucky and **taught** Latin and Greek to support the family.

Exercise 7.2

1. In 1861, the Civil War **began** with Confederate victories at Fort Sumter and Bull Run.
2. For many months after that, the timid Northern generals **ran** away or **did** nothing.
3. Early in 1862, Ulysses S. Grant **came** to President Lincoln's attention as the first Northern general to win a battle.
4. He **led** his troops in the bloody but indecisive battles at Shiloh and Antietam.
5. Then, in the following year, Grant **saw** a chance to win control of the Mississippi Valley.
6. On July 4, 1863, he **drank** a victory toast at Vicksburg, and his troops **sang** *Yankee Doodle* on the banks of the Mississippi.
7. After this triumph, the tide of the war **swung** in favor of the North.

Answers

Exercise 7.3

They **bought** They **brought** They **caught** They **taught** Spell these verbs with **AUGHT** or with **OUGHT** in the past tense.	They **stole**. They **rose**. They **froze**. They **chose**. Spell these verbs with **O** in the past tense.
They **threw**. They **knew**. They **grew**. Spell these verbs with **EW** in the past tense.	They **said**. They **laid**. They **paid**. Spell these verbs with **AID** in the past tense.
They **quit**. They **cut**. They **hit**. They **hurt**. They **put**. These verbs have **no** change in the past tense.	They **rang**. They **swam**. They **began**. They **drank**. They **sang**. Spell these verbs with **A** in the past tense.
They **sent**. They **lost**. They **spent**. They **slept**	They **kept**. They **felt**. They **left**. Spell these verbs with **T** in the past tense

Exercise 7.4

1. According to Joseph Smith, in 1829 an angel **presented** him with a book which he **called** *The Book of Mormon.*
2. This book **inspired** him to found the Mormon Church.
3. Because he and his followers **practiced** polygamy, an angry mob **lynched** him in 1844.
4. The leadership of the Church **passed** to Brigham Young.
5. Thousands of Mormon converts **followed** Young to Salt Lake City, where they **established** a new community.

Exercise 7.5

1. Gracia **planted** a garden and **grew** tomatoes.
2. The shortstop **stole** third base and then **scored** the winning run.
3. Mr. Erickson **taught** my high school Spanish class and **passed** all his students with a B.
4. The child **caught** chicken pox and **developed** a high fever.
5. Everybody **sat** in her seat and **pretended** to be working.

Exercise 7.6

1. During the 1940s, American factories **relied** on millions of women workers while their men **carried** arms in World War II.
2. Most of these women **enjoyed** their earning power and independence, but **buried** these feelings when their husbands and sweethearts returned.
3. Then throughout the 1950s, most wives **stayed** home and once again **played** a traditional role.
4. The post-war baby boom **delayed** feminism for an entire generation.

Exercise 7.7

After the bank **collapsed**, the investigators **laid** the entire blame on the bank officials. They **said** that the officers **relied** on inside information about stock investments and **delayed** paying interest on loans. As usual, the officers **denied** the charges, but the depositors **paid** dearly for these illegal practices.

Exercise 7.8

1. I **hoped** to get a B in my philosophy course last semester, but I didn't really expect to.
   Edmund **hopped** four miles last year to win a bet.
2. Somebody **robbed** the liquor store on the corner last week.
   The graduates **robed** in the hall before the ceremony.
3. Who **rapped** on my door a minute ago?
   The Romans **raped** the Sabines (that is, they carried them away).
4. That group **planned** the conference two years in advance.
   The carpenter **planed** the door so it would fit better.
5. We **stared** at each other in disbelief.
   The film **starred** William Hurt and Glenn Close.

Exercise 7.9 Underlining is optional.

As the storm battered the coast, the men on board the small fishing boat grasped the ropes and furled their sails. Desperately, they flashed distress signals to the shore. But the waves surged savagely, overturned their boat, and threatened to drown them. All night, they clutched the hull of their craft with aching fingers, and tried to stay hopeful. At dawn, while the storm still raged helicopter pilots risked their lives when they hovered over the fishermen, dropped ladders, and plucked them out of the sea.

Exercise 7.10

1. Millions **used to die** of smallpox.
2. Some middle-income folks **used to have** cooks and chauffeurs.
3. Some retired Americans **used to save** money by living abroad.

Exercise 7.11

Last week when I stepped out of the elevator in my apartment building, Sam the janitor warned me to be careful. He reminded me about the rise in street crime during this past year. I just laughed as I pushed open the front door. When I reached the sidewalk, I stopped, buttoned up my coat, pulled on my gloves, and gathered up all my packages again. It never occurred to me to see if I had everything. I entered the bank on the corner and asked to apply for a credit card. The guard opened the gate into the office area. I went inside and picked up an application to fill out. But when I reached for my lavender purse to get a pen, nothing lavender appeared among my packages. I started to **scream**. I kicked the gate and yelled, "Somebody stole my purse! Somebody robbed me!" The guard told me to **stop** for a minute and to try to think. I admitted to him, "Yes, maybe I left it on the street when I stopped and put my gloves on." In a panic, I dashed all the way home. Just inside the open door, Sam stared at me with my purse in his hand. He said with a look of astonishment, "Some stranger spotted your purse behind the door and handed it to me." This week Sam switched the topic of his conversation from crime to the weather.

Exercise 7.12

"Where **were** you when Kennedy was shot?" This **was** a familiar question when I **was** a child, and the answers **were** always interesting. We **were** at my parents' house last November 22nd, and a replay of the shocking events in Dallas in 1963 **was** on TV again. My small daughter suddenly looked up and asked, "Who **was** Jack Kennedy?"

Exercise 7.13

We **were** new at our jobs as bank tellers, so a counterfeit bill **was** hard for us to detect. But in this bank there **were** older tellers who **had** index fingers which **were** as sensitive as lie detectors. To their sharp eyes, a presidential face on a large bill **was** as familiar as their own. Presidents with crooked noses or bent ears **were** as obvious to them as the false smiles on the faces of thieves.

Exercise 7.14

1. We **weren't** sure of the answer.
2. My mother **wasn't** able to finish college.
3. You **weren't** there when we called.

Exercise 7.15

1. There **were** two terrible bus accidents in South America in 1991.
2. There **was** a huge celebration for the United States Bicentennial in 1976.
3. There **was** no cure for that disease before 1943.
4. There **was** just one person in the room then.

Exercise 7.16 Underlining which shows tense is optional.

1. Before my brother moved to Chicago, he **bought** a new car.
   Every time my brother makes a big change in his life, he **buys** a new car.
2. Whenever their parents disapprove of something, Maggie and Joan **are** eager to do it.
   Although their parents disapproved, Maggie and Joan **were** eager to become models.
3. If a person is ambitious, she **does** the best job possible.
   Because Latrelle was ambitious, she always **did** her best work.
4. When Ping's husband comes home, she **asks** him how he **feels**.
   When Ping's husband came home, she **asked** him how he **felt**.
5. Whenever she had time, Mrs. Franklin **stopped** and **bought** a newspaper to read on her way to work.
   Whenever she has time, Mrs. Franklin **stops** and **buys** a newspaper to read on her way to work.

Exercise 7.17 Underlining which shows tense is optional.

1. Last year, many people **dropped** their senile parents at the door of an emergency room and **drove** away.
2. If Congress **passes** that controversial bill, the President says that he will veto it when it **reaches** his desk.
3. Whenever I work at my computer, time **flies**, and I **lose** myself in my work.
4. A working mother often **shops** for groceries on the way home, and **rushes** to make supper before her husband arrives.

5. Then, while he **washes** the dishes, she lies down on the sofa and **watches** TV.
6. A deranged man **hid** a hammer under his coat, and then attacked Michaelangelo's famous statue of David and **chipped** its toe.
7. When the doorbell **rang**, Brenda looked to see who was there before she **unlocked** the door.
8. A young child is hard to live with because she **asks** questions constantly and **gets** into a lot of mischief.
9. There **are** several drugs which prolong the lives of AIDS victims, but until doctors **find** a cure, the disease will continue to spread.
10. Before the game started, Roseanne **sang** The Star-Spangled Banner off key and almost **caused** a riot.

Exercise 7.18

1. Yes, he **stood** up, **started** an argument, and **stalked** away.
2. Yes, she **worries** about money, **shops** very carefully, and **pays** all her bills.
3. Yes, she **attends** school, **keeps** house for her family, and **studies** every weekend.
4. Yes, it **rang**, **stopped** and **began** ringing again.
5. Yes, I **wake** up at 9am, **have** breakfast, **listen** to the morning news, and **go** back to bed.
6. Yes, he **prayed**, **read** from the Bible, **led** a hymn, and **said** the benediction.

Exercise 7.19 Underlining which shows tense is optional.

1. Doctors tell us that the pressures of modern life **are** a threat to health.
2. Before the Revolution began, the principal religion of the Chinese people **was** Confucianism.
3. Because the point of many of his jokes **is** basically cruel, I dislike Professor Keys.
4. The loudspeaker announced that nobody **was** a clear winner in yesterday's competition.
5. The mayor claims that the number of violent crimes in our city **is** relatively low.
6. Several books from that set **were** on the table before the moderator arrived.
7. When I registered, not one of the delegates to this convention **was** in the hall.
8. I **am** furious with him about the way he's acting.

Exercise 7.20 Underlining which shows tense is optional.

1. Julian wonders why he **was** so shy when he was a child.
2. My grandparents seldom talk about the olden days, when they **were** young.
3. I sometimes forget that my little girl **is** all grown up now.
4. Do you remember the time last year when we **were** almost late for the plane?

Exercise 7.21 Underlining which shows tense is optional.

When I **was** a small boy, my friends **were** always eager to hear my grandfather's war stories. This **was** Chapter One in his collection of stories: "Who **am** I? Well, sonny, my name **is** Bill Williams, and I **am** 99 years old. In World War I, I **was** a fighter pilot. The Red Baron and I **were** up there, stalking each other in the clouds. Fragments of shrapnel **were** all around me, but I **was** not one bit scared. Here **is** an old photograph of me in my uniform. I **was** 19 years old at the time. Those campaign ribbons on my chest **were** my pride and joy then, and they still **are** now. And here on this table **are** some more souvenirs, a couple of old brass artillery shells that now **are** lamps. It **is** hard to believe, but these shells **were** once in a German cannon. And now here they **are**, looking pretty in my living room. I **was** one high flyer in the Great War, child, and I still **am**."

Exercise 7.22

Aunt Mattie, like many people over sixty, thinks that all her young relatives need to know how great the good old days were – before TV, when she and her sisters were growing up. Every Sunday, when my brother Jake watches her coming up the block, he frowns and mutters that trouble is on the way. She always rushes into our kitchen with a big hello, but then she acts like a lady preacher. There are a thousand things she likes to criticize. While we eat dinner, Auntie M. tries to get our attention, and if she doesn't, she thumps the table, demands silence, and begins to preach a sermon against modern times. She says it's a scandal that girls these days are wearing sexy jeans and that boys are kissing girls they don't even know. And there are those boom boxes all over the place! When she was a girl, she declares, things were a lot different. She says life was better when times were harder. And then she asks what I am doing with all the money that I earn. We try to be polite, but she really tests our patience. Jake usually jumps up and leaves the room at some point long before Aunt Mattie's final amen. The next time she wants to visit, we are ready to tell her that we have to go out!

Exercise 7.23

I was not a suspicious person, but I knew that something was wrong. Whenever I left the house, someone followed me. I never saw him, but I knew that he was there. I heard the sound of feet behind me when I walked. As I stopped to glance into shop windows, I caught a glimpse of someone who stood off to one side, but when I turned around, he was not there. I felt his presence in crowds. As I chose a magazine, he looked over my shoulder. As I bought toothpaste or paid for my groceries, he passed near and counted my change. As I hurried home, I felt his eyes on my back. I went out less and less. He watched me through my windows. When the phone rang I never answered. I slept very little. My friends thought that I was paranoid, but I wondered if they were in league with him.

Exercise 7.24

The 14 leading cars carried tents and equipment, and the next seven transported the animals. In the fading light of June 22, 1918, the crew hitched the four sleeping cars to the end of the train. The flagman signaled to the engineer, and the Hagenbeck-Wallace Circus clattered out of Michigan City. In the wooden sleepers, 300 circus people chatted and played cards, or climbed into their bunks and dreamed of the next day's opening performance in Hammond, Indiana.

Near the town of Ivanhoe, the circus train pulled into a side track while the crew tried to fix an overheated brake box. The Pullman cars extended out onto the main track, so Ernest Trimm, the flagman, propped up emergency flares and checked to make sure that the signal lights were flashing warnings. Suddenly, an unscheduled troop train thundered down the track, hurtling toward the circus cars. Asleep at the throttle, Engineer Alonso Sargent never slowed down. As the oncoming train passed through the yellow caution lights, Trimm waved his lantern frantically and then hurled it through the engineer's window. But the speeding locomotive ripped past the red stop lights and plowed into the fragile wooden sleeping cars, crushing and killing most of the performers. Gas lights started fires in the wreckage, and the animals bellowed in terror as the flames licked toward them. Trapped in their cages, some burned to death. Their roars terrified the townspeople, and hysterical reports traveled from house to house. According to so-called eyewitnesses, lions and tigers jumped from the train and roamed the streets.

On the evening after the wreck, though, the circus opened on schedule. Performers and acts from all over the country rushed to Indiana and substituted for the victims of the crash.

For years afterwards, the people of Ivanhoe used to sit around on summer evenings, talking about that terrible night when one exhausted man destroyed almost an entire circus.

Exercise 7.25 Brackets are optional.

In the Middle Ages, marriage customs used to be strange and cruel, especially for women. While brides were still in their cradles, their parents used to arrange their weddings. Sometimes a girl never saw her husband until they met at the altar rail, and all too often this meeting turned out to be quite a shock. But no matter how she felt about him, the marriage contract made it clear that he had to have an heir. If the wife failed to deliver a child within a year or two, her husband often used to get an annulment, and then he married someone else. The man was free to take a mistress, but if his wife even looked at another man, he beat her. Some women thought that it was better not to marry at all, and chose to enter the convent instead.

Exercise 7.26

My grandmother grew up in the Depression of the 1930s, when it cost just eight cents to buy a loaf of bread. Even with such low prices, her parents were too poor to put a good meal on the table every day. She and her family saw some really hard times. Since almost everybody was in the same boat, though, they laughed off their troubles, and waited for the economy to **recover**. They and their neighbors were right to believe what President Roosevelt always said on his weekly radio broadcasts, that prosperity was just around the corner. Compared to the Great Depression, recent years seem prosperous to most people. Parts of the economy are thriving, and one of my own neighbors has two BMWs and a vacation home. But the lives of many working people today aren't much different from my grandmother's. For example, my nephew, a recent high school graduate, is having a hard time finding a decent job, and not one of his friends owns a car. There are people in the middle, like me and my husband. We pay our bills and drive an old station wagon, but our dream of owning our own home gets dimmer and dimmer. Our future seems just as likely to get worse as it is to get better, as America moves into the 21st century.

Module 8: *Recognizing and Fixing Run-ons*

Exercise 8.1

1. The TV station canceled its regular programs, it was having a fund-raising drive.
    2 simple sentence(s) with **0** connecting word(s) is a ☐ sentence ☒ run-on.
    +
    The TV station canceled its regular programs because it was having a fund-raising drive.
    2 simple sentence(s) with **1** connecting word(s) is a ☒ sentence ☐ run-on.
2.   +
    Some volunteers were answering phone calls, and others were praising the station.
    2 simple sentence(s) with **1** connecting word(s) is a ☒ sentence ☐ run-on.
    Some volunteers were answering phone calls, others were praising the station.
    2 simple sentence(s) with **0** connecting word(s) is a ☐ sentence ☒ run-on.
3. An actor asked for large contributions, he had starred in some popular programs.
    2 simple sentence(s) with **0** connecting word(s) is a ☐ sentence ☒ run-on.
          +
    An actor who had starred in some popular programs asked for large contributions.
    2 simple sentence(s) with **1** connecting word(s) is a ☒ sentence ☐ run-on.

4.   +

As telephones rang, he looked into the camera, he pleaded for funds.
3 simple sentence(s) with **1** connecting word(s) is a ❑ sentence ☒ run-on.

   +

As telephones rang, he looked into the camera and pleaded for funds.
2 simple sentence(s) with **1** connecting word(s) is a ☒ sentence ❑ run-on.

Exercise 8.2

¹ In big cities, taxi driving has changed in recent years.   ¹SENTENCE

   +

² For one thing, it has become so dangerous that women rarely
drive cabs any more, most cabbies are now men. ³ For another,   ²RUN-ON
25 years ago most taxi drivers spoke fluent English, today

   +

many taxi drivers are immigrants who speak English poorly.   ³RUN-ON

   +

⁴ When passengers ask to go to Broad Street, they sometimes
end up at Broadway. ⁵ In New York City, taxi drivers must   ⁴SENTENCE
take classes at the Taxi Driver Institute, it teaches geography,
American manners, and traffic rules to its immigrant students.   ⁵RUN-ON
⁶ In just a few weeks, they can learn Taxi English, it's a
language with only 177 words and phrases.   ⁶RUN-ON

Exercise 8.3

¹ Many African Americans became educated and
prosperous during the later decades of the 19ᵗʰ century.   ¹SENTENCE

   ✓

² However, around 1900 the "Jim Crow" segregation laws were

   ✓

passed, then the social and economic fortunes of all blacks
rapidly declined. ³ Under the Jim Crow laws, not even the most   ²RUN-ON

   ✓

gifted blacks were admitted to the better schools, also, they were

   +

prohibited from owning property, even if they had more than
enough money to buy it. ⁴ They were turned away from   ³RUN-ON
restaurants and hotels and forced to sit in the backs of buses and

   ✓

trolleys, moreover, their dignity as human beings was wounded
even more deeply by "Whites Only" signs on restrooms, water

   ✓

fountains, playgrounds, and other public facilities. ⁵ Finally,   ⁴RUN-ON
these laws were removed from the books in the 1950s and 1960s

   +

after civil disturbances erupted from coast to coast.   ⁵SENTENCE

   ✓

⁶ Nevertheless, the Jim Crow laws caused psychological and

   +

economic scars which are still obvious everywhere in American
society.   ⁶SENTENCE

Exercise 8.4

1. Owning a house is a lot of trouble. There are too many expensive problems.
2. Mrs. Kim rents an old house. Sometimes something breaks.
3. However, it never costs her anything. She just calls the owner. He fixes everything.

Exercise 8.5

1.
The snow was already eight inches deep, **and** it was still falling.
2.
Two feet of snow were predicted by morning, **so** people were told to stay home.
3.
Rajendra worried about leaving the house, **but** he wanted to rent a video.
4.
He decided to go anyway, **so** he started up his car.
5.
He got out of the garage, **but** he made it only halfway down the driveway.
6.
His car slid onto his neighbor's lawn, **and** it hit a big oak tree.
7.
Rajendra's trip was very expensive, **and** he never did get to see that video.

Exercise 8.6

1.
Sandra was nervous, (**because** she was supposed to sing a solo in church in a week).
2.
She decided to keep practicing, (**until** she could sing her solo perfectly).
3.
(**When** Sunday arrived), she felt pretty confident.
4.
(**Even though** the organist made many mistakes), Sandra sang beautifully anyway.

Exercise 8.7

1.
Jerome dropped the rock, (**which** landed on his foot).
2.
We rushed him to the doctor, (**who** said that his foot was broken).
3.
She put on a cast, (**which** he'd have to wear for a month).
4.
Jerome always exercised by swimming, (**which** he could no longer do).
5.
The lack of exercise was not good for Jerome, (**who** had always had a weight problem).
6.
Finally the doctor removed the cast (**which** she had put on a month earlier).
7.
Jerome could no longer fit into the swimsuit (**which** he had worn before the accident).

Exercise 8.8

1. That car, (**which** was repaired just yesterday), refused to start again this morning.

2. The battery, (**which** was just replaced), seemed to be dead.

3. The mechanic (**who** repaired my car yesterday) sent out a tow truck.

4. Now the alternator, (**which** keeps the battery charged), needs replacing.

5. These constant repair bills (**which** I have to pay) are driving me crazy.

Exercise 8.9

Although Albert Einstein was perhaps the greatest scientist of all time, he was a very simple human being. To his teachers, he seemed a normal child who grasped things rather slowly. After he became a renowned physicist, his colleagues at Princeton smiled in disbelief when he asked them to pause and repeat their statements because his mind understood new things so slowly. Before he joined the Institute for Advanced Study, he was told to name his own salary. The director had to plead with him to accept more money because he asked for such an impossibly small amount. When famous scientists and world leaders visited him, he greeted them wearing an old sweater, baggy pants, and a pair of sandals which he wore on all occasions. When some children came knocking at his door one Christmas Eve, he followed them through the streets of Princeton while he accompanied their carols on his violin.

Exercise 8.10

1. For the best coffee, you should buy whole coffee beans. They will stay fresh longer than ground coffee.

   For the best coffee, you should buy whole coffee beans, because they will stay fresh longer than ground coffee.

   For the best coffee, you should buy whole coffee beans, which will stay fresh longer than ground coffee.

2. You should also store them in the freezer. They will stay fresh even longer.

   You should also store them in the freezer, so that they will stay fresh even longer.

You should also store them in the freezer, where they will stay fresh even longer.

3.   Then you should grind the beans fresh every morning. This process takes time. It produces the best-tasting coffee.

Then you should grind the beans fresh every morning. This process takes time, but it produces the best-tasting coffee.

Then you should grind the beans fresh every morning. Although this process takes time, it produces the best-tasting coffee.

4.   Finally, you should always use cold water. This will give you the best-tasting coffee.

Finally, you should always use cold water, because this will give you the best-tasting coffee.

Finally, you should always use cold water, which will give you the best-tasting coffee.

Exercise 8.11

Many African Americans became educated and prosperous during the later decades of the 19th century. However, around 1900 the "Jim Crow" segregation laws were passed. Then, the social and economic fortunes of all blacks rapidly declined. Under the Jim Crow laws, not even the most gifted blacks were admitted to the better schools. Also, they were prohibited from owning property, even if they had more than enough money to buy it. They were turned away from restaurants and hotels and were forced to sit in the backs of buses and trolleys. Moreover, their dignity as human beings was wounded even more deeply by "Whites Only" signs on restrooms, water fountains, playgrounds, and other public facilities. Finally, these laws were removed from the books in the 1950s and 1960s after civil disturbances erupted from coast to coast. Nevertheless, the Jim Crow laws caused psychological and economic scars which are still obvious everywhere in American society.

Exercise 8.12

Many African Americans became educated and prosperous during the later decades of the 19th century. However, around 1900 the "Jim Crow" segregation laws were passed.

✓

then, the social and economic fortunes of all blacks rapidly declined. Under the Jim

✓

Crow laws, not even the most gifted blacks were admitted to the better schools; also,

+

they were prohibited from owning property, even if they had more than enough money

to buy it. They were turned away from restaurants and hotels and were forced to sit in

✓

the backs of buses and trolleys; moreover, their dignity as human beings was wounded

even more deeply by "Whites Only" signs on restrooms, water fountains, playgrounds,

✓

and other public facilities. Finally, these laws were removed from the books in the 1950s

+ ✓

and 1960s after civil disturbances erupted from coast to coast. Nevertheless, the Jim

+

Crow laws caused psychological and economic scars which are still obvious everywhere
in American society.

Exercise 8.13

1.

+

Americans seem very health-conscious, but most of us eat diets full of sugar and fat anyway.

+

Although Americans seem very health-conscious, most of us eat diets full of sugar and fat anyway.

✓

Americans seem very health-conscious; nevertheless, most of us eat diets full of sugar and fat anyway.

2.

+ ✓

We know that fast food restaurants are unhealthy; however, we often go there for supper.

+ +

We know that fast food restaurants are unhealthy, but we often go there for supper.

+ +

Although we know that fast food restaurants are unhealthy, we often go there for supper.

3.

+

We eat greasy hamburgers and french fries, and we drink sugar-laden soda pop.

+

We eat greasy hamburgers and french fries, while we drink sugar-laden soda pop.

✓

We eat greasy hamburgers and french fries; moreover, we drink sugar-laden soda pop.

4.

+

We talk about losing weight, but we continue to eat junk food.

✓

We talk about losing weight; nevertheless, we continue to eat junk food.

+

Although we talk about losing weight, we continue to eat junk food.

Answers

Exercise 8.14 Your answers may be slightly different. Check that your sentences are correct by marking them as you have learned to.

       In big cities, taxi driving has changed in recent years. For one thing, it has become so dangerous that women rarely drive cabs any more, **so** most cabbies are now men. For another, 25 years ago most taxi drivers spoke fluent English, **but** today many taxi drivers are immigrants who speak English poorly. When passengers ask to go to Broad Street, they sometimes end up at Broadway. In New York City, taxi drivers must take classes at the Taxi Driver Institute, **which** teaches geography, American manners, and traffic rules to its immigrant students. In just a few weeks, they can learn Taxi English, **which** is a language with only 177 words and phrases.

Exercise 8.15

       Our ancestors died of many diseases which the modern world knows little about, like bubonic plague and smallpox. In the Middle Ages, bubonic plague killed thousands; in fact, the populations of entire cities died of this scourge, which recurred every few generations. In despair, because they knew that there were no cures, doctors told the officials to lock the city gates. People shuddered when anyone mentioned its gruesome name; indeed, they even nicknamed it "Black Death." Up to the 18th century, smallpox was another killer. Even if the victims recovered, the pockmarks which it left on their faces disfigured them for life. This disease was particularly dreadful for women. However, modern medicine has discovered vaccines, sanitation, and antibiotics, so that smallpox, like bubonic plague, has become merely a memory; moreover, past successes in eliminating these diseases encourage researchers who now are seeking cures for AIDS and cancer.

Module 9: *Recognizing and Fixing Fragments*

Exercise 9.1

1. Information from books, magazines, and the Internet.
    This ❑ has ☒ doesn't have both a verb and a subject, so it is a ❑ sentence ☒ fragment.
    [Students] (get) information from books, magazines, and the Internet.
    This ☒ has ❑ doesn't have both a verb and a subject, so it is a ☒ sentence ❑ fragment.
2. [Students] (can access) the Internet from computers at school.
    This ☒ has ❑ doesn't have both a verb and a subject, so it is a ☒ sentence ❑ fragment.
    Or from computers at home.
    This ❑ has ☒ doesn't have both a verb and a subject, so it is a ❑ sentence ☒ fragment.
3. [Books] and [magazines] (may be) lost or checked out from the library.
    This ☒ has ❑ doesn't have both a verb and a subject, so it is a ☒ sentence ❑ fragment.
    But (are) always available on the Internet.
    This ❑ has ☒ doesn't have both a verb and a subject, so it is a ❑ sentence ☒ fragment.
4. Information available 24 hours a day.
    This ❑ has ☒ doesn't have both a verb and a subject, so it is a ❑ sentence ☒ fragment.
    [Information] (is) available 24 hours a day.
    This ☒ has ❑ doesn't have both a verb and a subject, so it is a ☒ sentence ❑ fragment.
    Sometimes too much information.
    This ❑ has ☒ doesn't have both a verb and a subject, so it is a ❑ sentence ☒ fragment.

Exercise 9.2

[1] [Lawrence] (used) to eat at a local diner.   [1] SENTENCE
[2] Really (enjoyed) the great tasting food.   [2] FRAGMENT
[3] Also of course the low prices. [4] Then [he] (read) a   [3] FRAGMENT
Health Department report on the kitchen.   [4] SENTENCE
[5] Roaches, greasy pots, and a filthy refrigerator, all   [5] FRAGMENT
frighteningly obvious. [6] [It] (was) hard to believe.   [6] SENTENCE
[7] But better not to take chances with his health.   [7] FRAGMENT
[8] [He] (found) another place to have lunch.   [8] SENTENCE

Exercise 9.3

[1] In the 17th century, religious [persecution] (was)
(spreading) in England, France, Holland, and other European
countries. [2] To escape this persecution, religious groups   [1] SENTENCE
emigrating to the New World. [3] Puritans to worship in their   [2] FRAGMENT
simple churches in the New England countryside.   [3] FRAGMENT
[4] [Quakers] (gathered) in their meeting-houses in Pennsylvania.   [4] SENTENCE
[5] Later on, Irish [Catholics] (began) sailing for Boston and
Baltimore. [6] Each [group,] alone in its new location, (rejoiced)   [5] SENTENCE
in its freedom to practice its faith openly. [7] But after a few   [6] SENTENCE
decades sometimes (refused) to extend the same tolerance to
newcomers of different religions. [8] By the end of the   [7] FRAGMENT
century, religious persecution becoming nearly as intense in
the New World as in the Old.   [8] FRAGMENT

Exercise 9.4 Your answers may be slightly different. Check that your sentences are correct by marking them as you have learned to.

Lawrence used to eat at a local diner. **He** really enjoyed the great tasting food. Also of course **he enjoyed** the low prices. Then he read a Health Department report on the kitchen. **The inspectors found** roaches, greasy pots, and a filthy refrigerator, all frighteningly obvious. It was hard to believe. But **it was** better not to take chances with his health. He found another place to have lunch.

Exercise 9.5 Your answers may be slightly different. Check that your sentences are correct by marking them as you have learned to.

In the 17ᵗʰ century, religious persecution was spreading in England, France, Holland, and other European countries. To escape this persecution, religious groups **were** emigrating to the New World. Puritans **worshipped** in their simple churches in the New England countryside. Quakers gathered in their meeting-houses in Pennsylvania. Later on, Irish Catholics began sailing for Boston and Baltimore. Each group, alone in its new location, rejoiced in its freedom to practice its faith openly. But after a few decades sometimes **they** refused to extend the same tolerance to newcomers of different religions. By the end of the century, religious persecution **was** becoming nearly as intense in the New World as in the Old.

Exercise 9.6

Some athletes need more than athletic skills to **succeed, especially** a black man like Jackie Robinson. He was a superb **athlete, starring** in football, basketball, track, and baseball in college. He had been playing baseball for many years, but not of course in the Major Leagues. The racism of many players and owners had limited him to the Negro Leagues. In 1957, Branch Rickey, owner of the Brooklyn Dodgers, chose Robinson to break the color **barrier by** integrating his team. Robinson could hit, throw, and catch as well as (or better than) most white **players, and** was a gentleman as **well, with** a quiet but strong self-control. He needed all his inner strength to resist the taunts of hostile fans and other players. He ignored their curses and **threats, and** concentrated on proving himself to the world. In just his second year, he was named to the All-Star **team, and** in his third year became the Most Valuable Player. Jackie Robinson earned the respect of players and fans throughout the **country for** both his dignity and his athleticism. He was the right man to integrate Major League **baseball, and** in 1962 the Baseball Hall of Fame.

Exercise 9.7

1.   +
   Although the meeting started late.
   1 simple sentence(s) with **1** connecting word(s) is a ❏ sentence ☒ fragment.
         +
   Although the meeting started late, it ended early.
   2 simple sentence(s) with **1** connecting word(s) is a ☒ sentence ❏ fragment.

2.   +
   Because nobody from the Elections Committee attended
   1 simple sentence(s) with **1** connecting word(s) is a ❏ sentence ☒ fragment.
         +
   Because nobody from the Elections Committee attended the meeting ended early.
   2 simple sentence(s) with **1** connecting word(s) is a ☒ sentence ❏ fragment.

3. +
    If we don't have an election next week.
    1 simple sentence(s) with **1** connecting word(s) is a ☐ sentence ☒ fragment.

                                    +
    We won't be able to meet legally if we don't have an election next week.
    2 simple sentence(s) with **1** connecting word(s) is a ☒ sentence ☐ fragment.

Exercise 9.8

1.   +
    Everyone will be able to hear if the audio system operates properly.
2.   +
    However, the audience was getting rowdy because they couldn't hear anything.
3.   +
    When the audio system gets fixed, things should calm down.

Exercise 9.9

1.   +   +
    Before Bertha arrived they turned off the lights because they wanted to surprise her.
2.   +   +
    When Bertha walked in the door and they shouted "Surprise!" she was frightened
        +
    so that she dropped her purse.
3.   +   +
    The clasp broke so that everything fell out on the floor, and a small bottle of perfume broke.
4. +   +
    After they cleaned up the mess, everyone just laughed because the presents included a new purse
    and some perfume.

Exercise 9.10

        +
    When the brutal emperor Caligula ruled Rome, he had complete power to do
anything, no matter how inhuman. On the hottest days, he often removed the canopies at
                                                      +
the outdoor theater. He then refused to let anyone leave, so that the spectators collapsed
        +   +
from sunstroke. When Caligula was sick once, a friend promised to commit suicide if the
                                    +
gods spared the emperor's life. Later after Caligula got well, he compelled his friend to
                                                      +
keep that promise. He forced important administrators to trot beside his chariot because
                        +
he enjoyed making them look ridiculous. When two officials failed to announce his
                                    +
birthday, he removed them from office and sent them into exile. If he liked the looks of a
                        +   +
woman, he took her home with him, even if she was unwilling. Until he died at the
                                    +

hands of an assassin, Caligula continued to brutalize others, because other people's suffering was, for him, the best entertainment.

Exercise 9.11

1.
   +
   VCRs (which are hard to program).
   The expansion ❑ is ☒ isn't connected to a sentence, so this is a ❑ sentence ☒ fragment.

   +
   Most people own VCRs (which are hard to program).
   The expansion ☒ is ❑ isn't connected to a sentence, so this is a ☒ sentence ❑ fragment.

2.
   +
   The time, (which constantly blinks 12:00).
   The expansion ❑ is ☒ isn't connected to a sentence, so this is a ❑ sentence ☒ fragment.

   +
   Often they can't set the time, (which constantly blinks 12:00).
   The expansion ☒ is ❑ isn't connected to a sentence, so this is a ☒ sentence ❑ fragment.

3.
   +
   They can't even record programs (which they are watching on TV).
   The expansion ☒ is ❑ isn't connected to a sentence, so this is a ☒ sentence ❑ fragment.

   +
   Programs (which they are watching on TV).
   The expansion ❑ is ☒ isn't connected to a sentence, so this is a ❑ sentence ☒ fragment.

4.
   +   +
   People (who invent VCRs) (which are easier to use).
   The expansion ❑ is ☒ isn't connected to a sentence, so this is a ❑ sentence ☒ fragment.

   +   +
   People (who invent VCRs) (which are easier to use) will make a lot of money.
   The expansion ☒ is ❑ isn't connected to a sentence, so this is a ☒ sentence ❑ fragment.

Exercise 9.12

1.
                                      +
   There once was a Greek mathematician (who was named Zeno).
2.
                          +
   He thought of a paradox (which has puzzled people ever since).
3.
                +
   Somebody (who wants to cross a room) has to cross half the room first.
4.
                                  +
   Then he has to cross half of the half (that is remaining).
5.
            +   +
   No matter (how far he goes), there still remains half of the distance (which he has yet to cross).
6.
                        +
   How can he ever get to the wall (which always remains half of some distance away)?

Exercise 9.13

¹ Animals have elaborate communication systems
(which resemble human speech). ² And (which some people describe as language). ³ Certainly most animals communicate fear and sexual desire through movement and sounds.
⁴ Like the songs (that birds sing). ⁵ Sounds like these do have some of the qualities of human speech. ⁶ Each melody (which we hear) signals food, danger, or a sense of territory.
⁷ Furthermore, tapes of the sounds (that dolphins make).
⁸ These tapes reveal vibrations like the pulses of Navy sonar equipment. ⁹ Some scientists consider them to be the equivalent of human speech. ¹⁰ Also, the complicated dances
(which bees perform). ¹¹ These dances tell other bees about sources of nectar. ¹² Now scientists are studying animals
(which seem to be able to learn actual human language). ¹³ A woman (who invented a signal system like the finger talk of the deaf). ¹⁴ Later she taught it to a chimpanzee (which now has a vocabulary of over 100 words). ¹⁵ However, not even this smart monkey uses language like that of humans. ¹⁶ Language
(that expresses general and original ideas).

¹ SENTENCE
² FRAGMENT
³ SENTENCE
⁴ FRAGMENT
⁵ SENTENCE
⁶ SENTENCE
⁷ FRAGMENT
⁸ SENTENCE
⁹ SENTENCE
¹⁰ FRAGMENT
¹¹ SENTENCE
¹² SENTENCE
¹³ FRAGMENT
¹⁴ SENTENCE
¹⁵ SENTENCE
¹⁶ FRAGMENT

Exercise 9.14 Your answers may be slightly different. Check that your sentences are correct by marking them as you have learned to.

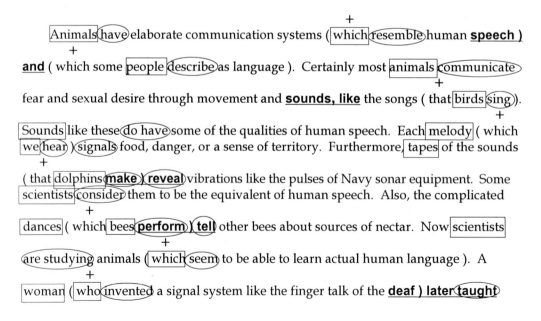

Animals have elaborate communication systems (which resemble human **speech)** **and** (which some people describe as language). Certainly most animals communicate fear and sexual desire through movement and **sounds, like** the songs (that birds sing).

Sounds like these do have some of the qualities of human speech. Each melody (which we hear) signals food, danger, or a sense of territory. Furthermore, tapes of the sounds (that dolphins **make) reveal** vibrations like the pulses of Navy sonar equipment. Some scientists consider them to be the equivalent of human speech. Also, the complicated dances (which bees **perform) tell** other bees about sources of nectar. Now scientists are studying animals (which seem to be able to learn actual human language). A woman (who invented a signal system like the finger talk of the **deaf) later taught** it to a chimpanzee (which now has a vocabulary of over 100 words). However, not even

this smart monkey uses language like that of **humans, language** (that expresses general and original ideas).

Exercise 9.15

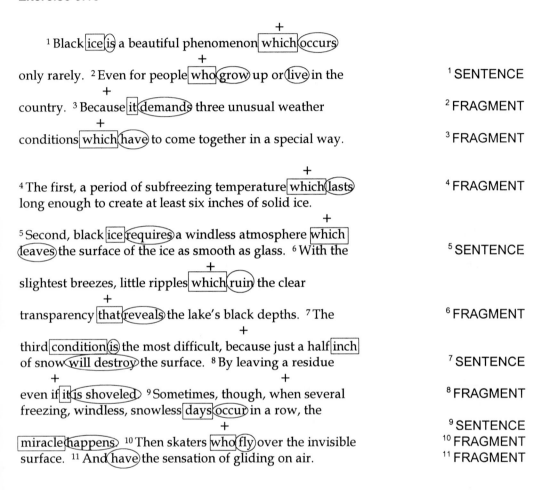

¹ Black ice is a beautiful phenomenon which occurs only rarely. ² Even for people who grow up or live in the country. ³ Because it demands three unusual weather conditions which have to come together in a special way.

⁴ The first, a period of subfreezing temperature which lasts long enough to create at least six inches of solid ice.

⁵ Second, black ice requires a windless atmosphere which leaves the surface of the ice as smooth as glass. ⁶ With the slightest breezes, little ripples which ruin the clear transparency that reveals the lake's black depths. ⁷ The third condition is the most difficult, because just a half inch of snow will destroy the surface. ⁸ By leaving a residue even if it is shoveled ⁹ Sometimes, though, when several freezing, windless, snowless days occur in a row, the miracle happens ¹⁰ Then skaters who fly over the invisible surface. ¹¹ And have the sensation of gliding on air.

¹ SENTENCE

² FRAGMENT

³ FRAGMENT

⁴ FRAGMENT

⁵ SENTENCE

⁶ FRAGMENT

⁷ SENTENCE

⁸ FRAGMENT

⁹ SENTENCE
¹⁰ FRAGMENT
¹¹ FRAGMENT

Exercise 9.16 Your answers may be slightly different. Check that your sentences are correct by marking them as you have learned to.

Black ice is a beautiful phenomenon which occurs only **rarely, even** for people who grow up or live in the **country, because** it demands three unusual weather conditions which have to come together in a special way. The first is a period of subfreezing temperature which lasts long enough to create at least six inches of solid ice. Second, black ice requires a windless atmosphere which leaves the surface of the ice as smooth as glass. With the slightest breezes, little ripples appear which ruin the clear transparency that reveals the lake's black depths. The third condition is the most difficult, because just a half inch of snow will destroy the **surface by** leaving a residue even if it is shoveled Sometimes, though, when several freezing, windless, snowless days occur in a row, the miracle happens. Then skaters fly over the invisible **surface and** have the sensation of gliding on air.

Exercise 9.17 Your answers may be slightly different. Check that your sentences are correct by marking them as you have learned to.

In 1935 Charles Richter, an American scientist, developed a **scale that** uses numbers to measure the intensity of earthquakes. Few people feel an earthquake that's rated number 1 unless they re very sensitive to faint tremors. Most people do notice a number **2, even** though nothing seems to move. Almost everyone sees and feels the effects of a number 3 **earthquake, which** makes hanging objects swing. Beginning with number 4, an earthquake makes sounds. Dishes rattle. Glasses clink. Sometimes they even tumble from the shelf. A number 5 earthquake is **frightening because** it's strong enough to break windows and to crack walls. A number 6 injures **people and** can even kill them when loose bricks and weak chimneys come crashing down. A number 7 turns whole buildings into **rubble which** can bury **everyone who** is inside. A number 8 shakes the earth **strongly, so** that even hills move Although more violent earthquakes are theoretically possible, none which was stronger than a number 8 has ever been recorded.

Module 10: *Mastering Verb Phrases I*

Exercise 10.1

1. You will see us tomorrow.
2. Alvin may not accept your nomination.
3. I might not paint my house until spring.
4. You simply must meet Mr. Fowler.
5. We shall always remember this occasion.
6. Denise never could find that committee list.
7. Can Felix ever finish his homework on time?
8. She would never forget your birthday.
9. You should not leave the scissors on that table.

Exercise 10.2

1. Your brother can **borrow** my motorcycle.
2. He must **return** it by Friday.
3. He should **replace** the gas he uses.

Exercise 10.3 Underlining which shows tense is optional.

1. By this afternoon we **will** be ready to go.
   We promised an hour ago that we **would** be ready to go by 3:00.
2. I think now that I **may** do it.
   Yesterday I thought that I **might** do it.
3. Last year, students could not major in business at that school.
   This year, they can major in business or computers.

Exercise 10.4

1. They **would appreciate** a card.
   She **would appreciate** a card.
2. Alice **might need** more time.
   Alice and Ray **might need** more time.
3. You **can complete** this form quickly.
   He **can complete** this form quickly.

Exercise 10.5

1. She **would** prefer not to talk about that.
   She'**d** prefer not to talk about that.
2. He **will** be there before midnight.
   He'**ll** be there before midnight.
3. They **would** rather fight than switch.
   They'**d** rather fight than switch.
4. I **will** be home soon.
   I'**ll** be home soon.

Exercise 10.6

1. Aurelia usually does very nice work.
   Of course, Kristie sometimes does earn higher job ratings.
2. First I did the dishes.
   I always do try to finish all my chores before watching TV.
3. Those two skaters do perform beautifully together.
   They do the spins in perfect unison.

Exercise 10.7

1. Rena really **does** like Hiroshi.
   Both Rena and her sister really **do** like Hiroshi.
2. These stereos **do** certainly need a few repairs.
   That stereo **does** certainly need a few repairs.

Answers

3. Yes, I do have a nasty temper.
    Yes, she does have a nasty temper.

Exercise 10.8

1. Today Delma does not have enough money to buy lunch.
2. Her sisters do not have lunch money either.
3. They did not have lunch money all week.

Exercise 10.9

1. Does she want me to call her back?
2. Did you really need a receipt?
3. Do their parents ever return their calls?

Exercise 10.10

1. She does always want you to call her back immediately.
2. You do really need your receipt to get that refund.
3. Their parents never did return that call.

Exercise 10.11

1. Joyce and John did not enjoy their trip last year.
    Joyce does enjoy traveling when John stays home.
2. When we bought these chairs, they did not need repairs.
    Even now one of them still does not need repairs.
3. Did those stores offer senior discounts last week?
    Do those stores still offer discounts on unpopular items?

Exercise 10.12

1. Those new shirts don't look good on you.
2. This typewriter doesn't work well.
3. That teacher didn't try to help.

Exercise 10.13 Time words like *always, often,* and *usually* usually interrupt a negative verb phrase, like *don't often catch* in the third sentence. But *often don't catch* would also be correct.

Marjorie doesn't always impress me with her skill at tennis. She certainly doesn't understand how to keep her opponents off balance. Her drop shots, for example, don't often catch them off guard. And after a drop shot, she doesn't hit long. Her serves don't usually land deep in the court, and her opponents don't find it hard to return them. Her friends don't want her as a partner and don't fear her as an opponent. All in all, Marjorie's skill on the tennis court doesn't really overwhelm me.

Exercise 10.14

1. Don't those new shirts look good on you?
2. Didn't this typewriter work well?
3. Doesn't that teacher try to help?

394

Exercise 10.15

1. Someone has my notebook.
    Someone has taken my notebook by mistake.
2. No one had the answer.
    No one had answered the last question before the end of the hour.
3. Many cities have financial problems.
    Many cities have grown smaller in population recently.

Exercise 10.16

1. Poland **has** begun to trade with the West.
    Poland and Czechoslovakia **have** begun to trade with the West.
2. Pavel **has** beaten the computer at chess seven times.
    Most of the time the computer **has** beaten me at chess.
3. My brother **has** had to borrow money.
    I **have** had to borrow money.

Exercise 10.17

1. Before the 1995 Oklahoma City bombing, many people **had** defended unlimited freedom of speech.
    Since the bombing, those same people **have** been less ready to defend it.
2. This town **had** had almost no commercial development up until the Civil War.
    But it **has** become famous for its antique shops since then.
3. Just before that big storm last winter, Jonas **had** put a new roof on his house.
    He **has** had a much dryer house for the last year.
4. Since 1998, I **have** sold women's shoes.
    Up until 1997, I **had** hoped to be a professional basketball player.
5. Sampson **had** been a suspect in this murder case until Gelman was arrested.
    Sampson **has** been a suspect in three murder cases for the last seven years.

Exercise 10.18

1. saw   seen
2. went   gone
3. bought   bought
4. paid   paid
5. had   had
6. was or were   been

Exercise 10.19

1. By the end of the 1970s, though, sales of American cars **had gone** down.
2. Before we knew it, Japan **had taken** the lead.
3. By the end of the 1980s, prices **had risen** and profits **had shrunk**.
4. Up until 1990, American companies **had chosen** to ignore the problem.
5. Lately, however, we **have had** to change our old ways.
6. Consequently, the trade outlook for the USA **has been** more encouraging recently.
7. But at this time, Congress still **has** not **done** enough about this problem.

Exercise 10.20

1. Up until the 1950s, infant mortality **had increased** slowly.
2. But since then, doctors **have learned** how to save premature babies.
3. For the last 50 years, modern medicine **has prevented** many childhood diseases.

Exercise 10.21

Over the centuries, *triskaidekaphobia,* the fear of the number 13, has **terrorized** many people, and has **caused** them to act in strange ways. In all ages and in all countries, people have **refused** to hold celebrations on the 13th of the month, and in some societies, they have **drowned** children born on this evil day. Recently, architects have **learned** to deal with *triskaidekaphobia* by giving the number 14 to the floor after 12. In this way, also, hospitals have **tricked** patients into accepting beds on the 13th floor. Yet despite this superstition, for two centuries Americans have saluted a flag with 13 stripes, and immigrants have **flocked** from all over the world to pledge allegiance to it.

Exercise 10.22

This winter, some serious accidents **have occurred** in my apartment building. Several elderly tenants **have slipped** on icy sidewalks. They **have applied** to the landlord for compensation. Because he **has denied** any responsibility, the tenants organization **has planned** a protest meeting for next week.

Exercise 10.23

1. Dr. Deer **specializes** in treating hantavirus disease.
   Dr. Deer **has specialized** in this disease for eight years.
2. In recent decades, attitudes toward sex **have changed** radically.
   Sexual behavior sometimes **changes** more slowly than attitudes.
3. The high rate of crime in the USA sometimes **discourages** tourism.
   The murder of several tourists **has discouraged** tourism in Florida since 1997.
4. Our newly widowed friend **is** in a state of shock.
   Since his wife's death, our friend **has been** in a state of shock.

Exercise 10.24

1. In the early 1990s, we **saw** sudden changes in Eastern Europe.
   Until then, we **had seen** nothing to warn us about this turn of events.
2. In 1990, the two Germanys once more **became** one nation.
   Before that, several Communist countries **had become** democracies.
3. The people of Vienna **buried** Beethoven with pomp and ceremony.
   Several decades earlier, they **had buried** Mozart in a pauper's grave.
4. In his first year in office, President Clinton **raised** taxes.
   But three years earlier, President Bush **had raised** them even more.
5. Until the invention of synthetic fibers, housewives **had spent** many hours ironing.
   My grandmother **spent** every Tuesday ironing back in the 1950s.
6. Before the cold weather, my daughter's health **had been** fine.
   But she **was** quite ill in January.

Exercise 10.25

1. Pilar **has liked** Rafael <u>for six months.</u>
    Pilar **had liked** Tomas <u>until she saw him with Emilia.</u>
2. Ruby and Dee **have been** friends <u>for years</u>; they live next door to one another.
    Ruby and Vikki **had been** best friends <u>until Vikki married Ruby's brother.</u>
3. Stavros **has taken** the bus to work <u>every day this week.</u>
    Stavros **had taken** his bicycle to work <u>until somebody stole it.</u>
4. My sister **has baked** three sweet potato pies <u>so far this week.</u>
    My sister already **had baked** two apple pies <u>before we arrived at her house last night.</u>

Exercise 10.26

For the past three months, Heinrich Schlegel, the retired school headmaster, **has visited** the west bank of the blue Danube. His neighbors **have noticed** that Hilde Hindenberg, the banker's widow, **has gone** to the same spot at almost the same hour. Behind their shuttered windows these nosy neighbors **have whispered** about the secret meetings. But all this gossip **has been** nonsense. Whenever these two **have gone** to the embankment, they **have sat** about three meters apart. The widow **has closed** her eyes for a snooze. The headmaster **has waited** for her first snore before he **has rolled** up his pants to the knee for a sunbath. Then he **has buried** his head in a book, while she **has snored** gently on. If he **has felt** the slightest interest in her plump form, he certainly never **has given** any sign of it.

Exercise 10.27

1. Last week, Minnie **drove** to work.
    For the past month, Minnie **has driven** to work.
    Until she wrecked her car, Minnie **had driven** to work.
2. Last year, Pedro **was** the store manager.
    For the last five years, Pedro **has been** the store manager.
    Before the store was closed, Pedro **had been** the store manager.
3. Last month, Noreen **read** romance magazines and **wrote** in her diary.
    For the last six months, Noreen **has written** romance magazines and **has written** in her diary.
    Until she eloped, Noreen **had written** romance magazines and **had written** in her diary.
    [The second helping verb may be omitted.]

Exercise 10.28

1. Last week, Charlene **made** her rounds as a traffic patrol officer. She **checked** parking meters, and she **wrote** tickets for violators. Drivers often **were** angry with her. But Charlene never **relented** for she **was** proud of her reputation as a heartless meter maid.
2. For the last six months, Charlene **has made** her rounds as a traffic patrol officer. She **has checked** parking meters, and she **has written** tickets for violators. Drivers often **have been** angry with her. But Charlene **has** never **relented** for she **has been** proud of her reputation as a heartless meter maid.
3. Until a driver attacked her, Charlene **had made** her rounds as a traffic patrol officer. She **had checked** parking meters, and she **had written** tickets for violators. Drivers often **had been** angry with her. But Charlene **had** never **relented** for she **had been** proud of her reputation as a heartless meter maid.

Module 11: *Mastering Verb Phrases II*

Exercise 11.1

1. Charlotte is an excellent pianist.
   Charlotte is playing the piano in the studio.
2. I am ready to leave.
   I am going to the store.
3. It was snowing last night.
   The temperature was below freezing.

Exercise 11.2

1. Right now I am planning to move to California.
2. My children are grumbling because they must make new friends.
3. My husband is trying to help them adjust.

Exercise 11.3

1. As crime and poverty rose in Russia, Boris Yeltsin's popularity was slipping.
2. I was expecting a promotion when I was fired.
3. Were you making more money on your last job?

Exercise 11.4

1. For a change, my husband is **cooking** dinner tonight.
2. During the blackout, the defendant was **robbing** the store.
3. Those clerks are **filing** our computer output.
4. I am **meeting** her for lunch today.
5. Bertram is **planning** to go to Trinidad this winter.
6. Itzak was **taking** notes during the lecture.

Exercise 11.5 Underlining which shows tense is optional.

1. I **am working** for a computer software company <u>now</u>.
2. Those departments **are cutting** employees <u>so that they can save money</u>.
3. Irina **is trying** to start her own business <u>because she wants more money</u>.
4. <u>Today</u> I **am being** very careful not to annoy you.

Exercise 11.6 Underlining which shows tense is optional.

1. <u>Until recently,</u> unemployment **was declining**.
2. <u>Just before the explosion occurred,</u> I **was hurrying** to catch the bus.
3. <u>After the sales increased,</u> they **were hoping** for a raise.
4. <u>Last night</u> I **was being** very careful not to annoy you.

Exercise 11.7 Underlining which shows tense is optional.

1. <u>By next month,</u> unemployment **will be declining**.
2. I **will be leaving** for Dallas <u>as soon as the letter arrives</u>.
3. They **will be attending** that concert <u>tomorrow night</u>.

4.   I will be watching that game as soon as the TV set is repaired.

Exercise 11.8   Underlining which shows tense is optional.

1.   I was hurrying when I twisted my ankle.
2.   My two sisters were planning to go skating yesterday.
3.   We are trying right now to finish this job.
4.   They were paying too much for car insurance last year.
5.   Linda was writing some e-mail when the phone rang.
6.   Next year these companies will be going out of business.
7.   I was working in the supermarket last year, but now I am selling computers.

Exercise 11.9

1.   My friend Jewel is studying Spanish and hoping to make a career as a bilingual secretary.
2.   The oncoming drivers were slowing their cars and staring at the accident.
3.   The chickens were pecking at my legs and clucking furiously.
4.   That raging blizzard is moving down from northern Canada and burying the upper Midwest in snow.

Exercise 11.10

1.   Those volunteers are answering the phones and are accepting donations.
2.   The cheerleaders were screaming and were leaping into the air as the crowd was filling the bleachers.
3.   The student government is preparing petitions, is collecting signatures, and is organizing a campaign for a new day care center on campus.

Exercise 11.11

1.   Extremes of heat and cold from one day to the next are occurring regularly now.
2.   We're experiencing higher sea levels and hotter winds every year. But are these events due to normal climate variation?
3.   People around the world are ever more anxiously asking the big question: Is global warming really happening, or are the signs of a warming trend merely accidental?
4.   Climate scientists have measured climate variation over many centuries, and are finally reaching firm conclusions: The symptoms of global warming are multiplying too rapidly to be normal.
5.   Heat-trapping gases from increased manufacturing activity are preventing solar heat from escaping into space and are raising the global temperature a fraction of a degree each year, so that during the next 100 years the earth's temperature will be rising between 1.5 and 6 degrees Fahrenheit.
6.   If the human race does nothing to prevent this disaster, it's eventually going to become extinct.

Exercise 11.12

These days, baby toys are selling briskly, and toy manufacturing is big business. In the past, toys for infants were mostly simple plastic rattles and terry-cloth balls. Now toy makers are constantly trying to come up with new gimmicks that will appeal to parents. In fact, they've turned for inspiration to research on babies, even on unborn babies. Investigators have recently discovered that soft music is able to soothe not only a pregnant woman but also her unborn child. So an ingenious manufacturer is now selling "Babyphones," lightweight stereo speakers that an expectant mother wears around her waist. A cassette player hooks onto her pocket or purse. If the fetus starts kicking, the mother switches on the "womb tunes" (as the maker calls these tapes). What else does the fetus hear besides violins or guitars? One favorite is a home-made tape of Mom and Dad singing lullabies. Then, to help the newborn baby to make the transition from the familiar womb to the scary outside world, toy makers have thought up yet another helpful invention. For nine months a baby has listened to the sounds of its mother's body and the beat of her heart. After birth, the parents are able to buy a tape player to put in the baby's bed, where it plays the same comforting rhythms. Toy manufacturers are also publicizing the discovery that babies enjoy the high contrast of black and white. Now zebras, pandas, and other black-and-white animals are making big bucks for them. They're also promoting black-and-white mobiles to hang on the crib. In this age of the consumer, the manufacturers exploit the idea that nobody is too young for an expensive toy.

Exercise 11.13

1. Dr. Hermann will teach the business seminar.
   The subject ☒ is ☐ is not doing the action, so the sentence is ☒ active ☐ passive.
   The business seminar will be taught by Dr. Hermann.
   The subject ☐ is ☒ is not doing the action, so the sentence is ☐ active ☒ passive.
   Dr. Hermann is admired by the students in his seminar.
   The subject ☐ is ☒ is not doing the action, so the sentence is ☐ active ☒ passive.
2. A small committee planned the conference.
   The subject ☒ is ☐ is not doing the action, so the sentence is ☒ active ☐ passive.
   The conference was planned by a small committee.
   The subject ☐ is ☒ is not doing the action, so the sentence is ☐ active ☒ passive.
   A small committee was appointed to plan the conference.
   The subject ☐ is ☒ is not doing the action, so the sentence is ☐ active ☒ passive.
3. The shortstop was throwing the ball.
   The subject ☒ is ☐ is not doing the action, so the sentence is ☒ active ☐ passive.
   The ball was thrown too late.
   The subject ☐ is ☒ is not doing the action, so the sentence is ☐ active ☒ passive.
   The shortstop was thrown out of the game for fighting.
   The subject ☐ is ☒ is not doing the action, so the sentence is ☐ active ☒ passive.

Exercise 11.14 Underlining which shows tense is optional.

1. Somebody is injured almost every day in this playground.
2. Benita was promoted twice last year.
3. The arsonists were sentenced last month after a short trial.
4. They are now locked up in a maximum security prison.
5. Even now, I am still surprised at the speedy verdict.

Exercise 11.15 Underlining which shows tense is optional.

1. Every day the same routine tasks are performed by dozens of workers.
2. Fortunes are lost on Wall Street every day.
3. That old trunk is used as a coffee table now.
4. Usually, sardines are caught in nets.
5. Emily was annoyed by that remark yesterday.
6. Last week, his windshield was broken by a rock.

Exercise 11.16 Underlining which shows tense is optional.

1. When I was a child, I was fascinated by complicated puzzles.
    I am still fascinated by puzzles that are hard to solve.
2. These days teenagers are often influenced by peer pressure.
    In the past, teenagers were influenced most by their families.
3. This opera was sung by Richard Tucker in 1960.
    Today it is often sung by Roberto Alagna.
4. The author of *Alice in Wonderland* was once suspected of child molestation.
    He is considered innocent by modern scholars.

Exercise 11.17 Underlining which shows tense is optional.

1. Last night, Ali was robbed in front of his own house.
    Last night, Ali got robbed in front of his own house.
2. Miss Holder is paid much less than she deserves these days.
    Miss Holder gets paid much less than she deserves these days.
3. Basil and Vera were divorced just two months after they were married last year.
    Basil and Vera got divorced just two months after they got married last year.

Exercise 11.18

In every culture, people are forbidden to perform certain acts which are called taboos. Some modern taboos were not always considered evil in the past. In ancient Egypt, royal siblings often got married to each other. American Indian warriors used to eat the hearts of enemies that they had killed to show respect for their courage. Now both incest and cannibalism have become almost universal taboos. We are horrified by incest. And if anyone eats human flesh today, that person is condemned as a monster. In 1972 a famous plane crash in the Andes illustrated how strongly this taboo is felt in modern times. Although some survivors kept themselves alive by eating the bodies of the passengers who had perished in the crash, the taboo against cannibalism was too strong for most of them. Instead they chose to die of starvation.

Exercise 11.19

In 1981, President Reagan **chose** the renowned doctor, C. Everett Koop, as Surgeon General of the United States, not because he was famous, but because he had openly opposed abortion. But once the Senate had **confirmed** his appointment, this conservative doctor astonished everyone. The President had **asked** him to write a report showing that abortion was harmful to women's health. Koop believed that abortion was morally wrong, but, when he studied the evidence, he saw that it failed to prove that abortion necessarily caused physical or psychological damage to women. So he explained to the President that he, as an honest and competent scientist, could not write this report. Then he turned his attention to smoking and AIDS. The Administration had not expressed much interest in these problems, but, according to Koop, they were health hazards which the Surgeon General's office could and should do something about. Within a few years, his warnings on cigarette packages had **caught** the attention of every smoker, and many had **kicked** the habit. Next, his report on AIDS showed that for the first time someone in the government had taken the deadly virus seriously. He strongly encouraged early sex education and the use of condoms. The Administration was angry, and the liberals were happy. Both said that he had **changed**. Koop answered mildly that he had not budged from his original position on any issue. By the time he left office in 1989, many of his early opponents had turned into supporters, and some of his former supporters claimed that he had **betrayed** them. In TV interviews after his retirement, Dr. Koop insisted that his views had never altered. The problem, he said, was that nobody had **bothered** to learn what his convictions really were in the first place.

Exercise 11.20

Geraldine wants to lose weight. She plans exactly what food she will buy, and how much of it. She has even memorized the layout of the supermarket, because she knows that if she can stay away from the ice cream and candy, she will lose five pounds in one week. She says that she is going to stick to her diet until she can get into every outfit which is hanging in her closet, especially those velvet slacks which she hasn't been able to wear for years. But, of course, Geraldine has made these plans before. Her friends don't think that she will actually lose a pound.

Exercise 11.21

Mickey hasn't been a very satisfactory dog. As a puppy, he **didn't know** when to stay on his training paper. As a one-year-old, he wouldn't chew his plastic bone and couldn't abstain from the upholstery. At two, he couldn't tell the difference between friend and foe, and **didn't growl** or wag his tail appropriately. So the mailman and meter reader especially **didn't** cherish this canine. Now at three, Mickey isn't the most popular dog on the block. He can't fetch the newspaper. He won't heel on command. And he **doesn't** even **know** when to leave people in peace. His owner **doesn't** often brag about him. To her, Mickey isn't the perfect pet. You **shouldn't mention** his name, because she won't beam with delight.

Exercise 11.22

Since my wife and I **began** to do crossword puzzles together, we have bought a lot of reference books, including a new edition of *The Guinness Book of World Records*. This book has certainly helped us with our puzzles, but it has also been a source of fascinating information. It **doesn't** just tell about recent sports records. Each edition tries to include every amazing and amusing feat of the human race. Here are some we will always remember. ① Although Strombo the Maniac has **established** the longest official record of 65 hours for lying on a bed of nails, that record was totally demolished by Silki the Fakir, who did the same thing for 101 days—but only his followers saw him do it. ② Lightning has **struck** one living man seven times—Roy Sullivan, a Shenandoah park ranger. His body was hit in five different places, and twice his head was **burned** bald. ③ Steve Weldon of Texas has **eaten** the longest meal in the shortest time: 100 yards of spaghetti in 28 seconds. ④ By the time he died in 597 AD, St. Simon Stylites had **chalked** up the all-time pole-sitting record: 45 years on top of a stone pillar. ⑤ And what book has **sold** the most copies in the past 25 years? *The Guinness Book of World Records*, of course!

Exercise 11.23

My mother has often tried to tell me that crime **doesn't** pay. But then, my mother has never run for office. I have never told her about what happened when I was a sophomore in high school. I had **campaigned** hard to be class president, and election day had finally arrived. Just before the vote was taken our teacher reminded us, "You shouldn't vote for yourself. Each student must **write** down somebody else's name on the ballot." But I was **scared** that I might lose the election by one vote. I knew that I should not have **done** it, but when the slips were passed around, I voted for myself. I have never forgotten the moment when the votes were all counted, and our teacher said, "There are 31 votes for Mary Williams and one vote for Ted Collins." As soon as the teacher announced the results, Ted jumped up to say that I had not cast my vote for him. But then he sat down even more quickly. It took me a day to figure out that Ted had voted for himself, too. He could not accuse me without accusing himself. So even if I did **commit** a crime, on that occasion I wasn't punished. In fact, I was praised for voting for my opponent.

Module 12: *Mastering Expansion*

Exercise 12.1

1. We sent a thank-you note to <u>my grandfather's friends</u>.
   They were friends of **my grandfather**.
2. <u>The new government's policy</u> was announced at a press conference.
   The policy had been formulated by **the new government**.
3. An old union motto is, "Work one day for <u>one day's pay</u>."
   The pay was for **one day**.
4. <u>The theater company's next play</u> is going to be <u>Shakespeare's</u> *Othello*.
   The next play will be given by **the theater company**.
   Othello was written by **Shakespeare**.

Exercise 12.2

1. the silk scarves belonging to <u>Jennifer</u>
   The noun that can be written in the possessive form is **Jennifer**
   To make it possessive, add   ❑ apostrophe only   ☒ apostrophe + *S* ending
   Jennifer's silk scarves
   The ending has   ❑ no sound added   ☒ ZZZ or SSS added
2. the shiny equipment used by <u>some cooks</u>
   The noun that can be written in the possessive form is **cooks**
   To make it possessive, add   ☒ apostrophe only   ❑ apostrophe + *S* ending
   some **cooks'** shiny equipment
   The ending has   ☒ no sound added   ❑ ZZZ or SSS added
3. razor blades intended for <u>men</u>
   The noun that can be written in the possessive form is **men**
   To make it possessive, add   ❑ apostrophe only   ☒ apostrophe + *S* ending
   men's razor blades
   The ending has   ❑ no sound added   ☒ ZZZ or SSS added
4. the lyric poems written by <u>Robert Frost</u>
   The noun that can be written in the possessive form is **Frost**
   To make it possessive, add   ❑ apostrophe only   ☒ apostrophe + *S* ending
   Robert **Frost's** lyric poems
   The ending has   ❑ no sound added   ☒ ZZZ or SSS added
5. cocktail dresses designed for <u>women</u>
   The noun that can be written in the possessive form is **women**
   To make it possessive, add   ❑ apostrophe only   ☒ apostrophe + *S* ending
   women's cocktail dresses
   The ending has   ❑ no sound added   ☒ ZZZ or SSS added

6. a frustrating delay of <u>three days</u>
    The noun that can be written in the possessive form is **days**
    To make it possessive, add   ☒ apostrophe only   ❏ apostrophe + *S* ending
    three **days'** frustrating delay
    The ending has   ☒ no sound added   ❏ ZZZ or SSS added

Exercise 12.3

1. my **brother's** dirty tools
    my **brothers'** dirty tools
2. one **woman's** expanding career
    many **women's** expanding careers
3. one **person's** strong opinion
    many **people's** strong opinions
4. a **man's** heavy responsibilities
    men's heavy responsibilities

Exercise 12.4

1. **Tess's** multimedia computer
2. **Harry's** new pen
3. one **class's** hard assignments
4. that **family's** brand new house
5. **Jesus's** profound teachings

Exercise 12.5

      Our grandparents' big old house was crowded. In the recreation room, **Tasha's stereo** was blaring rap music while the cousins checked out **each other's new dance steps**. In the kitchen, **the roast turkey's wonderful aroma** wafted from **Grandma's oven** while **Uncle Joe's yam casserole** and **Aunt Betty's mince pies** were displayed for **the assembled guests' approval**. In the living room, **our grandparents' photo albums** were being passed around, to **everyone's amusement**. "Look at **our aunts' miniskirts**! Get a load of **Joe's haircut**!" From the den, where **Granddad's television** was tuned to a football game, came the occasional roar of **men's voices**. **The family's Thanksgiving reunion** was in full swing.

Exercise 12.6

1. Valerie says that her sister's cooking is better than **hers** and even better than mine.
2. My **family's** friends are staying at my **brother's** house.
3. The jury asked **its** foreman to request a copy of the judge's instructions.
4. Sid's brother and sister-in-law were each married for the second time, and they always joked that their children were "his, **hers** and **ours**."

Exercise 12.7

1. **Who's** the person who wanted to borrow **Melvin's** notebook?
2. We **haven't** seen any apartment as attractive as ours, except perhaps **yours**.
3. **It's** been predicted that the finance committee will deliver its report only after the **Senate's** last meeting of the year.

Exercise 12.8

It's becoming almost a habit: The University raises its tuition nearly every year, and when it does, **it's** certain that a small group of students will protest against the **administration's** decision. They lock themselves into the **President's** office and hang banners out the windows. News reporters come to interview the **strikers'** leaders. After a **week's** delay and negotiation, the administrators call the police. They always say that the decision **hasn't** been easy, but that the students **who've** gone on strike are interfering with other **students'** right to an education.

Exercise 12.9

1. Both **applicants' acceptances** arrived yesterday.
2. **Teachers' salaries** were raised last year.
3. Those **stores' customers** all objected to the loss of parking.

Exercise 12.10

My twin **sisters' babies** were born just three **weeks** apart, so the **children** grew up together. **Rosa's** little girl and **Chita's** little boy were both healthy **infants**, but their **mothers** often wondered why the **children's personalities** were so very different. **Roberto's** temperament was sunny, but his cousin **Estella's tantrums** became famous in the family. Still, the two **children** got along very well together. Perhaps **opposites** attract. At any rate, they never fought over each **other's toys**, and they happily shared their **cookies** and **treats**. In fact, their **relatives** always called them "the junior **twins**."

Exercise 12.11

Some movies can make boring lawsuits seem **really** interesting. A **particularly** good example is *Erin Brockovich*, directed **brilliantly** by Steven Soderbergh. In this true story, an untrained legal secretary **meticulously** assembles bits and pieces of **carefully** concealed evidence which **ultimately** exposes the **criminally** negligent behavior of a gas company. It becomes obvious, as the plot **gradually** unfolds, that Soderbergh has done **well** in choosing Julia Roberts as the star. To achieve his best effects, the director leans **heavily** on both her comedic and dramatic talents. **Instantly**, as the movie begins, she challenges her viewers to reconsider what's **really** important to them as they drift **thoughtlessly** through life. In her role as Erin, Roberts dresses **tastelessly**, talks **obscenely**, and behaves **crudely** and sometimes even **disgustingly**, and yet **simultaneously** she remains dedicated to an **unquestionably** noble cause. Only Julia Roberts could have turned a movie about sifting through musty files into both a moral challenge and a **vastly** entertaining experience.

Exercise 12.12

1. The union members **cast almost 300** votes in favor of the strike.
2. Actually, they **needed only 174** to approve the strike proposal.
3. When they finally got a new contract, they **achieved nearly all** their goals.

Exercise 12.13

Viola always looked **beautiful**, with **long**, **lustrous** hair and **bright**, **white** teeth. She dressed **attractively** and moved **gracefully**. She enjoyed living **extravagantly**, so she looked **carefully** for a **smart** man who was becoming rich **quickly**. She behaved **stupidly** by picking Caspar, who had **little** charm and **few** brains. After six months in a **fashionable** part of town, Caspar began to trade stocks

recklessly and made a **bad** decision. After moving into a **dumpy** neighborhood, the couple had **little** to look forward to and **much** to regret.

Exercise 12.14

Katherine always looked **more beautiful** than Viola, with **longer, more lustrous** hair and **brighter, whiter** teeth. She dressed **more attractively** and moved **more gracefully**. She enjoyed living **more extravagantly**, so she looked **more carefully** for a **smarter** man who was becoming rich **more quickly** than Caspar was. She behaved **more stupidly** than Viola by picking Brad, who had **less** charm and **fewer** brains than Caspar. After six months in a **more fashionable** part of town, Brad began to trade stocks **more recklessly** than Caspar and made a **worse** decision. After moving into a **dumpier** neighborhood, the couple had **less** to look forward to than Viola and Caspar and **more** to regret.

Exercise 12.15

Diane always looked **the most beautiful** of the three women, with **the longest, most lustrous** hair and **the brightest, whitest** teeth. She dressed **the most attractively** and moved **the most gracefully**. She enjoyed living **the most extravagantly**, so she looked **the most carefully** for **the smartest** man who was becoming rich **the most quickly** of the three men. She behaved **the most stupidly** of the three women by picking Duncan, who had **the least** charm and **the fewest** brains of the three men. After six months in **the most fashionable** part of town, Duncan began to trade stocks **the most recklessly** of the three men and made **the worst** decision. After moving into **the dumpiest** neighborhood, the couple had **the least** to look forward to of the three couples and **the most** to regret.

Exercise 12.16

1. Jane served **samosas, (which** her guests ate **greedily), at** her open house.
2. All the **guests (who** were **vegetarians) wanted** the recipe.
3. Later Jane realized that the open **house, (which** she had **spent almost a** fortune **on), hadn't** been a success.

Exercise 12.17

1. In his first draft of the Declaration of Independence, a **man (owning** two hundred **slaves) wrote** a **paragraph (denouncing slavery).**
2. Benjamin **Franklin, (fearing** that the patriots from the southern colonies would refuse to sign the **Declaration), crossed** out this paragraph.
3. Thomas Jefferson, the author of the document, claimed that the **blacks (living** under his paternal **care) could** not survive in a hostile white world.
4. Modern **historians, (reviewing** Jefferson's words and **behavior), wonder** about his sincerity.

Exercise 12.18

1. A **man (wearing** a special brand of **shoes) left** a bloody footprint at the crime scene.
2. Some **photos (showing** the defendant in this expensive **footgear) were** exhibited to the jury.
3. The defense **lawyer, (vehemently** dismissing the photos as **fakes), spoke** to the judge.

Exercise 12.19

1. **(Hoping** for a **promotion), Miss** Solgars flirted with her boss.
2. She was happy to find his very positive performance **evaluation (lying** on top of his **desk).**

3. **(Entering** the **room), Christopher** recognized the picture.
4. Christopher recognized the **picture (hanging** on the **wall).**
5. **(Soaring** into the last **row), the** foul ball hit a spectator.
6. The foul ball hit a **spectator (sitting** in the last **row).**

Exercise 12.20

1. **(Hoping** to save not just billions but **trillions), we** are building unmanned space vehicles.
2. **(Operatin**g without expensive life-support **systems), they** travel light and on the cheap.
3. **(Responding** to commands from Mission Control at **Houston), they** perform elaborate experiments on distant planets.
4. **(Containing** tiny but powerful **cameras), they** beam brilliant pictures back to Earth.

Exercise 12.21

1. The tea was delicious. It was **iced**.
   The (iced) tea was delicious.
2. The bridge is a landmark. It was **covered**.
   The (covered) bridge is a landmark.
3. The patient took tranquilizers. He was **depressed**.
   The (depressed) patient took tranquilizers.
4. Leroy repaired the stereo. It was **used**.
   Leroy repaired the (used) stereo.
5. The banker refused to lend me money. He was **prejudiced**.
   The (prejudiced) banker refused to lend me money.

Exercise 12.22

1. **Diana, (enraged** by her question about **Charlie), abruptly** hung up on Nancy.
2. **(Irritated** by Nancy's **insensitivity), Diana** talked to her neighbor, Betty Windsor.
3. Betty tried to calm down her **friend, (so** easily irked by a simple **inquiry).**

Exercise 12.23

1. **(Puzzled** by his **grade), he** made an appointment with her.
2. **(Assaulted** recently by a disgruntled **student), she** hesitated to see him.
3. **(Surprised** by each other's quiet **reasonableness), however**, they actually enjoyed their chat.
   [OR **However, (surprised** by each other's quiet **reasonableness), they** actually enjoyed their chat.]

Exercise 12.24

1. Thousands watched the dramatization of Mary Ann Evans's Victorian novel *Middlemarch,* **(condensed** into six brief episodes for **TV).**
2. George Henry Lewes was deeply in love with *Middlemarch's* supremely ugly but superbly gifted **author, (described** by her contemporaries as a homely, horse-faced **woman).**
3. The pen-name George **Eliot, (suggested** by her lover's first **name), protected** the feminine identity of this writer.
4. **(Still** married to his despised wife, but forbidden by a quirk of the law to divorce **her), Lewes** lived with this talented **writer (until** he **died).**

Exercise 12.25

1. **(Eager** to know the latest horse-racing **results), Uncle** Boris picked up this morning's **newspaper, (abandoned** on the bar room **counter).**
2. Immediately a huge **headline (on** the financial page, which he read in **disbelief), informed** him that his most recent stock investment had plummeted.
3. **Then, (still** turning the pages in search of the sports **news), he** noticed the obituary of a favorite drinking companion.
4. **Discovering (at** the bottom of the last **page) that** his horse had indeed won, my poor **uncle, (who** boasts that he never forgets **anything), remembered** that he'd forgotten to place his bet.

Exercise 12.26 Your answers may be slightly different. Check carefully to make sure that your sentences are at least as clear as these.

    Some animal **lovers, (carried** away by their enthusiasm for animal **rights), seem** to ignore the best interests of both beasts and humans. For example, **some (white-tailed) deer, (now** multiplying into the **hundreds), and** a community of Long Island home-**owners, (trapped** together on a small peninsula a few miles **wide), have** become a menace to each other. Angry **residents, (bitten** by deer **ticks) (carrying** Lyme **disease), stare** bitterly at **their (devastated) gardens, (devoured** by (**starving) deer). Nevertheless, (driven** by an irrational **zeal), animal activists (living** in distant, **deer-free) towns** lobby against all attempts to control the deer population in this community. **These (dedicated) animal lovers, (relentlessly** reminding us that the woods and plains once belonged to these **animals), continue** to oppose any **laws (favoring** the rights of humans over animals).

Exercise 12.27 Your answers may be slightly different. Check carefully to make sure that your sentences are at least as clear as these.

1. Dorothy's dinner turns cold **as she is watching TV**.
2. Ignored by her friends, **Dorothy has a lonely life**.
3. Dorothy's health is poor, **because she never goes out or gets any exercise**.
4. Contacted recently by her granddaughter, **Dorothy may have a brighter future**.

Exercise 12.28

1. For Clara, getting ready to retire was a great experience, mentally, physically, and **emotionally**.
2. It was a pleasure to clear out her desk, to turn in her office keys, and **to say** goodbye to her workaholic friends.
3. As for her other co-workers — the hypocrites, the **liars**, and the snobs — she would just send them dazzling postcards from her new home.
4. To her surprise, her grumpy boss stopped for a moment, smiled, and even **shook** her hand.
5. Of course, she still had to decide whether to drive to her new home, to take the bus, or **to** go on the train.
6. As for her dilapidated car, it needed a new transmission, a complete tune-up, and four **replacement tires**.
7. Maybe it would save money in the long run to buy a new car rather than **to repair** that old one.
8. One thing she had already decided: Walking on the beach is more fun than **answering** phones or entering data into the company's computer.
9. Clara looked forward to Monday morning when she would turn off the lights, collect her bags, and then **leave** for her new life.

Exercise 12.29

1. Tomorrow I will read books, listen to CDs, watch videos, and play computer games.
2. Yesterday I read my books, listened to my CDs, watched my videos, and played my computer games.
3. I have read your books, listened to your CDs, watched your videos, and played your computer games.
4. I have books to read, CDs to listen to, videos to watch, and computer games to play.
5. I will need some exercise after reading Audrey's books, listening to her CDs, watching her videos, and playing her computer games.
6. These have all enriched my life: the books that I've read, the CDs that I've listened to, the videos that I've watched, and the computer games that I've played.
7. I rarely go out because I have so many books to read, [so many] CDs to listen to, [so many] videos to watch, and [so many] computer games to play.
    [The repetitions of *so many* may be omitted.]

Index

Abbreviations 40
Addresses 47
Adjective clauses 122
Adjectives 309
Adverbial clauses 103
Adverbs 309
Apostrophes 38, 306
Base form, definition 77
Capitalization 35
Contractions 38, 79, 179, 299
Coordinating conjunctions 103
Copying xxii
Dates 43
Dependent clauses 103
Drafting 8
Editing 23
Expansion 73, 96, 217, 299
    Dangling expansion 327
    Misplaced expansion 315
Expansion words 96
Fragments 231
Free writing 12
GET in passive sentences 290
Homonyms 54
ING words 81
Joining words 90
Main point 9
Misplaced modifiers 315
Modifiers 299
Noun clauses 119, 122
Noun-expansion words 111
Nouns   Determiners 131
    Irregular 138
    Noncount 142
    Plural 134
    Possessive 305
    Singular 131
    Spelling 133
Numbers, when to spell out 42
Of/of the phrases 139
One-word/two-word forms 43
Paragraphing 34
Parallel parts 329
Possessives 300
Prepositions 150
Pronouns   Case 150
    Person 152
    Possessive 305
    Reflexive 151
    Sexist 153
    Singular/Plural 146
Proofreading xviii, 25
Punctuation   Complex sentences 100, 109, 119

Punctuation   Compound sentences 93
Quotation marks 39
Relative pronouns 122
Revising 16
Run-ons 209
Sentences   Active 279
    Complex 96, 111, 217, 238, 241
    Compound 90, 216
    Emphatic 258
    Negative 257
    Passive 287
    Questions 257
    Simple 67
Spelling rules 46
Subjects 73
Subordinate clauses 103
Subordinating conjunctions 103
Tenses   Continuous 280
    Future 40, 250
    Past 186
    Perfect 262, 263
    Present 161
    Progressive 280
Topic sentence 9
Transitional words 213, 222
Two-word/one-word forms 43
Used to 193
Verbs   *BE*
        Past tense 195
        Present tense 178
    Helping verbs
        BE 277
        DO 256
        HAVE 261
        modals 250
    Past participles 264, 289, 322
    Past tense
        Irregular 186
        Regular 189
        Spelling 191
    Present participle 317
    Present tense
        Agreement 163
        Spelling 167
    Verb phrases 69, 76, 277
Who vs. *which* 119
Writing conventions 31
Writing process 1
Wrong words   *It's/Its* 56
        Than/Then 55
        Their/There/They're 58
        To/Too/Two 55
        You're/Your 57